# The Grimm Family of Sheboygan and Taylor Counties, Wisconsin

Maryellen Anderson

In loving memory of
Gladys Grimm Doriot
The greatest woman I ever knew

Gladys was the sharpest, bravest, most stoic person I ever met. Over the almost fourteen years that I knew this amazing woman, Gladys spoke of the good times, rewards, personal grief, and regrets during the many private, candid conversations that she and I shared. A very special bond grew between us. She once told me that, no matter what happened, she was always going to keep me. I never called her mom, but she was the best mom I never had. How apropos that the first time I met her was on Mother's Day.

This is for you Gladys – because you always told me that there weren't many branches or leaves on your tree.

I love you and miss you dearly,

Maryelllen

# Table of Contents

# TABLE OF ILLUSTRATIONS

# TABLE OF TEXTBOXES

# ACKNOWLEDGMENTS

Thank you to everyone who assisted and cooperated with the my efforts to gather the data for this work. There are just too many of you to name individually. The majority of the original documents and pictures contained herein were found among the paperwork and other effects left behind by Clara Anderson Grimm. Without her foresight in collecting and keeping the myriad of memorial cards, obituaries, photos, notes, invitations, and a plethora of other such items, this work would have been much more difficult to bring to fruition.

# Grimm

Nickname for a dour and forbidding individual, from Old High German grim 'stern', 'severe' from a Germanic personal name from grima 'mask', 'helmet'.

Source: Dictionary of American Family Names
©2013, Oxford University Press

# PART I

Grimms in America

# COMING TO AMERICA

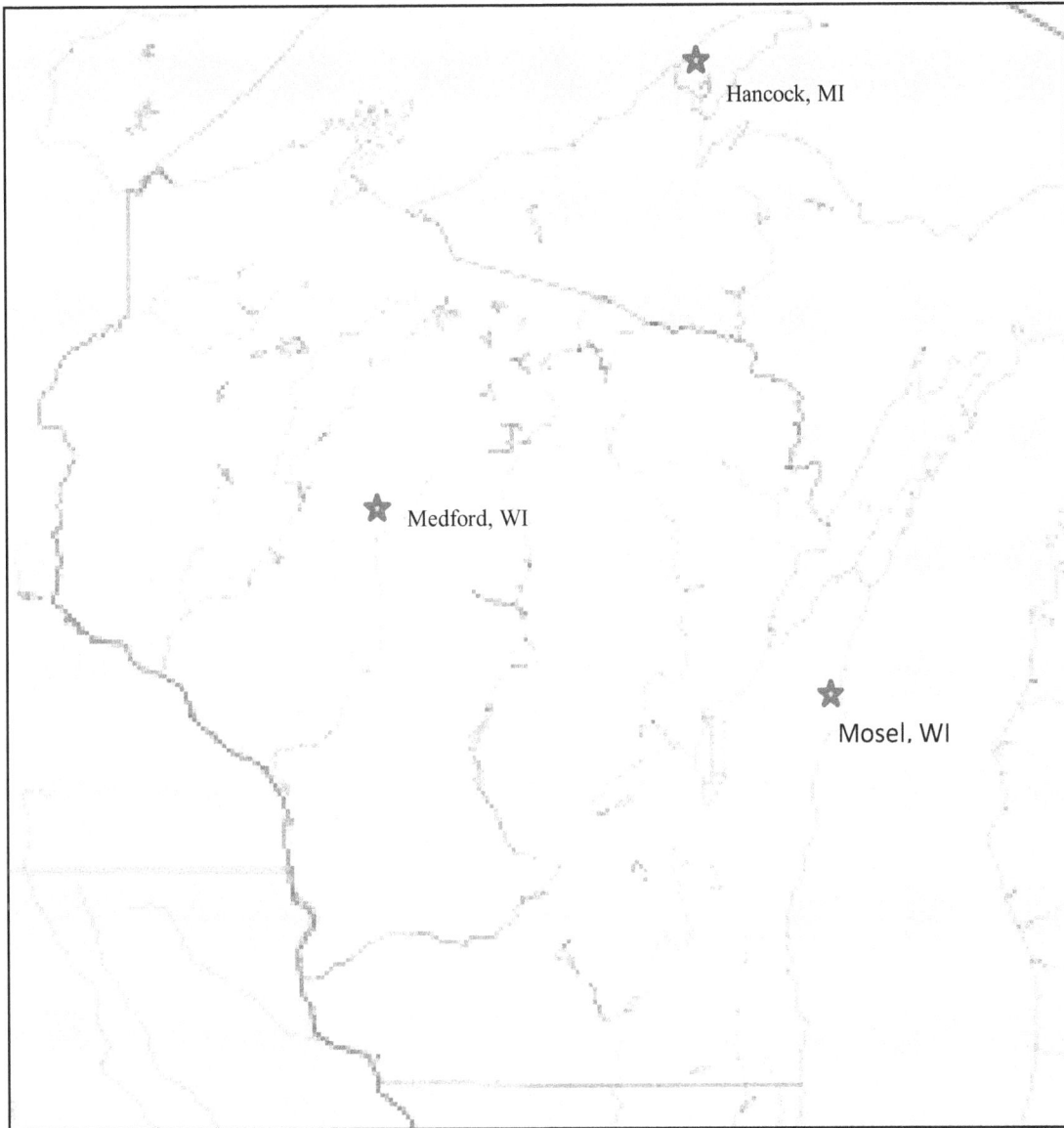

1: Map of Wisconsin showing proximity of Medford to Mosel, WI and Hancock, MI

The Napoleonic Wars had left the European continent in a state of social, political and economic upheaval. By 1848, uprisings against the oppression and tyranny of their governments were beginning. People were ripe for revolt and the citizens of Paris were the first to do so. By May of that same year, the seeds of revolution had spread to Germany, which consisted of fragmented and quasi-feudal states. The German people wanted a unified Germany, a national constitution, and increased basic rights. A National Assembly was formed and convened in response to these demands. However, infighting caused the Assembly to quickly fail and disperse.[1] It was amidst this atmosphere of social unrest and revolution that 32 year old Heinrich Ludwig Grimm made the decision to immigrate to the United States of America.

---

[1] Anderson, K., Burian, E., & Kemper, T. (Unknown). Wisconsin Mosaic: The Activists – The '48s. Retrieved August 21, 2013 from Htt://comminfo.rutgers.edu/~dalbello/FLVA/activists/48ers.html

That same year, the California gold rush began and Wisconsin had just gained statehood as the 30th state of the union. The failure of the revolution created a great influx of thousands of German revolutionaries fleeing their homeland to immigrate to America, rumored to be the land of opportunity and prosperity. Some of these immigrants settled in Wisconsin, enticed by the fledgling state's constitution, which allowed the foreign-born suffrage after just one year of residency[2]. The influence of the Saxon immigrants would indelibly change the culture and history of mid-nineteenth century Wisconsin. It was here with "an emerging community of Saxon immigrants who shared their dialect [and] their Calvinist reformed beliefs"[3] that Heinrich Grimm chose to settle with his family.

The U.S. Congress implemented a law in 1820 that called for a complete manifest of all passengers aboard ships entering the country to be completed by the ship's master and presented to the customs officer at the port of arrival before any passengers disembarked the vessel.[4] A record for "Ludwig Grimm" shows that he departed aboard the ship "Miles" from Hamburg, Germany in the year 1848, his place of origin Deutschland.[5] With him were his wife, Elizabeth Schneider, and his 3 year old son, Frank.

### New York, Passenger and Immigration Lists, 1820-1850

| | |
|---|---|
| Name: | Ludwig Grim |
| Arrival Date: | 4 Sep 1848 |
| Age: | 32 |
| Gender: | M (Male) |
| Port of Arrival: | New York |
| Port of Departure: | Hamburg, Germany |
| Place of Origin: | Deutschland |
| Ship: | Miles |
| Family Identification: | 1159132 |
| Microfilm Serial Number: | M237 |
| Microfilm Roll Number: | 75 |

2: New York Passenger and Immigration List showing arrival date of Ludwig Grimm

---

[2] Anderson, K., Burian, E., & Kemper, T. (Unknown). Wisconsin Mosaic: The Activists – The '48s. Retrieved August 21, 2013 from Htt://comminfo.rutgers.edu/~dalbello/FLVA/activists/48ers.html

[3] Knipping, Mark H. / *A history of the 27th Wisconsin Volunteer Infantry Regiment in the War of the Rebellion, 1862-1865* (2001); (pub. Unknown); Introduction p.2

[4] Morgan, George G. (2007). The Official Guide to Ancestry.com; p. 186; Ancestry Publishing; Canada

[5] Ancestry.com . *New York, Passenger and Immigration Lists, 1820-1850* [Database online ] Provo, UT, USA. Ancestry.com Operations Inc. 2013. Original source: New York, Registers of Vessels Arriving at the Port of New York from Foreign Ports, 1789-1919, Washington, D.C.: National Archives and Records Administration; MSN: M237, Roll #75

# SETTLING IN AMERICA

Ludwig Grimm settled on a farm in Mosel, Sheboygan County, Wisconsin, where the rich clay loam promised excellent farming. Frederich, the first Grimm in the family to be born on American soil, was born in 1849. Five more children were born into the family by 1862, all born in Sheboygan County except the third, a son, who was born in Michigan. Since most women at that time gave birth on average of every two years, the five year span between the second and third child suggests the possibility that Ludwig's wife, Elizabeth, may have lost one or two children between them. The 1855 Wisconsin State Census shows the family residence as being Mosel, Wisconsin[6], the year Bernhart was born in Michigan. Perhaps Barbara (Mertz) Schneider, living in Houghton Co., Michigan, was a sister-in-law to Elizabeth and she went there for help with the pregnancy?

H. Ludwig Grimm was born in Germany in 1816 and married Elizabeth Lucetta/Lisette Schneider, also born in Germany 1819. Their marriage probably occurred around 1844 since their oldest child was three years old when they immigrated to America in 1848. The couple had six children, four boys and 2 girls, the oldest born in Prussia, the third born in Michigan, and the other four born in Wisconsin. The 1855 Wisconsin State Census lists Ludwig Grimm living in

## MOSEL

*The town of Mosel contains only eighteen full and six fractional sections and is the smallest in the county. It has no villages.*

*In 1853 the town was separated from Sheboygan.... At the time that settlements were made in Mosel there were no roads to Sheboygan except by way of the Green Bay road to Sheboygan Falls and thence by a road to Sheboygan. The first settlers came in the summer of 1847... The sole industry of Mosel town is agriculture and the population is practically all German. In 1910 the population was 884.*

3: Excerpt from "History of Sheboygan County, Wisconsin, past and present Vol.1, 1912.
Zillier, Carl, b. 1838 (ed); Chap XIV: Towns and Villages, Mosel, pp. 164-265

Children of Ludwig Grimm and Elizabeth Schneider:

i.  Franziscus Gustav Grimm, born Dec 1844 in Germany; died 1911 in Portland, Multnomah Co., OR. Married 1873, Wilhelmina "Minnie" Schalk, born Jan 1847 in Germany and died about Nov 1934 in Portland, Multnomah Co., OR. They had six children.

ii. Frederich "Fred" Theodore Grimm, born 05 Sep 1849 in Sheboygan Co., WI; died 1930 in Reedsville, Manitowoc Co., WI. Married 1879 Augusta Emma Fischer, born 10 Mar 1858 in Mosel, Sheboygan Co., WI and died Mar 1939 in Reedsville, Manitowoc Co., WI. They had five children.

iii. Bernhart Grimm, born Mar 1855 in Hancock, Houghton Co., MI; died 1924 in Astoria, Clatsop Co., OR. Never married.

iv. Albert A. Grimm, born Oct 1856 in Wisconsin; died 05 Jun 1946 in Red Lake Co., MN. Married Mary S. Schellman, born about 1865 in Pennsylvania and died in 1936 in Red Lake Co., MN. They had ten children.

---

[6] Ancestry.com. Wisconsin, Compiled Census and Census Substitutes Index, 1820-1890 [database on-line]. Provo, UT, USA: Ancestry.com Operations Inc, 1999. Original data: Jackson, Ron V., Accelerated Indexing Systems, comp.. Wisconsin Census, 1820-1890. Compiled and digitized by Mr. Jackson and AIS from microfilmed schedules of the U.S. Federal Decennial Census, territorial/state censuses, and/or census substitutes.

> v. Anna Margaret Grimm, born 05 Feb 1860 in Sheboygan Co., WI; died 19 Oct 1952 in Santa Rosa, Sonoma Co., CA. Married 11 Aug 1895 in Mount Angel, Marion Co., OR. Carl F. Schmelzer, born Mar 1860 in Wisconsin and died 1931 in California.

> vi. Carolina "Carrie" Theresa Grimm, born 06 Jan 1862 in Sheboygan Co., WI; died 16 Jun 1952 in Dayton, Yamhill Co., OR. Married 22 Aug 1882 in Hancock, Houghton Co., MI, Louis Elmer Penrose, born 02 Oct 1861 in Brookfield, Waukesha Co., WI and died 22 Dec 1921 in Fort Rock, Lake Co., OR. They had six children.

The birth of his two youngest children places the family in Sheboygan Co. between 1860-1862. These were the early years of the Civil War. Over 90,000 men from Wisconsin served in the Union armed forces during the Civil War. Of the 240 Grimms that enlisted in the Civil War, 220 of them were Union. The other 20 were Confederate.[7] Although Ludwig's eldest son, Frank, age 18, would have been eligible to enlist, and the second son, Frederick, though four years younger, could still have enlisted later, neither claimed to be Civil War Veterans on the 1910 US Federal Census. There is a record of a Ludwig Grimm, Wisconsin, who enlisted in the 1st Wisconsin Infantry, Co. H, at the rank of private.[8] The record should be researched to determine if this was Henry Ludwig Grimm, born 1816. Ludwig would have been about 46 years old at the time.

Three years after the Civil War ended, Heinrich Ludwig Grimm was granted his petition to become a naturalized citizen on 25 November 1868 at the age of fifty-two.[9] The certificate (No. G-650) was issued at the Circuit Court in Sheboygan, Wisconsin. A woman's citizenship status was still governed by her husband's at that time, so it wasn't necessary for Elizabeth to file as well.

4: Naturalization Certificate of Ludwig Grimm (G-650 No. 109)

---

[7] e-Reference Desk (Website); Guide to State Resources: Wisconsin, Counties, Sheboygan Couny; Retrieved 19 August 20, 2013 from http://www.e-referencedesk.com/resources/counties/wisconsin/sheboygan.html

[8] Ancestry.com *US Civil War Soldiers, 1861-1865*; [database online] Provo, UT, USA. Ancestry.com Operations Inc. 2010. ; #M559, Roll 11

[9] Ancestry.com. *U.S. Naturalization Record Indexes, 1791-1992 (Indexed in World Archives Project)* [Database online.] Provo, UT, USA. Ancestry.com Operations Inc. 2010. Original source: Selected U.S. Naturalization Records, Washington D.C.: National Archives and Records Administration; 25 Nov 1868; Circuit Court, Sheboygan, Wisconsin; Certificate #G-650

Historical events that Ludwig and his family were witness to, besides the Civil War, were the building of the US Transcontinental Railroad (1863-1869); the assassination of President Lincoln (1865); and the building of the Suez Canal in Egypt (1869). By 1870, the demographics of the town of Mosel were changing as well. The Germans were the first to settle Mosel beginning over thirty years earlier. The Polish began to arrive in 1870 and conflict between the two groups was inevitable.[10]

Ludwig moved his family to Iowa in 1868, probably to Westbury, Buchanan County, where the family owned property and were farming in 1880. Althrough they couldn't be located in either the 1860 or 1870 US Fedeeral census records, Minnie Schalk (1860) and Emma Fischer (1870) , the eventual wifes of Ludwig's two oldest sons, were found living with their respective families in Mosel, Wisconsin during those two population censuses. The Grimms moved to "the upper peninusla of Michigan[11] where they resided for about two years." It is probable that they lived in Houghton County, possibly in the town of Hancock, where Elizabeth had family. A land record issued to Ludwig Grimm for property in Taylor County, Wisconsin, indicates that the family had returned to Wisconsin by May 1892. The 160 acre farm, located Chelsea (Twp 31N, Range 1E, Section 4, at the 4pm, 1831 MN/WI)[12] would remain in the family for six generations.

5: Location of Westburg (later Independence) in Buchanan Co., Iowa

[10] Kittel, Sis. Teresita; ca. 1976; *"Ghost Parishes of Manitowoc County; Manitowoc, Wisconsin"*; (Cass 977.567) 00:09:36-Part 11; State of Wisconsin Collection; Manitowoc Local History Collection; Kathy Schmidt, Submitter: Manitowoc Public Library

[11] Falge, Dr. L. "History of Manitowoc County Wisconsin, 1911-1912 (Manitowoc County Wisconsin Genealogy – People Who Lived in Manitowoc County, Wisconsin Primarily Before 1901); Manitowoc County Personal Sketches; Fred T. Grimm, v.2, p.321-322. Retrieved 19 Aug 2013 from http://www.2manitowoc.com

[12] Ancestry.com. U.S. General Land Office Records, 1796-1907 [database online]. (Provo, UT, USA. Ancestry.com Operations Inc) 2008. Document #4588, Accession No. WI0360_.492; Authority: May 20,1862: Homestead Entry Original (12 Stat.392). Original data: United States, Bureau of Land Management, General Land Office Records. Automated Records Project; Federal Land Patents, State Volumes. Http://www.glorecords.blm.gov/. Springfield, Virginia: Bureau of Land Management, Eastern States, 2007.

Ludwig died the following month, in June1892, at the age of seventy-six. He had lived to see four of his six children married and with families of their own. He had fourteen grandchildren at the time of his death and one who had preceded him. His wife Elizabeth traveled to Marion Co., Oregon about 1895, with four of her children: Frank, Bernhart, Caroline, and Anna. She died in the year 1900 and is buried in Mount Angel, Marion Co., Oregon.[13]

6: Henry Ludwig and Elizabeth (Schneider) Grimm

7: Headstone of Elizabeth L.. Grimm, Mount Angel, Marion Co., OR

---

[13] Ancestry.com. *Web: Oregon, Find A Grave Index, 1819-2012;* [Database online].(Provo, UT, USA; Ancestry.com Operations Inc.) Record added: May 08, 2012; Memorial# 89817881. Photo by Patty C.

# GRIMMS COME OF AGE

Franziscus "Frank" Gustav Grimm, Ludwig and Elizabeth's oldest son, married Wilhelmina "Minnie" Schalk in 1873. Frank's family and that of his father, Ludwig, were listed in Westburg (Independence), Buchanan Co., Iowa in 1880[14] where they were living and farming side-by-side. It's probable that both families moved to Westburg together before the birth of Frank's first child born in Iowa in 1871. His three brothers were still living at home working as laborers, presumably on the family farm, as well as his two sisters, who assisted their mother.

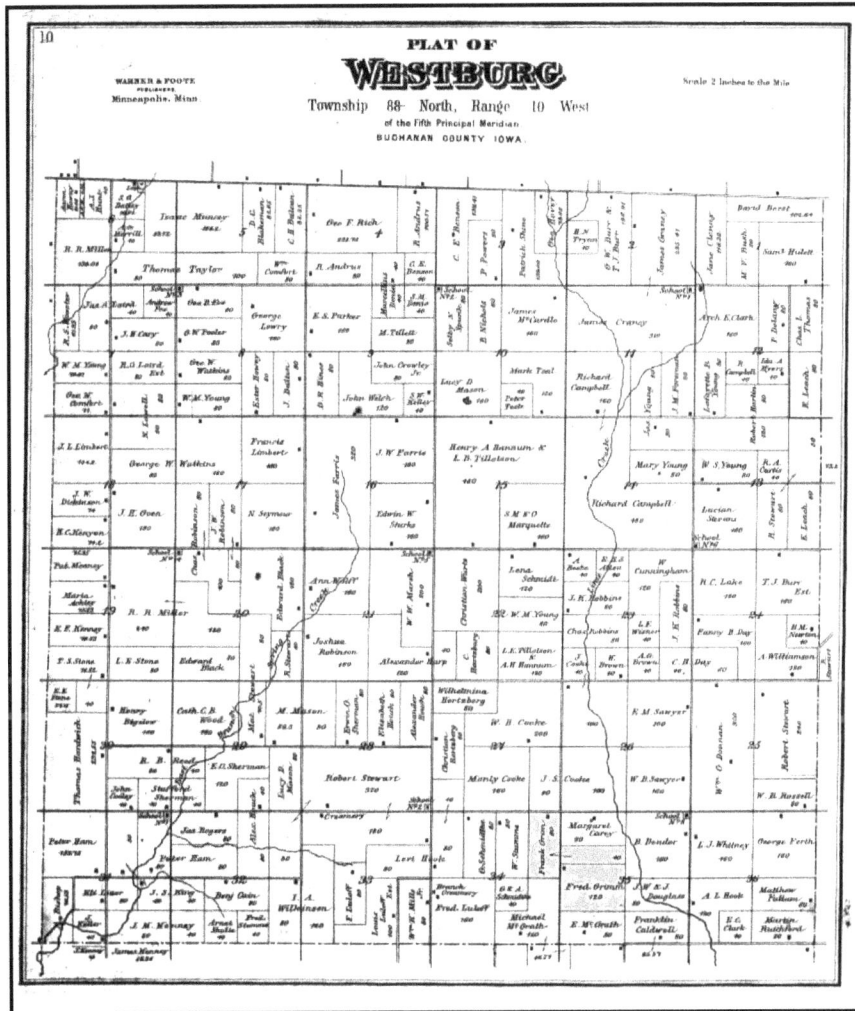

8: 1886 Plat map of Westburg, Buchanan Co., IA
Indicating the adjacent farms of Frank and Fred Grimm

The following year, Fred married Augusta Emma Fischer, daughter of Johann Heinrich Fischer and Augusta Rosina Oswald of Mosel, Wisconsin. Fred and Emma made their first home in Westburg on a farm adjacent to his brother Frank.[15] Caroline was the next to leave, marrying Louis Penrose in 1882. They made their first home in Michigan, probably in or near Hancock, Houghton County, where the Grimms had relatives. Albert A. Grimm, the fourth child, married Mary S. Schellman, daughter or John Schellman and Barbara Mertz, the following year in Houghton.

---

[14] Ancestry.com. *1880 United States Federal Census*. (Provo, UT, USA; Ancestry.com Operations Inc.) www.ancestry.com [Database Online]. Year: 1880. Westburg, Buchanan Co., Iowa; p. ED:97, p.9A, L.6-19, Dwelling 81/82, Family 81/82.

[15] Ancestry.com. *U.S., Indexed County Land Ownership Maps 1860-1918;* [database on-line]. 2010. Collection #G&M_79; Roll # 79. Westburg, Buchanan Co., IA, 1886.Original data: Various publishers of County Land Ownership Atlases. Microfilmed by the Library of Congress, Washington, D.C.

9: 1880 United States Federal Census, Westburg, Buchanan Co., Iowa[16]

[16] Ancestry.com. *1880 United States Federal Census* [database on-line].( Provo, UT, USA. Ancestry.com Operations Inc) Year: *1880*; *Westbury, Buchanan, Iowa; Roll 329; FHL: 1254329*; Page: *606A*; ED: *97*; Original data: Tenth Census of the United States, 1880. (NARA microfilm publication T9.) Records of the Bureau of the Census, Record Group 29. National Archives, Washington, D.C.

# GRIMMS ON THE MOVE

Wilhelmina "Minnie" Schalk was born in Mosel, Wisconsin. The U.S. Federal Census lists her as living there with her German immigrant parents, Christa and Sophia Schalk, in 1860. This was the same town in which Franziscus "Frank" Gustav Grimm spent his childhood after immigrating to America with his parents in 1848 at the age of three. He is the only known child of Ludwig and Elizabeth Grimm's children who was born in Germany. Frank married Minnie Schalk in 1873. The newlywed couple made their home in Westburg, Buchanan Co., Iowa on a farm they shared with Frank's parents. Their first child, Frank A, was born there in 1872, followed in close succession by five other siblings: Anna L., Wilhelm A., Ludwig A., Heinrich W., and Edward C. Their property description was listed as Twp. 88, Range [10], Sect. 34, NE NE.[17] The family moved to Marion Co., Oregon, probably sometime between 1892, when his father Ludwig died, and 1895, the year his sister, Anna, married in there.

10: Frank and Wilhelmina Grimm
(circa unknown)

In 1900, Frank and Minnie were living on a farm in Monitor, Marion Co., Oregon. Their two youngest sons, Heinrich and Edward, were still living at home working on the family farm, which was owned free of mortgage.[18] Frank had also applied and submitted papers for naturalization. All six of their children were still living. Frank died in Portland, Oregon at the age of sixty-six in 1911. Minnie is listed in the Portland, Clackamas County, Oregon City Directories between 1913 and 1918. She was living with her youngest son, Edward in Heyburn, Minidoka Co., ID in 1920 and with him in Anaheim, Orange Co., California in 1930. She returned to Portland, Oregon before 1934, where she died in November that year. She is buried in the Rose City Cemetery, Portland, Oregon.

11 Frank Grimm, Sr.
Rose City Cemetery, Portland, OR

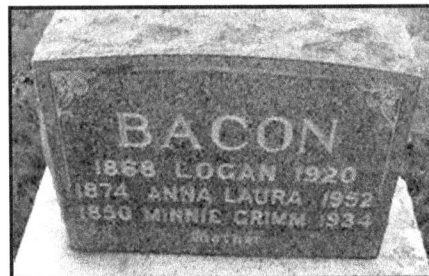

12: Wilhelmina Schalk Grimm,
Rose City Cemetery, Portland, OR

---

[17] Ancestry.com. *1885 Iowa State Census*. (Provo, UT, USA; Ancestry.com Operations Inc.) http://www.Ancestry.com [Database Online]. Year: 1885. Westburg, Buchanan Co., Iowa; p. 5; Line 1-8; Dwelling 23; Family 23.

[18] Ancestry.com. *1885 Iowa State Census*. (Provo, UT, USA; Ancestry.com Operations Inc.) http://www.Ancestry.com [Database Online]. Year: 1885. Westburg, Buchanan Co., Iowa; p. 5; Line 1-8; Dwelling 23; Family 23

Children of Frank Grimm and Wilhelmina Schalk:

i.       Frank A. Grimm, born 20 Feb 1872 in Iowa; died 14 Apr 1925, Paul, Minidoka Co., ID. Married (1) 12 Apr 1898 in Mount Angel, Marion Co., OR, Minnie Beigal, born 19 Sep 1876 in Wisconsin and died 11 Sep 1902. They had one son who died in infancy in 1901. Married (2) in 1904, Alma Helen Bauman, born 1879 in Wisconsin and died 28 Apr 1961 in Portland, Multnomah Co., OR. They had three children. Frank was a proprietor of a hotel in Paul, MN.

ii.      Anna Laura Grimm, born 24 Sep 1873 in Independence, Buchanan Co., IA; died 13 Aug 1952 in CA. Married (1) 12 Apr 1898 in Mount Angel, Marion Co., OR, Logan J. Bacon, born 02 Jun 1868 in MO and died 28 May 1920 in Minidoka Co., ID. They had two children. Married (2) before 1930, Charles A. McKee, born about 1864 in OR and died before 1935. Married (3) Ernest Stansbery.

iii.    Wilhelm Albert Grimm, born Mar 1874 in IA; died 21 Sep 1952 in Portland, Multnomah Co., OR and buried in Trinity Lutheran Church Cemetery, Portland, OR. Married (1) before May 1902, Emily C. Kreidt, born 09 Nov 1881 and died 20 Jan 1919 in Marion Co., OR. They had four children. Married (2) 01 May 1920 in Multnomah Co., OR, Mildred Idella [Unknown], born about 1890 in MN and died 03 May 1951 in Clackamas Co., OR. They had one child.

iv.    Ludwig "Louis" Alexander Grimm, born 10 Jan 1877 in IA; died before 1920. Married 27 Feb 1900 in Portland, Multnomah Co., OR, Ida C. Bruns, born May 1880 in Freedom, Lafayette Co., MO and died 03 Nov 1961 in Portland, Multnomah Co., OR. They had four children. Ida never remarried. She was a widow and living on a farm with two of her children in Paul, Minidoka Co., ID in 1920.[19] In 1940, she was living with her daughter, Leona Arronson, in Portland, OR. Louis worked as a grocer for a while and Ida was a piano teacher.

v.      Heinrich "Henry" William Grimm, born 06 Jun 1879 in Independence, Buchanan Co., IA; died 17 Dec 1945 in Boise, Ada Co., ID. Married 07 Dec 1902 in Woodburn, Marion Co., OR, Rosa Elma M Otjen, born 05 Mar 1883 in Silverton, Marion Co., OR and died 03 Nov 1921 in Burley, Cassia Co., ID. They had three children.

vi.    Edward Christoph Grimm, born 23 Jul 1881 in Independence, Buchanan Co., IA; died 26 Apr 1941 in Fullerton, Orange Co., CA. Married (1) 24 Nov 1910 in Mount Angel, Marion Co., OR, Minnie Marie Hug, born 1894 in Burt, Kossuth Co., IA and died 1920 in Burley, Cassia Co., ID. They had three children. Married (2) about 1935 in Orange Co., CA, Dora H [Unknown], born about 1895 in Wisconsin.

13: Frank and Minnie Grimm Family Portrait.
Back row, L-R: Ed, Henry, Frank Jr., Louis, William.
Front row, L-R: Anna, Frank Sr., Minnie (circa unknown)

[19] Ancestry.com. *1920 United States Federal Census*. (Provo, UT, USA; Ancestry.com Operations Inc.) www.ancestry.com [Database Online]. Year: 1920. Paul, Minidoka Co., Idaho. ED:__ , p.5B, L.96-98, Dwelling 108, Family 115.

By 1906, Frank and Minnie's grown children began to move out of Oregon and into Idaho. Anna, Henry, and Edward were the first to go. Anna and her husband, Logan Bacon settled on a farm in Acequia, Lincoln County, where they had a child born in 1907. Logan was involved with "moving pictures" in 1920. He probably ran the town movie theater. Henry and Edward settled in Heyburn, Lincoln County, where the two brothers farmed stock and hay. Henry became the proprietor of a feed store in Paul Village, Minidoka County by 1930. Edward moved to southern California where he began working as a distributor for the Times newspaper. Frank Jr. and Louis moved to Paul, Minidoka County about 1915. Frank became the proprietor of a hotel there. Louis worked as a grocer and farmer but died a few years later, leaving his young widow to care for their farm. Wilhelm was the only son who remained behind in Oregon. He was a grocer in 1900 and turned to farming by 1910.

Bernhart "Bernard" Grimm moved with the family to Oregon and was living near his brother, Frank, in Mount Angel, Marion Co., in 1900.[20] He was living in Astoria, Clatsop Co., in 1904, where he lived until he died in 1924. He never married.

Anna Margaret Grimm married Carl F. Schmelzer, of Wisconsin, in Mount Angel, Oregon, in 1895. In 1900, she had one daughter, Hilda C., and was caring for her aging father-in-law, on a mortgaged farm.[21] Carl moved his family to Anaheim, Orange Co., CA, before 1910, where he bought another farm.[22] By 1920, they have moved to Oakdale, Stanislaus Co, CA, to still another farm.[23] They owned a poultry farm in Santa Rosa, Sonoma Co., CA, in 1930. Hilda was grown and had been married for a couple of years to Laurin Cook, a bus driver for the city, and had a daughter of their own.[24] They lived nearby. After her father died in 1931, Hilda and her husband moved in with her mother and took over management of the poultry farm.

Child of Carl and Anna Schmelzer:

i.    Hilda C. Schmelzer, born 30 Jun 1896 in Mount Angel, Marion Co., OR; died Jul 1986 in Sandersville, Washington Co., GA. Married about 1928 Laurin F. Cook, born 07 Aug 1896 in Santa Rosa, Sonoma Co., CA and died May 1981 in Santa Rosa, Sonoma Co., CA. They had three children.

14: Carl and Anna Schmelzer
(circa unknown)

Carolina "Carrie" Theresa Grimm, Ludwig and Elizabeth's youngest daughter, married Louis Elmer Penrose in 1882, Hancock, Houghton Co., Michigan, where the Grimms had relatives. She and her husband made their home there until after their third child was born in 1885. They may possibly have traveled with her other siblings to the west coast when the family emigrated there after her father Ludwig's death. Her fourth child was born in 1890 in Tacoma, Pierce Co., WA, however, her last two children were born in Salem, Marion Co., Oregon, in 1891 and 1894. The gap between the last two births is probably when Carrie may given birth to and lost a child. The 1910 census indicates that she had given birth to seven children but only six were living by then.[25]

---

[20] Ancestry.com. *1900 United States Federal Census*. (Provo, UT, USA; Ancestry.com Operations Inc.) www.ancestry.com [Database Online]. Year: 1900. Mount Angel, Marion Co., Oregon. ED: 137, p.16A, L. 1, Dwelling 296, Family 296.

[21] Ancestry.com. *1900 United States Federal Census*. (Provo, UT, USA; Ancestry.com Operations Inc.) www.ancestry.com [Database Online]. Year: 1900. Mount Angel, Marion Co., Oregon. ED: 137, p.13B, L. 54-57, Dwelling 255, Family 255.

[22] Ancestry.com. *1910 United States Federal Census*. (Provo, UT, USA; Ancestry.com Operations Inc.) www.ancestry.com [Database Online]. Year: 1910. Anaheim, Orange Co., California. ED: 43, p. 12B, L. 79-82.

[23] Ancestry.com. *1920 United States Federal Census*. (Provo, UT, USA; Ancestry.com Operations Inc.) www.ancestry.com [Database Online]. Year: 1920. Oakdale, Stanislaus Co., CA. ED: 179, p.8B, L.93-96, Dwelling 166, Family 167.

[24] Ancestry.com. *1930 United States Federal Census*. (Provo, UT, USA; Ancestry.com Operations Inc.) www.ancestry.com [Database Online]. Year: 1930. Santa Rosa, Sonoma Co., CA. ED: 56, p.2B, L.78-79, Dwelling 34, Family 34; ED:50, p.3B, L.93-95, Dwelling 90, Family 100.

[25] Ancestry.com. *1900 United States Federal Census*. (Provo, UT, USA; Ancestry.com Operations Inc.) www.ancestry.com [Database Online]. Year: 1900. Spring Valley, Polk Co., Oregon. ED: 178, p.7A, L. 6-12, Dwelling 69, Family 69.

Carrie and Louis rented a house in Spring Valley, Polk Co., Oregon, one county over from her siblings in Marion County, in 1900. Louis worked as a day laborer and Carrie took care of the five children that were still at home.[26] Their oldest child, seventeen year old Minnie, was living with the Robert Dent family as a servant.[27] By 1910, Carrie and Louis had moved to a farm they shared with their daughters Rose and Minnie, and their respective families, in Silver, Lake Co., Oregon.[28] Ten years later they owned and were operating a lodging house in Bend, Deschutes Co., Oregon.[29] Louis died the following year in December 1921. Carrie moved back to Oregon and lived with her daughter, Rose Stoutenberg, and her family, in Hopewell, Yamhill Co.[30] She died in Dayton, Yamhill County, in 1952. She was preceded in death by her son, Louis Jr., possibly from the influenza pandemic in 1917, and her youngest daughter, Hazel in 1938.

15: Louis and Carrie Penrose
(circa unknown)

Children of Louis and Caroline Penrose:

i.      Minnie Gertrude Penrose, born 01 Sep 1882 in Hancock, Houghton Co., MI; died 11 May 1973, Salem, Marion Co., OR. Married 13 Sep 1902 in Salem, Marion Co., OR, Walter Boomer Hunt, born 31 Jan 1877, Salem, Marion Co., OR, died 22 Jan 1959, Salem, Marion Co., OR. They had three children.

ii.     Rose Carrie Penrose, born 26 Apr 1884 in Hancock, Houghton Co., MI; died 21 Jun 1975, Salem, Marion Co., OR. Married 19 Sep 1905 in Dayton, Yamhill Co., OR, Roy Ethelbert Stoutenberg, born 20 Jul 1884 in Unionvale, Yamhill Co., OR and died 16 Sep 1968 in Dayton, Yamhill Co., OR. They had four children.

iii.    Lewis William Penrose, born 13 Nov 1885 in Hancock, Houghton Co., MI; died 20 Oct 1917 in Fort Rock, Lake Co., OR. Married 11 Oct 1908 in Unionvale, Yamhill Co., OR, Arka Antrim, born 09 Aug 1890 in Boise, Ada Co., ID and died 12 Oct 1942 in Newberg, Yamhill Co., OR. They had four children.

iv.     Lillian Ann Penrose, born 28 Mar 1890 in Tacoma, Pierce Co., WA; died 08 Sep 1974 in Salem, Marion Co., OR. Married 24 mar 1909 in Dayton, Yamhill Co., OR, Ralph E. Nelson, born 27 Dec 1883 in Fairmount, Richland Co., ND and died 28 Apr 1970 in Salem, Marion Co., OR. They had six children.

v.      Esther Martha Penrose, born 06 Dec 1891 in Salem, Marion Co., OR; died 15 mar 1992 in Woodburn, Marion Co., OR. Married 14 Jun 1910 in Corvallis, Benton Co., OR, Horace Minor Propst, born 20 Oct 1885 in Albany, Benton Co., OR and died 08 Apr 1988 in Woodburn, Marion Co., OR. They had two children.

vi.     Hazel Glenn Penrose, born 29 Dec 1894 in Oregon; died 08 Aug 1938 in Deschutes Co., OR. Married 1914 George Earl Menkenmaier, born 12 May 1892 in SD and died 23 Dec 1938 in Portland, Multnomah Co., OR. They had two children.

---

[26] Ancestry.com. *1900 United States Federal Census*. (Provo, UT, USA; Ancestry.com Operations Inc.) www.ancestry.com [Database Online]. Year: 1900. Spring Valley, Polk Co., Oregon. ED: 178, p.4A, L.6-12, Dwelling 69, Family 69.

[27] Ancestry.com. *1900 United States Federal Census*. (Provo, UT, USA; Ancestry.com Operations Inc.) www.ancestry.com [Database Online]. Year: 1900. Spring Valley, Polk Co., Oregon. ED: 142, p.2A, L. 84, Dwelling 39, Family 39.

[28] Ancestry.com. *1910 United States Federal Census*. (Provo, UT, USA; Ancestry.com Operations Inc.) www.ancestry.com [Database Online]. Year: 1910. Silver, Lake Co., Oregon. ED: 138, p.6B, L.87-90, Dwelling 90, Family 92.

[29] Ancestry.com. *1920 United States Federal Census*. (Provo, UT, USA; Ancestry.com Operations Inc.) www.ancestry.com [Database Online]. Year: 1920. Bend, Deschutes Co., Oregon. ED: 35, p.4B, L.75-76, Dwelling 97, Family 108.

[30] Ancestry.com. *1930 United States Federal Census*. (Provo, UT, USA; Ancestry.com Operations Inc.) www.ancestry.com [Database Online]. Year: 1930. Precinct 11, Yamhill Co., Oregon. ED: 36, p.5A, L. 25-28, Dwelling 117, Family 113.

Number of Grimm families

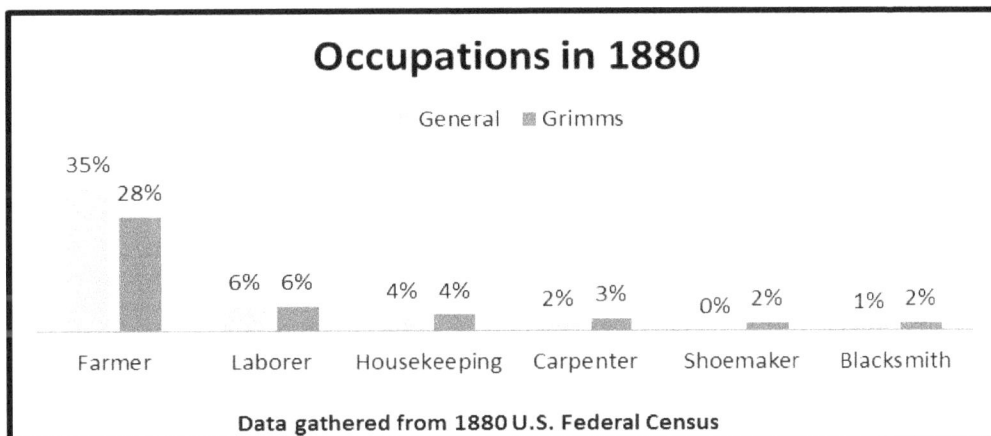

## Occupations in 1880

General ■ Grimms

| | | | | | |
|---|---|---|---|---|---|
| 35% | | | | | |
| 28% | | | | | |
| | 6% 6% | 4% 4% | 2% 3% | 0% 2% | 1% 2% |
| Farmer | Laborer | Housekeeping | Carpenter | Shoemaker | Blacksmith |

**Data gathered from 1880 U.S. Federal Census**

16: Distribution and occupations of Grimms in the U.S. in 1880
(All data derived from 1880 U.S. Federal Census Records)

Although they were predominantly farmers by trade, many changes were occurring in America that had an affect upon the future generations of Grimms. The world was changing around them and so were the dynamics of the Grimm family. Education levels began to increase from the standard four to eight years. By 1940, more individuals were going to and completing high school; some were beginning to go onto college. Grimms began moving away from the agrarian lifestyle of their progenitors and taking jobs in the cities. New inventions brought about new jobs: electric bill collectors, truck drivers, and salesman of manufactured goods Some turned to work in the saw mills. One was involved with "moving pictures". A few became accountants, newspaper distributors, policemen, and musicians. There was another change too. Women in the Grimm family began to take jobs outside the home as telephone operators, stenographers, waitresses, sales persons, and retail shop managers. Farming eventually became the exception rather than the rule.

## BROTHERS GRIMM IN WISCONSIN

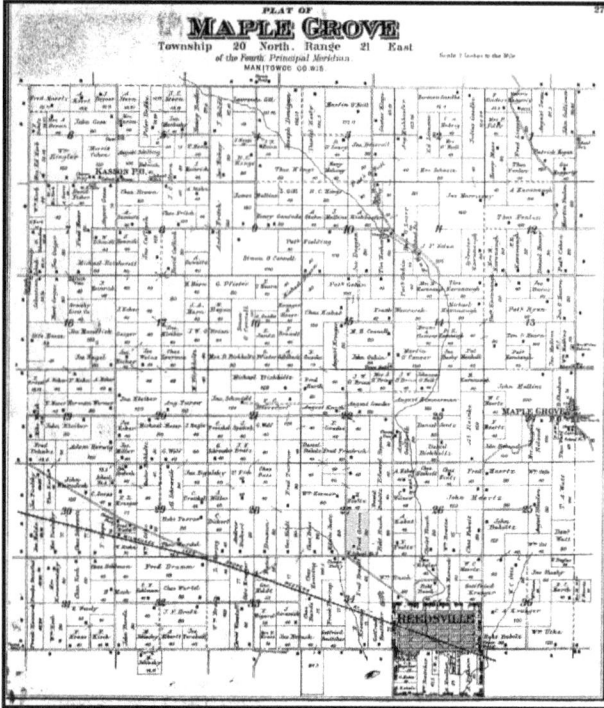

17: 1893 Plat map of Maple Grove,
Manitowoc Co., WI

There were two sons of Ludwig and Elizabeth who decided not to follow the path of their siblings to travel west to Oregon. These brothers chose to stay in Wisconsin and make a living off the land. They were Frederich and Albert.

The 1885 Iowa state census lists Fred and his family living on a farm adjacent to that of his brother Frank in Independence, Buchanan County, Twp. 88, Range [10], Sect. 35, S ½, SW NW.[31] Fred Grimm and his wife, Emma, lived their lives out on a farm in Maple Grove (Reedsville), Manitowoc Co., Wisconsin where the couple had five sons.

Fred returned to Wisconsin between 1885-1900 where he bought 100 acres of farmland in section 27 of Maple Grove (Reedsville), Manitowoc Co., and 140 acres in section 22. In 1900, Otto (17) and Reinhard (11) were already working as farm laborers to help out on the farm. It was acceptable and usual practice for older children to work outside the home at an early age to earn money to help pay off a mortgage and make ends meet. For fifteen-year-old Adolph there was no exception. He was living and working as a servant two houses away with the August Burcholtz family.[32] By 1920, Fred and Emma were still living on the farm; however, they were listed as members of

Reinhardt's family, along with their son Otto. Reinhard, Adolph, and Anton were each head of their own household on the property and each owned a portion of the farm.[33] Reinhard and Anton were married and had children of their own.

Dr. L. Falge mentioned Fred Grimm and his farm in "History of Manitowoc County Wisconsin, 1911-1912". He wrote that Fred cultivated about 75 acres of his farm. *"The fences are all barbed wire, and the premises kept in first-class condition. He manufactures dairy products, milking twenty-two cows of graded stock. He breeds to Percheron and Clyde horses, and raises hay, grain and clover seed. The basement of his barn is forty-four by sixty-eight feet, and was built in 1896. The floor of this is of cement and modern appliances have been put in as they were required. The water supply for all purposes comes from open wells....He is a modern farmer who thoroughly appreciates the value of scientific methods, and his premises and farm show the results of his intelligent care."*[34]

18: Fred and Emma Grimm
(circa unknown)

[31] Ancestry.com. *U.S., Indexed County Land Ownership Maps 1860-1918;* [database on-line]. 2010. Collection #G&M_79; Roll # 79. Westburg, Buchanan Co., IA, 1886.Original data: Various publishers of County Land Ownership Atlases. Microfilmed by the Library of Congress, Washington, D.C.

[32] Ancestry.com. *1900 United States Federal Census.* (Provo, UT, USA; Ancestry.com Operations Inc.) www.ancestry.com [Database Online]. Year: 1900. Maple Grove, Manitowoc Co., Wisconsin. ED: 80, p.5A, L. 29, 41-45, Dwelling 77/79, Family 78/80.

[33] Ancestry.com. *1920 United States Federal Census.* (Provo, UT, USA; Ancestry.com Operations Inc.) www.ancestry.com [Database Online]. Year: 1920. Maple Grove, Manitowoc Co., Wisconsin. ED: 113, p.5B, Dwelling 92, Family 93, line 51-52.

[34] Flage, Dr. L' "History of Manitowoc County Wisconsin, 1911-1912. (Manitowoc County Wisconsin Genealogy – People Who Lived in Manitowoc County, Wisconsin Primarily Before 1901); Manitowoc County Personal Sketches: Fred T. Grimm, v.2, p.321-322. Retrieved 19 Aug 2013 from http://www.2manitowoc.com

19: 1920 U.S. Federal Census for Maple Grove, Manitowoc Co., WI
listing Grimm family. Fred and Emma are listed at the top of the following page. (p. 5A/B)

Fred and Emma were living in town in Reedsville Village by the next population census in 1930. Fred was eighty years old and Emma was seventy-two. Their son Otto had been institutionalized at the Manitowoc County Insane Asylum where he would spend the remainder of his life.[35] By 1940, their other three sons had continued to live on the farm with their families. Adolph was working for the WPA while Reinhard and Anton ran the farm.[36]

Children of Fred and Emma Grimm:

    i.      Herman Heinrich Ludwig, born 08 Aug 1882 in Sheboygan Co., WI; died before 1885.

    ii.     Otto William Grimm, born 06 Aug 1883 in IA. Otto was institutionalized in the Manitowoc Insane Asylum by 1930, probably because his elderly parents could no longer care for him. He died there 06 Mar 1963 at the age of 79 and is buried in the hospital section of the Manitowoc County Cemetery.

    iii.    Adolph H, born 20 May 1885 in Spring Creek, Black Hawk Co., IA; died 09 Jun 1970 in Reedsville, Sheboygan Co., WI. Married 20 Dec 1915, Clara Etzler, born 06 Sep 1889 in Reedsville, Manitowoc Co., WI and died 06 Jan 1980 in Green Bay, Brown Co., WI. They had six children.

    iv.    Reinhard Franz, born 19 May 1889 in Independence, Buchanan Co., IA; died 31 May 1966 in Reedsville, Manitowoc Co., WI. Married 06 Jul 1918 in Manitowoc, Manitowoc Co., WI, Ella Pautz, born between 1899-1901 in WI and died 03 Jan 1957 in Manitowoc Co., WI. They had ten children.

    v.     Anton H., born 25 Jun 1893 in Maple Grove, Manitowoc Co., WI; died 25 Jul 1977 in Sheboygan, Sheboygan Co., WI.

---

[35] Ancestry.com. *1930 United States Federal Census*. (Provo, UT, USA; Ancestry.com Operations Inc.) www.ancestry.com [Database Online]. Year: 1930. Manitowoc, Manitowoc Co., Wisconsin. ED: 22, p.1A, L. 24, Manitowoc County Insane Asylum, patient.
[36] Ancestry.com. *1940 United States Federal Census*. (Provo, UT, USA; Ancestry.com Operations Inc.) www.ancestry.com [Database Online]. Year: 1940. Maple Grove, Manitowoc Co., Wisconsin. ED:34, p.3B/5A, L.66-71/35-44, Dwelling 56/85.

20: Letter written by Fred Grimm to his brother Albert in Medford.
The date 08 April 1908 is stamped on the back of the envelope.

21: 1912 Panoramic view of Medford, Taylor Co., WI
(Photo from National Archives Collection)

Albert A. Grimm was the fourth Grimm son. He was born in Oct 1856 in Wisconsin. He married Mary S. Schellman in Hancock, Houghton Co., Michigan in 1883. Mary was born about 1865 in Pennsylvania to German immigrants, John Schellman and Barbara Mertz. Albert and Mary's oldest son, Albert Phillip Henry Grim, was born there the following year.

Albert purchased and moved his family to a farm in Medford, Taylor Co., Wisconsin, soon after the birth of Albert Jr. The legal description of the property was: S½SE, Sec. 2, Twp. 36 N, RN 2 E, 4th pm, signed 23 March 1892.[37] Their second child, Lydia, was born in Medford two years later. William Max, however, was born in 1888 in Phillips, Price Co., Wisconsin. The couple's last seven children were again born in Taylor County so it is possible Mary was only temporarily in Phillips when she delivered her third child. The couple eventually had a total of ten children.[38, 39]

Albert and Mary's oldest daughter Lydia was married and living in Lambert, Red Lake County, Minnesota in 1910 and may have been a reason her parents decided to move their family there sometime between 1910-1913. Albert left the family farm to his recently married son, Albert Jr., and bought another farm in Lambert. William Max stayed with his parents and eventually took over the farm from them and lived out the remained of his life there. Albert died on 05 Jun 1946 at the age of ninety. Mary preceded him by ten years.

Their daughter Rose married and settled in Medford with her family. Lydia returned to Medford after the death of her first husband, Alfred Schubert. Alvina returned to Wisconsin at an undetermined date and lived in Park Falls, Price County according to information obtained from an entry in an address book once kept by Clara (nee Anderson) Grimm, the wife of Alvina's nephew, Alvin Grimm.

Gustav continued to live in Minnesota in the town of Lessor after he married but eventually moved his family to Salem, Oregon sometime before 1940. His sister Elsie Pederson followed him to Marion County, arriving about 1942, after living for a few years in Spokane, WA. Caroline went to Pennsylvania. Circumstances regarding Alma's life after 1910 are unknown at this writing.

22: Albert A. and Mary Grimm
Immanuel Lutheran Cemetery,
McIntosh, MN

---

[37] Ancestry.com. U.S. General Land Office Records, 1796-1907 [database online]. (Provo, UT, USA. Ancestry.com Operations Inc) 2008. Document #4588, Accession No. WI0360_.492; Authority: May 20,1862: Homestead Entry Original (12 Stat.392). Original data: United States, Bureau of Land Management, General Land Office Records. *Automated Records Project; Federal Land Patents, State Volumes. Http://www.glorecords.blm.gov/.* Springfield, Virginia: Bureau of Land Management, Eastern States, 2007.

[38] Ancestry.com. *1900 United States Federal Census.* (Provo, UT, USA; Ancestry.com Operations Inc.) www.ancestry.com [Database Online]. Year: 1900. Medford Twp., Taylor Co., Wisconsin. ED: 181, p.__, L.102-110.

[39] Ancestry.com. *1905 Wisconsin State Census.* (Provo, UT, USA; Ancestry.com Operations Inc.) http://www.Ancestry.com [Database Online]. Year: 1905. Medford, Taylor Co., Wisconsin; p.23; Line 64-73; Dwelling 13.

Children of Albert and Mary Grimm:

i.     Albert Philip Henry Grimm, born 24 Oct 1884 in Hancock, Houghton Co., MI; died 14 Mar 1981 in Medford, Taylor Co., WI. Married 19 Aug 1908 in Medford, Taylor Co., WI, Anna Steiner, born 09 Aug 1890 in Marshfield, Fond du Lac Co., WI and died 15 Mar 1956 in Marshfield, Fond du Lac Co., WI. They had four children.

ii.    Lydia Louise Grimm, born 27 May 1886 in Medford, Taylor Co., WI; died 14 Apr 1973 in Medford, Taylor Co., WI. Married (1) 22 Jun 1904 in Taylor Co., WI, Alfred Schubert, born 19 Mar 1878 in Germany and died 12 Jun 1929. Married (2) before 27 Jul 1931 in Taylor Co., WI, Charles Henry Louis Strebig, born 07 May 1876 in Germany and died 15 Nov 1950. Lydia and Alfred had five children; no issue from the second marriage.

iii.   William Max Grimm, born 03 Mar 1888 in Phillips, Price Co., WI; died 19 Feb 1990 in McIntosh, Polk Co., MN. Married 31 Aug 1910 in Medford, Taylor Co., WI, Anna Duesing, born 10 Jan 1889 in Hancock, Houghton Co., MI and died 19 Feb 1977 in McIntosh, Polk Co., MN. They had six children.

iv.    Rosette Elisabeth Grimm, born 01 Mar 1890 in Medford, Taylor Co., WI. Married (1) 25 Nov 1908 in Taylor Co., WI, Paul F. Schubert, born 02 Aug 1887 in Wisconsin. Married (2) bet. 1920-1930, [Unknown] Johnson, died before Apr 1930. Married (3) [Unknown] Evans. No other information.

v.     Lisette Susanna Ferdinanda Franciscka Grimm, born 08 May 1892 in Taylor Co., WI; died before 1905.

vi.    Alma Augusta Karolina Albertina Grimm, born 1894 in Taylor Co., WI. No other information.

vii.   Gustav August Grimm, born 22 Jul 1896 in Medford, Taylor Co., WI; died 30 Nov 1989 in Salem, Marion Co., Oregon. Married before 1930, Ella O. [Unknown], born Mar 1893 in Minnesota and died 23 Sep 1975 in Salem, Marion Co., OR.

viii.  Caroline Wilhelmina Grimm, born 20 May 1899 in Medford, Taylor Co., WI; died Oct 1982 in York, York Co., PA.

ix.    Elsie Maria Grimm, born 25 Dec 1901 in Medford, Taylor Co., WI; died 07 Jun 1989 in Salem, Marion Co., OR. Married 21 Dec 1917 in McIntosh, Polk Co., MN, Nels Pederson, born 20 Mar 1896 in McIntosh, Polk Co., MN and died 31 May 1959 in Salem, Marion Co., OR. They had eight children.

x.     Alvina Anna Augusta Barbara Grimm, born before 28 Apr 1907 in Wisconsin. She married Arthur [Unknown]. No other information.

23: Albert A. Grimm Family four generations: (L-R): William, Albert St., Lavern, and Larry

Five brothers and sisters were all present at the 100th Anniversary Birthday Party for Willie Grimm, held Saturday, March 12th at the McIntosh Manor. L-r: Orville Grimm (TRF), LaVerne Grimm (Brooks), Evelyn Nelson (TRF), Doris Nelson (Oklee) and Violet Ferden (McIntosh). Seated in front of them is their father, Willie Grimm, 100 years old.

24: 100th Birthday celebration of William Max Grimm with five of his living children in 1998 taken at the Mac Manor Nursing Home in McIntosh, MN where he was residing at the time. William lived for another two years.

25: 100th Birthday celebration of William Max Grimm taken with a niece and seven nephews at the nursing home he was residing in at McIntosh, MN

# WILLIAM GRIMM CELEBRATES 100TH BIRTHDAY

On Thursday, March 3rd, relatives and friends joind William Grimm at Mac Manor Nursing Home to help him celebrate his 100th birthday. Cake, ice ream, nuts, mints, coffee and punch were served to the guests. Entertainment for the afternoon was by the McIntosh Swingers Kitchen Band, who played several good old time songs. Also, Acitivity Director, Linda Nyland, who was the Master of Ceremonies. She did a great job!

Willie received several cards and gifts. He received a special 100th year birtday card from President Ronald and Nancy Reagan. The day was enjoyed by all.

Another birthday party was held on Saturday, March 12th, at Mac Manor Nursing Home honoring Willie with over 100 relatives attending.

Willie received two beautiful decorated birthday cakes given by granddauther Gail and Dean Stom and family of McIntosh and Mr. and Mrs. Vincent Anderson of Oklee. He also received many beautiful cards, gifts, and flowers.

Cake, coffee, and punch were served in the afternoon. Many family pictures were taken and the special event was also video taped. Later a poluck supper was served at Immanuel Lutheran Church, McIntosh.

Guests attending were from Covina, Calif., Fargo, N.Dak., Havre, Chinook, Great Falls, Monatan, Rochester, Anoka, Northfied, Cannon Falls, Spicerr, Thief River Falls, St. Hilaire, Argyle, Warren, Kennedy, Warroad, McIntosh, Fosston, Winger, Mentor, Erskine, Red Lake Falls, Brooks, Gully, Trail, Olkee, NM.

## THE MEDFORD GRIMMS

26: Aerial view of the Grimm family farm in Medford, Taylor Co., WI 1979.
(Photographer unknown)

The day was Friday, 24 October 1884, when Albert and Mary Grimm of Hancock, Houghton County, Michigan, welcomed their first child into the world. Nine more children were born follow over the next twenty-three years. Three weeks later, the infant was baptized Albert Philip Henry Grimm by his uncle, the Reverend Philip Henry Wambsganss. Reverend Wambsganss had been ordained a few years back and was then the pastor of Saints Peter and Paul Lutheran Church in nearby Houghton, Michigan. Twenty years and one month after baptizing his nephew, this same man went on to found the Lutheran Hospital in Fort Wayne, Indiana.

Wisconsin was considered "America's breadbasket" from 1840-1880 when it was producing one-sixth of the nation's wheat. However, competition from Minnesota and Iowa, crop diseases, and diminished crops negatively affected the economic viability of wheat as a cash crop. The chinch bug disaster of the 1860's forced farmers to seriously consider other ways to farm profitably. Dairy farming began to immerge as a better alternative and by 1899 more than 90% of Wisconsin farmers were raising dairy cows. German and Scandinavian immigrants were quick to convert to dairy farming. By 1915, Wisconsin had successfully changed from a wheat-producing state, to becoming the leading producer of butter and cheese in the nation. It was in this state of agricultural flux during which the Grimms began dairy farming in Medford.[40]

27: Wedding portrait of Albert Grimm
and Annie Steiner 18 Aug 1908

---

[40] Wisconsin State Historical Society. *The History of Wisconsin, Vols. 1 &2*. Retrieved 17 Nov 2013 from http://www.wisconsinhistory.org/turningpoints

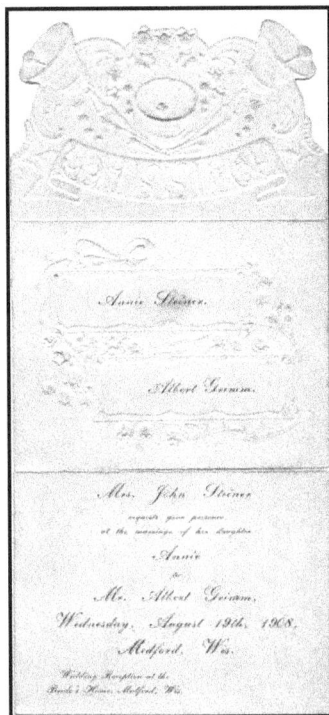

28: Wedding invitation of
Anna Steiner and Albert
Grimm 1908

Albert's family moved to Medford, Taylor County, Wisconsin before he was two years old. It was here that he grew up and spent his entire life. Albert literally married the "girl next door", the daughter of John August Steiner and Louise "Muna" Rouder. Annie was the sixth of nine children and was born 09 August 1890 in Marshfield, Fond du Lac County, Wisconsin. She was the second child of her family to be born in America. Her parents had immigrated from Tirol, Austria with her four oldest siblings the year before Albert was born.

Albert was a member of Trinity Lutheran Church in Whittlesey, not far from the family farm. He was confirmed there at the age of fourteen on 23 April 1899 by Rev. Frederick Moecker.[41] It was there that Albert and Annie were married on 19 August 1908 with a reception that followed at the bride's home. [42,43] He was twenty-three, she was eighteen. Their marriage would last almost thirty eight years until Anna died at the age of fifty-six. As the cycle of life went on and their family grew, Trinity Church oversaw many of the baptisms, confirmations, marriages, and burials of the couple's children and grandchildren.

Annie gave birth to their first child nine months after she and Albert wed. Two daughters quickly followed over the next two years. However, their second child, Sophia, born 17 July 1910, died the day after she was born. Anna gave birth to their last child, Everett, later in life at the age of thirty-seven, sixteen years after his sister, Erma was born in 1911.

Albert and his young bride lived with Albert's family during the early years of their marriage. Annie's brother Joe took care of the farm for his widowed mother, while Albert and his other three brother-in-laws worked as woodsmen at a nearby lumber camp.[44]

Albert's family had survived the influenza pandemic that had taken an estimated 40-50 million lives worldwide and reached every corner of the globe between 1918 and 1920.[45] Another crisis loomed to threaten the family during that same time. World War I had broken out in Europe. Thirty-three year old Albert was eligible to be drafted and was required to register with the local draft board. The war ended quickly and Albert was never called upon to serve. His draft registration card described him as medium height, stout build, with brown eyes and dark hair[46].

Albert owned his own dairy farm free of mortgage according to the 1920 population census. Anna had a live-in servant, fifteen-year old Selma Foss, to help her with the home and her two children.[47] By the next census in 1930, their 20-year old son Alvin, who was single and still living at home, was working on the dairy farm as well. Their daughter Erma had married Siegfried Krausse and was raising her own family in on a farm in Molitor, Taylor County.

29: Alvin and
Erma Grimm
(circa 1914)

---

[41] Newton, Jerome, Rev. *Memorial Service of Albert P. Grimm* (Trinity Lutheran Church, Whittlesey, WI). March 1981. Typed sermon with "From Church" written at top of page.

[42] Newton, Jerome, Rev. *Memorial Service of Albert P. Grimm* (Trinity Lutheran Church, Whittlesey, WI). March 1981. Typed sermon with "From Church" written at top of page.

[43] Wedding invitation of Anna Steiner and Albert Grimm.

[44] Ancestry.com. *1910 United States Federal Census*. (Provo, UT, USA; Ancestry.com Operations Inc.) www.ancestry.com [Database Online]. Year: 1910. Medford Twp., Taylor Co., Wisconsin. ED: 167, p.3B, Dwelling 52, Family 52, L.62-69.

[45] Taubenberger, Jeffery K.; Morens, David M. (January 2006). *1918 Influenza: The Mother of All Pandemics*. (Centers for Disease Control and Prevention; doi:10.3201/eid1201.050979. 2006. Retrieved 7 Nov 2013.

[46] Ancestry.com. *United States, Selective Service System, World War I Selective Service System Draft Registration Cards, 1917-1918,* Washington, D.C.: National Archives and Records Administration. [Database online] (Ancestry.com Operations Inc., Provo, UT, USA) 2005. Taylor Co., Wisconsin.

[47] Ancestry.com. *1920 United States Federal Census*. (Provo, UT, USA; Ancestry.com Operations Inc.) www.ancestry.com [Database Online]. Year: 1920. Medford Twp., Taylor Co., Wisconsin. ED: 203, p.6B, L.88-95.

30: World War I draft registration card C for Albert Grimm Jr. 12 Sep 1918

The biggest change in the Grimm family dynamic in 1930 was the addition of their last born child, Everett, who was then a two-year old toddler.[48] Everett was just eighteen years old when his mother died of thrombosis. She was fifty-six. Albert Grimm lived another thirty-five years before he died at the age of ninety-six.

31: Confirmation portrait of Everett Grimm ( 1942)

Everett was drafted into the U.S. Army in May 1952 during the Korean War. He did his basic training at Fort Sill, Oklahoma where he was trained as a Combat Engineer in the use field artillery guns. Six months later, Private Grimm was assigned to a platoon in the 31st Infantry Regiment, Seventh Infantry Division and sent to the front line in Korea. Once there, he was put in charge of a 4.2 mortar platoon of twenty-four men. There were others present that outranked him – notably two sergeants and a corporal – but no one else wanted to take responsibility for the platoon. Everett spent eight months as Platoon Leader. His platoon participated in numerous battles to gain control of a prominent hill referred to as "Old Baldy" that dominated the terrain. Some troops named it "Suicide Hill" since battles were so intense, with heavy casualties on both sides. Possession of the hill changed hands several times during the infamous battles. A few days after rotating out to headquarters while waiting to be processed back to the U.S., the hill was overtaken by the Chinese again and was never regained by the Allied troops.

*"Feb 1953, the company commander brought out a second lieutenant to be in charge of my platoon. The commander told me he wanted a commissioned officer to be responsible for the equipment: one jeep and trailer, four ¾ ton trucks and trailers, four 4.2 mortars and one 8" mortar, plus all ammo and a 50 cal. machine gun. Later this same night I received a call from my forward observers that something was happening again. I relayed the message to the lieutenant, thinking he would take over the radio, but he stayed in his little room. The first thing I knew the enemy passed over my observers again. This time the enemy jammed my radio. Just before the radio was jammed, the observers called for fire*

---

[48] Ancestry.com. *1930 United States Federal Census.* (Provo, UT, USA; Ancestry.com Operations Inc.) www.ancestry.com [Database Online]. Year: 1930. Medford Twp., Taylor Co., Wisconsin. ED: 60, p.3B, L.88-91.

*power on a location between our position and the observers. At this time the blood starts to boil! This is not good – having to fire this close to my observers and my position. This lieutenant still stayed in his room. Now higher headquarters had called for a bombing mission on "No Man's Land" and enemy side. I gave my platoon orders to cease firing, take sights off the mortar tubes, and take up defensive positions with our small arms rifles and 50 caliber machine gun. The Air Force bombed for hours on end... [In the morning] the radio was working so the commander was notified. The two observers were missing. The commander was on his way to my platoon. He told me he tried to make contact during the night, telling me to...retreat. I never received the message with our radio being jammed. The commander was at the platoon for half an hour or so, when here comes my two observers scrambling down the mountain.... At this time I informed the commander of the lieutenant not assuming responsibility. I asked him to get the lieutenant the hell out of the platoon! He gladly took him along and reassigned him to another position." ------*
*Everett Grimm*

32: Sgt. Everett Grimm (circa 1960)

When Everett re-enlisted, he was assigned to Battalion Headquarters, 5-2 Section, Intelligence and Reconnaissance. He spent the next two years constructing cement foundations for Quonset buildings at Camp Clay Banks in Michigan. It was during his time there that Everett volunteered to attend an "Escape and Evasion" school in Alameda, CA. A couple of years later, in 1960, he requested a change of duty. He was assigned as an Army recruiter for the town of Sheboygan in his home state of Wisconsin. However, one short year later, Sergeant Grimm was pulled off recruiting duty and sent to Crailsheim, Germany, where he was assigned to the 12th Engineer Battalion, 4th Armored Division.

Germany had been separated into East and West after the second World War. The communists occupied East Germany as well as East Berlin, the city being divided by the heavily patrolled Berlin Wall. The year was 1961. Unbeknownst to Everett and his platoon, the Berlin Crisis – when East Germany was trying to block air transportation to the free world – was in full swing. Sgt.First Class Grimm was ordered to head a mission to Check Point Charlie which was located at the Berlin Wall. His assignment was a direct result of the training he had received at the school in Alameda. In the event that he was captured, his training in escape and evasion would theoretically enable him to get back to the Army and provide inside information. Tensions were high on both sides as the platoon made its way through check points across East Germany. They spent an uncomfortable two months in Berlin before they were able to return to Crailsheim. He was reassigned to recruiting duty upon the completion of his mission in East Germany.[49]

33: Everett Grimm and Gertrude Baeur (circa 1961)

Everett made the decision not to re-enlist at the end of his tour of duty. He was honorably discharged from the Army in March 1963. Seven medals decorated his uniform: National Defense Service, Army Commendation, Army Good Conduct, Korean Service medal (two bronze stars), Korean Defense Service, United Nations Korean Service, and Combat Infantry badge.

Everett was on his way back to Medford, Wisconsin, and his family home when the train he was riding stopped in Elkhart, Indiana. He picked up a newspaper and read an ad that a local company was looking for truck drivers to haul mobile homes. That began his post-Army career of driving trucks for Morgan Drive-a-Way from 1963 to 1974. He worked for Jayco hauling RVs from 1974 to 1984. Over the next five years, until his retirement in 1989, he drove a truck for various companies.

Everett met Gertrude "Trudl" Baeur while he was in Germany. She had been born in Karlsrude, Baden-Wurttemberg, Germany but had immigrated to the United States in 1948. She had returned to Germany and was temporarily living with her parents when she and Everett met. The couple was married in 1965 and made their home in Middlebury, Elkhart Co., Indiana. They had no children.

---

[49] Grimm, Everett. *Everett Grimm's Military Service*. 2005. Middlebury, Elkhart Co., Indiana.

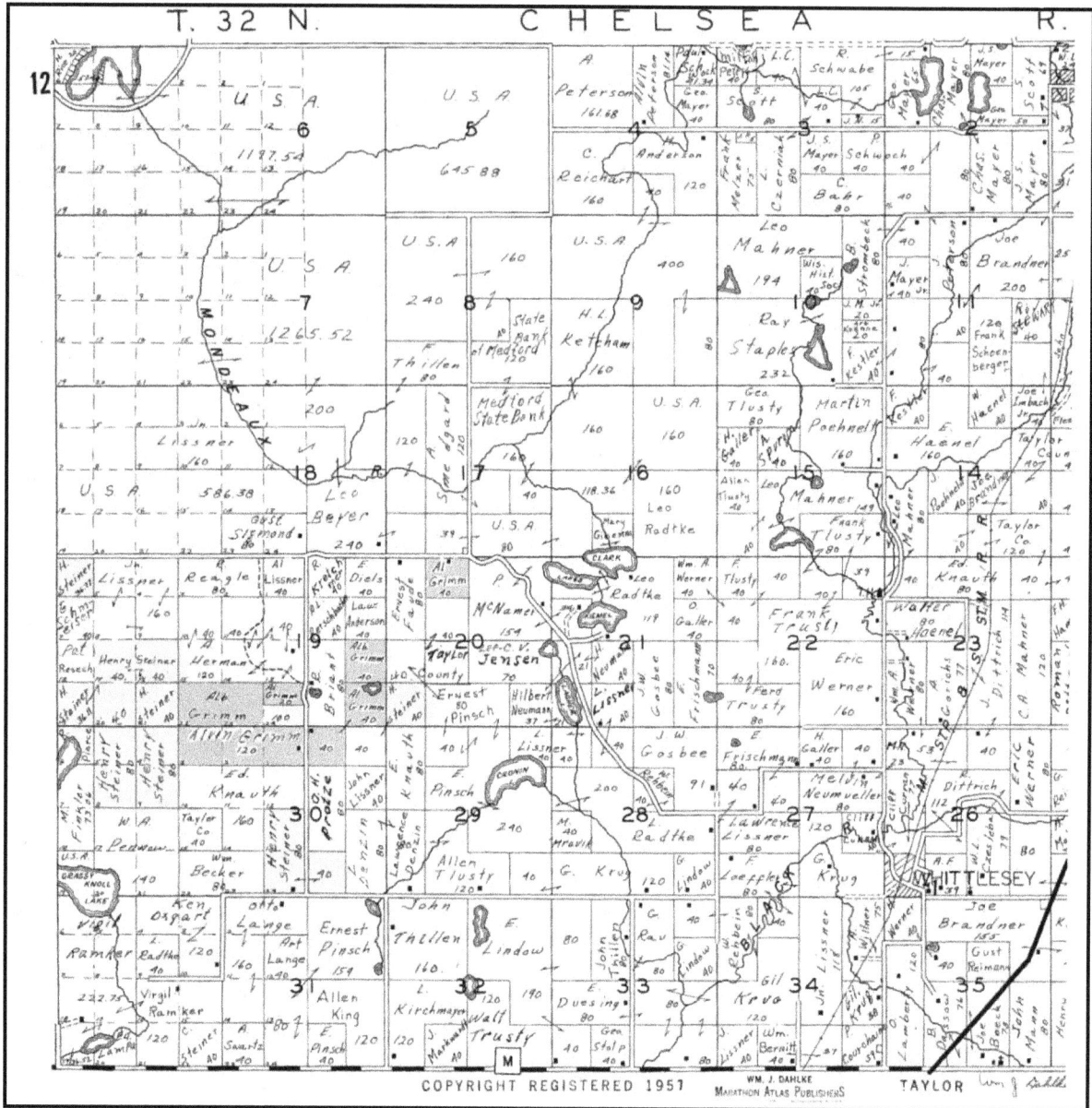

34: 1951 Plat map of Chelsea (Medford), Taylor Co., WI depicting Grimm property.

*"The original farm was a 220 acre homestead. Albert took over the farm from his father...probably through a will. [Everett] bought that property in 1950. Alvin bought 120 acres across the road from his father's farm but sold it back to his father when he moved into town. [Everett] next bought 40 acres a short distance away from the family farm but sold it to his brother Alvin when he was drafted into the Army in 1952. Albert and Alvin farmed all of the property together. Albert moved into the "little house" on Alvin's property after his wife Annie died and Alvin and Clara moved into the farmhouse. [Everett] eventually bought Alvin's original 120 acres across the road in 1970 to use as a place to hunt."*[50]

---

[50] Grimm, Everett. 2013.Middlebury, Elkhart Co., Indiana. Interview by Maryellen Anderson..

Children of Albert and Annie Grimm:

i.      Alvin Albert William Grimm, born 08 May 1909 May1908 in Chelsea (Medford), Taylor Co., WI; died 24 June 2003 in Vancouver, Clark Co., WA. Married 09 Nov 1933 in Medford, Taylor Co., WI, Clara Mathilda Anderson, born 09 Jan 1912 in Little Black, Taylor Co., WI and died 05 May 1997 in Medford, Taylor Co., WI. They had one child.

ii.     Sophia Grimm, born 17 July 1910 Taylor Co., WI; died 18 July 1910, Taylor Co., WI. Buried in Medford, Taylor Co., WI; Evergreen Cemetery.

iii.    Erma Helen Grimm, born 11 Nov 1911 in Chelsea, Taylor Co., WI; died 02 Jun 1991 in Stoughton, Dane Co., WI. Married 29 Feb in Medford, Taylor Co., WI, Siegfried Krausse, born 18 Feb 1903 in Molitor, Taylor Co., WI and died 21 Mar 1950 in Molitor, Taylor Co., WI. They had three children.

iv.    Everett Reuben Grimm, born 13 Nov 1927, Medford, Taylor Co., WI. Married (1) Florence Twa, born 1921 in Watersmeet, Gogebic Co., MI. Married (2) Gertrude "Trudl" Baeur, born 23 Dec 1929 in Karlsrude, Baden-Wurttemberg, Germany and died 08 Mar 1996 in Goshen, Elkhart Co., Indiana. Married (3) Joanna Ulrich, born 25 Mar 1930 in Middlebury, Elkhart Co., IN. Everett never had any children.

### Erma H. Krausse
### (1911-1991)

Funeral services will be held here at 10 a.m. Friday at St. Paul's Lutheran Church for Mrs. Erma H. Krausse, 79, Edgerton, a former Town of Molitor resident who died Sunday night at Skaalen Sunset Nursing Home in Stoughton where she had resided the past three days.

Rev. Warren Behling will officiate and burial will take place in Evergreen Cemetery. Ed, Tim and Tom Krausse and Craig Mason will serve as pallbearers.

The body will repose from 5 to 8 p.m. Thursday at the Hemer Funeral Home in Medford and then after 8 a.m. Friday at the church until time of services.

The former Erma Helen Grimm, daughter of the late Albert and Anne (Steiner) Grimm, was born November 10, 1911, in the Medford area where she received her education.

Her marriage to Siegfried Krausse, who preceded her in death March 21, 1950, took place in February of 1929 at Medford.

She had resided in the Town of Molitor most of her life, working as a homemaker. For the past three years she had resided at Edgerton with her son.

Mrs. Krausse was a member of St. Paul's Lutheran Church at Medford.

Surviving her are a son, LeRoy (Ann), Edgerton; two daughters, Mrs. Bernice Kuklinski, Milwaukee, and Elaine, Mrs. Jim McNeil, Marshall; two brothers, Everett, Middlebury, Ind., and Alvin, Medford, six grandchildren and nine great grandchildren.

35: Obituary of Erma Grimm Krausse (Star News, Medford, WI)

36: Obituary of Annie Grimm (Star News, Medford, WI)

**In Memory Of**

ALBERT P. GRIMM
Age 96

**BORN**
October 24, 1884

**DIED**
March 14, 1981

**SERVICES**
Tuesday, March 17, 1981  2:00 PM
Trinity Lutheran Church
Whittlesey, Wisconsin

**CLERGYMAN**
Rev. Jerome Newton

**INTERMENT**
Medford Evergreen Cemetery

Hemer Funeral Service, Inc.
Medford, Wisconsin

38: Memory card of Albert P. Grimm

37: Albert and Annie Grimm Evergreen Cemetery Medford, Taylor Co. WI

### Mrs. Albert Grimm, 56 Buried Here Yesterday

Mrs. Albert Grimm, 56, was buried in the Medford Evergreen cemetery yesterday afternoon, following services at the home and at Trinity Lutheran Church, town of Chelsea. She died Friday evening at 9:15 at St. Joseph's hospital at Marshfield. Services were conducted by Rev. C. F. Lutdtke, pastor of the family church.

She is survived by her husband, a well known town of Chelsea farmer; Also by three children: Alvin, on a farm in Chelsea; Mrs. Siegfried Krausse, Molitor; and Everett, at the home farm with his father; Also four brothers and two sisters: Louis and Joe and Mrs. Otto Lange, Chelsea; William, Owen; Frank, Sheboygan Falls; and Mrs. Otto Lechner, Bend, Oregon; Also by four grandchildren. One child preceded her in death, and her brother John died last fall. *John died 1944*

The funeral was largely attended by relatives and friends from a distance, whose names will be available for publication in the next issue of the Star News.

39: Clara (Anderson), Alvin, Erma (Grimm) Krausse, Gertrude (Baeur), Everett Grimm.
Trinity Lutheran Church, Whittlesey, Taylor Co., WI

40: Gladys (Grimm) Doriot, Alvin Grimm, Tracy Doriot,
Albert P. Grimm (seated). Four generations.
Chelsea, WI (circa 1971)

41: Trinity Lutheran Church
Whittlesey, Taylor Co., Wisconsin
(circa 1899). Photo from "Trinity
Centennial 1883-1993" (p. 15)

## THE LAST DAIRY FARMER

Alvin Grimm was born on 09 May 1909 in Medford, Taylor Co., Wisconsin.[51] Two months later, he was baptized Alvin Albert Wilhelm at Trinity Lutheran Church in Whittlesey.[52] Barbara Schellman and Wilhelm Grimm were the sponsors. Alvin spent almost the entire next eighty-five years living on the family farm. Young Alvin grew up helping his father run and maintain the dairy farm. He was a young man during the Great Depression. Times were lean; Alvin took a job working in road construction during that time. Although he worked the dairy farm every day, it became secondary to his trade as a bricklayer. He was a member of the United Brotherhood of Carpenters and Joiners of America from 1948 until December 1952 when he resigned.[53,54]

42: Alvin Grimm
(circa 1909)

Alvin's future wife, Clara Mathilda Anderson, was born a few miles away on 09 Jan 1912[55] in the town of Little Black. Her parents, August Nikolaus Anderson and Marie Olson had their daughter, the sixth of their eventual ten children, baptized at the Scandinavian Lutheran Church of Pine Creek and Little Black (later known as Our Saviour Lutheran), in Holway, Taylor Co., Wisconsin.[56] August was a dairy farmer, born 20 March 1875, in Green Bay, Brown Co., Wisconsin. Marie "Mary" Olson, was born in Christiana, Norway, on 15 Sep 1880.

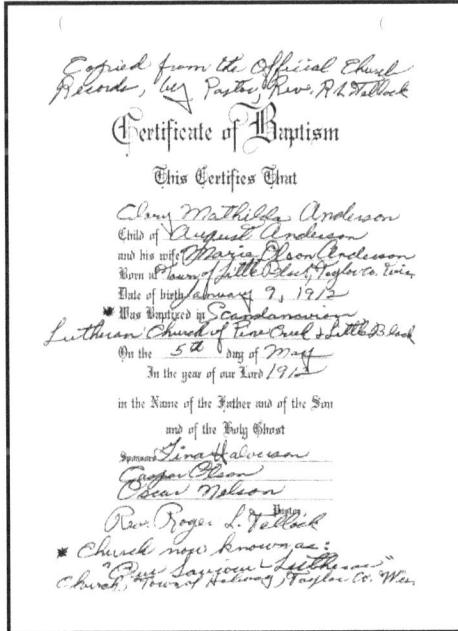

43: Baptism record of Clara Anderson
Scandinavian Lutheran Church
Holway, WI 05 May 1912

44: Alvin Grimm baptismal
Trinity Lutheran Church
Whittlesey, Taylor Co., WI
02 July 1909

---

[51] Baptismal Record, Trinity Lutheran Church, Whittlesey, Taylor Co., WI; 02 July 1909; date of birth 08 May 1909.
[52] Baptismal Record, Trinity Lutheran Church, Whittlesey, Taylor Co., WI; 02 July 1909 (date of baptism). Performed by Rev. Richard E. Heschke.
[53] United Brotherhood of Carpenters and Joiners of America, Local Union #1025, Medford, Taylor Co., WI; Dues Book; 14 Sep 1948.
[54] United Brotherhood of Carpenters and Joiners of America, Local Union #1025, Medford, Taylor Co., WI; Resignation Card; 30 December 1952.
[55] Certificate of Baptism, Scandinavian Lutheran Church of Pine Creek and Little Black; Holway, Taylor Co., WI; 05 May 1912; date of birth 09 Jan 1912.
[56] Certificate of Baptism, Scandinavian Lutheran Church of Pine Creek and Little Black; Holway, Taylor Co., WI; 05 May 1912; date of birth 09 Jan 1912 (date of baptism); Performed by Rev. Roger L. Tellock.

Alvin and Clara were married on 09 Nov 1933 at Trinity Lutheran Church parsonage.[57] They celebrated their golden wedding anniversary at Chelsea Conservation Clubhouse fifty years later. Present at the gathering were two guests of the original wedding party and witnesses on their marriage certificate: Clara's sister, Elva, and her brother-in-law, Arthur Lange.

### CLARA ANDERSON, ALVIN GRIMM MARRIED THURSDAY

Miss Clara Anderson, daughter of Mr. and Mrs. August Anderson, Little Black, and Alvin Grimm, son of Mr. and Mrs. Albert Grimm, Medford, were married at three o'clock Thursday afternoon, November 9, at the Whittlesey Lutheran church, by Rev. J.H. Steitler. Miss Alva Anderson, a sister of the bride, and Arthur Lange, a cousin, acted as attendants.

The bride wore an ankle length dress of orchid satin, white slippers, a headband of pearls and orange blossoms, and carried a bouquet of asters and white mums. Her bridesmaid wore a gown of wine colored silk crepe, and dark slippers, and carried a bouquet similar to that of the bride.

The marriage was a quiet affair, with only members of the immediate family present. Supper was served at the bride's home, and in the evening a wedding dance was held at Spreen's Interlaken Pavilion at Lake Esadore.

The young couple will make their home with the groom's parents. (Star News, Medford, WI; abt. 10 Nov 1933)

45: Mr. and Mrs. Alvin Grimm
Trinity Church Parsonage
Whittlesey, WI 09 Nov 1933

The newlyweds first home was a small house across the road from Alvin's parents' farm. A year later, their daughter Gladys Ann was born. She was the only child the couple would have. Clara was afflicted with tuberculosis which she lost a sister to in 1922, and necessitated Clara to spend the early years of her marriage away from home for treatment at a tuberculosis sanatorium. Alvin and his young daughter made regular trips to visit Clara until she could return home in August 1940. The 1940 U.S. Federal Census shows Alvin and Gladys living alone at their farm in April and Clara as a patient at Mt. View Sanatorium in Stettin, Marathon Co., Wisconsin.[58, 59]

46: Grimm farm mailbox. The house that Alvin and Clara first lived in can be seen in the background. (Photo by M. Anderson Oct 2003)

---

[57] State of Wisconsin, Dept. of Health, Bureau of Vital Statistics, Taylor Co., WI; Certificate of Marriage, #1601, 06 Nov 1933.
[58] Ancestry.com. 1940 U.S. Federal Census; Chelsea, Taylor Co., WI; ED 60, p.5B, Dwelling #78, L.44-45.
[59] Ancestry.com. 1940 U.S. Federal Census; Stettin, Marathon Co., WI; ED 37, p.11B, Dwelling #199.

47: Mt. View Sanatorium, Stettin, Marathon Co., Wisconsin (circa 1939)

48: Autographs written on newsletter
from Mt. View Sanatorium
Vol. VIII, No. 1)
Stettin, Marathon Co., WI

49: Clara Grimm Mt.
View Sanatorium
(circa 1939)

# Wisconsin Anti-Tuberculosis Association, Demonstration Chest Clinic

**SOCIAL AND STATISTICAL HISTORY**

Number _21_ Date _7-22_ City _Medford_ Age _10_ Sex M (F) (S) M W D  Family physician _Clinic,_
Color _white_  Referred by _Co. N._
Name _Clara Anderson_  Nativity _Am._  Employer
Occupation { Present _at school_  Education _In 4th gr._
Address _Medford R 2._  { Former  How long in County _10 yrs_
Stopped working when?

**FAMILY HISTORY**—(Give deaths of tuberculosis and pneumonia, age, and how long ago, of all relatives.)
(Give facts of any living relative having Tbc., and how long and how closely patient was associated.)

_1 sister - tb. - (1922 - death)_

**PERSONAL HISTORY**—Breast or bottle fed—Influenza—Bronchitis—Whooping cough—Typhoid—Pneumonia—Pleurisy—Colds—
(Underline with date above) Tonsilitis—Bone and Joint Disease—Swollen Glands—Fistula
Other Diseases—operations—  Tbc. ever diagnosed? _No_ Where?  When?

**PRESENT ILLNESS** (Underline Symptoms) Fatigue—Loss of appetite—Irregular bowels—Weight (loss or gain)—Pain in Chest—
Hoarseness—Cough—Expectoration—Hemoptysis—Sleeplessness—Indigestion—Amenorrhea—Palpitation—Night Sweats

Has patient served in Army, Navy, Marine Corps? _No_ When?  Life Insurance? Kind and Company. _No._

_h.59_  Historian

**PHYSICAL EXAMINATION**, Temp. { A.M. _98.8_ P.M. Pulse _99_ Weight (Past____ Present _54_) Height _49½_ Thyroid _Simple goitre_
Gen. appearance _Healthy_  HEART _neg._  Blood pressure
Teeth _neglect_ Tonsils _N_ Pharynx _Adenoids_ _Yes._ Mucous mem.____ Glands _enlarged_ Bone and Joint____
Spine____

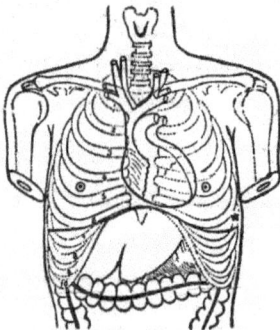

Impaired resonance / Dullness / Flatness / Voice Conduction (+)(—)(A) / Prolonged expiration / Pectoriloquy / Broncho-Vesicular B. / Bronchial B. / Harsh inspiration / Feeble B. / Amphoric B / Sibilant—Sonorous Rales / Fine, medium, coarse, moist Rales / Rhonchi—friction rub

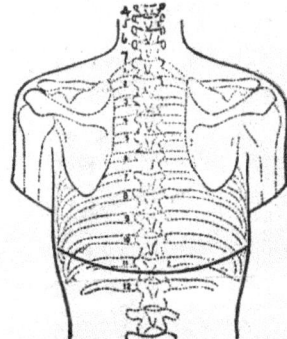

Sputum Ex. _none_ Wasserman  Urine Ex.  Other
Diagnosis: _(De espnae's sign present.)_
Treatment: San.  Referred to Physician  Follow up  No follow up
_For treatment of goitre; obs. + removal of goitre._
Additional Remarks: _Should have more milk, veg., rest, no coffee._

_R. L. Harrington_ Examiner

50: Clara Anderson medical exam July 1922

The Grimms were a musically-inclined family and they formed a band called The Grimm Orchestra. Alvin played the accordion, saxophone, trumpet, guitar, and piano. Clara and Alvin's father, Albert, played the guitar. Albert also played the harmonica and he and Alvin took turns playing the drums. Erma and Everett were also part of the band. They played guitar and accordion. The band began entertaining the locals when another band didn't show at the Pine Tree Pavilion dance hall in Chelsea one evening. The proprietor, knowing the Grimms' could play, asked them to entertain in the other band's stead. The Grimm Orchestra was such a success that they were invited back as a regular gig at the Pine Tree Pavilion and other local dances halls around Chelsea, Medford, and Little Black.. Their repertoire included waltzes, polkas, and popular songs of the day.

Alvin often hunted in the woods on their farm. He and Clara often went camping and fishing. They especially enjoyed ice fishing at Horseshoe Lake, located about five miles northeast of their farm. Alvin also enjoyed word search puzzles until he was almost ninety-years old. Clara enjoyed gardening and cooking. But it was family and friends that was most important to her. She collected a myriad of invitations, pictures and cards, letters, newspaper clippings, obituaries, documents, and other items that chronicled the lives and events of her family and friends.

51: Alvin Grimm playing horn (circa 1924)

52: Alvin Grimm standing outside his ice-fishing hut
Horseshoe Lake, Chelsea, WI
(circa unknown)

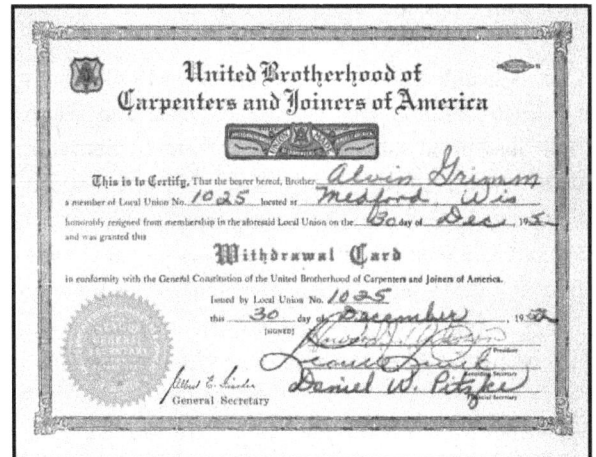

53: Union card of Alvin Grimm
UBCJA, Resignation 30 Dec 1952
Medford, Wisconsin

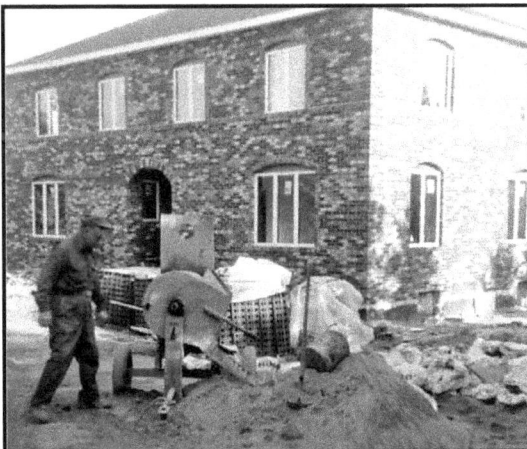

54: Alvin Grimm at work laying brick
(circa unknown)

Alvin was a hard worker. Every morning, for the majority of his life, he rose early to tend to his twenty-five head of milk cows before heading off to work laying bricks all day. In the evening, he would return home and feed and milk his cows again. When spring came, he would plow 40-acre plots of land under and plant crops.

*"Harvest was in the summer. Crops varied. [Alvin planted] predominately hay to feed the cattle, but also oats. After the oats were harvested, he would bale the stalks which were straw for bedding the cattle in the winter. I remember corn at different times in parts of the field." – Tracy Doriot* [60]

55: Tracy Doriot sitting on Alvin Grimm's Case tractor outside the barn at the family farm in Chelsea, WI Oct 2003. Tracy took the tractor to Washougal, WA with him after his grandfather's death. (Photo by M. Anderson Oct 2003)

Alvin continued to manage his dairy farm into the 1970s when he was nearing retirement age. In his later years, he leased some of his acreage to other farmers in the area to help supplement the his income. These other farmers used Alvin's fields to grow their own crops and to use as pasture for their livestock.

Clara's health began to fail in the early 1990's due to Chronic Obstructive Pulmonary Disease (COPD) and sclerosis of the right lung from tuberculosis. Alvin moved his wife into town where they lived for the next five years so Clara could be near her doctors. Neither would ever return to the farm they loved again. Clara died of congestive heart failure at the age of eighty-five at the Medford Nursing Home in Medford on 05 May 1997.[61,62] She was buried at Trinity Church where she and Alvin had been married almost sixty-four years earlier.[63]

Albert and Clara had rented their farm to relatives before they moved into Medford. Albert was eighty-three years old and could no longer manage the farm on his own. He continued to reside at the apartment in Medford for a while after Clara's death. A few months later, his daughter, Gladys Doriot, took him to live with her and her family in Ridgefield, Clark Co., Washington.

56: Clara Anderson obituary
(Star News, Medford, WI May 1997)

## CLARA M. GRIMM (1912-1997)

Clara M. Grimm, 85, Medford, formerly of the Town of Chelsea, died Monday, May 5, at memorial Nursing Home in Medford where she had resided for one month. Funeral services were held Saturday, May 10, at Trinity Lutheran Church in Whittlesey with Rev. Rand Jeppesen officiating.

Burial was held in the church cemetery. Pallbearers were Tracy and Orrin Doriot, John Drolshagen, Jim Neuman, Roland Neumann, and Paul Anderson.

Hemer funeral Home in Medford assisted the family with arrangements.

The former Clara M. Anderson was born January 9, 1912, in the Town of Little Black to August and Mary (Olson) Anderson. She attended the Medford High School. Her marriage to Alvin W. Grimm took place on November 10, 1933, in Whittlesey.

She and her husband farmed in the town of Chelsea. They had recently moved to Medford. She was a member of Trinity Lutheran Church.

Survivors include her husband, Alvin of Medford; a daughter, Gladys Doriot of Ridgefield, Wash., one sister, Elva Drohlshagen of Medford; two brothers, Robert and Arthur Anderson, both of Okanogan, Wash., four grandchildren, Tracy Doriot of Washougal, Wash., Orrin and Cathy Doriot, both of Ridgefield, Wash., and Lorie Harbour of Eureka, Calif.; and one great-grandchild, Brandon Doriot of Ridgefield.

She was preceded in death by her parents; two brothers, Casper and Elmer; and four sister, Olive, Myrtle, Emma, and Florence. (Star News, Medford, WI; abt May 12 1997)

---

[60] Doriot, Tracy. *Interview with Maryellen Anderson.* Nov 2013. Washougal, WA
[61] The Star News. *Clara M. Grimm (1912-1997)* circa 11 May 1997. (The Star News, Medford, Taylor Co., WI) Obituary of Clara M. Grimm.
[62] State of Wisconsin. Death Certificate of Clara Mathilda Grimm. May 1997. (State of Wisconsin, Department of Health and Social Services, Register of Deed; Madison, Dane Co., WI). Vol. 32 p.35.
[63] Hemer Funeral Service, Inc. *Memorial Card for Clara M. Grimm.* 10 May 1997. (Hemer Funeral Service, Inc., Medford, Taylor Co., WI)

Gladys placed an easy chair in front of the picture window of her home for her father. Iit was from that vantage point that Alvin would sit and watch the comings and goings of family and friends every day. When he wasn't in his chair, he could be found raiding the kitchen. Alvin had a particular fondness for Kit Kat bars and could drink a six pack of soda pop in a day. His general health was good despite his fondness for sweets. However, he became more feeble and unsteady on his feet as he grew older. He required constant supervision and was unable to be left alone. Gladys, who was contending with her own dire health issues, eventually had to make the difficult decision to place her father in a nearby nursing home.

*"Grandpa was in pretty good physical condition till the end. His dementia was the issue, as he would wander out of Mom's house and end up falling on the hundreds of fall hazards that exist in a hillside 3-story house. The most famous was making his way down the stairs and down to the old house (Cathy's now) and falling in a pit full of blackberries and broken concrete! Aside from various cuts and bruises, he was fine ! My Grandpa was a tough guy!"*

57: Alvin Grimm
(circa unknown)

*"In all the years I knew my Grandpa...I never saw him get angry. He had the patience of a Saint and always indulged my every whim. No matter what hare-brained scheme I came up, he always did everything he could to make it happen. From my earliest memories my time with Grandpa and Grandma and those wondrous summers of my youth are among my fondest memories."[64] – Tracy Doriot*

Alvin's brother Everett claimed his older brother only got angry with him once his whole life – when he was shooting birds out of a tree with his bb gun. His daughter Gladys said her father was a saint on earth. His grandchildren adored him. All who knew him said he was the kindest man they had ever known. Everyone loved Alvin – the man with the twinkle in his eyes.

Alvin's daughter and grandchildren made frequent visits to the nursing home, often taking him a can of soda pop and a box of Kit Kat bars which he would consume one after the other during their visit. Sometimes his grandson, Tracy, would bring him a can of beer instead which brought a grin to Alvin's face and brightened the twinkle in his eyes. He didn't care for the food that was served but, just as he had at home, he often *raided the sweet snacks off the nurses' carts when they were making their rounds.*

### ALVIN GRIMM (1909-2003)

Chelsea native and former Medford resident Alvin William Grimm, 94, Ridgefield, Wash., died Jun 24, 2003 in Vancouver, Wash. A memorial service will be held Friday, Oct 3 at Trinity Lutheran church in Whittlesey at 11 a.m. Burial of cremains will be in Trinity Lutheran Cemetery in Whittlesey.

Hemer Funeral Service of Medford is assisting the family with

58: Alvin Grimm obituary
(Star News, Medford, WI Oct 2003)

Alvin began developing dementia as he aged and, as it progressed in his last years, Alvin slowly faded away from the family that loved him so much. He often forgot his daughter's and grandchildren's names. However, he knew who his brother was when Everett came to visit him a couple of months before his death. He was completely unresponsive during his last week of life. Nonetheless, when a woman from hospice care offered to say "The Lord's Prayer" for him, Alvin, his eyes still closed, lifted his hand toward the ceiling and kept it there until the final amen. He was surrounded by those who loved him the most when he passed away in the late afternoon on 24 June 2003.

Gladys, accompanied by her children and her grandson, flew back to Medford, Wisconsin where a memorial service was held. She had her father's cremains buried beside her mother at the Trinity Lutheran Church in Whittlesey. When she sold the family farm a few years later, it was the end of the Grimm presence in Medford. Alvin was the last Grimm dairy farmer in Taylor Co, Wisconsin.

---

[64] Doriot, Tracy. *Interview with Maryellen Anderson.* Nov 2013. Washougal, WA

## ALVIN GRIMM MEMORIAL SERMON
By Rev. Randal Jeppesen October 3, 2003
John 14:6 "At Home - Forever"

Friends and family, and especially to you Gladys,

After waiting over 94 years, our Lord knew it was time for Alvin Grimm to come home, to come to his new home in Heaven, a home that would last forever.

Today, we gather to say our final goodbyes to your father, your grandfather and our friend. As we do so, we are reminded that Alvin Grimm is at home forever with his Lord.

On May 9, 1909, Alvin's parents, Albert and Anna, were blessed with the gift of a son. At that particular time, Alvin had no idea what events would transpire in his life. He didn't know he would be milking cows or working as a brick mason. Nor did he have any clue that nearly all of his life would be spent living in the home where he was born and raised. Yet God had all those events carefully planned. As God blessed Alvin's life, He saw to it that everything worked out so that Alvin could spend over 85 years in the same home, that he and his wife, Clara, could raise their daughter, Gladys, in the same home that Alvin was raise in many years earlier.

Alvin and Clara spent their married life living on their farm northwest of Medford. As I visited them on the farm, we would spend time talking about how the house used to look, where Alvin had slept as a child, and what had changed over the years. Whether it was summer, fall, or winter talking about their home and their farm was a common part of our conversations. When God called Alvin's wife, Clara home in 1997, it left an empty place in Alvin's life. For several years prior to that time, Alvin had done what he could to care for Clara as she faced her health issues. As the winter months would arrive, Alvin was always concerned about the winter weather and what he would need to do if the electricity went out. There was no doubt that Alvin enjoyed his farm, no doubt that Alvin was proud to live in the same home for over 85 years. It was all possible because God had it in His blueprint for Alvin Grimm's life.

Throughout Alvin's life, God blessed him in many ways. Alvin's greatest blessing came at a time Alvin didn't even remember. On July 2, 1909, God had a plan that would provide Alvin with a home forever. On that day, God brought Alvin into His family through Baptism. From that moment on, Alvin held the keys to a home that would last forever, a home where he would never have to move, never age, never face any health issues, a perfect mansion in Heaven. Yet Alvin had to wait over 94 years to receive his mansion in Heaven. But Alvin was content to wait and as he waited, God blessed him in many ways. Some days, those blessings were opportunities to go hunting in his woods or ice fishing. Other days, it was playing the piano, the guitar, or the accordion in the Grimm Orchestra. Throughout his life on the farm, God blessed him in many ways. As we look at the blessings God provided to Alvin Grimm, we can't help but realize that receiving his crown of life on June 24, 2003 was the greatest blessing of his life. After several years of declining health and nursing home care, after waiting over five years to see his wife, Clara, again, God granted Alvin the blessing of eternal life in Heaven, the blessing of being at home forever. Today, Alvin Grimm is at home forever. Today, Alvin is enjoying all the blessings God had planned for him since before his birth.

Today, Alvin may not be looking out the picture window on the south side of his house watching the deer in the field, but he is enjoying an even better setting as he enjoys his mansion in Heaven, an eternal home that far exceeds the simple farm setting northwest of town. Today, Alvin Grimm has what he needed most - relief from his difficulties on this earth and a home that lasts forever.

Alvin Grimm is at home today. No matter what the future may bring, Alvin will never have to move again, never have to relocate due to health, never have to wonder about what the future will bring. He is at home - forever.

Throughout Alvin and Clara's lives, it was faith that kept them going. It was faith that enabled Alvin to adjust to Clara's loss. It was faith that enabled Alvin to remain faithful to his God his entire life....

As I knew Alvin, he was a quiet man with a simple faith, yet a faith that enabled him to be an example for others. As I knew Alvin, he always seemed to be a patient person. To enjoy hunting and fishing and word search books, he had to have been very patient.

Alvin Grimm spent nearly his entire life on the farm northwest of town, yet today, he is at home, at home forever with his Lord. While we wait for our mansion in Heaven by faith, may we never forget that when that time comes, we too will be at home - forever. Amen

Alvin Grimm and Clara Anderson had one child:

i.       Gladys Ann Grimm was born on 10 Dec 1934 in Chelsea, Taylor Co., Wisconsin, USA. She died at home on 04 Mar 2011 in Ridgefield, Clark Co., Washington, USA (Complications from breast cancer; age 76). She married James Maynard Doriot, son of Charles Henry Doriot and Catherine Belle McDonald on 16 Oct 1971 in Reno, Washoe Co., Nevada, USA. He was born on 04 Oct 1913 in Manitowish Waters, Vilas Co., Wisconsin, USA. He died on 10 Feb 1992 in Clackamas, Clackamas Co., Oregon, USA. Gladys was buried next to her husband, James, in Ridgefield Cemetery, Ridgefield, Clark County, USA.

60: Alvin and Clara Grimm
Trinity Lutheran Church Cemetery Whittlesey,
Taylor Co., Wisconsin

61: Grimm family farmhouse Chelsea, Taylor Co., WI
just north of Medford, where the Grimms had been
dairy farmers for four generations.

# RETURN TO THE NORTHWEST

Gladys Ann Grimm was the only child born to Alvin and Clara (Anderson) Grimm on 10 Dec 1935. She spent her childhood living on the same dairy farm in Chelsea, Taylor Co., Wisconsin where her father had spent his entire life. Both her maternal and paternal grandparents lived nearby on farms adjacent to their family farm. She was raised in the Lutheran faith and most likely attended the same church in Whittlesey that her parents were life-time members of. However, she received her confirmation at Evangelical Lutheran Church in Medford, Wisconsin.

Gladys attended Medford schools. She didn't participate in any club activities but was a member of the high school band. She played a number of wind instruments; the saxophone was her instrument of choice. At home, she learned to play the accordion and occasionally played the instrument in her later years. Gladys graduated from Medford High School in 1952, the same school where her mother had graduated some twenty-five years earlier.

62: Gladys Ann Grimm
Confirmation
(circa 1948)

63: Gladys Grimm
in her band uniform
(circa 1952)

64: Medford High School, Medford, Wisconsin
(Photo: Maryellen Anderson 2003)

As a high school graduation present, Gladys' parents bought her a ticket to Okanogan, Washington where she spent that summer visiting with family relatives. She got a job at a local restaurant called the Loop Loop Café in Okanogan where she worked as a waitress along with her cousin Donna Anderson. She met and fell in love with a young man named Woody Morris and,although she returned to Medford at the end of the summer without him, she never forgot her first love.

Gladys got a job as a nurse's aide at the Medford Hospital in downtown Medford when she returned home. Not long after, she met Jim Doriot, the man she would marry, and gave up her job so she could travel west with him. Every summer the couple would make the drive back to the Grimm farm in Wisconsin, where Jim would leave his family while he returned to his job. He retuned at the end of the summer to pick them up and take them home again.

65: Gladys Ann Grimm 1952
senior picture Age 17

Gladys' husband worked as a welder on the trans-continental pipeline. His job required him to travel to wherever the work was being done. While living in Bend, Oregon, Jim worked as a laborer at Oregon Woodwork and Gladys helped supplement their income by taking a job as a waitress at the Pilot Butte Inn, a popular restaurant in town. All four of her children were born in Bend. Other places the family lived were Bowling Green, Virginia, Medford, Wisconsin, and Reno, Nevada for varying periods of time. Jim accepted a job as a knife grinder with the Pacific Wood Treating Plant in Ridgefield, Washington. He moved his family there about 1963. The sleepy little town of Ridgefield was never the same after Gladys Grimm Doriot arrived and permanently settled there.

66: Gladys in her waitress uniform.
Pilot Butte Inn, Bend, OR (Circa 1960)

Gladys became a founding officer of the now defunct PWT Federal Credit Union that was once located in downtown Ridgefield. However, her legacy and the indelible mark she left on the town was when she and a few close friends founded the annual Ridgefield 4th of July Parade. The parade and celebration grew to become a much anticipated and major regional event every year. She also helped found the annual Ridgefield Easter Egg Hunt.

Once all four of her children were in attending school, Gladys took a job driving a school bus for the Ridgefield School District. She also became a dispatcher for the Kalama, Woodland, Ridgefield and La Center School District Student Transportation Co-op (KWRL) in nearby Woodland, Washington. Part of her duties was to be responsible for determining the road conditions for the bus routes during inclement weather. In the pre-dawn winters, she would drive the routes and radio in her findings. Decisions to delay, change, or cancel bus routes and

67: Mayor Gladys Doriot
(circa 2002)

school days would be determined based on the reports she and other dispatchers sent back to headquarters.[65] Gladys eventually became Secretary, then Director, of Transportation for KWRL. She worked there from 1976 until she retired in 2002.

68: Mayor Gladys Doriot
at a council mMeeting
Ridgefield, Clark Co., WA
(circa 2002)

Gladys was actively involved in other public service for her community as well. She served as President for the Washington Association for Pupil Transportation (1986-87) and served on it's Board of Directors for five years (1987-1992). She sat on the Board of Directors of Clark Transportation (CTRAN) during the same time period. She was also a Department of Transportation Third Party Commercial Driver's License Examiner. In 1991, Gladys was elected a member of the Ridgefield City Council and as the town's mayor in 2002. She retired in 2006 for health reasons after having served the council for a total of sixteen years. Not one to sit still, Gladys continued to serve her community after her retirement by volunteering for the Red Cross Foundation once a week. She was honored in 2002 with Ridgefield's Outstanding Citizen award "in recognition of her exemplary community service."[66]

Gladys enjoyed camping and fishing when she visited her family and relatives in Wisconsin during the summer. She was an avid collector of Native American artwork and artifacts that she proudly displayed throughout her home. She enjoyed hunting for Indian arrowheads around the back country of Bend, Oregon and exploring abandoned mining and ghost towns. She used this same prowess in her retirement years to hunt for the next "great find" at local area Goodwill stores – and Gladys knew where *every* one in the area was and what the best days to shop at them were. She especially enjoyed traveling and was able to visit the majority of the states in the continental U.S. Her favorite place of all was the City of New Orleans, Louisiana.

---

[65] "Warrior of the Road", Lewis River News, La Center, WA;20 Jan 1993
[66] Doriot, Tracy. Gladys Doriot's Memorial Eulogy. May 2011.

Gladys was first diagnosed with breast cancer in the late 1970s. Surgery and chemotherapy took its toll on her for a while but Gladys recovered and jumped right back into her life after completing the course of treatment. When she wasn't dispatching for KWRL, examining a class C driver, going to a meeting somewhere, or prowling a Goodwill store, Gladys enjoyed going to Spirit Mountain casino with a friend to play the nickel machines all night. Sadly, the cancer returned in 2006. She retired from her public life as the disease progressed. By 2010, all viable means of treatment had been exhausted; Gladys knew she was losing the battle. Her trips to the casino became less frequent but she continued to volunteer for the Red Cross up to a month before her death. She continued to enjoy frequent visits from friends and family. Gladys Ann passed away peacefully in her bed at home on May 2011 with her family at her bedside.

James Maynard Doriot and Gladys Ann Grimm had the following children:

i.    TRACY OWEN DORIOT was born on 01 April 1956 in Bend, Deschutes Co., Oregon. He married (1) Mary Katherine Herdener on 22 May 1982 in Vancouver, Clark Co., Washington, USA (St. James Catholic Church). She was born on 06 Apr 1955 in Vancouver, Clark Co., Washington, USA. Divorced; no issue. He married (2) Terry Lynn Miller on 12 Jul 2013 in Vancouver, Clark Co., Washington, USA. She was born on 31 May 1955 in Washington, USA. He had no children from either marriage.

ii.    LORIE ANN DORIOT was born on 01 Mar 1959 in Bend, Deschutes Co., Oregon, USA (St. Charles Memorial Hospital). She married Daniel A Harbour about 1987. He was born on 27 Aug 1956 in Los Angeles, Los Angeles Co., California, USA. Divorced; They had no children.

iii.    ORRIN LEE DORIOT (son of James Maynard Doriot and Gladys Ann Grimm) was born on 10 Oct 1960 in Bend, Deschutes Co., Oregon, USA. He married Julia A Purdem on 30 Aug 1986 in Reno, Washoe Co., Nevada, USA. She was born on 03 Dec 1966.

Orrin Lee Doriot and Julia A Purdem had the following child:

i.    BRANDON MICHAEL3 DORIOT was born on 16 Mar 1987 in Vancouver, Clark Co., Washington, USA.

iv.    CATHY LYNN DORIOT (daughter of James Maynard Doriot and Gladys Ann Grimm) was born on 03 Jun 1966 in Bend, Deschutes Co., Oregon, USA. She never married.

69: Doriot family portrait (L-R): Lori, Orrin, Gladys, Jim, Tracy, and Cathy. Vancouver, Clark Co., WA. May 1982

70: James and Gladys Doriot,
Ridgefield Cemetery,
Ridgefield, WA

71: Doriot home in Ridgefield, Clark Co., Washington.
Before and after pictures of remodel conducted by their son, Tracy Doriot
with help from his family in 1984.
(Photos courtesy of Doriot Construction, Washougal, WA)

# HOURGLASS CHART OF ALVIN WILLIAM GRIMM

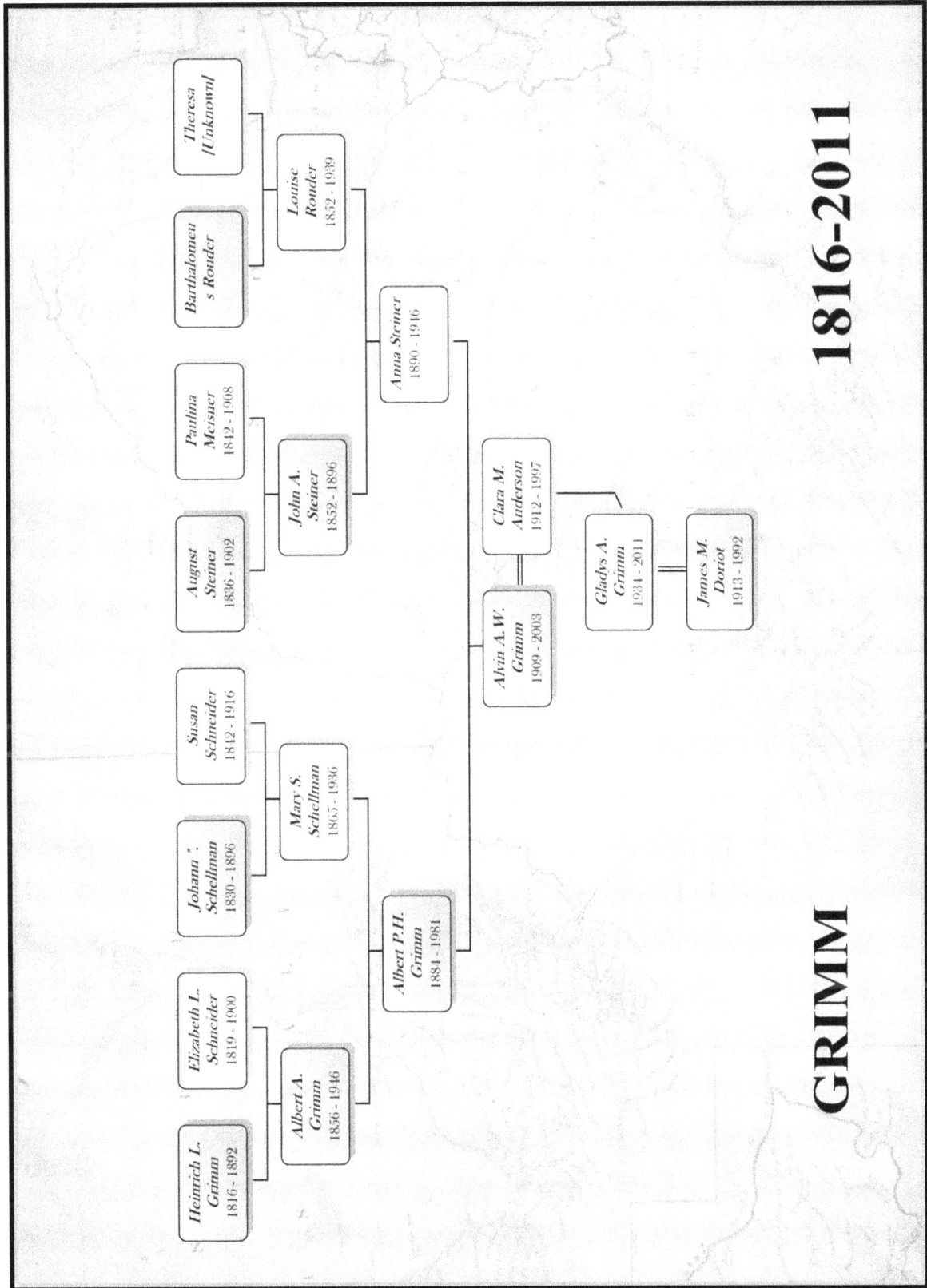

**1816-2011**

**GRIMM**

Theresa [Unknown]

Bartholomews Rouder

Louise Rouder
1852 - 1939

Paulina Meisner
1842 - 1908

Anna Steiner
1890 - 1916

August Steiner
1836 - 1902

John A. Steiner
1852 - 1896

Clara M. Anderson
1912 - 1997

Alvin A.W. Grimm
1909 - 2003

Gladys A. Grimm
1934 - 2011

James M. Doriot
1913 - 1992

Susan Schneider
1812 - 1916

Johann ? Schellman
1830 - 1896

Mary S. Schellman
1865 - 1936

Albert P.H. Grimm
1884 - 1981

Elizabeth L. Schneider
1819 - 1900

Albert A. Grimm
1856 - 1946

Heinrich L. Grimm
1816 - 1892

## PEDIGREE CHART OF GLADYS ANN GRIMM

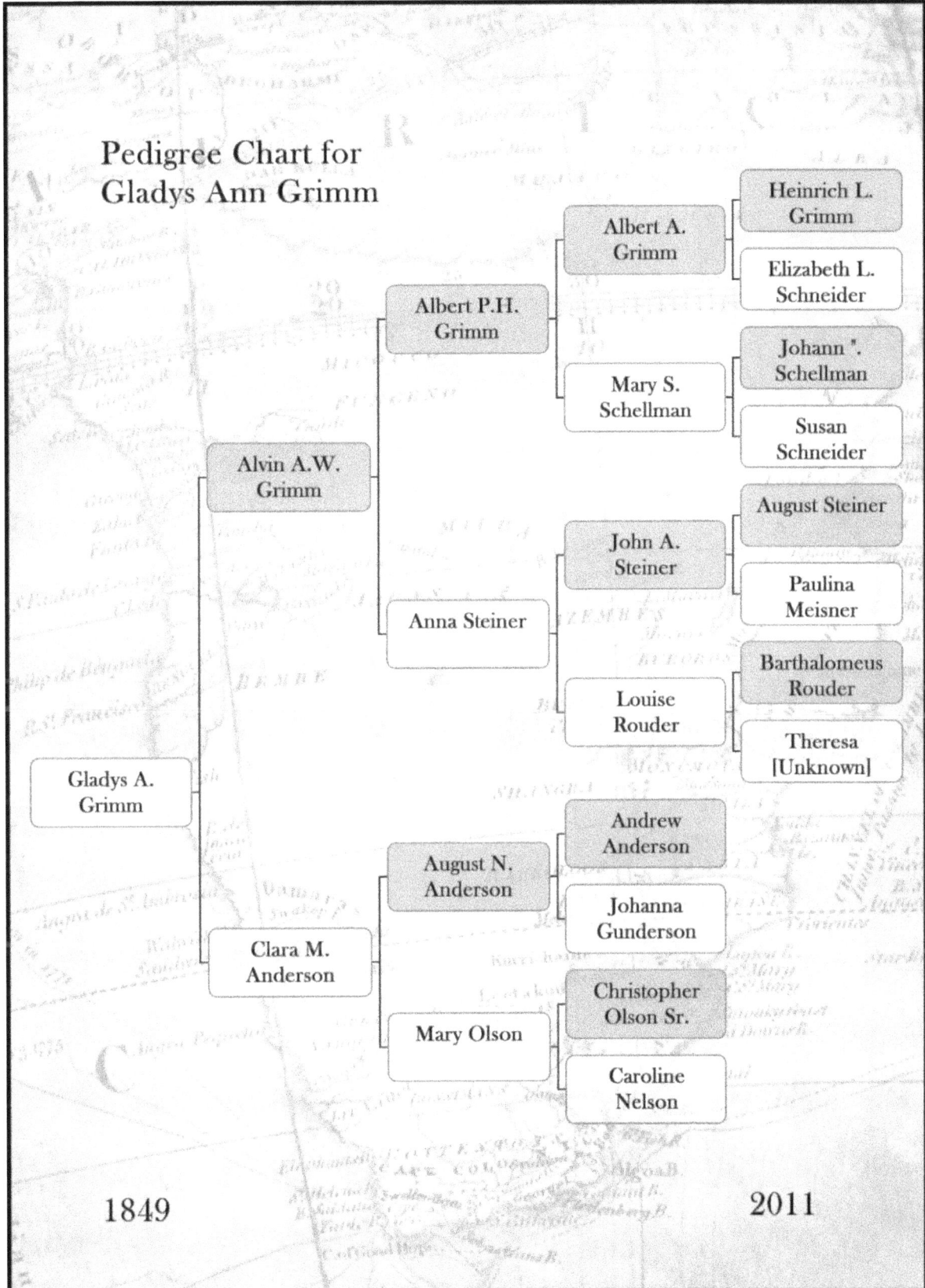

Pedigree Chart for
Gladys Ann Grimm

Gladys A. Grimm

Alvin A.W. Grimm

Albert P.H. Grimm

Albert A. Grimm

Heinrich L. Grimm

Elizabeth L. Schneider

Mary S. Schellman

Johann ". Schellman

Susan Schneider

Anna Steiner

John A. Steiner

August Steiner

Paulina Meisner

Louise Rouder

Barthalomeus Rouder

Theresa [Unknown]

Clara M. Anderson

August N. Anderson

Andrew Anderson

Johanna Gunderson

Mary Olson

Christopher Olson Sr.

Caroline Nelson

1849

2011

# PART II

## Genealogy Reports of
## Grimm and Collateral Families

# DESCENDANTS OF HENRY LUDWIG GRIMM

## Generation 1

1.   HEINRICH LUDWIG[1] "HENRY LOUIS" GRIMM was born in 1816 in Germany. He died in Jun 1892 in Wisconsin, USA (Age 76). He married Elizabeth Lucetta "Lisette" Schneider. She was born in 1819 in Germany. She died on 09 May 1900 in Marion Co., Oregon, USA (Probably) (Age 71). Elizabeth Schneider was buried after 09 May 1900 in Mount Angel, Marion Co., Oregon, USA.

Note: Ludwig Grimm's death date is per other family trees found on Ancestry.com. However, I have not been able to find any evidence verify this data.

Military Service Notes: Two of Henry's daughters were born in Sheboygan Co., Wisconsin during the early years of the Civil War. Henry would have been about 46 years old at the time. There is a record of a Ludwig Grimm, Wisconsin, who enlisted in the 1st Wisconsin Infantry, Co. H, at the rank of private. (US Civil War Soldiers, 1861-1865; [database online] #M559, Roll 11). The record would need to be researched to determine if this was Henry Ludwig Grimm b. 1816. His oldest son, Frank, age 18, would have been eligible to enlist. His second son, Frederick, though 4 years younger, could still have enlisted at a later date and fought in the war. However, neither Frank nor Fred claimed to be Civil War Veterans on the 1910 US Federal Census.

Heinrich Ludwig "Henry Louis" Grimm and Elizabeth Lucetta "Lisette" Schneider had the following children:

2.   i.    FRANZICUS GUSTAV[2] "FRANK" GRIMM was born in Dec 1844 in Germany. He died in 1911 in Portland, Multnomah Co., Oregon, USA. He married Wilhelmina Schalk in 1873. She was born in Jan 1847 in Germany. She died about Nov 1934 in Portland, Multnomah Co., Oregon, USA.

3.   ii.   FREDERICH THEODORE GRIMM was born on 05 Sep 1849 in Sheboygan Co., Wisconsin, USA. He died in 1930 in Reedsville, Manitowoc Co., Wisconsin, USA. He married Augusta Emma Fischer, daughter of Johann Heinrich Fischer and Augusta Rosina Oswald about 1881 in Manitowoc Co., Wisconsin, USA. She was born on 10 Mar 1858 in Mosel, Sheboygan Co., Wisconsin, USA. She died in Mar 1939 in Reedsville, Manitowoc Co., Wisconsin, USA.

     iii.  BERNHART GRIMM was born in Mar 1855 in Michigan, USA. He died on 02 May 1924 in Clatsop Co., Oregon, USA.

4.   iv.   ALBERT A GRIMM was born in Oct 1856 in Wisconsin, USA. He died on 05 Jun 1946 in Red Lake Co., Minnesota, USA (Probably; Age: 90). He married Mary S Schellman, daughter of John Schellman and Susan Schneider in 1883. She was born in Jul 1865 in Hancock, Houghton Co., Michigan, USA. She died in 1936 in Minnesota, USA (probably) (Age 71).

5.   v     ANNA MARGARET GRIMM was born on 05 Feb 1860 in Sheboygan Co., Wisconsin, USA. She died on 19 Oct 1952 in Santa Rosa, Sonoma Co., California, USA. She married Carl F Schmelzer on 11 Aug 1895 in Mount Angel, Marion Co., Oregon, USA. He was born in Mar 1860 in Wisconsin, USA. He died in 1931 in California, USA.

6.   vi.   CAROLINA THERESA GRIMM was born on 06 Jan 1862 in Sheboygan Co., Wisconsin, USA. She died on 16 Jun 1952 in Dayton, Yamhill Co., Oregon, USA. She married Louis Elmer Penrose on 22 Aug 1882 in Hancock, Houghton Co., Michigan, USA. He was born on 02 Oct 1861 in Brookfield, Waukesha Co., Wisconsin, USA. He died on 22 Dec 1921 in Fort Rock, Lake Co., Oregon, USA.

## Generation 2

2.  FRANZICUS GUSTAV[2] "FRANK" GRIMM (Heinrich Ludwig[1] "Henry Louis") was born in Dec 1844 in Germany. He died in 1911 in Portland, Multnomah Co., Oregon, USA. He married Wilhelmina Schalk in 1873. She was born in Jan 1847 in Germany, daughter of Christa and Sophia, Mosel, Sheboygan, WI. She died about Nov 1934 in Portland, Multnomah Co., Oregon, USA. Wilhelmina Schalk was buried on 16 Nov 1934 in Portland, Multnomah Co., Oregon, USA, at Rose City Cemetery.

Franziscus Gustav "Frank" Grimm and Wilhelmina "Minnie, Mena" Schalk had the following children:

2.  i.  FRANK A[3] GRIMM was born on 20 Feb 1872 in Iowa, USA. He died on 14 Apr 1925 in Paul, Minidoka Co., Idaho, USA. He married (1) Minnie Beigal on 12 Apr 1898 in Mount Angel, Marion Co., Oregon, USA. She was born on 19 Sep 1876 in Wisconsin, USA. She died on 11 Sep 1902. He married (2) Alma Helen Bauman, daughter of Albert Bauman and Wilhelmina [Unknown] in 1904. She was born in 1879 in Wisconsin, USA. She died on 28 Apr 1961 in Portland, Multnomah Co., Oregon, USA.

3.  ii.  ANNA LAURA GRIMM was born on 24 Sep 1873 in Independence, Buchanan Co., Iowa, USA. She died on 13 Aug 1952 in California, USA. She married (1) Logan J Bacon on 12 Apr 1898 in Mount Angel, Marion Co., Oregon, USA. He was born on 02 Jun 1868 in Missouri, USA. He died on 28 May 1920 in Minidoka Co., Idaho, USA. She married (2) Charles A Mckee before 1930. He was born about 1864 in Oregon, USA. He died before 1935. She married (3) Ernest Stansbery.

4.  iii.  WILHELM ALBERT "WILLIAM" GRIMM was born in Mar 1874 in Iowa, USA. He died on 21 Sep 1952 in Portland, Multnomah Co., Oregon, USA. He married (1) Mildred Idella [Unknown] on 01 May 1920 in Multnomah Co., Oregon, USA. She was born about 1890 in Minnesota, USA. She died on 03 May 1951 in Clackamas Co., Oregon, USA (Age: 58). He married (2) Emily C Kreidt before May 1902. She was born on 09 Nov 1881 in Iowa, USA and died on 20 Jan 1919 in Marion Co., Oregon, USA.

5.  iv.  LUDWIG ALEXANDER "LOUIS" GRIMM was born on 10 Jan 1877 in Iowa, USA. He died before 1920. He married Ida C Bruns on 27 Feb 1900 in Portland, Multnomah Co., Oregon, USA (probably). She was born in May 1880 in Freedom, Lafayette Co, Missouri, USA. She died on 03 Nov 1961 in Portland, Multnomah Co., Oregon, USA.

11.  v.  HEINRICH WILLIAM "HENRY" GRIMM was born on 06 Jun 1879 in Independence, Buchanan Co., Iowa, USA. He died on 17 Dec 1945 in Boise, Ada Co., Idaho, USA. He married Rosa Elma M Otjen on 07 Dec 1902 in Woodburn, Marion Co., Oregon, USA. She was born on 05 Mar 1883 in Silverton, Marion Co., Oregon, USA. She died on 03 Nov 1921 in Burley, Cassia Co., Idaho, USA.

12.  vi.  EDWARD CHRISTOPH GRIMM was born on 23 Jul 1881 in Independence, Buchanan Co., Iowa, USA. He died on 26 Apr 1941 in Fullerton, Orange Co., California, USA. He married (1) Minnie Marie Hug on 24 Nov 1910 in Mount Angel, Marion Co., Oregon, USA. She was born in 1894 in Burt, Kossuth Co., Iowa, USA (Near Algona Co.). She died in 1920 in Burley, Cassia Co., Idaho, USA. He married (2) Dora H [Unknown] about 1935 in Orange Co., California, USA (probably). She was born about 1895 in Wisconsin, USA.

3.  FREDERICH THEODORE[2] GRIMM (Heinrich Ludwig[1] "Henry Louis") was born on 05 Sep 1849 in Sheboygan Co., Wisconsin, USA. He died in 1930 in Reedsville, Manitowoc Co., Wisconsin, USA. He married Augusta Emma Fischer,

daughter of Johann Heinrich Fischer and Augusta Rosina Oswald about 1881 in Manitowoc Co., Wisconsin, USA. She was born on 10 Mar 1858 in Mosel, Sheboygan Co., Wisconsin, USA. (Marriage record gave her year of birth as 1855). She died in Mar 1939 in Reedsville, Manitowoc Co., Wisconsin, USA.

Frederich Theodore Grimm and Augusta Emma Fischer had the following children:

i.   HERMAN HENRICH LUDWIG[3] GRIMM was born on 08 Aug 1882 in Sheboygan Co., Wisconsin, USA. He died before 1885.

ii.   OTTO WILLIAM GRIMM was born on 06 Aug 1883 in Iowa, USA. He died on 26 Mar 1963 in Manitowoc, Manitowoc Co., Wisconsin, USA. He was buried on 28 Mar 1963 in Manitowoc, Manitowoc Co., Wisconsin, USA, at Manitowoc County Cemetery (hospital section, row 8. lot 12).

13.   iii.   ADOLPH H GRIMM was born on 20 May 1885 in Spring Creek, Black Hawk Co., Iowa, USA. He died on 09 Jun 1970 in Reedsville, Manitowoc Co., Wisconsin, USA (Age 85). He married Clara Etzler on 20 Dec 1915. She was born on 06 Sep 1889 in Reedsville, Manitowoc Co., Wisconsin, USA. She died on 06 Jan 1980 in Green Bay, Brown Co., Wisconsin, USA.

14.   iv.   REINHARD FRANZ GRIMM was born on 19 May 1889 in Independence, Buchanan Co., Iowa, USA. He died on 31 May 1966 in Reedsville, Manitowoc Co., Wisconsin, USA. He married Ella Pautz on 06 Jul 1918 in Manitowoc, Manitowoc Co., Wisconsin, USA. She was born between 1889-1901 in Wisconsin, USA. She died on 03 Jan 1957 in Manitowoc Co., Wisconsin, USA.

v.   ANTON H. "AMBROSE" GRIMM was born on 25 Jun 1893 in Maple Grove, Manitowoc Co., Wisconsin, USA. He died on 25 Jul 1977 in Sheboygan, Sheboygan Co., Wisconsin, USA (We Care Nursing Home.). Anton H. "Ambrose" Grimm was buried on 27 Jul 1977 in Reedsville, Manitowoc Co., Wisconsin, USA.

4.   ALBERT A[2] GRIMM (Heinrich Ludwig[1] "Henry Louis") was born in Oct 1856 in Wisconsin, USA. He died on 05 Jun 1946 in Red Lake Co., Minnesota, USA (Probably; Age: 90). He married Mary S Schellman, daughter of John Schellman and Susan Schneider in 1883. She was born in Jul 1865 in Hancock, Houghton Co., Michigan, USA. She died in 1936 in Minnesota, USA (Probably; Age 71). Albert A Grimm was buried after 05 Jun 1946. Both he and Mary Schellman were buried in McIntosh, Polk Co., Minnesota, USA, at Immanuel Lutheran Cemetery.

Albert A Grimm and Mary S Schellman had the following children:

15.   i.   ALBERT PHILIP HENRY[3] GRIMM was born on 24 Oct 1884 in Hancock, Houghton Co., Michigan, USA. He died on 14 Mar 1981 in Medford, Taylor Co., Wisconsin, USA (Medford Hospital; Age 96). He married Anna Steiner, daughter of John August Steiner and Louise "Muna" Rouder on 19 Aug 1908 in Medford, Taylor Co., Wisconsin, USA, at Trinity Lutheran Church of Whittlesey. She was born on 09 Aug 1890 in Marshfield, Fond du Lac Co., Wisconsin, USA. She died on 15 Mar 1946 in Marshfield, Fond du Lac Co., Wisconsin, USA (Age 56).

16.   ii.   LYDIA LOUISE GRIMM was born on 27 May 1886 in Medford, Taylor Co., Wisconsin, USA. She died on 14 Apr 1973 in Medford, Taylor Co., Wisconsin, USA. She married (1) Alfred Schubert on 22 Jun 1904 in Taylor Co., Wisconsin, USA. He was born on 19 Mar 1878 in Germany. He died on 12 Jun 1929. She married (2) Charles Henry Louis Strebig before 27 Jul 1931 in Taylor Co., Wisconsin, USA. He was born on 07 May 1876 in Germany. He died on 15 Nov 1950 (Age: 74).

17.   iii.   WILLIAM MAX GRIMM was born on 03 Mar 1888 in Phillips, Price Co., Wisconsin, USA. He died on 19 Feb 1990 in McIntosh, Polk Co., Minnesota, USA (Age 101 yrs. 11 mo. 16 dyes). He married Anna Duesing on 31 Aug 1910 in Medford, Taylor Co., Wisconsin, USA (Whittlesey Lutheran Church). She was born on 10 Jan 1889 in Houghton, Houghton Co., Michigan, USA. She died on 19 Feb 1979 in McIntosh, Polk Co., Minnesota, USA (Age 90).

18.   iv.   ROSETTE ELISABETH GRIMM was born on 01 Mar 1890 in Medford, Taylor Co., Wisconsin, USA. She married (1) [Unknown] Evans. She married (2) Paul Fred Schubert on 25 Nov 1908 in Taylor Co., Wisconsin, USA. He was born on 02 Aug 1887 in Wisconsin, USA. She married (3) [Unknown] Johnson between 1920-1930. He died before Apr 1930.

      v.   LISETTE SUSANNA FERDINANDA FRANZISKA GRIMM was born on 08 May 1892 in Taylor Co., Wisconsin, USA. She died before 1905.

      vi.   ALMA AUGUSTA KAROLINA ALBERTINA GRIMM was born in 1894 in Taylor Co., Wisconsin, USA.

      vii.   GUSTAV AUGUST GRIMM was born on 22 Jul 1896 in Medford, Taylor Co., Wisconsin, USA. He died on 30 Nov 1989 in Salem, Marion Co., Oregon, USA (Age 93). He married Ella O. [Unknown] before 1930. She was born in Mar 1893 in Minnesota, USA. She died on 23 Sep 1975 in Salem, Marion Co., Oregon, USA. Gustav August Grimm was buried in Dec 1989 in Salem, Marion Co., Oregon, USA, at City View Cemetery.

      viii.   CAROLINE WILHELMINE GRIMM was born on 20 May 1899 in Medford, Taylor Co., Wisconsin, USA. She died in Oct 1982 in York, York Co., Pennsylvania, USA.

19.   ix.   ELSIE MARIA GRIMM was born on 25 Dec 1901 in Medford, Taylor Co., Wisconsin, USA. She died on 07 Jun 1989 in Salem, Marion Co., Oregon, USA. She married Nels Pederson on 21 Dec 1917 in McIntosh, Polk Co., Minnesota, USA. He was born on 20 Mar 1896 in McIntosh, Polk Co., Minnesota, USA. He died on 31 May 1951 in Salem, Marion Co., Oregon, USA.

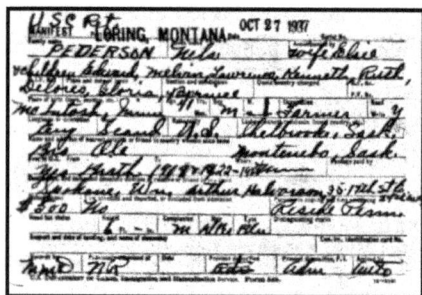

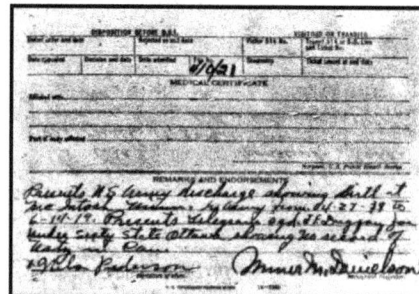

72: Border Crossing of Nels Pederson and his family
into Canada to visit his brother in 1937.

      x.   ALVINA ANNA AGUSTA BARBARA GRIMM was born before 28 Apr 1907 in Wisconsin, USA. She married Arthur [Unknown].

5.  ANNA MARGARET[2] GRIMM (Heinrich Ludwig[1] "Henry Louis") was born on 05 Feb 1860 in Sheboygan Co., Wisconsin, USA. She died on 19 Oct 1952 in Santa Rosa, Sonoma Co., California, USA. She married Carl F Schmelzer on 11 Aug 1895 in Mount Angel, Marion Co., Oregon, USA. He was born in Mar 1860 in Wisconsin, USA. He died in 1931 in California, USA. Carl F Schmelzer was buried in 1931 in Santa Rosa, Sonoma Co., California, USA.

Carl F Schmelzer and Anna Margaret Grimm had the following child:

20.   i.   HILDA C[3] SCHMELZER was born on 30 Jun 1896 in Mount Angel, Marion Co., Oregon, USA. She died in Jul 1986 in Sandersville, Washington Co., Georgia, USA. She married Laurin Frederick Cook about 1928. He was born on 07 Aug 1896 in Santa Rosa, Sonoma Co., California, USA. He died in May 1981 in Santa Rosa, Sonoma Co., California, USA.

6.  CAROLINA THERESA[2] GRIMM (Heinrich Ludwig[1] "Henry Louis") was born on 06 Jan 1862 in Sheboygan Co., Wisconsin, USA. She died on 16 Jun 1952 in Dayton, Yamhill Co., Oregon, USA. She married Louis Elmer Penrose on 22 Aug 1882 in Hancock, Houghton Co., Michigan, USA. He was born on 02 Oct 1861 in Brookfield, Waukesha Co., Wisconsin, USA. He died on 22 Dec 1921 in Fort Rock, Lake Co., Oregon, USA. Caroline Theresa Grimm was buried in Dayton, Yamhill Co., Oregon, USA; Unionvale Cemetery. Louis Elmer Penrose was buried in Oregon, USA; Unionvale Cemetery.

73: Lewis and Carrie Penrose

Louis Elmer Penrose and Carolina Theresa Grimm had the following children:

21.   i.   MINNIE GERTRUDE[3] PENROSE was born on 01 Sep 1882 in Hancock, Houghton Co., Michigan, USA. She died on 11 May 1973 in Salem, Marion Co., Oregon, USA. She married Walter Boomer Hunt on 13 Sep 1902 in Salem, Marion Co., Oregon, USA. He was born on 31 Jan 1877 in Salem, Marion Co., Oregon, USA. He died on 22 Jan 1959 in Salem, Marion Co., Oregon, USA.

22.   ii.   ROSE CARRIE PENROSE was born on 26 Apr 1884 in Houghton Co., Michigan, USA. She died on 21 Jun 1975 in Salem, Marion Co., Oregon, USA (Sherwood Park Nursing Home; Age 91). She married Roy Ethelbert Stoutenburg on 19 Sep 1905 in Dayton, Yamhill Co., Oregon, USA (Dayton Parsonage). He was born on 20 Jul 1884 in Unionvale, Yamhill Co., Oregon, USA. He died on 16 Sep 1968 in Dayton, Yamhill Co., Oregon, USA.

23.   iii.   LEWIS WILLIAM PENROSE was born on 13 Nov 1885 in Hancock, Houghton Co., Michigan, USA. He died on 20 Oct 1917 in Fort Rock, Lake Co., Oregon, USA. He married Arka Antrim on 11 Oct 1908 in Unionvale, Yamhill Co., Oregon, USA. She was born on 09 Aug 1890 in Boise, Ada Co., Idaho, USA. She died on 12 Oct 1942 in Newberg, Yamhill Co., Oregon, USA.

24.   iv.   LILLIAN ANN PENROSE was born on 28 Mar 1890 in Tacoma, Pierce Co., Washington, USA. She died on 08 Sep 1974 in Salem, Marion Co., Oregon, USA. She married Ralph E Nelson on 24 Mar 1909 in Dayton, Yamhill Co., Oregon, USA. He was born on 27 Dec 1883 in Fairmount, Richland Co., North Dakota, USA. He died on 28 Apr 1970 in Salem, Marion Co., Oregon, USA.

25.   v.   ESTHER MARTHA PENROSE was born on 06 Dec 1891 in Salem, Marion Co., Oregon, USA. She died on 15 Mar 1992 in Woodburn, Marion Co., Oregon, USA. She married Horace Minor Propst on 14 Jun 1910 in Corvallis, Benton Co., Oregon, USA. He was born on 20 Oct 1885 in Albany, Benton Co., Oregon, USA. He died on 08 Apr 1988 in Woodburn, Marion Co., Oregon, USA.

26.     vi.     HAZEL GLENN PENROSE was born on 29 Dec 1894 in Oregon, USA. She died on 08 Aug 1938 in Deschutes Co., Oregon, USA. She married George Earl Menkenmaier in 1914. He was born on 12 May 1892 in South Dakota, USA. He died on 23 Dec 1938 in Portland, Multnomah Co., Oregon, USA.

## Generation 3

7.  FRANK A[3] GRIMM (Franziscus Gustav[2] "Frank", Heinrich Ludwig[1] "Henry Louis") was born on 20 Feb 1872 in Iowa, USA. He died on 14 Apr 1925 in Paul, Minidoka Co., Idaho, USA. He married (1) Minnie Beigal on 12 Apr 1898 in Mount Angel, Marion Co., Oregon, USA. She was born on 19 Sep 1876 in Wisconsin, USA. She died on 11 Sep 1902. He married (2) Alma Helen Bauman, daughter of Albert Bauman and Wilhelmina [Unknown] in 1904. She was born in 1879 in Wisconsin, USA. She died on 28 Apr 1961 in Portland, Multnomah Co., Oregon, USA. Frank A. Grimm was buried on 18 Apr 1925; Alma Bauman was buried on 02 May 1961. Both are buried in Portland, Multnomah Co., Oregon, USA, at Rose City Cemetery.

Frank A Grimm was employed as a Photographer in 1900 in Portland, Multnomah Co., Oregon, USA. Alma Helen Bauman was employed as a Nurse in 1931 in Portland, Multnomah Co., Oregon, USA.

> GRIMM/BEIGEL - F. A. Grimm, over 21 of Multnomah Co., OR & Minnie Biegel, over 18, m 12 April 1898 at house of Franz Grimm by Ed Doering, M.G. Aff: L. Bacon. Wit: Louie Grimm & Alma Bauman.( 5468 p. 152)

Frank A Grimm and Minnie Beigal had the following child:

        i.      EDDIE[4] GRIMM was born in 1901 in Mount Angel, Marion Co., Oregon, USA. He died on 25 Nov 1901, Oregon, USA. Eddie Grimm was buried after 25 Nov 1901 in Mount Angel, Marion Co., Oregon, USA; Trinity Lutheran Church.

> **ALMA HELEN GRIMM**
>
> GRIMM - Alma Helen, 39th NE 102, mother of Mildred Domnisse, Lawrence A., and Harold F. Grimm; sister of Thelma L. Haynes, and Albert Baumann; 4 grandchildren, 6 great-grandchildren. Services Tuesday 10 a.m. at Colonial Mortuary, Sandy Blvd at 14th. Internment at Rose City Cemetery. (Sunday Oregonian, Portland, Oregon; 30 April 1961.

Alma was listed in the Portland, Oregon City directory as a widow in 1931.

Frank A Grimm and Alma Helen Bauman had the following children:

27.     i.      MILDRED A GRIMM was born in 1906 in Oregon, USA. She died on 28 Oct 1969 in Portland, Multnomah Co., Oregon, USA. She married (1) Elmore Addison Johns on 18 Oct 1924 in Multnomah Co., Oregon, USA. He was born on 01 Feb 1896 in Oregon City, Clackamas Co., Oregon, USA. He died on 12 Oct 1951 in Clackamas, Clackamas Co., Oregon, USA (Age: 55). She married (2) John Nicholas "Jack" Domnisse on 03 Aug 1952 in Oregon, USA. He was born on 31 Jul 1887 in Council Bluffs, Pottawattamie Co., Iowa, USA. He died on 29 Jul 1976 in Portland, Multnomah Co., Oregon, USA (Age 89).

28.    ii.    LAWRENCE A GRIMM was born on 03 Sep 1908 in Oregon, USA. He died on 11 Jun 1986 in Portland, Multnomah Co., Oregon, USA (Age: 77). He married Varina Mae [Unknown] between 1929-1931. She was born on 28 Feb 1910 in Washington, USA. She died on 01 Sep 1989 in Portland, Multnomah Co., Oregon, USA.

      iii.    HAROLD F. GRIMM was born about 1914 in Oregon, USA.

74: Logan and Anna Bacon
April 1898

8.    ANNA LAURA[3] GRIMM (Franziscus Gustav[2] "Frank", Heinrich Ludwig[1] "Henry Louis") was born on 24 Sep 1873 in Independence, Buchanan Co., Iowa, USA. She died on 13 Aug 1952 in California, USA. She married (1) Logan J Bacon on 12 April 1904 in Mount Angel, Marion Co., Oregon, USA. He was born on 2 Jun 1868 in Missouri, USA. He died on 28 May 1920 in Minidoka Co, Idaho, USA. She Married (2) CHARLES A Mckee before 1930. He was born about 1864 in Oregon, USA. He died before 1935. She married (3) Ernest Stansbery. Anna Laura Grimm was buried after 13 Aug 1952 in Portland, Multnomah Co., Oregon, USA, at Rose City Cemetery.

Logan J Bacon was employed as a Barber in 1900 in Portland, Multnomah Co., Oregon, USA. He was buried after 28 May 1920 in Portland, Multnomah Co., Oregon, USA, at Rose City Cemetery.

BACON/GRIMM – L. Bacon, over 21 of Multnomah Co., OR & Anna L. Grimm, over 18, m. 12 April 1904 at house of Franz Grimm by Ed Doering, M.G., Lutheran Pastor. Aff: F.A. Grimm. Wit: W. Grimm & Emma Gpecht. (5467 p. 151)

STATE OF OREGON, COUNTY OF MULTNOMAH

I, Anna McKee, being first duly sworn say that I am a sister of William Albert Grimm, that said William Albert Grimm was born about five or six miles from Independence in Buchanan County, Iowa on April 8, 1877. That our father's name was Frank Grimm and our mother's maiden name was Minnie Shelk. That I was born in the same place, which was our father's farm, on November 1875. Anna McKee

Subscribed and sworn to before me this 7th day of January 1943
N. Watts, Notary Public for Oregon

Logan J Bacon and Anna Laura Grimm had the following children:

      i.    EVADNA I[4] BACON was born in 1903 in Oregon, USA. She died on 15 Jan 1968 in Portland, Multnomah Co., Oregon, USA. She married (1) Ralph Frank "Spence" Spencer before Aug 1952. He was born on 07 May 1899 in Canada. He died on 28 Jan 1981 in Portland, Multnomah Co., Oregon, USA. She married (2) Hueston Leon "Hugh" Rosebrook on 24 Dec 1924 in Clark Co., Washington, USA. He was born on 24 Oct 1899 in New York, USA. He died in May 1974 in Spokane, Spokane Co., Washington, USA.

SPENCER - Evadna I., Rt. 2 Box 203, Portland; wife of Ralph F. Spencer. Services Wednesday, Jan 16, 1:30 p.m. at Riverview Abbey Chapel. Member of Eastern Star. Arrangements by Davy Sunnyside Funeral Home.

ii.     VERNA R BACON was born on 03 May 1906 in Idaho, USA. She died on 19 Sep 1967 in San Bernardino, San Bernardino Co., California, USA (Age: 61). She married (1) Horace C Teuber on 18 Jul 1930 in Clark Co., Washington, USA. He was born on 14 Dec 1896 in North Dakota, USA. He died on 20 Dec 1938 in Seattle, King Co., Washington, USA. She married (2) [Unknown] Field between 1948-1952.

9.   WILHELM ALBERT[3] "WILLIAM" GRIMM (Franziscus Gustav[2] "Frank", Heinrich Ludwig[1] "Henry Louis") was born in Mar 1874 in Iowa, USA. He died on 21 Sep 1952 in Portland, Multnomah Co., Oregon, USA. He married (1) Mildred Idella [Unknown] on 01 May 1920 in Multnomah Co., Oregon, USA. She was born about 1890 in Minnesota, USA. She died on 03 May 1951 in Clackamas Co., Oregon, USA (Age: 58). He married (2) Emily C Kreidt before May 1902. She was born on 09 Nov 1881 in Iowa, USA. She died on 20 Jan 1919 in Marion Co., Oregon, USA. Wilhelm Albert "William" Grimm was buried on 24 Sep 1952 in Portland, Multnomah Co., Oregon, USA, at Trinity Lutheran Church Cemetery. Mildred Idella [Unknown] was in Oregon City, Clackamas Co., Oregon, USA, at Mountain View Cemetery. Emily C. Kreidt was buried on 24 Jan 1919 in Portland, Multnomah Co., Oregon, USA.

> GRIMM - William A., Sept 21, late of 4232 NE 72nd. Father of Alvin and Elmer Grimm, Mrs. Max Doblie and Mrs. Lova Jean Hendrix; 6 grandchildren, 2 great-grandchildren. Member of Calvary Lutheran Church. Services Wednesday, Sept 24, 1 p.m. at the Pearson Funeral Church, NE Knott at Union. Friends invited. Graveside services 3 p.m. Wednesday, standard time at the Trinity Lutheran Church Cemetery, Mt. Angel, OR. Vault interment.

Wilhelm Albert "William" Grimm and Emily C Kreidt had the following children:

29.     i.    ALVIN EDWARD GRIMM was born on 31 May 1902 in Portland, Multnomah Co., Oregon, USA. He died on 03 Mar 1994 in Los Angeles, Los Angeles Co., California, USA (Age: 91). He married Emilie L [Unknown]. She was born about 1906 in Nebraska, USA.

        ii.   ELMER HENRY GRIMM was born on 17 Feb 1905 in Mount Angel, Marion Co., Oregon, USA. He died on 07 Sep 2000 in Portland, Multnomah Co., Oregon, USA (Age: 95). He married (1) Bettylee SAPP on 28 Dec 1965 in Del Norte, California, USA. She was born on 06 Jan 1927. She died in Sep 1980 in Portland, Multnomah Co., Oregon, USA. He married (2) Ruby H [Unknown] in 1929. She was born about 1911 in Texas, USA. She died on [unknown].

        Elmer Henry Grimm was employed as a Salesman in 1933 in San Diego, San Diego Co., California, USA. He served in the military on 17 Mar 1941 (US Army; Age: 36).

        iii.  HERMAN F GRIMM was born on 26 Jan 1907 in Mount Angel, Marion Co., Oregon, USA. He died on 17 Feb 1917 in Portland, Multnomah Co., Oregon, USA (Age: 11). Herman F Grimm was buried in Mount Angel, Marion Co., Oregon, USA.

30.     iv.   BERTHA WILHELMINA GRIMM was born on 07 Oct 1909 in Mount Angel, Marion Co., Oregon, USA. She died on 19 Nov 2011 (Age: 102). She married (1) Max Irvin Doblie on 15 Feb 1942 in Portland, Multnomah Co., Oregon, USA. He was born on 28 Oct 1907 in Concordia, Lafayette Co., Missouri, USA. He died on 04 Apr 2000 in Portland, Multnomah Co., Oregon, USA. She married (2) [Unknown] Buxton before 1938.

Wilhelm Albert "William" Grimm and Mildred Idella [Unknown] had the following child:

     v.    LOVA JEAN*4* GRIMM was born on 20 Nov 1927 in Mount Angel, Marion Co., Oregon, USA. She died on 23 Jul 1992 in Clackamas Co., Oregon, USA. She married Aubrey Hendrix.

10.    LUDWIG ALEXANDER*3* "LOUIS" GRIMM (Franziscus Gustav*2* "Frank", Heinrich Ludwig*1* "Henry Louis") was born on 10 Jan 1877 in Iowa, USA. He died before 1920. He married Ida C Bruns on 27 Feb 1900 in Portland, Multnomah Co., Oregon, USA (Probably). She was born in May 1880 in Freedom, Lafayette Co, Missouri, USA. She died on 03 Nov 1961 in Portland, Multnomah Co., Oregon, USA. Ida C. Bruns was buried in Portland, Multnomah co., Oregon, USA, at Rose City Cemetery.

> GRIMM - Ida C., late of 2824 N. Bryant; mother of Wilbert L. Grimm, Wilma E. Huffman, Leonard R. Grimm, Leona P. Arronson; 4 grand and 2 great-grandchildren; sister of Albert H. Bruns, Mrs. Richard Kuhnau, and Stanley Hall. Funeral services Monday November 6, 3 p.m. at Zeller Chapel of Roses, NE 21st and Broadway. Internment Rose City Cemetery.(The Oregonian, Portland, Oregon, 05 Nov 1961)

Ludwig Alexander "Louis" Grimm was employed as a Clerk in 1918 in Portland, Multnomah Co., Oregon, USA. WWI Draft Registration: Sep 1918 in Rupert, Minidoka Co., Idaho, USA

Louis' wife, Ida, is listed on the 1920 US Federal Census in Paul, Minidoka Co., ID as a widow.

Ludwig Alexander "Louis" Grimm and Ida C Bruns had the following children:

31.    i.    WILBERT LOUIS*4* GRIMM was born on 07 Jan 1902 in Oregon, USA. He died on 31 Dec 1986 in Shasta, Shasta Co., California, USA. He married Hannah Kraus. She was born in 1905 in Russia.

32.    ii.    WILMA EDITH GRIMM was born on 29 Jul 1904 in Oregon, USA. She died on 15 Oct 1980 in Portland, Multnomah Co., Oregon, USA. She married James Edward Huffman in 1926. He was born on 31 Dec 1895 in Malheur, Malheur Co., Oregon, USA. He died on 22 May 1970 in Portland, Multnomah Co., Oregon, USA.

    iii.    LEONARD R. GRIMM was born on 19 Sep 1907 in Oregon, USA. He died on 20 Oct 1972 in Concord, Contra Costa Co., California, USA. He married Lucile N [Unknown]. She was born in 1909 in Oregon, USA.

    iv.    LEONA FLORENCE GRIMM was born on 11 Nov 1911 in Portland, Multnomah Co., Oregon, USA. She died on 23 Sep 1988 in Portland, Multnomah Co., Oregon, USA. She married Alfred Eric Arronson on 24 Mar 1940 in Portland, Multnomah Co., Oregon, USA. He was born on 05 Jan 1918 in Oregon, USA. He died on 14 Dec 1996 in Portland, Multnomah Co., Oregon, USA. Leona Florence Grimm was buried in Portland, Multnomah Co., Oregon, USA, at Skyline Memorial Gardens.

11.    HEINRICH WILLIAM*3* "HENRY" GRIMM (Franziscus Gustav*2* "Frank", Heinrich Ludwig*1* "Henry Louis") was born on 06 Jun 1879 in Independence, Buchanan Co., Iowa, USA. He died on 17 Dec 1945 in Boise, Ada Co., Idaho, USA. He married Rosa Elma M Otjen, daughter of Henry Otjen Sr., on 07 Dec 1902 in Woodburn, Marion Co., Oregon, USA. She was born on 05 Mar 1883 in Silverton, Marion Co., Oregon, USA. She died on 03 Nov 1921 in Burley, Cassia Co., Idaho, USA. Heinrich William "Henry" Grimm was buried in Paul, Minidoka Co., Idaho, USA; Paul Cemetery. Rosa Elma Otjen was buried in Mount Angel, Marion Co., Oregon, USA; Lutheran Cemetery. Heinrich William Grimm WWI Draft Registration: 12 Sep 1918 in Minidoka Co., Idaho, USA.

HENRY GRIMM, OLD-TIME CITIZEN OF MINIDOKA COUNTY DIES IN BOISE.

Suffering a heart attack in Boise Monday, Henry William Grimm, pioneer of the Paul community, died a few minutes later in St. Luke's Hospital where he was rushed following the attack.

He had been taken to Boise by his son Monroe Grimm to receive treatment for the heart ailment and had just alighted from the car at the corner of Eighth and Main streets when he collapsed from the attack. Rushed to the hospital, he never regained consciousness, and died at 4 p.m.

Born in Iowa June 6, 1879, Mr. Grimm was 66 years old at the time of his death. When six* years old he moved with his parents to Oregon where he made his home until 1905 when he came to the Minidoka project. He homesteaded on a farm near Paul and lived there until World War I when he moved into Paul to operate a hotel. The establishment was considered one of the best in this section of the country at the time.

His wife, the former Rosa Otjen whom he married in Woodburn, Ore., in 1902, preceded him in death in 1921.

A progressive farmer, Mr. Grimm experimented with many farm methods, some of which were universally adopted. He tried growing hops with some success; raised registered livestock, and was one of the first and largest beet growers when the Amalgamated Sugar Company was soliciting acreage for the Rupert-Paul plant.

He is survived by one son, Monroe Grimm, two daughters, Mrs. Mathilda Kock and Mrs. Viola Bill, all of Paul; 15 grandchildren; one sister Mrs. Anna Stansberry, of Portland, OR., and a brother, William Grimm of Oregon City, OR. One grandson, Pfc. Junior Kock, was killed in action in Germany in World War II.

Funeral services will be held Friday at 2:00 p.m. at the Lutheran Church in Rupert. (Rupert News, Rupert, Idaho; 20 Dec 1945)

*Note: Henry's father didn't move to Oregon until about 1892.

Heinrich William "Henry" Grimm and Rosa Elma M Otjen had the following children:

33.     i.    MATHILDA ALICE[4] GRIMM was born on 22 May 1904 in Mount Angel, Marion Co., Oregon, USA. She died on 28 Aug 1951 in Paul, Minidoka Co., Idaho, USA. She married Adolph Koch on 30 Jul 1922 in Paul, Minidoka Co., Idaho, USA. He was born on 14 Dec 1901 in Kolpe, Russia. He died in Jan 1985 in Paul, Minidoka Co., Idaho, USA.

34.     ii.   VIOLA ANNA WILHEMINA GRIMM was born on 11 Oct 1907 in Idaho, USA. She died on 04 Sep 1946 in Paul, Minidoka Co., Idaho, USA. She married Amos Bill on 23 Nov 1923 in Paul, Minidoka Co., Idaho, USA. He was born on 19 Dec 1901 in Illinois, USA. He died on 13 May 1984 in Paul, Minidoka Co., Idaho, USA.

35.     iii.  MONROE HENRY FRANK GRIMM was born on 28 Aug 1910 in Idaho, USA. He died on 03 Nov 1960. He married Ruth Virginia Hofhine on 23 Jul 1927 in Blackfoot, Bingham Co., Idaho, USA. She was born on 29 Nov 1909 in Oregon, USA. She died on 21 May 2004 in Idaho, USA.

12  EDWARD CHRISTOPH[3] GRIMM (Franziscus Gustav[2] "Frank", Heinrich Ludwig[1] "Henry Louis") was born on 23 Jul 1881 in Independence, Buchanan Co., Iowa, USA. He died on 26 Apr 1941 in Fullerton, Orange Co., California, USA. He married (1) Minnie Marie Hug, daughter of William Hug and Mary [Unknown], on 24 Nov 1910 in Mount Angel, Marion Co., Oregon, USA. She was born in 1894 in Burt, Kossuth Co., Iowa, USA (Near Algona Co.). She died in 1920 in Burley, Cassia Co., Idaho, USA. He married (2) Dora H [Unknown] about 1935 in Orange Co., California, USA (probably). She was born about 1895 in Wisconsin, USA. Minnie Marie Hug was buried in Mount Angel, Marion Co., Oregon, USA, at Trinity Lutheran Church Cemetery.

Edward Christoph Grimm WWI Draft Registration: 12 Sep 1918 in Minidoka Co., Idaho, USA.

Edward Christoph Grimm and Minnie Marie Hug had the following children:

i.  CORRINE ILETA[4] GRIMM was born on 12 Jan 1913 in Paul, Minidoka Co., Idaho, USA. She married Charles A Raid on 14 Dec 1935 in Portland, Multnomah Co., Oregon, USA. He was born in 1910. He died in 2002 in Oregon, USA.

ii.  HERBERT EDWARD GRIMM was born on 24 Sep 1915 in Paul, Minidoka Co., Idaho, USA. He married Eunice [Unknown] about 1937. She was born about 1919 in Wisconsin, USA.

iii.  RAYMOND WILLARD GRIMM was born on 04 Oct 1917 in Paul, Minidoka Co., Idaho, USA.

13.  ADOLPH H[3] GRIMM (Frederich Theodore[2], Heinrich Ludwig[1] "Henry Louis") was born on 20 May 1885 in Spring Creek, Black Hawk Co., Iowa, USA. He died on 09 Jun 1970 in Reedsville, Manitowoc Co., Wisconsin, USA (Age 85). He married Clara Etzler, daughter of Charles Etzler and Carline Braun, on 20 Dec 1915. She was born on 06 Sep 1889 in Reedsville, Manitowoc Co., Wisconsin, USA. She died on 06 Jan 1980 in Green Bay, Brown Co., Wisconsin, USA. Adolph H. Grimm was buried on 11 Jun 1970 in Reedsville, Manitowoc Co., Wisconsin, USA, at St John-St James Evangelical Lutheran Cemetery.

Adolph Grimm WWI Draft Registration: Bet. 1918-1942 in Reedsville, Manitowoc Co., Wisconsin, USA

Adolph H Grimm and Clara Etzler had the following children:

i.  [DAUGHTER][4] GRIMM was born on 11 Aug 1916. She died on 11 Aug 1916.

ii.  ELEANOR GRIMM was born in 1918 in Wisconsin, USA. She married Jerome Kane.

iii.  HELEN GRIMM was born on 06 Feb 1923 in Wisconsin, USA. She died on 11 Apr 1982 in Green Bay, Brown Co., Wisconsin, USA. She married Francis Kennedy on 05 Nov 1941. He died in Feb 1962.

iv.  JUNE GRIMM was born on 17 Sep 1924 in Maple Grove, Manitowoc Co., Wisconsin, USA. She died on 19 Nov 2007 in Madison, Dane Co., Wisconsin, USA. She married Ervin Arthur Emil Kasten in 1945. He was born on 12 Nov 1919 in Maple Grove, Manitowoc Co., Wisconsin, USA.

v.  BETTY GRIMM was born in 1927 in Wisconsin, USA. She married Edmond Bielinski.

vi.  ERVIN L GRIMM was born on 23 Oct 1932 in Maple Grove, Manitowoc Co., Wisconsin, USA. He died on 07 Aug 1997. He married Mildred A Luedtke on 06 Feb 1954 in Morrison, Brown Co., Wisconsin, USA. She died after Aug 1997.

GRIMM

Adolph Grimm, 85, of 152 Coolidge St., Green Bay, died Tuesday morning at Bellin Memorial Hospital, Green Bay.

Funeral services will be at 2 p.m. Thursday at St. John-St. James Evangelical Lutheran Church, Reedsville. The Rev. Robert Wendland will officiate and burial will be in the church cemetery.

Mr. Grimm was born May 22, 1885, in Iowa, son of the late Fred and Emma Fischer Grimm. He married Clara Etzler Miller Dec. 20, 1915. They resided at Rt. 1, Reedsville on a farm, retiring 15 years ago.

Survivors include his wife; a son, Ervin, of Rt. 1, Reedsville; four daughters, Mrs. Jerome (Eleanor) Kane and Mrs. Helen Kennedy of Rt. 1, Maribel, Mrs. June Kasten of De Pere and Mrs. Edmund (Betty Bielinski of Green Bay; a step-son, Dr. C. G. Miller, of Sarasota, Fla.; a brother, Anton, of Rt 1, Reedsville; 25 grandchildren and 11 great grandchildren. A daughter and two brothers preceded him in death.

Friends may call at Reedsville Funeral Home after 7 o'clock this Wednesday evening until 10:30 a.m. Thursday and then at the church until the time of services. (Manitowoc Herald Times (Two Rivers Reporter T-13); Manitowoc, WI; 10 June 1970)

14. REINHARD FRANZ[3] GRIMM (Frederich Theodore[2], Heinrich Ludwig[1] "Henry Louis") was born on 19 May 1889 in Independence, Buchanan Co., Iowa, USA. He died on 31 May 1966 in Reedsville, Manitowoc Co., Wisconsin, USA. He married Ella Pautz on 06 Jul 1918 in Manitowoc, Manitowoc Co., Wisconsin, USA. She was born between 1889-1901 in Wisconsin, USA. She died on 03 Jan 1957 in Manitowoc Co., Wisconsin, USA.

Reinhard Franz Grimm was employed as a Farmer in 1921 in Maple Grove, Manitowoc Co., WI, USA.

Reinhard Franz Grimm and Ella Pautz had the following children:

    i.      ROSE IRENE[4] GRIMM was born in May 1920 in Manitowoc Co., Wisconsin, USA. She died before 2004. She married Elmer Kroening.

    ii.     ETHEL MAY GRIMM was born on 23 Feb 1921 in Manitowoc Co., Wisconsin, USA. She died on 19 Feb 2004 in Manitowoc Co., Wisconsin, USA. She married Lester H Pautz on 03 Oct 1942 in Reedsville, Manitowoc Co., Wisconsin, USA. He was born on 20 Apr 1921. He died on 26 Nov 1986. Ethel May Grimm was buried on 21 Feb 2004 in Manitowoc Co., Wisconsin, USA, at Knollwood Mausoleum.

    iii.    VICTOR FREDERICK GRIMM was born on 23 Nov 1923 in Manitowoc Co., Wisconsin, USA. He married Verona [Unknown].

    iv.    LLOYD EUGENE GRIMM was born on 31 May 1925 in Manitowoc Co., Wisconsin, USA. He died on 19 Mar 1997 in Reedsville, Manitowoc Co., Wisconsin, USA.

    v.     REINHARD FRANZ GRIMM JR was born on 03 Nov 1926 in Manitowoc Co., Wisconsin, USA.

    vi.    FERN ELIZABETH GRIMM was born on 12 Sep 1928 in Manitowoc Co., Wisconsin, USA. She married Albert Wolf.

    vii.   FREDERICK JOHN GRIMM was born on 25 Jan 1932 in Manitowoc Co., Wisconsin, USA.

    viii.  RONALD ALBERT GRIMM was born on 12 Dec 1942 in Manitowoc Co., Wisconsin, USA. He married Joan [Unknown].

ix.     DORIS IDA GRIMM was born on 08 Jan 1946 in Manitowoc Co., Wisconsin, USA. She married Roland Polzin.

x.      KAREN ANN GRIMM was born on 06 Oct 1946 in Manitowoc Co., Wisconsin, USA. She married [Unknown] Blish.

---

GRIMM- Reinhard Grimm, 77, Town of Maple Grove resident, died Tuesday afternoon at Memorial Hospital, Manitowoc.

Funeral services will be 2 p.m. Friday at St. John and St. James Evangelical Lutheran Church, Reedsville, the Rev. Harvey Heckendorf officiating. Burial will be in West Side Cemetery, Reedsville.

Mr. Grimm was born May 19, 1889, at Springcreek, Iowa, son of the late Fred and Emma Fischer Grimm. He married the former Ella Pautz July 6, 1918. She preceded him in death Jan 3, 1957. He farmed in the town of Maple Grove and was clerk of Brookside School, Maple Grove, for 25 years. He was also supervisor for the town of Maple Grove School for four years.

Survivors include five sons, Victor and Reinhard Jr., of Reedsville, Lloyd and Fredrick of Rt. 1 Reedsville, and Ronald of Manitowoc; five daughters, Mrs. Elmer Kroening and Mrs. Lester Pautz of Rt 1 Reedsville, Mrs. Albert Wolf of Green Bay, Mrs. Roland Polzin and Miss Karen Grimm of Manitowoc; two brothers, Adolph and Anton of Rt 1, Reedsville; 29 grandchildren and two great-grandchildren. A brother also preceded him in death.

Friends may call after 4 p.m. Thursday at Reedsville Funeral Home until 10:30 a.m. Friday when the casket will be removed to the church where the body will lie in state until the hour of the service. (Herald-Times Reporter, Manitowoc, Wisconsin; 01 June 1966)

---

15. ALBERT PHILIP HENRY[3] GRIMM (Albert A[2], Heinrich Ludwig[1] "Henry Louis") was born on 24 Oct 1884 in Hancock, Houghton Co., Michigan, USA. He died on 14 Mar 1981 in Medford, Taylor Co., Wisconsin, USA (Medford Hospital; Age 96). He married Anna Steiner, daughter of John August Steiner and Louise "Muna" Rouder on 19 Aug 1908 in Medford, Taylor Co., Wisconsin, USA (Trinity Lutheran Church of Whittlesey). She was born on 09 Aug 1890 in Marshfield, Fond du Lac Co., Wisconsin, USA. She died on 15 Mar 1946 in Marshfield, Fond du Lac Co., Wisconsin, USA (Age 56). Albert Philip Grimm was buried on 17 Mar 1981 in Medford, Taylor Co., Wisconsin, USA, at Evergreen Cemetery. Annie Steiner was buried in Medford, Taylor Co., Wisconsin, USA, at Evergreen Cemetery.

Albert Philip Henry Grimm was employed as a Farmer, Logger between 1900-1940. WWI Draft Registration: Sep 1918 in Medford, Taylor Co., Wisconsin, USA.

Albert Philip Henry Grimm and Anna Steiner had the following children:

36.     i.      ALVIN ALBERT WILLIAM[4] GRIMM was born on 08 May 1909 in Chelsea, Taylor Co., Wisconsin, USA. He died on 24 Jun 2003 in Vancouver, Clark Co., Washington, USA (Age 94). He married Clara Matilda Anderson, daughter of August Nikolaus Anderson and Mary Olson on 09 Nov 1933 in Medford, Taylor Co., Wisconsin, USA (Whittlesey Lutheran Church Parsonage). She was born on 09 Jan 1912 in Little Black, Taylor Co., Wisconsin, USA. She died on 05 May 1997 in Medford, Taylor Co., Wisconsin, USA (Age 85). Both are buried at Trinity Lutheran Church Cemetery, Whittlesey, Taylor Co., Wisconsin.

        ii.     SOPHIA GRIMM was born on 17 Jul 1910 in Taylor Co., Wisconsin, USA. She died on 18 Jul 1910 in Taylor Co., Wisconsin, USA. Sophia was buried at Evergreen Cemetery, Medford, Taylor Co., Wisconsin.

37.     iii.    ERMA HELEN GRIMM was born on 11 Nov 1911 in Chelsea, Taylor Co., Wisconsin, USA. She died on 02 Jun 1991 in Stoughton, Dane Co., Wisconsin, USA (Age: 79). She married Siegfried Krausse in Feb 1929 in Medford, Taylor Co., Wisconsin, USA. He was born on 18 Feb 1903 in Molitor, Taylor Co., Wisconsin, USA. He died on 21 Mar 1950 in Medford, Taylor Co., Wisconsin, USA (Age: 48).

iv. EVERETT REUBEN GRIMM* was born on 13 Nov 1927 in Medford, Taylor Co., Wisconsin, USA. He married (1) Florence Twa between 1949-1950 in Medford, Taylor Co., Wisconsin, USA. She was born in 1921 in Watersmeet, Gogebic Co., Michigan, USA. He married (2) Gertrude E "Trudl" [Unknown] in Jul 1965 in South Bend, St Joseph Co., Indiana, USA. She was born on 23 Dec 1929 in Karlsruhe, Baden-Württemberg, Germany. She died on 08 Mar 1996 in Goshen, Elkhart Co., Indiana, USA (Age 66). He married (3) Joanne Aulrich on 30 Dec 1999 in Middlebury, Elkhart Co., Indiana, USA. She was born on 25 Mar 1930 in Middlebury, Elkhart Co., Indiana, USA.

Everett Reuben Grimm served in the military between May 1952-Mar 1963 in Medford, Taylor Co., Wisconsin, USA (U.S. Army; 31st Infantry Reg, 7th Infantry Div; SFC).

15. LYDIA LOUISE³ GRIMM (Albert A², Heinrich Ludwig¹ "Henry Louis") was born on 27 May 1886 in Medford, Taylor Co., Wisconsin, USA. She died on 14 Apr 1973 in Medford, Taylor Co., Wisconsin, USA. She married (1) Alfred Schubert on 22 Jun 1904 in Taylor Co., Wisconsin, USA. He was born on 19 Mar 1878 in Germany. He died on 12 Jun 1929. She married (2) Charles Henry Louis Strebig before 27 Jul 1931 in Taylor Co., Wisconsin, USA. He was born on 07 May 1876 in Germany. He died on 15 Nov 1950 (Age: 74). Lydia Louise Grimm was buried in Medford, Taylor Co., Wisconsin, USA; Evergreen Cemetery. Alfred Schubert was buried in Medford, Taylor Co., Wisconsin, USA, at Evergreen Cemetery as was Charles Henry Louis Strebig.

Alfred Schubert WWI Draft Registration: Sep 1918 in Red Lake Co., Minnesota, USA.

Alfred Schubert is listed in *U.S., Burial Registers, Military Posts and National Cemeteries, 1862-1960* (p. 350, entry 3). It gives the details of the military company he was attached to, the date of his death, his age being 51, and that his body was shipped to Medford, Wisc. His widow applied for a military veteran's headstone on 02 Jul 1929 and requested it be shipped to Medford, Taylor Co., WI where Alfred was interned at the Evergreen Cemetery.

Lydia returned to Taylor County, WI after Alfred's death and filed a Civil War Widow's Pension [App #1645.82, Cert #A9-12-29 WI] in his name on 28 Jun 1929 and a another claim [App #1698.734, Cert #A9-10-6-31 WI] on 27 Jul 1931 for her minor children. The second claim has her listed as Lydia Strebig.

Alfred Schubert and Lydia Louise Grimm had the following children:

i. ALVIN⁴ SCHUBERT was born on 06 Jun 1905 in Medford, Taylor Co., Wisconsin, USA. He died in Jan 1982 in Mesa, Maricopa Co., Arizona, USA (Age: 76).

ii. OLIVER SCHUBERT was born on 15 Apr 1907 in Medford, Taylor Co., Wisconsin, USA.

iii. ESTHER SCHUBERT was born about 1918 in Minnesota, USA.

38. iv. LUCILLE SCHUBERT was born about 1924 in Minnesota, USA. She died after 2004. She married Vernon J. Frey on 18 Jul 1942 in Medford, Taylor Co., Wisconsin, USA (Immanuel Evangelical Lutheran Church). He was born on 10 Aug 1920 in Browning, Taylor Co., Wisconsin, USA. He died on 21 Nov 2004 in Medford, Taylor Co., Wisconsin, USA (Age: 84).

39. v . LLOYD G SCHUBERT was born on 04 Mar 1927. He died on 02 May 2000 (Age: 73). He was buried after 02 May 2000 in Medford, Taylor Co., Wisconsin, USA, at Evergreen Cemetery

Lloyd G Schubert served in the military on 13 Apr 1945 (US Navy; Age: 18).

17. WILLIAM MAX[3] GRIMM (Albert A[2], Heinrich Ludwig[1] "Henry Louis") was born on 03 Mar 1888 in Phillips, Price Co., Wisconsin, USA. He died on 19 Feb 1990 in McIntosh, Polk Co., Minnesota, USA (Age 101 yrs. 11 mo. 16 dyes). He married Anna Duesing, daughter of Ferdinand Duesing and Emilie Lindow, on 31 Aug 1910 in Medford, Taylor Co., Wisconsin, USA (Whittlesey Lutheran Church). She was born on 10 Jan 1889 in Houghton, Houghton Co., Michigan, USA. She died on 19 Feb 1979 in McIntosh, Polk Co., Minnesota, USA (Age 90). William Max Grimm was buried on 24 Feb 1990 in McIntosh, Polk Co., Minnesota, USA, at Immanuel Lutheran Cemetery. Anna Duesing was buried in McIntosh, Polk Co., Minnesota, USA, at Immanuel Lutheran Cemetery.

65: William Max and Annie Grimm
Immanuel Lutheran Cemetery
McIntosh. Polk Co.. MN

William Max Grimm and Anna Duesing had the following children:

39.   i.  ORVILLE GUST[4] GRIMM was born on 28 May 1912 in Brooks, Red Lake Co., Minnesota, USA. He died on 09 Feb 2005 in McIntosh, Polk Co., Minnesota, USA (McIntosh Manor Nursing Home). He married Marie L. Magoon on 05 Nov 1931 in McIntosh, Polk Co., Minnesota, USA. She was born on 08 Jul 1912 in Minnesota, USA. She died on 17 Oct 1977 in Red Lake Co., Minnesota, USA.

40.   ii.  LAVERN ALBERT GRIMM was born on 23 Nov 1914 in Minnesota, USA. He died on 04 Jul 2008 in Brooks, Red Lake Co., Minnesota, USA. He married Nora Irene Nelson on 10 Oct 1936 in McIntosh, Polk Co., Minnesota, USA. She was born on 01 Jan 1919 in Hill River Township, Polk Co., Minnesota, USA. She died on 09 Apr 1995 in Brooks, Red Lake Co., Minnesota, USA.

      iii.  EVELYN GRIMM was born on 24 Jul 1917 in Red Lake Co., Minnesota, USA. She died on 12 Nov 1997 in Red Lake Falls, Red Lake Co., Minnesota, USA. She married Edwin P. Nelson in Dec 1935.

41.   iv.  BEVERLY DORIS GRIMM was born on 11 Jan 1922 in Red Lake Co., Minnesota, USA. She married Melvin Johnson.

42.   v.  VIOLETTE M. GRIMM was born on 21 Aug 1927 in Minnesota, USA. She died on [Deceased]. She married Maynard Ferden. He was born in 1916 in Illinois, USA. He died on 14 May 2007 in Sycamore, De Kalb Co., Illinois, USA.

      vi.  WILBUR GRIMM. He died between 1974-1979.

18. ROSETTE ELISABETH[3] GRIMM (Albert A[2], Heinrich Ludwig[1] "Henry Louis") was born on 01 Mar 1890 in Medford, Taylor Co., Wisconsin, USA. She married [Unknown] Evans. She married (2) Paul Fred Schubert on 25 Nov 1908 in Taylor Co., Wisconsin, USA. He was born on 02 Aug 1887 in Wisconsin, USA. She married (3) [Unknown] Johnson between 1920-1930. He died before Apr 1930. Rosette Elisabeth Grimm was buried in 1973 in Park Falls, Price Co., Wisconsin, USA, at Nola Cemetery (Block O, Lot 67).

Paul Fred Schubert WWI Draft Registration: Paul Fred Schubert in 1918 in Taylor Co., Wisconsin, USA

Paul Fred Schubert and Rosette Elisabeth Grimm had the following children:

      i.  VIOLA E[4] SCHUBERT was born in 1910 in Wisconsin, USA.

      ii.  ALVINA SCHUBERT was born about 1912 in Wisconsin, USA.

iii.    RAYMOND PAUL SCHUBERT was born on 04 Aug 1915 in Wisconsin, USA. He died on 12 Aug 1993 in Hennepin Co., Minnesota, USA. Raymond Paul Schubert was buried after 12 Aug 1993 in Park Falls, Price Co., Wisconsin, USA, at Nola Cemetery (Block O, Lot 54).

iv.    EVERETT SCHUBERT was born about Apr 1919 in Wisconsin, USA.

19.  ELSIE MARIA[3] GRIMM (Albert A[2], Heinrich Ludwig[1] "Henry Louis") was born on 25 Dec 1901 in Medford, Taylor Co., Wisconsin, USA. She died on 07 Jun 1989 in Salem, Marion Co., Oregon, USA. She married Nels Pederson on 21 Dec 1917 in McIntosh, Polk Co., Minnesota, USA. He was born on 20 Mar 1896 in McIntosh, Polk Co., Minnesota, USA. He died on 31 May 1951 in Salem, Marion Co., Oregon, USA.

Nels Pederson and Elsie Maria Grimm had the following children:

i.    EVERT NELS[4] PEDERSON was born on 14 Dec 1918 in Brooks, Red Lake Co., Minnesota, USA. He died on 05 May 1998 in Salem, Marion Co., Oregon, USA. He married Marie [Unknown].

ii.    MELVIN PEDERSON was born on 10 Dec 1923. He died on 16 Apr 2007 in Salem, Marion Co., Oregon, USA.

Melvin Pederson served in the military between 15 Aug 1943-26 Apr 1946.

iii.    LAWRENCE PEDERSON was born about 1925.

iv.    DELORIS GLADYS PEDERSON was born on 04 Nov 1927 in McIntosh, Polk Co., Minnesota, USA. She died on 01 May 1994 in Salem, Marion Co., Oregon, USA. She married [Unknown] on 22 Jun 1963 in Hennepin Co., Minnesota, USA.

v.    KENNETH MORRIS PEDERSON was born on 19 Nov 1929. He died on 11 Dec 2002 in Salem, Marion Co., Oregon, USA (Age: 73). He married Joann [Unknown]. Kenneth Morris Pederson was buried after 11 Dec 2002 in Salem, Marion Co., Oregon, USA.

vi.    RUTH PEDERSON was born about 1931.

vii.    GLORIA PEDERSON was born about 1933.

viii.    SHIRLEY BERNICE PEDERSON was born on 29 Dec 1936 in Canada. She died on 04 Feb 1990 in Santa Clara, Santa Clara Co., California, USA. She married Chester Evanoff on 25 May 1954 in Marion Co., Oregon, USA.

20.  HILDA C[3] SCHMELZER (Anna Margaret[2] Grimm, Heinrich Ludwig[1] "Henry Louis" Grimm) was born on 30 Jun 1896 in Mount Angel, Marion Co., Oregon, USA. She died in Jul 1986 in Sandersville, Washington Co., Georgia, USA. She married Laurin Frederick Cook about 1928. He was born on 07 Aug 1896 in Santa Rosa, Sonoma Co., California, USA. He died in May 1981 in Santa Rosa, Sonoma Co., California, USA.

Laurin Frederick Cook and Hilda C Schmelzer had the following children:

i.    BARBARA ANN[4] COOK was born on 27 Feb 1929 in Santa Rosa, Sonoma Co., California, USA. She married William Wiggins on 09 Mar 1943. He was born on 03 Jul in Sandersville, Washington Co., Georgia, USA.

ii.     KENNETH F COOK was born on 27 Dec 1932 in Santa Rosa, Sonoma Co., California, USA. He married Marie Dykes on 20 Apr 1957 in California, USA. She was born on 09 Aug 1932 in Hood River, Hood River Co., Oregon, USA.

iii.    RICHARD K COOK was born on 26 Dec 1933 in Santa Rosa, Sonoma Co., California, USA. He married Joyce Cheathane Collins. She was born on 25 Jan 1938 in Oklahoma, USA. She died on 02 Nov 1986 in Santa Clara, Santa Clara Co., California, USA.

21. MINNIE GERTRUDE[3] PENROSE (Carolina Theresa[2] Grimm, Heinrich Ludwig[1] "Henry Louis" Grimm) was born on 01 Sep 1882 in Hancock, Houghton Co., Michigan, USA. She died on 11 May 1973 in Salem, Marion Co., Oregon, USA. She married Walter Boomer Hunt on 13 Sep 1902 in Salem, Marion Co., Oregon, USA. He was born on 31 Jan 1877 in Salem, Marion Co., Oregon, USA. He died on 22 Jan 1959 in Salem, Marion Co., Oregon, USA.

Walter Boomer Hunt and Minnie Gertrude Penrose had the following children:

76: Walter and Minnie Hunt
(circa unknown)

43.     i.      FRANCES L[4] HUNT was born on 23 Jan 1905 in Salem, Marion Co., Oregon, USA. She died on 19 Aug 2004 in Salem, Marion Co., Oregon, USA. She married Theodore E. Burns on 07 Nov 1925 in Salem, Marion Co., Oregon, USA. He was born on 22 Sep 1905 in Winona, Emmons Co., North Dakota, USA. He died on 08 Jul 1972 in Bend, Deschutes Co., Oregon, USA.

ii.     KENNETH ROY HUNT was born on 31 Jan 1915 in Fort Rock, Lake Co., Oregon, USA. He died on 28 Mar 2003 in Dallas, Polk Co., Oregon, USA. He married Alice May Turner on 17 Jul 1937. She was born on 16 May 1918 in Salem, Marion Co., Oregon, USA. Kenneth Roy Hunt was buried in Polk Co., Oregon, USA, at Zena Cemetery.

iii.    HELEN MURIEL HUNT was born on 11 Mar 1921 in Salem, Marion Co., Oregon, USA. She married Lawrence Fremont McClure on 24 Sep 1939. He was born on 12 Sep 1919 in Notus, Canyon Co., Idaho, USA.

22 ROSE CARRIE[3] PENROSE (Carolina Theresa[2] Grimm, Heinrich Ludwig[1] "Henry Louis" Grimm) was born on 26 Apr 1884 in Houghton Co., Michigan, USA. She died on 21 Jun 1975 in Salem, Marion Co., Oregon, USA (Age 91). She married Roy Ethelbert Stoutenburg, son of Dingeman Stoutenburg and Margaret Galloway on 19 Sep 1905 in Dayton, Yamhill Co., Oregon, USA (Dayton Parsonage). He was born on 20 Jul 1884 in Unionvale, Yamhill Co., Oregon, USA. He died on 16 Sep 1968 in Dayton, Yamhill Co., Oregon, USA. Rose Carrie Penrose was buried on 24 Jun 1975 in Hopewell, Yamhill Co., Oregon, USA, at Hopewell Cemetery. Roy E. Stoutenburg was buried in Hopewell, Yamhill Co., Oregon, USA, at Hopewell Cemetery.

Roy E. Stoutenburg WWI Draft Registration: 1917-1918 in Yamhill Co., Oregon, USA.

77: Roy and Carrie Stoutenburg
(circa unknown)

STOUTENBURG, ROSE CARRIE [Shares stone w/Roy E. Stoutenburg] Age 91: 21-6-4 b. 26r 1884 Quincy, Michigan d. 21 Jun 1975 Keizer, Oregon

Funeral services for Mrs. Rose Carrie Stoutenburg were held at the Hopewell Community Church, Tuesday afternoon, June 24, at 2 p.m., with Rev. Walter Rowley of Silverton of the Hopewell and Unionvale Churches, officiating. Interment was in the Hopewell Cemetery beside her husband, Roy E. Stoutenburg who died Sept 16, 1968.

Rose Carrie Stoutenburg, the daughter of Louis E. Penrose and Carrie Teresa Grimm Penrose, was born in Quincy, Mich., April 26, 1884. When she was three years old, her parents moved to Zena, and lived in Hopewell and Unionvale areas, until she was married to Roy E. Stoutenburg on Sept. 1905. Their daughter, Elsie Webster of Kelso, Wash., was born in Pleasantdale, and the family moved to Fort Rock, Eastern Oregon, where daughter Esther Palmer was born and daughter Mildred, who was killed in a car accident when she was 16. The fourth daughter, Muriel Dodd of Reno, Nev., was born after the family returned to the Willamette Valley, living in Sheridan and Unionvale, until 1935, they moved to Grand Island, where she lived all the rest of her life.

She died June 20, 1975, at the Sherwood Park Nursing Home in Salem. She is survived by three daughters, five grandchildren, 14 great-grandchildren, a 2 great-great-granddaughters, and a sister, Mrs. Esther Propst, Woodburn. She was a member of the Unionvale Community Church. ( Dayton Tribune, Dayton, Oregon, June 26, 1975)

Roy and Carrie Stoutenburg celebrated their 60th wedding anniversary on 19 Sep 1965 at the recreation hall in the Unionvale Church.

Roy Ethelbert Stoutenburg and Rose Carrie Penrose had the following children:

i.    ELSIE MAE[4] STOUTENBURG was born on 08 Jul 1908 in Dayton, Yamhill Co., Oregon, USA. She died on 02 Mar 1987 in Longview, Cowlitz Co., Washington, USA. She married Harold Webster on 18 Sep 1926 in Dayton, Yamhill Co., Oregon, USA. He was born on 06 Sep 1902 in Wisconsin, USA.

ii.   ESTHER MARGARET STOUTENBURG was born on 19 Sep 1910 in Fort Rock, Lake Co., Oregon, USA. She died on 02 Sep 2004 in McMinnville, Yamhill Co., Oregon, USA (Oakwood Country Place). She married Raymond Isaac Palmer on 06 Jun 1929 in Dayton, Yamhill Co., Oregon, USA. He was born on 12 Apr 1908 in Fallon, Churchill Co., Nevada, USA. He died on 17 Apr 1984 in McMinnville, Yamhill Co., Oregon, USA. Esther Margaret Stoutenburg was buried in Hopewell, Yamhill Co., Oregon, USA (Hopewell Cemetery).

iii.  MILDRED LUCILLE STOUTENBURG was born on 20 Jan 1913 in Fort Rock, Lake Co., Oregon, USA. She died on 20 Jul 1929 in Dayton, Yamhill Co., Oregon, USA. Mildred Lucille Stoutenburg was buried after 20 Jul 1929 in Hopewell, Yamhill Co., Oregon, USA, at Hopewell Cemetery.

      Notes for: Mildred Lucille Stoutenburg: Auto accident when the auto turned over on her while riding outside of the car.

iv.   MURIEL LOIS STOUTENBURG was born on 27 Mar 1919 in Sheridan, Yamhill Co., Oregon, USA. She died on 02 Mar 2001 in Woodburn, Marion Co., Oregon, USA. She married John Raymond Dodd. He was born on 01 Aug 1896 in Charles City, Floyd Co., Iowa, USA. He died on 04 Nov 1983 in Reno, Washoe Co., Nevada, USA.

23.  LEWIS WILLIAM[3] PENROSE (Carolina Theresa[2] Grimm, Heinrich Ludwig[1] "Henry Louis" Grimm) was born on 13 Nov 1885 in Hancock, Houghton Co., Michigan, USA. He died on 20 Oct 1917 in Fort Rock, Lake Co., Oregon, USA. He married Arka Antrim, daughter of George Antrim and Olive Harvey, on 11 Oct 1908 in Unionvale, Yamhill Co.,

Oregon, USA. She was born on 09 Aug 1890 in Boise, Ada Co., Idaho, USA. She died on 12 Oct 1942 in Newberg, Yamhill Co., Oregon, USA. Lewis William Penrose was buried in Dayton, Yamhill Co., Oregon, USA; Hopewell Cemetery. Arka Antrim was buried in Yamhill Co., Oregon, USA; Hopewell Cemetery.

Lewis William Penrose was buried after 20 Oct 1917 in Dayton, Yamhill Co., Oregon, USA (Hopewell

Lewis William Penrose and Arka Antrim had the following children:

78: Lewis and Arka Penrose (circa unknown)

    i.    BERNETTA ELEANOR[4] PENROSE was born on 12 Sep 1913 in Dayton, Yamhill Co., Oregon, USA. She died on 09 Jun 1939 in Salem, Marion Co., Oregon, USA. She married Fred Bethune. He was born in 1896. He died in 1975.

    ii.    GEORGE LEWIS PENROSE was born on 13 Apr 1915 in Fort Rock, Lake Co., Oregon, USA. He died on 04 Dec 1987 in Tigard, Washington Co., Oregon, USA. He married Eleanor Sterrett Shields on 06 Nov 1937 in Portland, Multnomah Co., Oregon, USA. She was born on 08 Mar 1913 in Portland, Multnomah Co., Oregon, USA. She died in 1993 in Washington, USA.

    iii.    MELVIN LLOYD PENROSE was born on 02 Nov 1916 in Fort Rock, Lake Co., Oregon, USA. He died on 08 Oct 1968 in Portland, Multnomah Co., Oregon, USA. He married Evelyn Helen Sandin on 14 Sep 1940 in Vancouver, Clark Co., Washington, USA. She was born on 01 Sep 1918 in Woodland, Clark Co., Washington, USA.

    iv.    ERWIN CLARK PENROSE was born on 15 May 1918 in Unionvale, Yamhill Co., Oregon, USA. He died on 30 Sep 1997 in McMinnville, Yamhill Co., Oregon, USA. He married Violette Estelle Bunn on 13 Jul 1936 in Vancouver, Clark Co., Washington, USA. She was born on 15 Nov 1917 in Dayton, Yamhill Co., Oregon, USA. She died on 22 Sep 2006 in Salem, Marion Co., Oregon, USA.

24. LILLIAN ANN[3] PENROSE (Carolina Theresa[2] Grimm, Heinrich Ludwig[1] "Henry Louis" Grimm) was born on 28 Mar 1890 in Tacoma, Pierce Co., Washington, USA. She died on 08 Sep 1974 in Salem, Marion Co., Oregon, USA. She married Ralph E. Nelson on 24 Mar 1909 in Dayton, Yamhill Co., Oregon, USA. He was born on 27 Dec 1883 in Fairmount, Richland Co., North Dakota, USA. He died on 28 Apr 1970 in Salem, Marion Co., Oregon, USA.

79: Ralph and Lillian Penrose ( March 1909)

Ralph E Nelson and Lillian Ann Penrose had the following children:

    i.    LILLIAN MAY[4] NELSON was born on 13 Mar 1910 in Corvallis, Benton Co., Oregon, USA. She died on 16 Oct 1989 in New York, New York, USA. She married Alfred J Schwartz on 26 Oct 1932 in Corvallis, Benton Co., Oregon, USA. He was born on 25 Aug 1906 in Rochester, Ulster Co., New York, USA. He died on 07 Mar 1985 in New York, New York, USA.

    ii.    EDWARD W NELSON was born on 29 Dec 1914 in Corvallis, Benton Co., Oregon, USA. He died on 16 Feb 2001 in Lebanon, Linn Co., Oregon, USA. He married Mary Tyler on 07 Jun 1941. She was born on 22 Apr.

iii.  WALTER LEWIS NELSON was born on 14 Jan 1917 in Wren, Benton Co., Oregon, USA. He died on 12 Apr 2002 in Lebanon, Linn Co., Oregon, USA. He married Etta Ione Robertson on 26 Jun 1940. She was born on 30 Jan 1909 in Waterloo, Linn Co., Oregon, USA. She died on 20 Mar 1997 in Lebanon, Linn Co., Oregon, USA.

iv.  LEWIS ELMER NELSON was born on 01 Feb 1922 in Watauga, Corson Co., South Dakota, USA. He married Stella M Bradbury on 03 Nov 1950 in Reno, Washoe Co., Nevada, USA. She was born on 13 Sep 1913 in Little Rock, Pulaski Co., Arkansas, USA.

v.  EDITH ROSE NELSON was born on 06 Sep 1924 in Watauga, Corson Co., South Dakota, USA. She died on 12 Apr 1973 in Portland, Multnomah Co., Oregon, USA. She married James Reuben Dey on 23 Jun 1944 in Vancouver, Clark Co., Washington, USA. He was born on 30 Sep 1924 in Dayton, Yamhill Co., Oregon, USA.

vi.  HAZEL ELIZABETH NELSON was born on 06 Dec 1929 in Watauga, Corson Co., South Dakota, USA. She married (1) Dan Selvage in 1948 in Montana, USA. She married (2) Kenneth Edward Allen on 23 May 1949. He died on 15 Mar 1964 in Portland, Multnomah Co., Oregon, USA. She married (3) Ted James Klee on 24 Dec 1959 in Dayton, Yamhill Co., Oregon, USA. He was born on 15 Jul 1933 in Hood River, Hood River Co., Oregon, USA.

25.  ESTHER MARTHA[3] PENROSE (Carolina Theresa[2] Grimm, Heinrich Ludwig[1] "Henry Louis" Grimm) was born on 06 Dec 1891 in Salem, Marion Co., Oregon, USA. She died on 15 Mar 1992 in Woodburn, Marion Co., Oregon, USA. She married Horace Minor Propst on 14 Jun 1910 in Corvallis, Benton Co., Oregon, USA. He was born on 20 Oct 1885 in Albany, Benton Co., Oregon, USA. He died on 08 Apr 1988 in Woodburn, Marion Co., Oregon, USA. Horace Minor Propst was buried in Portland, Multnomah Co., Oregon, USA, at Riverview Abbey Mausoleum.

80: Horace and Esther Propst (circa unknown)

Horace Minor Propst and Esther Martha Penrose had the following children:

i.  GLEN MARION[4] PROPST was born on 14 Jun 1915 in Butte, Silver Bow Co., Montana, USA. He married Helen Pearl Dodds on 06 Sep 1942 in California, USA.

ii.  MELVIN RAY PROPST was born on 16 Oct 1926 in Portland, Multnomah Co., Oregon, USA. He married Elaine Ann Plieth on 29 Jul 1949 in Tigard, Washington Co., Oregon, USA. She was born in 1928 in Oregon, USA.

26.  HAZEL GLENN[3] PENROSE (Carolina Theresa[2] Grimm, Heinrich Ludwig[1] "Henry Louis" Grimm) was born on 29 Dec 1894 in Oregon, USA. She died on 08 Aug 1938 in Deschutes Co., Oregon, USA. She married George Earl Menkenmaier in 1914. He was born on 12 May 1892 in South Dakota, USA. He died on 23 Dec 1938 in Portland, Multnomah Co., Oregon, USA. Hazel Glenn Penrose and her husband, George Earl Menkenmaier are buried in Bend, Deschutes Co., Oregon, US George Earl Menkenmaier WWI Draft Registration: Sep 1918 in Lake Co., California.

George Earl Menkenmaier and Hazel Glenn Penrose had the following children:

i.  BEATRICE FRANCES[4] MENKENMAIER was born on 28 Jun 1918 in Deschutes Co., Oregon, USA. She died on 08 Nov 2004 in Harney Co., Oregon, USA. She married Hollie Franklin Schroeder on 25

Oct 1939 in Reno, Washoe Co., Nevada, USA. He was born on 11 Sep 1914 in Silver Lake, Lake Co., Oregon, USA. He died on 14 Jan 1999 in Hines, Harney Co., Oregon, USA.

ii.     GEORGE WILLIAM MENKENMAIER was born on 16 Jun 1927 in McMinnville, Yamhill Co., Oregon, USA. He died on 22 Aug 1958 in Prineville, Crook Co., Oregon, USA. He married Lola Oliver. George William Menkenmaier was buried in Burns, Harney Co., Oregon, USA.

---

### WILD PLUNGE OF HORSES KILLS RESIDENT OF FORT ROCK AREA
*Mrs. George Menkenmaier Fatally Hurt when Team
Runs Away; Rake, Mower Horse Pile Up*

Injured in an accident in a Fort Rock hayfield, Mrs. George Menkenmaier, long a resident of northern Lake County and owner of one of the largest collections of Indian artifacts in the Pacific Northwest, died in the St. Charles hospital here shortly before 3 o'clock yesterday afternoon.

Internal injuries were the cause of death, the attending physician said. Serious head injuries had also been received.

Mrs. Menkenmaier was operating a mowing machine on the Menkenmaier ranch near Fort Rock shortly before noon yesterday when the accident occurred. Ahead of Mrs. Menkenmaier, and also operating a mowing machine was her husband. Behind Mr. and Mrs. Menkenmaier was their 10-year-old son, George, driving a team attached to a rake. Suddenly, the boy's team bolted and plunged into the mowing machine outfit operated by Mrs. Menkenmaier. Horses and machinery were soon in a pile, with Mrs. Menkenmaier near the center of the pile up.

*Boy Not Hurt*

The boy escaped unhurt, but Mrs. Menkenmaier was trampled by the horses and bruised by the machinery. The team driven by Menkenmaier was not involved in the pile up, according to information from Fort Rock.

When it was determined that Mrs. Menkenmaier had been gravely hurt, she was placed in an automobile and brought to Bend. At the same time a call for Dr. J.W. Thom and an ambulance was received here. Ambulance and physician met the fatally injured woman south of here.

Death occurred at about 2:35.

Because of her interest in artifacts, Mrs. Menkenmaier's home was frequently the gathering place of students of ancient man in Oregon. Only recently, Dr. L.S. Cressman, University of Oregon anthropologist, and members of his party received valuable aid from Mrs. Menkenmaier when they were making their studies in the Fort Rock cave, only a short distance from the Menkenmaier ranch. Mrs. Menkenmaier was also active in grange work.

Aside from her husband and son, Mrs. Menkenmaier is survived by a daughter, Bernice, 19. Mrs. Menkenmaier, the former Hazel Penrose, was a member of a family that settled in Fort Rock valley some 30 years ago.

*Funeral to be Thursday*

Hazel Penrose was a native of Salem, having been born there on December 26, 1895. In 1914 she was married to George Menkenmaier, at Fort Rock. Aside from her husband and children, Mrs. Menkenmaier is survived by her mother, Mrs. Carrie Penrose of Dayton, and four sisters, Mrs. H.M. Propst, Portland; Mrs. R.E. Stoutenburg, Dayton; Mrs. Ralph Nelson, Lebanon; and Mrs. Walter Hunt, Salem.

Mrs. Menkenmaier was a member of the Fort Rock grange, secretary of the Marginal Land association of Fort Rock, and secretary-treasurer of the Fort Rock Telephone Co.

Services will be held from the Niswonger & Winslow Chapel in Bend Thursday afternoon at 2 o'clock. The Rev. George H. Redden will be in charge and burial will be in the Greenwood Cemetery (The Bulletin; Bend, Oregon. 09 August 1938).

---

## Generation 4

27. MILDRED A⁴ GRIMM (Frank A³, Franziscus Gustav² "Frank", Heinrich Ludwig¹ "Henry Louis") was born in 1906 in Oregon, USA. She died on 28 Oct 1969 in Portland, Multnomah Co., Oregon, USA. She married (1) Elmore Addison Johns on 18 Oct 1924 in Multnomah Co., Oregon, USA. He was born on 01 Feb 1896 in Oregon City, Clackamas Co., Oregon, USA. He died on 12 Oct 1951 in Clackamas, Clackamas Co., Oregon, USA (Age: 55). She married (2) John Nicholas "Jack" Domnisse on 03 Aug 1952 in Oregon, USA. He was born on 31 Jul 1887 in Council Bluffs, Pottawattamie Co., Iowa, USA. He died on 29 Jul 1976 in Portland, Multnomah Co., Oregon, USA (Age 89). Mildred A

Grimm was buried in Portland, Multnomah Co., Oregon, USA, at Riverview Cemetery. Elmore Addison Johns was buried on 18 Oct 1951 in Portland, Multnomah Co., Oregon, USA, at Willamette National Cemetery (Sec: G, Site: 2816).

Elmore Addison Johns served in the military on 03 Aug 1917 (Military: 05/20/1919; US Army; Chauffer; Age: 21).

Elmore Addison Johns and Mildred A Grimm had the following children:

      i.      MARGARET E$^5$ JOHNS was born about 1926 in Washington, USA.

      ii.     GERALDINE E JOHNS was born about 1927 in Oregon, USA.

      iii.    LAWRENCE A JOHNS was born about 1929 in Oregon, USA.

John Nicholas "Jack" Domnisse was employed as a Dohrman Hotel Supply Co., Manager in Portland, Multnomah Co., Oregon, USA.

28   LAWRENCE A$^4$ GRIMM (Frank A$^3$, Franziscus Gustav$^2$ "Frank", Heinrich Ludwig$^1$ "Henry Louis") was born on 03 Sep 1908 in Oregon, USA. He died on 11 Jun 1986 in Portland, Multnomah Co., Oregon, USA (Age: 77). He married Varina Mae [Unknown] between 1929-1931. She was born on 28 Feb 1910 in Washington, USA. She died on 01 Sep 1989 in Portland, Multnomah Co., Oregon, USA. Lawrence A. Grimm was buried in Portland, Multnomah Co., Oregon, USA, at Riverview Cemetery. Varina Mae [Unknown] was buried in Portland, Multnomah Co., Oregon, USA, at Riverview Cemetery.

Lawrence A. Grimm was employed as a Montgomery Ward (Dept. Store); Checker in 1931 in Portland, Multnomah Co., Oregon, USA.

Lawrence A. Grimm and Varina Mae [Unknown] had the following child:

      i.      SHARON$^5$ GRIMM was born about 1937 in Oregon, USA.

29   ALVIN EDWARD$^4$ GRIMM (Wilhelm Albert$^3$ "William", Franziscus Gustav$^2$ "Frank", Heinrich Ludwig$^1$ "Henry Louis") was born on 31 May 1902 in Portland, Multnomah Co., Oregon, USA. He died on 03 Mar 1994 in Los Angeles, Los Angeles Co., California, USA (Age: 91). He married Emilie L [Unknown]. She was born about 1906 in Nebraska, USA.

Note for: Alvin Edward Grimm: original surname of Kreidt.

Alvin Edward Grimm and Emilie L [Unknown] had the following children:

      i.      ALVIN CHARLES W$^5$ GRIMM was born about 1927 in Arizona, USA.

      ii.     FLOYD E GRIMM was born about 1930 in Arizona, USA.

      iii.    DALE L GRIMM was born about 1932 in Idaho, USA.

      iv.    MARLENE J GRIMM was born about 1934 in Idaho, USA.

      v.     KENNETH E GRIMM was born about 1936 in Idaho, USA.

30. BERTHA WILHELMINA[4] GRIMM (Wilhelm Albert[3] "William", Franziscus Gustav[2] "Frank", Heinrich Ludwig[1] "Henry Louis") was born on 07 Oct 1909 in Mount Angel, Marion Co., Oregon, USA. She died on 19 Nov 2011 (Age: 102). She married (1) Max Irvin Doblie on 15 Feb 1942 in Portland, Multnomah Co., Oregon, USA. He was born on 28 Oct 1907 in Concordia, Lafayette Co., Missouri, USA. He died on 04 Apr 2000 in Portland, Multnomah Co., Oregon, USA. She married (2) [Unknown] Buxton before 1938.

[Unknown] Buxton and Bertha Wilhelmina Grimm had the following child:

  i.  JAMES[5] "JAMIE" BUXTON was born about 1938 in Oregon, USA.

---

BERTHA GRIMM DOBLIE

  Doblie, Bertha Grimm 102 Oct. 07, 1909 Nov. 19, 2011 A memorial will be held at St. Michael's Lutheran Church, 6700 NE 29th Avenue, Portland, Jan. 7, 2012, at 1 p.m. Bertha is survived by a son, James "Jim" Buxton of Vernonia; grandchildren, Julie Mullen of Canby, Katherine Chakos of St. Helens, Elizabeth Andersen of Vancouver and Alexander "Woody" Buxton of Portland; seven great-grandchildren; and one great-great-grandchild. (The Oregonian, Portland, Oregon; 25 Dec 2011)

---

31. WILBERT LOUIS[4] GRIMM (Ludwig Alexander[3] "Louis", Franziscus Gustav[2] "Frank", Heinrich Ludwig[1] "Henry Louis") was born on 07 Jan 1902 in Oregon, USA. He died on 31 Dec 1986 in Shasta, Shasta Co., California, USA. He married Hannah Kraus. She was born in 1905 in Russia.

Wilbert Louis Grimm and Hannah Kraus had the following child:

  i.  ROBERT LOUIS[5] GRIMM was born on 18 Feb 1925 in Oregon, USA. He died on 09 May 1996 in Anderson, Shasta Co., California, USA. He married Julianne L [Unknown]. Robert Louis Grimm was buried after 09 May 1996 in Redding, Shasta Co., California, USA, at Lawncrest Memorial Park.

32. WILMA EDITH[4] GRIMM (Ludwig Alexander[3] "Louis", Franziscus Gustav[2] "Frank", Heinrich Ludwig[1] "Henry Louis") was born on 29 Jul 1904 in Oregon, USA. She died on 15 Oct 1980 in Portland, Multnomah Co., Oregon, USA. She married James Edward Huffman in 1926. He was born on 31 Dec 1895 in Malheur, Malheur Co., Oregon, USA. He died on 22 May 1970 in Portland, Multnomah Co., Oregon, USA. Wilma Edith Grimm was buried on 20 Oct 1980 in Portland, Multnomah Co., Oregon, USA, at Willamette National Cemetery. James Edward Huffman was buried in Portland, Multnomah Co., Oregon, USA, at Willamette National Cemetery.

James Edward Huffman was employed as a Farmer in 1917 in Vernonia, Columbia Co., Oregon, USA. He served in the military on 02 Oct 1917 (US Army; Private). He was employed as a laborer, rigger for a logging camp between 1920-1930 in Vernonia, Columbia Co., Oregon, USA. He was employed as a Oregon Shipbuilding Corp (St. Johns) in 1945 in Portland, Multnomah Co., Oregon, USA.

James Edward Huffman and Wilma Edith Grimm had the following child:

  i.  LEONARD JAMES[5] HUFFMAN was born on 18 Feb 1929 in Portland, Multnomah Co., Oregon, USA. He died on 14 Sep 2009 in Portland, Multnomah Co., Oregon, USA. Leonard James Huffman served in the U.S. Navy in 1946.

33. MATHILDA ALICE[4] GRIMM (Heinrich William[3] "Henry", Franziscus Gustav[2] "Frank", Heinrich Ludwig[1] "Henry Louis") was born on 22 May 1904 in Mount Angel, Marion Co., Oregon, USA. She died on 28 Aug 1951 in Paul, Minidoka Co., Idaho, USA. She married Adolph Koch, son of Peter Koch and Katherine Knopp, on 30 Jul 1922 in Paul,

Minidoka Co., Idaho, USA. He was born on 14 Dec 1901 in Kolpe, Russia. He died in Jan 1985 in Paul, Minidoka Co., Idaho, USA. Mathilda Alice Grimm was buried in Paul, Minidoka Co., Idaho, USA, at Paul Cemetery. Adolph Koch was buried in Paul, Minidoka Co., Idaho, USA, at Paul Cemetery.

Adolph Koch and Mathilda Alice Grimm had the following children:

    i.      ADOLPH[5] KOCH JR was born on 15 Oct 1924 in Idaho, USA. He died on 14 Apr 1945 in Germany. He was buried in Paul, Minidoka Co., Idaho, USA, at Paul Cemetery.

            Adolph Koch Jr. served in the military on 21 Mar 1944 in Fort Douglas, Salt Lake Co., Utah, USA; PFC 22 Infantry, 4 Division, WWII.

    ii.     ROSELLA KOCH was born in 1929 in Idaho, USA. She married [Unknown] Miller.

    iii.    SEYMOUR KOCH was born in 1931 in Idaho, USA.

    iv.    TRUMAN KOCH was born in 1932 in Idaho, USA.

    v.     BEATRICE KOCH was born in 1935 in Idaho, USA. She died before 1985.

    vi.    ARVILLA KOCH was born in 1937 in Idaho, USA. She married [Unknown] Howard.

---

ADOLPH KOCH

    Adolph Koch , 83, Paul, died Wednesday evening at Minidoka Memorial Hospital.He was born Dec. 14, 1901, in Kolpe, Russia, the son of Peter and Katherine Knopp Koch. He moved to America with his parents in 1902. They lived in Dayton, WA., until 1905 when they moved to Mud Lake. In 1910 they settled on a homestead north of Paul, where he attended the Frontier School. He married Mathilda Grimm in Paul in 1921. She died in 1951. He married Bessie Ward in Rupert in 1955. She died in 1964. He custom farmed in Rupert-Paul area and raised cattle and sheep. He was a member of the Lutheran Church.
    Surviving are two sons, Seymour Koch, Wendell, and Truman Koch, Paul; two daughters Rosella Miller, Highland, Utah, and Arvilla Howard, Murray, Utah; three brothers, Fred Koch, Richfield, Utah; Daniel Koch, Spokane, and Paul Koch, Cascade; four sisters, Sandra Koch and Rachael Shaffer, Paul; Pauline Neiwert, Rupert, and Emma Kulm, Spokane; 22 grandchildren; and 29 great-grandchildren.He was preceded in death by a son, a daughter, a granddaughter, three brothers and one sister.
    The funeral will be Saturday at 2 p.m. in the Burley Zion Lutheran Church, with the Rev. Ron L. Leder officiating. Burial will be in Paul Cemetery.Friends may call at Hansen Mortuary this evening and prior to the service on Saturday. The family suggests memorials may be made to the Zion Lutheran Church. (Times News, Twin Falls, Idaho)

---

34. VIOLA ANNA WILHEMINA[4] GRIMM (Heinrich William[3] "Henry", Franziscus Gustav[2] "Frank", Heinrich Ludwig[1] was born on 11 Oct 1907 in Idaho, USA. She died on 04 Sep 1946 in Paul, Minidoka Co., Idaho, USA. She married Amos Bill on 23 Nov 1923 in Paul, Minidoka Co., Idaho, USA. He was born on 19 Dec 1901 in Illinois, USA. He died on 13 May 1984 in Paul, Minidoka Co., Idaho, USA. Viola Anna Wilhelmina Grimm was buried after 04 Sep 1946 in Paul, Minidoka Co., Idaho, USA at Paul Cemetery. Amos Bill was buried in Paul, Minidoka Co., Idaho, USA.

Amos Bill and Viola Anna Wilhelmina Grimm had the following children:

    i.      HENRY A[5] BILL was born on 20 Jan 1925 in Paul, Minidoka Co., Idaho, USA. He died on 27 Aug 1997 in Burley, Cassia Co., Idaho, USA.

            Henry A Bill served in the military on 20 May 1943 in Pocatello, Bannock Co., Idaho, USA.

ii.     CLEO ROSE BILL was born in Mar 1926 in Paul, Minidoka Co., Idaho, USA. She died on 07 Oct 2008 in Paul, Minidoka Co., Idaho, USA. She married Ronald Lester Zemke. He was born on 24 Jul 1926. He died on 14 Feb 2010 in Paul, Minidoka Co., Idaho, USA. Cleo Rose Bill was buried in Paul, Minidoka Co., Idaho, USA at Paul Cemetery.

iii.    LEONA BILL was born in 1931 in Paul, Minidoka Co., Idaho, USA.

44.     iv.    LEO LEON BILL was born on 16 Jun 1934 in Paul, Minidoka Co., Idaho, USA. He died on 22 Jun 1997 in Rupert, Minidoka Co., Idaho, USA. He married Lauretta June Hodge on 29 Aug 1952 in Burley, Cassia Co., Idaho, USA. She was born on 20 Jun 1935.

35. MONROE HENRY FRANK[4] GRIMM (Heinrich William[3] "Henry", Franziscus Gustav[2] "Frank", Heinrich Ludwig[1] "Henry Louis") was born on 28 Aug 1910 in Idaho, USA. He died on 03 Nov 1960. He married Ruth Virginia Hofhine on 23 Jul 1927 in Blackfoot, Bingham Co., Idaho, USA. She was born on 29 Nov 1909 in Oregon, USA. She died on 21 May 2004 in Idaho, USA. Monroe Henry Frank Grimm was buried in Paul, Minidoka Co., Idaho, USA at Paul Cemetery. Ruth Virginia Hofhine is buried in Paul, Minidoka Co., Idaho, USA, at Paul Cemetery.

Monroe Henry Frank Grimm and Ruth Virginia Hofhine had the following children:

i.     RICHARD[5] GRIMM was born in 1929 in Paul, Minidoka Co., Idaho, USA.

ii.    FRANK GRIMM was born in Mar 1930 in Paul, Minidoka Co., Idaho, USA.

iii.   GLADYS GRIMM was born in 1932 in Paul, Minidoka Co., Idaho, USA.

iv.    DONNA GAY GRIMM was born on 21 Jan 1934 in Paul, Minidoka Co., Idaho, USA. She died on 14 Jan 2002 in Arkansas, USA. She married Carmen Eugene Hutson on 29 Aug 1949 in Prineville, Crook Co., Oregon, USA. Donna Gay Grimm was buried after 14 Jan 2002 in Fulton Co., Arkansas, USA, at Wild Cherry Cemetery.

v.     JOAN GRIMM was born in 1936 in Paul, Minidoka Co., Idaho, USA.

vi.    DOROTHY GRIMM was born in 1938 in Paul, Minidoka Co., Idaho, USA.

81: Monroe and Ruth Grimm
Paul, Minidoka Co., ID

36. ALVIN ALBERT WILLIAM[4] GRIMM (Albert Philip Henry[3], Albert A[2], Heinrich Ludwig[1] "Henry Louis") was born on 08 May 1909 in Chelsea, Taylor Co., Wisconsin, USA. He died on 24 Jun 2003 in Vancouver, Clark Co., Washington, USA (Age 94). He married Clara Matilda Anderson, daughter of August Nikolaus Anderson and Mary Olson on 09 Nov 1933 in Medford, Taylor Co., Wisconsin, USA (Whittlesey Lutheran Church Parsonage). She was born on 09 Jan 1912 in Little Black, Taylor Co., Wisconsin, USA. She died on 5 May 1997 in Medford; Taylor Co., Wisconsin, USA of congestive heart failure, Chronic Obstructive Pulmonary Disease (COPD) and sclerosis of the right lung due to

tuberculosis. (Age 85). Alvin Albert William Grimm was buried on 03 Oct 2003 and Clara Mathilda Anderson was buried 10 May 1997 in Medford, Taylor Co., Wisconsin, USA. Alvin Albert William Grimm was buried at Whittlesey, Taylor Co., Wisconsin, USA at Trinity Lutheran Church Cemetery. Clara Mathilda Anderson Grimm was buried at Whittlesey, Taylor Co., Wisconsin, USA at Trinity Lutheran Church Cemetery.

Burial Notes: Gladys Grimm Doriot flew her father's ashes back to Medford and had his cremains buried next to his wife, Clara, at Trinity Lutheran Church in Whittlesey where the couple had been married sixty-four years earlier.

---

**CLARA GRIMM**

MEDFORD - Clara M. (Anderson) Grimm, 85, Medford, died May 5 1997, at Memorial Nursing Home of Taylor County, Medford.

Funeral services will be at 11 a.m. Saturday at Trinity Lutheran church, Whittlesey. Burial will be in the parish cemetery.

Visitation will be from 4-9 p.m. Friday at Hemer Funeral Home, Medford, and at the church on Saturday from 9 a.m. until service time.

Mrs. Grimm was born Jan. 9, 1912, in the town of Little Black. She was a homemaker.

Survivors are her husband, Alvin W. Grimm of Medford; a daughter,, Gladys Doriot of Ridgefield, Wash.; four grandchildren and one great-grandson; a sister, Elva Drolshagen of Medford; and two brothers, Robert Anderson and Arthur Anderson, both of Okanogan, Wash. (Star News, Medford, WI; abt 07 May 1997)

---

**ALVIN W. GRIMM (Ridgefield)**

A fairy farmer and brick mason, Alvin William Grimm died Tuesday, June 24, in Vancouver. He was 94.

Mr. Grimm enjoyed fishing,, hunting, camping and picking berries. He was a member of the Grimm Orchestra and played accordion, piano, and guitar.

His wife, Clara, died in 1997.

He was born May 8,1909, in Chelsea, Wis., He lived in Wisconsin for many years before moving to Clark County five years ago.

Survivors include one daughter, Gladys Doriot of Ridgefield; one brother, Everett of Middlebury, Ind.; four grandchildren; and one great-grandchild.

There will be a memorial service in Whittlesey, Wis. Layne's Funeral Home in Battle Ground was in charge of arrangements.

Memorial contributions may be made to Hospice Southwest, P.O. Box 1600, Vancouver, WA 98668. (The Columbian, Vancouver, WA; 26 June 2003)

---

**ALVIN GRIMM (1909-2003)**

Chelsea native and former Medford resident Alvin William Grimm, 94, Ridgefield, Wash., died Jun 24, 2003 in Vancouver, Wash. A memorial service will be held Friday, Oct 3 at Trinity Lutheran church in Whittlesey at 11 a.m. Burial of cremains will be in Trinity Lutheran Cemetery in Whittlesey

Hemer Funeral Service of Medford is assisting the family with arrangements. (Star News, Medford, WI; 02 Oct 2003)

---

Alvin Albert William Grimm and Clara Matilda Anderson had the following child:

45.      i.   GLADYS ANN[5] GRIMM was born on 10 Dec 1934 in Chelsea, Taylor Co., Wisconsin, USA. She died on 04 Mar 2011 in Ridgefield, Clark Co., Washington, USA (At home; Complications from breast cancer; age 76). She married James Maynard Doriot, son of Charles Henry Doriot and Catherine Belle McDonald on 16 Oct 1971 in Reno, Washoe Co., Nevada, USA. He was born on 04 Oct 1913 in Manitowish Waters, Vilas Co., Wisconsin, USA. He died on 10 Feb 1992 in Clackamas, Clackamas Co., Oregon, USA. Gladys is buried in Ridgefield, Clark Co., USA at Ridgefield Cemetery. James Maynard Doriot is buried in Ridgefield, Clark Co., USA at Ridgefield Cemetery.

37. ERMA HELEN*⁴* GRIMM (Albert Philip Henry*³*, Albert A*²*, Heinrich Ludwig*¹* "Henry Louis") was born on 11 Nov 1911 in Chelsea, Taylor Co., Wisconsin, USA. She died on 02 Jun 1991 in Stoughton, Dane Co., Wisconsin, USA (Age: 79). She married Siegfried Krausse, son of Fred Krausse and Elsie Minna Agnes Mueller, in Feb 1929 in Medford, Taylor Co., Wisconsin, USA. He was born on 18 Feb 1903 in Molitor, Taylor Co., Wisconsin, USA. He died on 21 Mar 1950 in Medford, Taylor Co., Wisconsin, USA (Age: 48). Erma Helen Grimm was buried on 07 Jun 1991 in Medford, Taylor Co., Wisconsin, USA at Evergreen Cemetery.

Siegfried Krausse and Erma Helen Grimm had the following children:

46.    i.    LEROY SIEGFRED*⁵* KRAUSSE was born on 23 Jul 1929 in Molitor, Taylor Co., Wisconsin, USA. He died on 29 Jan 2000 in Edgerton, Rock Co., Wisconsin, USA. He married Annanelle [Unknown].

47.    ii.    BERNICE F KRAUSE was born on 02 Apr 1938 in Molitor, Taylor Co., Wisconsin, USA. She married Kenneth Kuklinsky on 02 Jun 1973 in Milwaukee, Milwaukee Co., Wisconsin, USA. He was born on 21 Apr 1927. He died on 15 Mar 1990.

48.    iii.    ELAINE LEONA KRAUSSE was born on 28 Oct 1943 in Molitor, Taylor Co., Wisconsin, USA. She married (1) Charles L. Mason in 1964. He was born in May 1933. She married (2) James Henry McNeil on 27 Aug 1988 in Milwaukee, Milwaukee Co., Wisconsin, USA. He was born in Sep 1933.

38. LUCILLE*⁴* SCHUBERT (Lydia Louise*³* Grimm, Albert A*²* Grimm, Heinrich Ludwig*¹* "Henry Louis" Grimm) was born about 1924 in Minnesota, USA. She died after 2004. She married Vernon J. Frey, son of William Frey and Wanda Schmoldt, on 18 Jul 1942 in Medford, Taylor Co., Wisconsin, USA (Immanuel Evangelical Lutheran Church). He was born on 10 Aug 1920 in Browning, Taylor Co., Wisconsin, USA. He died on 21 Nov 2004 in Medford, Taylor Co., Wisconsin, USA (Age: 84). Vernon J. Frey was buried on 24 Nov 2004 in Medford, Taylor Co., Wisconsin, USA at Evergreen Cemetery.

Vernon J. Frey served in the military between 1939-1945 in Medford, Taylor Co., Wisconsin, USA (US Army). He was employed as a Farmer about 1940 in Browning, Taylor Co., Wisconsin, USA.

Vernon J. Frey and Lucille Schubert had the following children:

    i.    DONNA*⁵* FREY. She married [Unknown] Flaherty.

    ii.    PAM FREY.

    iii.    SHELLEY FREY. She married [Unknown] Bruns.

    iv.    VERNON FREY JR. He married Carol [Unknown].

    v.    PATRICK FREY. He married Velome [Unknown].

    vi.    RANDALL FREY.

    vii.    JOHN FREY. He married Claire [Unknown]

VERNON J. FREY

Medford - Vernon J. Frey, 84, of Medford, formerly of the town of Browning, died Sunday, Nov. 21, 2004, at his home.

Funeral services will be at 11 a.m. Wednesday at Immanuel Evangelical Lutheran Church in Medford. Burial will follow in Medford Evergreen Cemetery II, with graveside military rites.

Visitation will be from 4 p.m. to 8 p.m. Tuesday at Hemer Funeral Home and from 9 a.m. until service time Wednesday at the church.

He was born Aug. 10, 1920, in the town of Browning to William Frey and Wanda Schmoldt. He attended Medford High School and served in the U.S. Navy during World War II from 1939 to 1945. He married Lucille Schubert on July 18, 1942, at Immanuel Evangelical Lutheran Church, Medford. He farmed in the town of Browning for 46 years.

He was a member of Immanuel Evangelical Lutheran Church, Medford, Klossner-Dietzler Veterans of Foreign Wars Post No. 5729, Medford, and Landau-Jensen America Legion Post No. 147, Medford.

He is survived by his wife, Lucille Frey of Medford; three daughters, Donna Flaherty of Oconomowoc, Pam Frey of Green Bay and Shelley Bruns of Minneapolis; four sons, Vernon (Carol) Frey Jr. of Colorado Springs, Colo., Patrick (Velome) Frey of Las Vegas, Randall Frey of Colorado Springs, Colo., and John (Claire) Frey of Green Bay; his brother, Gerald Frey of Stetsonville; eight grandchildren; and three great-grandchildren.

---

39. ORVILLE GUST[4] GRIMM (William Max[3], Albert A[2], Heinrich Ludwig[1] "Henry Louis") was born on 28 May 1912 in Brooks, Red Lake Co., Minnesota, USA. He died on 09 Feb 2005 in McIntosh, Polk Co., Minnesota, USA (McIntosh Manor Nursing Home). He married Marie L. Magoon on 05 Nov 1931 in McIntosh, Polk Co., Minnesota, USA. She was born on 08 Jul 1912 in Minnesota, USA. She died on 17 Oct 1977 in Red Lake Co., Minnesota, USA. Orville Gust Grimm was buried on 14 Feb 2005 in McIntosh, Polk Co., Minnesota, USA at Immanuel Lutheran Cemetery.

Doris is not mentioned with husband in William M. Grimm's obituary. Probably deceased.

Orville Gust Grimm and Marie L. Magoon had the following children:

   i.  LEROY[5] GRIMM was born in 1932 in Minnesota, USA.

49.  ii.  DUANE ERVIN GRIMM was born on 05 Jun 1933 in Minnesota, USA. He died on 23 Dec 2004 in Great Falls, Cascade Co., Montana, USA.

   iii.  PEARL GRIMM was born in 1934 in Minnesota, USA. She married Russell Johnson.

   iv.  DOUGLAS LAVERN GRIMM was born on 28 Dec 1935 in Minnesota, USA. He died on 17 Dec 1975 in Ramsey, Anoka Co., Minnesota, USA.

   v.  DOUGLAS LAVERN GRIMM was buried after 17 Dec 1975 in McIntosh, Polk Co., Minnesota, USA at Immanuel Lutheran Cemetery.

   vi.  DONALD LAVERN GRIMM was born on 28 Dec 1935 in Red Lake Co., MI, USA.

   vii.  JANICE MARIE GRIMM was born on 08 Jun 1937 in Red Lake Co., Minnesota, USA. She married Alvin Turner.

   viii.  RUBY VIOLET GRIMM was born on 09 Jun 1942 in Red Lake Co., Minnesota, USA. She married Irvin Christianson.

   ix.  CURTIS LEROY GRIMM was born on 13 Aug 1944 in Red Lake Co., Minnesota, USA. He died on 13 Aug 1944 in Red Lake Co., Minnesota, USA.

x.  EILEEN THEA GRIMM was born on 09 Mar 1946 in Red Lake Co., Minnesota, USA. She married Wallace Christianson.

xi.  DARREL LLOYD GEORGE GRIMM was born on 25 Jun 1947 in Red Lake Co., Minnesota, USA.

---

ORVILLE GRIMM

Orville Grimm, 92 of McIntosh, and formerly of Brooks, died on Wednesday, Feb 9 at the McIntosh Manor Nursing Home in McIntosh.

Funeral services were held at 11 a.m. on Monday, Feb 14 at Immanuel Lutheran Church in McIntosh, with the Rev. Dean Bell officiating. Honorary casket bearers included Orville's family and friends. Casket bearers included Orville's grandsons, Travis Christianson, Levie Nelson, Darrin Grimm, Corey Hanson, Brandon Tranby, Chad Christianson, Aaron Johnson, Micah Johnson, and Gideon Johnson. Interment will be held at Immanuel Lutheran Cemetery in McIntosh.

Orville Gust Grimm was born on May 28, 1912 in rural Brooks, to parents William and Annie (Duesing) Grimm. He grew up and attended rural school near Brooks. Orville was united in marriage to Marie L. Magoon on Nov. 5, 1931 in McIntosh by the Rev. C.F. Knauft. Following their marriage, they made their home and raised their family on the farm near Brooks.

During his working years, Orville farmed, worked on area mink farms, and mowed the sides of highway 2 for the State of Minnesota for many years. Marie passed away on October 17, 1977. In the spring of 1978, Orville moved to the Valley Home in Thief River Falls. He then lived at First Care Nursing Home in Fosston and most recently, the McIntosh Manor Nursing Home.

He was a member of Immanuel Lutheran Church in McIntosh.

Survivors include four daughters, Pearl Johnson and Janis Turner, both of McIntosh, Ruby (Irvin) Christianson of Trail, and Eileen Christianson of Oklee; one son, Darryl Grimm of Brooks; 14 grandchildren, 22 great-grandchildren, and two great-great grandchildren; one brother, Lavern Grimm of Brooks; and two sisters, Doris Nelson of Oklee, and Violet Ferden of McIntosh; nieces, nephews and cousins also survive.

He was preceded in death by his wife, parents, four sons, LeRoy, Duane, Douglas, and Curtis LeRoy; one grandson; sister, Evelyn Nelson; and three sons-in-law, Alvin Turner, Wallace Christianson, and Russell Johnson. (Tritimes, McIntosh, MN; 15 Feb 2005)

---

40.  LAVERN ALBERT⁴ GRIMM (William Max³, Albert A², Heinrich Ludwig¹ Grimm) was born on 23 Nov 1914 in Minnesota, USA. He died on 04 Jul 2008 in Brooks, Red Lake Co., Minnesota, USA. He married Nora Irene Nelson, daughter of Ole Nelson and Anne Strande, on 10 Oct 1936 in McIntosh, Polk Co., Minnesota, USA. She was born on 01 Jan 1919 in Polk Co., Minnesota, USA (Hill River Township). She died on 09 Apr 1995 in Brooks, Red Lake Co., Minnesota, USA. Lavern Albert Grimm was buried in McIntosh, Polk Co., Minnesota, USA. Nora Irene Nelson was buried on 13 Apr 1995 in McIntosh, Polk Co., Minnesota, USA; Immanuel Lutheran Cemetery.

Nora Irene Nelson was employed as a Oklee Public Schools; Cook before Apr 1995 in Oklee, Red Lake Co., Minnesota, USA.

Lavern Albert Grimm and Nora Irene Nelson had the following children:

50.  i.  LARRY LAVERN⁵ GRIMM was born on 06 Jan 1943 in Red Lake Co., Minnesota, USA. He married Erlyss [Unknown].

ii.  VICKIE GRIMM.

41. BEVERLY DORIS[4] GRIMM (William Max[3], Albert A[2], Heinrich Ludwig[1] Grimm") was born on 11 Jan 1922 in Red Lake Co., Minnesota, USA. She married Melvin Johnson.

Melvin Johnson and Beverly Doris Grimm had the following child:

    i.    JEFFREY[5] JOHNSON. He married Kathy [Unknown].

42. VIOLETTE M.[4] GRIMM (William Max[3], Albert A[2], Heinrich Ludwig[1] Grimm) was born on 21 Aug 1927 in Minnesota, USA. She died on Deceased. She married Maynard Ferden. He was born in 1916 in Illinois, USA. He died on 14 May 2007 in Sycamore, De Kalb Co., Illinois, USA. Violette M. Grimm was buried in McIntosh, Polk Co., Minnesota, USA, at Immanuel Lutheran Cemetery.

Maynard Ferden was employed as a Boy Scouts of America; Field Scout Executive in 1946 in Bloomington, McLean Co., Illinois, USA.

Maynard Ferden and Violette M. Grimm had the following children:

    i.    RONALD E[5] FERDEN was born in 1938 in Illinois, USA.

    ii.    BARBARA ANN FERDEN was born before Apr 1940 in Illinois, USA.

43. FRANCES L[4] HUNT (Minnie Gertrude[3] Penrose, Carolina Theresa[2] Grimm, Heinrich Ludwig[1] "Henry Louis" Grimm) was born on 23 Jan 1905 in Salem, Marion Co., Oregon, USA. She died on 19 Aug 2004 in Salem, Marion Co., Oregon, USA. She married Theodore E. Burns on 07 Nov 1925 in Salem, Marion Co., Oregon, USA. He was born on 22 Sep 1905 in Winona, Emmons Co., North Dakota, USA. He died on 08 Jul 1972 in Bend, Deschutes Co., Oregon, USA. Frances L Hunt was buried on 23 Aug 2004 in Salem, Marion Co., Oregon, USA, at Zena Cemetery.

Theodore E. Burns and Frances L Hunt had the following children:

    i.    MARIAN[5] BURNS was born on 06 Aug 1926 in Salem, Marion Co., Oregon, USA. She married Richard F Gitschlag on 16 Sep 1949 in West Salem, Polk Co., Oregon, USA. He was born on 16 Oct 1926 in Marshfield, Coos Co., Oregon, USA.

    ii.    VIOLA N. BURNS was born on 23 Feb 1928 in Salem, Marion Co., Oregon, USA. She married Norman J Noble on 09 Dec 1947 in Vancouver, Clark Co., Washington, USA. He was born on 25 Aug 1921 in Canada.

## Generation 5

44. LEO LEON[5] BILL (Viola Anna Wilhemina[4] Grimm, Heinrich William[3] "Henry" Grimm, Franziscus Gustav[2] "Frank" Grimm, Heinrich Ludwig[1] "Henry Louis" Grimm) was born on 16 Jun 1934 in Paul, Minidoka Co., Idaho, USA. He died on 22 Jun 1997 in Rupert, Minidoka Co., Idaho, USA. He married Lauretta June Hodge on 29 Aug 1952 in Burley, Cassia Co., Idaho, USA. She was born on 20 Jun 1935.Leo Leon Bill was buried after 22 Jun 1997 in Paul, Minidoka Co., Idaho, USA (Paul Cemetery). They had five children.

LEO LEON BILL

Leo Leon Bill, 63-years-old Rupert resident, passed away Sunday, June 22, 1997, at his home. Leo was born June 16, 1934, in Paul, the son of Amos and Viola Anna Wilhelmina Grimm Bill. He attended schools in Paul and graduated from Paul High School. He married Lauretta June Hodge on Aug 29, 1952, in Burley. He started working for the Amalgamated Sugar Co. in 1952, where he was employed until the time of his death.

He was a member of the LDS Church. He loved music, sports and gardening. He was a devoted loving father. He will be missed very much. We love you.

He is survived by his wife of Rupert; and seven children, Rebecca Lynn Holgate and Deborah Lorraine Baldez, both of Burley, Steven Leo Bill and Matthew Leon Bill, both of Rupert, Rachell Lee Kelsey of Paul, and Ruth Lachel Ellenberger and Sarah Louise Bill, both of Heyburn. He is also survived by a sister, Cleo Zemke of Paul; and a brother, Henry Bill, both of Burley. He had 23 grandchildren and three great-grandchildren. He was preceded in death by his parents, one sister and three grandchildren.

Services will be held at 10 a.m. Wednesday, June 25, 1997, at the Rupert West LDS Stake Center, with Rupert 2nd ward Counselor Lind Garner officiating, Burial will be at the Paul Cemetery. Friends may call one hour before the service today at the church. Arrangements are under the direction of the Hansen Mortuary Rupert Chapel. (Times News, (Twin Falls, Idaho)

45. GLADYS ANN[5] GRIMM (Alvin Albert William[4], Albert Philip Henry[3], Albert A[2], Heinrich Ludwig[1] "Henry Louis") was born on 10 Dec 1934 in Chelsea, Taylor Co., Wisconsin, USA. She died on 04 Mar 2011 in Ridgefield, Clark Co., Washington, USA from breast cancer. (Age 76). She married James Maynard Doriot, son of Charles Henry Doriot and Catherine Belle McDonald on 16 Oct 1971 in Reno, Washoe Co., Nevada, USA. He was born on 04 Oct 1913 in Manitowish Waters, Vilas Co., Wisconsin, USA. He died on 10 Feb 1992 in Clackamas, Clackamas Co., Oregon, USA of emphysema and an enlarged heart. (Age 78). Gladys Ann Grimm was cremated and buried in Ridgefield, Clark Co., Washington, USA, at Ridgefield Cemetery. James Maynard Doriot was cremated and buried on 13 Feb 1992 in Ridgefield, Clark Co., Washington, USA, at Ridgefield Cemetery. They had four children.

Gladys Ann Grimm was employed as a nurse's aide ("Candy Striper") at Medford Hospital, about 1952 in Medford, Taylor Co., Wisconsin, USA. She worked as a waitress at a local diner the summer of 1952 in Okanogan, Okanogan Co., Washington, and again in Bend, Deschutes Co., Oregon, in 1960. She held several jobs and positions after she moved to Ridgefield, Clark Co., Washington about 1967. She drove a school bus for the Ridgefield School District then was employed at Kalama/Woodland/Ridgefield/La Center (K.W.R.L) Transportation Co-op as a bus dispatcher. She worked her way up to Secretary of Transportation, then it's Director, between 1976-2002 in Woodland, Clark Co., Washington, USA. She volunteered for the American Red Cross after she retired (2008-2011) in Clark Co., Washington, USA. She also served the City of Ridgefield as a council member and as the Mayor of Ridgefield for her last six years of public life.

James Maynard Doriot served in the military on 15 Oct 1942 in Tacoma, Pierce Co., Washington, USA (U.S. Army Air Corp; 748th Basic Flying Training Squadron). He worked as a welder on the transcontinental pipeline when Gladys met him. He was employed as a laborer at Oregon Woodwork when they lived in Band, Deschutes County, Oregon about 1960. He retired as a Molder Operator from Pacific Wood Treating Plant in Ridgefield, Clark Co., Washington, USA, where he began working about 1967.

46. LEROY SIEGFRED[5] KRAUSSE (Erma Helen[4] Grimm, Albert Philip Henry[3] Grimm, Albert A[2] Grimm, Heinrich Ludwig[1] "Henry Louis" Grimm) was born on 23 Jul 1929 in Molitor, Taylor Co., Wisconsin, USA. He died on 29 Jan 2000 in Edgerton, Rock Co., Wisconsin, USA. He married Annanelle [Unknown]. Leroy Siegfried Krausse was buried in Edgerton, Rock Co., Wisconsin, USA. They had four children.

Leroy Siegfried Krausse served in the military between 01 Mar 1951-01 Mar 1953.

47. BERNICE F[5] KRAUSE (Erma Helen[4] Grimm, Albert Philip Henry[3] Grimm, Albert A[2] Grimm, Heinrich Ludwig[1] "Henry Louis" Grimm) was born on 02 Apr 1938 in Molitor, Taylor Co., Wisconsin, USA. She married Kenneth Kuklinsky, son

of Maximillian Kuklinsky and Josephine [Unknown], on 02 Jun 1973 in Milwaukee, Milwaukee Co., Wisconsin, USA. He was born on 21 Apr 1927. He died on 15 Mar 1990.

49. ELAINE LEONA[5] KRAUSSE (Erma Helen[4] Grimm, Albert Philip Henry[3] Grimm, Albert A[2] Grimm, Heinrich Ludwig[1] "Henry Louis" Grimm) was born on 28 Oct 1943 in Molitor, Taylor Co., Wisconsin, USA. She married (1) Charles L. Mason in 1964. He was born in May 1933. She married (2) James Henry Mcneil on 27 Aug 1988 in Milwaukee, Milwaukee Co., Wisconsin, USA. He was born in Sep 1933.

50. DUANE ERVIN[5] GRIMM (Orville Gust[4], William Max[3], Albert A[2], Heinrich Ludwig[1] "Henry Louis") was born on 05 Jun 1933 in Minnesota, USA. He died on 23 Dec 2004 in Great Falls, Cascade Co., Montana, USA. He had 2 children.

51. LARRY LAVERN[5] GRIMM (Lavern Albert[4], William Max[3], Albert A[2], Heinrich Ludwig[1] "Henry Louis") was born on 06 Jan 1943 in Red Lake Co., Minnesota, USA. He married Erlyss [Unknown].

# DESCENDANTS OF JOHANN "JOHN" SCHELLMAN

## Generation 1

1. JOHANN "JOHN"[1] SCHELLMAN was born on 30 Jun 1830 in Prussia (Germany). He died on 24 Oct 1896 in Hancock, Houghton Co., Michigan, USA (Age: 66). He married Susan Schneider, daughter of John Schneider and Barbara Mertz before 1860. She was born on 19 Aug 1842 in Stuttgart, Baden-Württemberg, Germany. She died on 30 Sep 1916 in Hancock, Houghton Co., Michigan, USA (Age: 74). Johann "John" Schellman was buried in Hancock, Houghton Co., Michigan, USAat the now defunct St Joseph Cemetery Susan Schneider was buried in Hancock, Houghton Co., Michigan, USA at Lakeside Cemetery.

82: Susan Schneider (circa unknown)

83: Barbara Mertz (circa unknown)

*St. Joseph Cemetery was kept by the local Roman Catholic churches in Hancock. In the 1970's it was decided since the area churches were consolidated into one parish, to build a new church. The site chosen was over the St. Joseph Cemetery after deliberation by the parish, the diocese and contacting the proper government authorities.*

*The families of those buried were contacted ahead of time to let them know of the plans and let them remove their family to different area cemeteries. The remaining grave markers were then removed after a recording was done and buried in a trench at the site of the present day church. The new church was started in 1975 and took in St. Ann, St. Joseph, and St. Joseph-St. Patrick parish churches at various times.*

Johann "John" Schellman and Susan Schneider had the following children:

84 John Schellman Jr. (circa unknown)

i. JOHN S[2] SCHELLMAN Jr. was born on 23 Apr 1860 in Hancock, Houghton Co., Michigan, USA. He died on 30 Sep 1916 in Hancock, Houghton Co., Michigan, USA. He married Barbara [Unknown] about 1884. She was born about 1859 in Germany. She died before 1940. John S Schellman was buried 18 Jan 1946 in Hancock, Houghton Co., Michigan, USA, at Lakeside Cemetery

Register No. 10; SCHELLMAN, JOHN; Born: Apr 23, 1860; Place of birth: Hancock; Date of death: Jan 16, 1946; Time of death: 4:00 a.m.; Age: 85 yrs. 8 m. 23 d.; Cause of death: cerebral hemorrhage; arteriosclerosis; Attended by signer from: Jan 14, 1945; Attended by signer to: Jan 16, 1946; Alive: Jan 14, 1946; Father: John Schellman; Birth place of father: Germany; Mother: Susan Snyder; Birth place of mother: Germany; Sex: male; Color or race: white; Marital status: widowed; Spouse: Barbara Schellman; Citizen of what country: no; Residence: 813 Summit St., Hancock, Houghton, Mich.; Occupation: carpenter; Type of occupation: retired; Informant: Mrs. Rose O' Leary. Hancock, Mich.; Hospital: county inf.; Duration: 15 min.; Operation: none; Autopsy: none; Signed: Leonard C. Aldrich, M.D.; Hancock, Mich.; Place of burial: Hancock, Hancock, Mich.; Date of burial: Jan 18, 1946; Undertaker: Maynard R. Hurlburt; Address of undertaker: Calumet, Mich. [Source: Michigan Find A Grave (database online) Find A Grave Memorial# 47985650]

ii. CAROLINE SCHELLMAN was born in Apr 1862 in Sheboygan, Sheboygan Co., Wisconsin, USA. She died in 1931 in Ohio, USA. She married Philipp Heinrich Wilhelm Wambsganss on 04 Jun 1880. He was born on 16 Feb 1857 in Preeble Town, Adams Co., Indiana, USA. He died in 1933 in Fort Wayne, Allen Co., Indiana, USA (Age: 76).

2. iii. MARY S SCHELLMAN was born in Jul 1865 in Hancock, Houghton Co., Michigan, USA. She died in 1936 in Minnesota, USA (Probably; Age 71). She married Albert A Grimm, son of Heinrich Ludwig Grimm and Elizabeth Lucetta Schneider in 1883. He was born in Oct 1856 in Wisconsin, USA. He died on 05 Jun 1946 in Red Lake Co., Minnesota, USA (probably). (Age: 90). (See "Descendants of Heinrich Ludwig Grimm")

3. iv. BARBARA O SCHELLMAN was born in Aug 1867 in Hancock, Houghton Co., Michigan, USA. She married Henry J Klasner in 1898. He was born in Aug 1867 in Michigan, USA.

v. WILLIAM SCHELLMAN was born in Sep 1869 in Hancock, Houghton Co., Michigan, USA. He died on 19 Jan 1891 in Hancock, Houghton Co., Michigan, USA (Age: 21).

vi. FREDRICKA "RICKA" SCHELLMANN was born about 1871 in Hancock, Houghton Co., Michigan, USA. She died on 10 Apr 1894 in Hancock, Houghton Co., Michigan, USA (Age: 23).

4. vii. PAULINA SCHELLMAN was born about 1873 in Hancock, Houghton Co., Michigan, USA. She married Adolph Vollmer about 1895. He was born about 1870 in Germany. He died before 1920.

5. viii. HANNAH SCHELLMAN was born in Nov 1874 in Hancock, Houghton Co., Michigan, USA. She died after 1962. She married Henry Kettenbiel. He was born in Feb 1871 in Michigan, USA. He died before 1940.

6. ix. ROSETTA SCHELLMAN was born on 15 Jun 1879 in Hancock, Houghton Co., Michigan, USA. She died on 28 Apr 1962 (Age: 83). She married Loyal Daniel O'leary. He was born on 05 Sep 1878 in Green Bay, Brown Co., Wisconsin, USA. He died on 01 Sep 1925 in Hancock, Houghton Co., Michigan, USA.

7. x. LYDIA SCHELLMAN was born on 10 Aug 1882 in Hancock, Houghton Co., Michigan, USA. She died on 29 Jul 1958 in Green Bay, Brown Co., Wisconsin, USA (Age 76). She married Peter Hansen Terp. He was born on 18 Nov 1871 in Denmark. He died on 29 Mar 1928 in Green Bay, Brown Co., Wisconsin, USA.

## Generation 2

2. CAROLINE B[2] SCHELLMAN (Johann "John"[1]) was born in Apr 1862 in Sheboygan, Sheboygan Co., Wisconsin, USA. She died in 1931 in Ohio, USA. She married Philipp Heinrich Wilhelm Wambsganss, son of Philipp Wambsganss Sr. and Elizabeth Hess, on 04 Jun 1880. He was born on 16 Feb 1857 in Preeble Town, Adams Co., Indiana, USA. He died in 1933 in Fort Wayne, Allen Co., Indiana, USA (Age: 76). Caroline Schellman was buried in 1931 in Fort Wayne, Allen Co., Indiana, USA. Philipp Heinrich Wilhelm Wambsganss was buried at Fort Wayne, Allen co., Indiana, USA. at Concordia Lutheran Cemetery.

Notes for Caroline Schellman: Entry found: Hodge, Robert and Lois A: 1994. "Index, Emporia Gazette Death Notices, 1892-1989". 1307 Trail Ridge Rd. Emporia, KS 66801. Description Microfilmed back files of the Emporia (Kansas)

Gazette newspaper found in the Emporia Public Library and the William Allen White Library of Emporia State University covering the period 1892 through 1989. [http://www.rootsweb.ancestry.com/~ksfhgslc/obitkirkou.html]

Koegeboehn, Caroline O. Wambsganss, Mrs. Henry (p3) 23 Mar 1932
Koegeboehn, Henry 15 Dec 1948
Koegeboehn, Sophia Elizabeth nee Wambsganss, Mrs. 08 Feb 1960

REV. PHILLIP WAMBSGANSS, JR., pastor of the German Lutheran SS. Peter and Paul Church, was born in Adams County, Ind., February 16, 1857. He was educated for the ministry at Concordia College, Fort Wayne, Ind., and at Concordia College, Springfield, Ill., spending six years at the former and three at the latter. He was ordained a minister of the German Lutheran Church by his father, the Rev. Phillip Wambsganss, Sr., in Sheboygan County, Wis., in 1879. Immediately after his ordination, he proceeded to Hancock, Lake Superior, to accept the pastorship of this church, and has since served as its pastor. Mr. Wambsganss was married at his father's house, in Sheboygan County, Wis., June 4, 1880, to Miss Carrie B., daughter of John Schellman, of Hancock, Lake Superior. Mrs. Wambsganss was born in Sheboygan County, Wis. [History of the Upper Peninsula of Michigan: Houghton County Pages 291-299 www.mfhn.com, 23 Jan 2010; Retrieved 29 Aug 2013 http://www.zoominfo.com/p/Phillip-Wambsganss/1442268319]

85: Rev. Philipp Wambsganss
(circa unknown)

*Dedication of the Lutheran Hospital...on Thanksgiving Day, November 24, 1904, ... the dedication and formal opening of Lutheran Hospital, a 25-bed facility that was formerly the Judge Lindley M. Ninde homestead at the corner of Fairfield and Wildwood Avenues. Little did they realize that with the dedication of this dream that they were creating much more than a hospital. They were laying the foundation for a tradition of service to all that would last well over a century. During the dedication ceremony on that late autumn day, the tone and definition for this mission was defined by The Reverend Phillip Wambsganss - then Pastor of Emmaus Lutheran Church - when he stated that all these efforts and the fruits of those labors were dedicated "to the service of suffering humanity and to the glory of God." Since then, the Reverend Wambsganss' words have been powerfully distilled into the Latin phrase "Soli Deo Gloria" - "To God Alone Be the Glory." [The Lutheran Foundation;: http://www.thelutheranfoundation.org/_pdf/history_book.pdf]*

Philipp Heinrich Wilhelm Wambsganss and Caroline Schellman had the following children:

8.    i.    FREDERICK PHILLIP ERNEST[3] WAMBSGANSS was born on 17 May 1881 in Hancock, Houghton Co., Michigan, USA. He died before 25 Nov 1957 in Fort Wayne, Allen Co., Indiana, USA (Age: 76). He married Mary L Rodenbeck on 25 Oct 1905 in Allen Co., Indiana, USA. She was born in 1881 in Indiana, USA. She died in 1960 in Fort Wayne, Allen Co., Indiana, USA.

        iii.    PHILIP WAMBSGANSS was born on 20 Apr 1883 in Michigan, USA. He died in 1920 in Fort Wayne, Allen Co., Indiana, USA (Age 37). He married Mathilda P Franke on 21 Jun 1911 in Allen Co., Indiana, USA. Philip Wambsganss was buried 1920 in Fort Wayne, Allen Co., Indiana, USA, at Concordia Lutheran Cemetery.

iv.     ELIZABETH WAMBSGANSS was born in Sep 1885 in Michigan, USA. She died in 1960 in Marshall, Harrison Co., Texas, USA. She married Gustave A Weber on 17 Aug 1909 in Allen Co., Indiana, USA. He was born on 03 Aug 1884 in New Orleans, Orleans Co., Louisiana, USA. He died in 1968 in Marshall, Harrison Co., Texas, USA. Elizabeth Wambsganss was buried in1960 in Marshall, Harrison Co., Texas, USA, at Algoma Cemetery North and South.

v.     INFANT WAMBSGANSS. Infant died before 1900.

vi.     HANNAH WAMBAGANSS was born on 19 Apr 1890 in Ohio, USA. She died in May 1969 in Fort Wayne, Allen Co., Indiana, USA (Age: 79). She married Paul W Hitzeman about 1914. He was born on 10 Jun 1892 in Indiana, USA (Age: 90). He died in Nov 1982 in Indiana, USA.

9.     vi.     WILLIAM ADOLPH. "BILL WAMBY" WAMBSGANSS was born on 19 Mar 1894 in Cleveland, Cuyahoga Co., Ohio, USA. He died on 08 Dec 1985 in Lakewood, Cuyahoga Co., Ohio, USA (Age: 91). He married Effie L Mulholland on 30 Jun 1917 in Cuyahoga Co., Ohio, USA. She was born on 21 Jul 1893 in Cleveland, Cuyahoga Co., Ohio, USA. She died in Apr 1977 in Lakewood, Cuyahoga Co., Ohio, USA (Age: 83). William A. Wambsganss was buried in Green Bay, Brown Co., Wisconsin, USA, at Concordia Cemetery. Effie L. Mulholland was buried in Green Bay, Brown Co., Wisconsin, USA, at Concordia Cemetery.

vii.     ROSA WAMBSGANSS was born in 1895. She died in 1896.

3.     MARY S[2] SCHELLMAN (Johann "John"[1]) was born in Jul 1865 in Hancock, Houghton Co., Michigan, USA. She died in 1936 in Minnesota, USA (Probably; Age 71). She married Albert A Grimm, son of Heinrich Ludwig "Henry Louis" Grimm and Elizabeth Lucetta "Lisette" Schneider in 1883. He was born in Oct 1856 in Wisconsin, USA. He died on 05 Jun 1946 in Red Lake Co., Minnesota, USA (Probably; Age: 90). (See "Descendants of Heinrich Ludwig Grimm")

4.     BARBARA O[2] SCHELLMAN (Johann "John"[1]) was born in Aug 1867 in Hancock, Houghton Co., Michigan, USA. She married Henry J Klasner in 1898. He was born in Aug 1867 in Michigan, USA.

Henry J Klasner and Barbara O Schellman had the following children:

i.     MYRTLE E[3] KLASNER was born on 28 May 1899 in Michigan, USA. She died on 22 Dec 1954 (Age: 55). She married William Joos. He was born on 15 Mar 1901 in Wisconsin, USA. He died on 21 Jun 1952 (Age: 51). Myrtle E Klasner was buried in Ontonagon, Ontonagon Co., Michigan, USA, at Riverside Cemetery

ii.     ETHEL KLASNER was born on 10 Dec 1900 in Hancock, Houghton Co., Michigan, USA. She died on 22 Oct 1974 in Flint, Genesee Co., Michigan, USA. She married LeRoy Earl Funkey about 1924. He was born on 07 Sep 1892 in Hancock, Houghton Co., Michigan, USA. He died on 29 May 1958. Ethel Klasner was buried Burial: Oct 1974 in Birch Run, Saginaw Co., Michigan, USA, Birch Run Cemetery

iii.     CLAUDE H KLASNER was born on 29 Apr 1903 in Michigan, USA. He died on 08 May 1972 (Age: 69). He married Leona Harriet [Unknown]. She was born on 16 Feb 1906. She died on 06 Sep 1982 in Jackson, Jackson Co., Michigan, USA. Claude H Klasner was buried in Jackson, Jackson Co., Michigan, USA, at Woodland Cemetery.

10.     iv.     HENRY J KLASNER JR was born on 27 Apr 1905 in Michigan, USA. He died on 06 Mar 1985 in Hancock, Houghton Co., Michigan, USA (Age: 79). He married Ina B [Unknown] about 1930. She was born in 1898. She died in 1938.

11.     v.   BARBARA L KLASNER was born on 15 May 1908 in Michigan, USA. She died on 06 Sep 2001 in Flushing, Genesee Co., Michigan, USA (Age: 93). She married Christian Brohn in 1934 in Flint, Genesee Co., Michigan, USA. He was born about 1906 in Michigan, USA. He died on 23 Oct 1971.

        vi.   WILLIAM KLASNER was born before May 1910 in Michigan, USA. He died before 2001. He married Esther Victoria [Unknown]. She was born about 1906 in Iowa, USA.

        vii.   JOHN LINCOLN KLASNER was born about 1912 in Michigan, USA. He died on 13 May 1930 in Genesee Co., Michigan, USA.

5. PAULINA[2] SCHELLMAN (Johann "John"1) was born about 1873 in Hancock, Houghton Co., Michigan, USA. She married Adolph Vollmer about 1895. He was born about 1870 in Germany. He died before 1920.

Adolph Vollmer and Paulina Schellman had the following children:

        i.   WILLIAM JOHN[3] VOLLMER was born on 11 Feb 1896 in Hancock, Houghton Co., Michigan, USA. He died in 1950 in Superior, Douglas Co., Wisconsin, USA (probably). He married Florence "Flossie" Laurine. She was born in 1897 in Michigan, USA. She died in 1987 in Superior, Douglas Co., Wisconsin, USA. William John Vollmer was buried in Superior, Douglas co., Wisconsin, USA, at Calvary Cemetery.

           Draft Registration: 1942 in Superior, Douglas Co., Wisconsin, USA; WWII

        ii.   HAROLD VOLMER was born about 1900 in Michigan, USA. He died on [unknown]

        iii.   HOWARD H VOLLMER was born on 22 Oct 1902 in Michigan, USA. He died on 09 Jun 1976 in Hancock, Houghton Co., Michigan, USA (Age: 73).

13.     iv.   CLARA J VOLLMER was born on 28 Jul 1904 in Michigan, USA. She died on 01 Oct 1994 in Akron, Summit Co., Ohio, USA (Age 90; Widow). She married (1) George H Repke about 1927. He was born about 1900. She married Alphonse Cyrille Cheney. He was born on 24 Dec 1901. He died on 07 Mar 1986.

6. HANNAH[2] SCHELLMAN (Johann "John"1) was born in Nov 1874 in Hancock, Houghton Co., Michigan, USA. She died after 1962. She married Henry Kettenbiel. He was born in Feb 1871 in Michigan, USA. He died before 1940.

Henry Kettenbiel and Hannah Schellman had the following children:

14.     i.   WALTER HERMAN[3] KETTENBEIL was born on 03 Aug 1895 in Schoolcraft, Houghton Co., Michigan, USA. He died on 11 Jul 1977 in Laurium, Houghton Co., Michigan, USA (Age 81). He married Flossie Cantin about 1916. She was born about 1897 in Michigan, USA.

        ii.   REUBEN KETTENBEIL was born on 19 Feb 1897 in Schoolcraft, Houghton Co., Michigan, USA. He died on 30 Sep 1903 in Lake Linden, Houghton Co., Michigan, USA (Age: 6).

        iii.   HAROLD KETTENBIEL was born in Jan 1898 in Michigan, USA.

15.     iv.   EDNA KETTENBIEL was born in 1899 in Michigan, USA. She married Robert Porell. He was born about 1898 in Michigan, USA.

16.    v.    HENRY KETTENBEIL JR was born on 21 Feb 1901 in Michigan, USA. He died in Apr 1970 in Lake
              Linden, Houghton Co., Michigan, USA (Age: 69). He married Margaret Birk. She was born on 08 Mar
              1905 in Michigan, USA. She died in Jan 1992.

17.    vi.   ELSA K. KETTENBIEL was born on 03 Mar 1903 in Michigan, USA. She died on 09 Dec 1993 in
              Portage, Kalamazoo Co., Michigan, USA (Age: 90). She married Garvin Peter Mitchell. He was born
              on 26 Aug 1897 in Hancock, Houghton Co., Michigan, USA. He died on 27 Dec 1985 in Oshtemo,
              Kalamazoo Co., Michigan, USA (Age: 88).

18.    vii.  ESTELLE KETTENBIEL was born in 1908 in Michigan, USA. She died [Unknown]

7.   ROSETTA[2] SCHELLMAN (Johann "John"1) was born on 15 Jun 1879 in Hancock, Houghton Co., Michigan, USA. She
     died on 28 Apr 1962 (Age: 83). She married Loyal Daniel O'leary. He was born on 05 Sep 1878 in Green Bay, Brown
     Co., Wisconsin, USA. He died on 01 Sep 1925 in Hancock, Houghton Co., Michigan, USA. Rosetta Schellman was
     buried in Forest Hill Cemetery

86: Rosetta Schellman
(circa unknown)

MRS. LOYAL O'LEARY

    Mrs. Loyal O'Leary, 83 of 821 Cloverland Drive, Died at 4:45 P.M. Friday at the Grand
View Hospital, where she had been a patient since April 10, when she suffered a stroke. The
former Rosetta Schellman was born Jan. 15 1879, in Hancock. She attended schools and was
married there to Loyal O'Leary. He died in 1925. She lived in Hancock until three years ago when
she came here to live with a daughter, Miss Olive R. O'Leary, Cloverland Drive. Mrs. O'Leary
was a member of the Evangelical Church of Hancock. Surviving are three daughters, Miss Olive
of Ironwood, Mrs. Andrew Heaischer of Atlantic Mine, Mrs. Christian Jauch of Baraboo, Wis., a
son Loyal of Hancock, and several grandchildren. Also surviving is a sister, Mrs. Hannah
Kettenbeil of Hancock. The remains were taken to the Thomas Funeral Home at Laurium with
funeral services set for Monday at the funeral home. Burial will be in Forest Lawn Cemetery at
Houghton. ( 28 Apr 1962)

Loyal Daniel O'Leary and Rosetta Schellman had the following children:

    i.    JULIA LYDIA[3] O'LEARY was born on 31 Jul 1902 in Hancock, Houghton Co., Michigan, USA. She
          died on 08 Aug 1926 in Hancock, Houghton Co., Michigan, USA. Julia Lydia O'Leary was buried in
          Houghton, Houghton Co., Michigan, USA, at Forest Hill Cemetery.

    ii.   IRENE JOHANNA O'LEARY was born on 05 Aug 1903 in Hancock, Houghton Co., Michigan, USA.
          She died on 06 Apr 1983 in Houghton, Houghton Co., Michigan, USA. She married Andrew John
          Haischer. He was born on 21 Oct 1898 in Atlantic Mine, Houghton Co., Michigan, USA. He died on 10
          Mar 1980 in Atlantic Mine, Houghton Co., Michigan, USA. Irene Johanna O'Leary was buried in
          Houghton Co., Michigan, USA, at Forest Hill Cemetery

IRENE HAISCHER

Atlantic Mine - Mrs. Irene Haischer, 79, Atlantic Mine, died Wednesday. Funeral services will Saturday at 1 p.m. from SS.
Peter and Paul Lutheran Church, Hancock, with the Rev. Robert Paul officiating. Spring burial will be at the Forest Hills
Cemetery. The body will be taken to the church at noon Saturday from the Mountain View Mortuary, South Range, which will
be open for visitation from 4-8 p.m. Friday.

iii.     OLIVE MINNA O'LEARY was born on 07 Oct 1904 in Hancock, Houghton Co., Michigan, USA. She died on 25 Aug 1987 in Madison, Dane Co., Wisconsin, USA.

---

OLIVE O'LEARY

Miss Olive R. O'Leary 76 Cloverland Dr. Ironwood, died Tuesday evening at Methodist Hospital, Madison, Wis., after a lengthy illness. Daughter of the late Mr. and Mrs. Loyal O'Leary, she was born Oct. 1904 at Hancock and graduated from High School there. She worked for Michigan Bell Telephone Co. 40 years at Houghton, Sault St. Marie, Marquette and at Ironwood from 1961 to 1963 when she retired. She was a member of Telephone Pioneers of America Club and while at Hancock a member of SS. Peter and Paul Lutheran Church.

Survivors include two sisters, Mrs. Irene Haischer, Atlantic Mine, and Mrs. (Rose) Jauch, Baraboo, Wis.; and one brother, Loyal, Hancock. The funeral will take place Friday at 1 p.m. at SS. Peter and Paul Lutheran Church with the Rev. Robert Paul officiating. Burial will be in Forest Hill Cemetery, Houghton. There will be visitation at Mountain View Mortuary, South Range, from 7 to 9 p.m. Thursday and at the church Friday from noon to service time

---

iv.     ROBERT FRANK O'LEARY was born on 14 Sep 1907 in Hancock, Houghton Co., Michigan, USA. He died on 30 Oct 1937 in Hancock, Houghton Co., Michigan, USA. Robert Frank O'Leary was buried in Houghton, Houghton Co., Michigan, USA, at Forest Hill Cemetery

87: Robert O'Leary
(circa unknown)

88: Ann Nutini
(circa unknown)

v.     LOYAL DANIEL O'LEARY JR was born on 05 Sep 1909 in Hancock, Houghton Co., Michigan, USA. He died on 08 Dec 1993 in Hancock, Houghton Co., Michigan, USA. He married Ann Nutini. She was born on 25 Jan 1913. She died on 01 May 2005. Loyal Daniel O'Leary Jr. was buried in Houghton, Houghton Co., Michigan, USA, at Forest Hill Cemetery

---

LOYAL D. O'LEARY

HANCOCK --- Mr. Loyal D. "Muht" O'Leary, 84, a lifelong Hancock resident died on Wednesday morning, December 8, 1993 at Portage View Hospital following a long illness. He was born on September 5, 1909, 1 son of Loyal and Rose (Schellman) O'Leary. On October 12, 1939 he married Ann Nutini of Hancock. He attended Hancock High School and began working for the city of Hancock in 1926. He was then employed at the Atlas Powder Company Dupont Plant in Senter until it's closing in 1960, and at the Houghton County Road Commission until his retirement in 1974.

He is survived by his wife, Ann; three children, Ann Marie (Ron) Harma of Westlake, Ohio, Donna O'Leary (Ron Steiner) of Madison, Wisc. and Loyal (Gretchen) of Lansing; three grandchildren; two great-grandchildren; a sister, Rose Jauch of Baraboo, Wisc.; and several nieces, nephews and cousins. He was preceded in death by his parents; a brother, Robert and sisters, Julia, Olive, and Irene (Haischer). Funeral services will be held at 11a.m. on Saturday at the O'Neill Funeral Home in Hancock with Rev. Robert Paul of St. Peter & Paul Lutheran Church to officiate. At the request of the deceased, there will be no visitation.

"A Dying man needs to die, as a sleepy man need to sleep, and there comes a time when it is wrong, as well as useless, to resist" ---Stewart Alsop

8. LYDIA*2* SCHELLMAN (Johann "John"*1*) was born on 10 Aug 1882 in Hancock, Houghton Co., Michigan, USA. She died on 29 Jul 1958 in Green Bay, Brown Co., Wisconsin, USA (Bellin Memorial Hospital; Age 76). She married Peter Hansen Terp. He was born on 18 Nov 1871 in Denmark. He died on 29 Mar 1928 in Green Bay, Brown Co., Wisconsin, USA. Lydia Schellman was in Brown Co., Wisconsin, USA; Woodlawn Cemetery. Peter Hansen Terp was buried in Allouez, Brown Co., Wisconsin, USA; Woodlawn Cemetery.

89: Lydia Schellman (circa unknown)

### LYDIA TERP

Mrs. Lydia Terp 76 of 2607 Nicholet Road Green Bay mother of J. W. and Leslie Terp of Two Rivers and Harold Terp of Manitowoc died early Tuesday at Bellin Memorial Hospital Green Bay after a year of Failing health. Funeral arrangements are incomplete and are being handled by Lyndahl Funeral Home, Green Bay. Mrs. Terp nee Lydia Schellman was born at Hancock, Mich. Aug. 11, 1891. Her husband, Peter Terp who was a Chiropractor, died at Green Bay in 1928. She leaves three daughters. Mrs. Merle Crabb and Mrs. Joseph Baeb of Green Bay, and Mrs. Cletus Berkin of De Pere, four other sons, Henry and William of Green Bay, Robert of Fond Du Lac and Woodrow of Los Angeles, Calif., two sisters, Hannah Kettenbeil and Mrs. Rose O'Leary of Hancock; 31 grandchildren and three great grandchildren. Friends may call at the funeral home after 2 p.m. Wednesday

Peter Hansen Terp and Lydia Schellman had the following children:

i. JOHN W*3* TERP was born on 26 Mar 1924 in Wisconsin, USA. He died on 29 Feb 2000 in Lake Forest, Orange Co., California, USA (Age at Death: 75). He married Kathleen C [Unknown]. She was born on 21 Mar 1921. She died on 13 Dec 2000 in Placerville, El Dorado Co., California, USA (Age 79).

ii. HENRY GEORGE LINCOLN TERP was born on 12 Feb 1905 in St Paul, Ramsey Co., Minnesota, USA. He died in Apr 1980 in Green Bay, Brown Co., Wisconsin, USA (Age: 75). He married (1) Mary Eileen C [Unknown] about 1937. She was born on 11 Jun 1916 in Wisconsin, USA. She died on 01 Nov 1995 in Green Bay, Brown Co., Wisconsin, USA (Age: 79). He married (2) [Unknown] between 1925-1930. She died before 1930.

iii. J. WILBERT "JW" TERP was born on 17 Sep 1906 in Green Bay, Brown Co., Wisconsin, USA. He died in May 1972 in Green Bay, Brown Co., Wisconsin, USA (Age: 66). He married Venita M. [Unknown]. She was born on 26 Jul 1914. She died on 26 Oct 2006 in Green Bay, Brown Co., Wisconsin, USA (Age: 92). Wilbert W "JW" Terp was buried in Green Bay, Brown Co., Wisconsin, USA, at Fort Howard Memorial Park.

iv. WILLIAM F TERP was born about 1907 in Wisconsin, USA. He married Rose A [Unknown].

v. ROBERT J TERP was born on 02 Aug 1908 in Wisconsin, USA. He died on 05 Jul 1981 in Manitowoc, Manitowoc Co., Wisconsin, USA (Age: 73). He married Bernice A [Unknown] between Apr 1940-1942. She was born on 10 Nov 1916. She died on 04 Dec 1990 in Manitowoc, Manitowoc Co., Wisconsin, USA (Age: 74). Robert J Terp was buried in Burial: Allouez, Brown Co., Wisconsin, USA, at Woodlawn Cemetery.

vi.   MAREN R TERP was born on 01 Nov 1910 in Wisconsin, USA. She died on 12 Jan 2003 in Green Bay, Brown Co., Wisconsin, USA (Age: 92). She married Merle Elton Crabb. He was born on 03 Jun 1908. He died on 29 Jan 1992 in Brown Co., Wisconsin, USA (Age: 83). Maren R Terp was buried in Green Bay, Brown Co., Wisconsin, USA, at Ashwaubenon Moravian Cemetery

18.   vii.   LUCILLE S TERP was born on 07 Oct 1912 in Wisconsin, USA. She died on 18 May 2004 in Green Bay, Brown Co., Wisconsin, USA (Age: 91). She married Joseph P Baeb on 26 Dec 1933. He was born on 29 Jul 1908. He died on 27 May 1988 in Green Bay, Brown Co., Wisconsin, USA (Age: 80).

viii.   WOODROW J TERP was born on 15 Mar 1915 in Wisconsin, USA. He died on 22 Jun 1983 in Glendale, Los Angeles Co., California, USA (Age: 68). He married Marian Virginia Dyce. She was born on 22 May 1918 in Wisconsin, USA. She died on 28 Jun 1993 in Los Angeles, Los Angeles Co., California, USA (Age: 75).

20.   ix.   LESLIE IVEN JEPSON TERP was born on 21 Dec 1916 in Minnesota, USA. He died on 18 Dec 1977 in Los Angeles, Los Angeles Co., California, USA (Age: 60). He married Eunice [Unknown] about 1948. She was born about 1919 in Wisconsin, USA.

x.   ELIZABETH C TERP was born on 29 Nov 1918 in Minneapolis, Anoka Co., Minnesota, USA. She died on 25 Feb 2008 in De Pere, Brown Co., Wisconsin, USA (At home; Age 89). She married Cletus J Berken on 22 Nov 1942. He was born on 13 May 1914 in Wisconsin, USA. He died on 03 May 1981 in De Pere, Brown Co., Wisconsin, USA (Age 67).

---

BERKEN, BETTY C.

Mrs. Cletus (Betty) Berken, 89, De Pere, died of a heart attack Monday, Feb. 25, 2008, at her home. She was born Nov. 29, 1918, to the late Peter and Lydia (Shellman) Terp in Minneapolis, Minn. On Nov. 22, 1942, she married Cletus Berken. He preceded her in death on May 13, 1981. Betty enjoyed spending time with her family and friends. She was a loving mother dedicated to caring for her family. It was a thrill for her to visit with classmates this summer at her 70th class reunion (West High).

---

21.   xi.   HAROLD JAMES TERP was born on 05 Dec 1919 in Wisconsin, USA. He died on 28 Nov 2002 in Francis Creek, Manitowoc Co., Wisconsin, USA (Age: 80). He married Viola Ann Vincent on 14 Mar 1947 in Dubuque, Dubuque Co., Iowa, USA. She was born on 18 Apr 1928 in Wisconsin, USA. She died on 07 Mar 1992 (Age: 63).


## Generation 3

9.   FREDERICK PHILLIP ERNEST[3] WAMBSGANSS (Caroline[2] Schellman, Johann "John"[1] Schellman) was born on 17 May 1881 in Hancock, Houghton Co., Michigan, USA. He died before 25 Nov 1957 in Fort Wayne, Allen Co., Indiana, USA (Age: 76). He married Mary L Rodenbeck on 25 Oct 1905 in Allen Co., Indiana, USA. She was born in 1881 in Indiana, USA. She died in 1960 in Fort Wayne, Allen Co., Indiana, USA. Frederick Phillip Wambsganss was buried in Fort Wayne, Allen Co., Indiana, USA, at Concordia Lutheran Cemetery. Mary L. Rodenbeck was buried in Fort Wayne, Allen Co., Indiana, USA, at Concordia Lutheran Cemetery.

Frederick Philip Wambsganss WWI Draft Registration: 1942 in Fort Wayne, Allen Co., Indiana, USA

Frederick Phillip Ernest Wambsganss and Mary L Rodenbeck had the following children:

 i.  FREDERICK R*⁴* WAMBSGANSS was born about 1907 in New Orleans, Orleans Co., Louisiana, USA. He died on 17 Apr 1961 in Fort Wayne, Allen Co., Indiana, USA (Greenlawn Memorial Park). He married Margaret B [Unknown]. She died before 04 Mar 1972 in Fort Wayne, Allen Co., Indiana, USA.

 ii.  ELFREIDA WAMBSGANSS was born on 01 Jun 1910 in New Orleans, Orleans Co., Louisiana, USA. She died on 27 Feb 1992 in Fort Wayne, Allen Co., Indiana, USA (Age 81). She married Jack D Baals. He was born on 14 Nov 1910 in Fort Wayne, Allen Co., Indiana, USA. He died on 20 Jun 2003 in Fort Wayne, Allen Co., Indiana, USA (Woodview Healthcare Center; Age 92). Elfreida Wambsganss was buried 01 Mar 1992 in Fort Wayne, Allen Co., Indiana, USA; Concordia Gardens.

---

 iii.

**ELFRIEDA M. BAALS**

Elfrieda M. Baals, 81, died yesterday at Lutheran Hospital. The New Orleans native had lived in Fort Wayne most of her life. She was a homemaker and a member of Emmaus Lutheran Church, the church's Ladies Aid and Lutheran Hospital Auxiliary.

Surviving are her husband, Jack; a daughter, Sara Witt of Fort Wayne; a son, David of Fort Wayne; sisters, Winifred Fritz and Eunice Smith, both of Fort Wayne; five grandchildren and one great-grandchild. Services are 10 a.m. tomorrow at the church, 2320 Broadway. Calling is 3 to 5 and 7 to 9 p.m. today at Klaehn, Fahl & Melton Funeral Homes, Winchester Road Chapel, 6424 Winchester Road, and 9 to 10 a.m. tomorrow at the church. Burial will be in Concordia Gardens. Preferred memorials are gifts to the church foundation or the donor's choice. (News-Sentinel, The (Fort Wayne, Indiana) - 28 Feb 1992)

---

 iii.  HILDEGARDE G WAMBSGANSS was born on 17 Nov 1914 in Indiana, USA. She died on 29 Nov 1983 in Steamboat Springs, Routt Co., Colorado, USA. She married Paul W Nelson. He was born on 08 Apr 1910. He died on 15 Jan 1975 in Steamboat Springs, Routt Co., Colorado, USA (Age 64). Hildegarde G Wambsganss was buried in Burial: Steamboat Springs, Routt Co., Colorado, USA. at Steamboat Springs Cemetery

 iv.  WINIFRED L WAMBSGANSS was born about 1927 in Indiana, USA. She married Douglas L Fritz. He was born on 10 Jul 1922. He died on 25 Dec 1990 in Fort Wayne, Allen Co., Indiana, USA (Age: 68).

 v.  EUNICE EVELYN WAMBSGANSS was born on 25 Jun 1928 in Fort Wayne, Allen Co., Indiana, USA. She died on 10 Jun 2007 in Fort Wayne, Allen Co., Indiana, USA (Age: 78). She married Jack Vernon Smith on 02 Sep 1950 in Allen Co., Indiana, USA. He was born on 17 May 1925 in Auburn, De Kalb Co., Indiana, USA. He died on 11 Nov 1990 in Indianapolis, Marion Co., Indiana, USA (Veterans Affairs Medical Center; Age: 65).

10. WILLIAM ADOLPH.*³* "BILL WAMBY" WAMBSGANSS (Caroline*²* Schellman, Johann "John"*¹* Schellman) was born on 19 Mar 1894 in Cleveland, Cuyahoga Co., Ohio, USA. He died on 08 Dec 1985 in Lakewood, Cuyahoga Co., Ohio, USA (Age: 91). He married Effie L Mulholland on 30 Jun 1917 in Cuyahoga Co., Ohio, USA. She was born on 21 Jul 1893 in Cleveland, Cuyahoga Co., Ohio, USA. She died in Apr 1977 in Lakewood, Cuyahoga Co., Ohio, USA (Age: 83). William A. Wambsganss was buried in Cleveland, Cuyahoga Co., Ohio, USA, at Calvary Cemetery.

Military Service: 1918 in Ohio, USA; Age: 24 Depot Brigade to 29 Aug 1918; 20 Co Central Officers' Training School Cp Gordon Ga to Discharge Corporal 1 Aug 1918. Honorable discharge 30 Nov 1918.

William Wambsganss was a professional baseball from 1914 to 1926. He played infielder/second baseman for the world champion Cleveland Indians between 1914-1923 and made history when he made the first ever unassisted triple play during the 1920 World Series. The first grand slam and home run by a pitcher during a Series occurred during that same game. The Indians won the series 8-1. Bill Wamby also played for the Boston Red Sox (1925-1925) and the Philadelphia Athletics (1926).

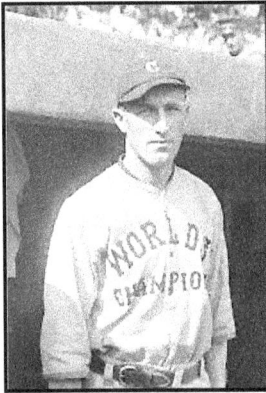

90: William "Bill Wamby"
Wambsganss
(circa 1920)

71: William Wambsganss 1976
Motorola Statistics Card
(autographed)
(National Archives Collection)

WILLIAM WAMBSGANSS

SECOND BASE          1914—1926
Only unassisted triple play in Series history.

TRIAC Triple Play —
from Motorola to Distributors to You!

92: Bill Wamby standing with the three Brooklyn Dodgers ballplayers he took out in an unassisted triple play during the 1920 World Series game .(Photo by : L.Van Oeyer, Library of Congress Archives)

BILL WAMBSGANSS
*Dies at 91; Made a Triple Play in Series*
*Lakewood, Ohio, Dec. 10*

William Adolph Wambsganss, one of the two remaining members of the 1920 world champion Cleveland Indians, died Sunday in Lakewood Hospital. He was 91 years old.

Wambsganss, whose name occasionally appeared in box scores as Bill Wamby, is celebrated in baseball lore as the man who made the only unassisted triple play in World Series history.

With runners on first base and second base, he caught a sharp line drive that had been hit just to the right of second by Clarence Mitchell of the Brooklyn Dodgers. Then Wambsganss stepped on second to double up Pete Kilduff and easily tagged out Otto Miller, who had been on first.

Wambsganss was the Indians' regular second baseman from 1914 to 1923. He remained with the Indians until being sent to Boston in 1924. He finished with Philadelphia in 1926, batting .352 in 54 games. (AP; 11: Dec1985)

William Adolph Wambsganss and Effie L Mulholland had the following children:

    i.      MARY C*4* WAMBSGANSS was born on 07 Oct 1918 in Ohio, USA. She died on 15 Nov 1989 in Rocky River, Cuyahoga Co., Ohio, USA (Age: 71). She married [Unknown] Brandes.

    ii.     LOIS WAMBSGANSS was born about 1924 in Ohio, USA.

    iii.    WILLIAM A WAMBSGANSS JR was born about 1933 in Ohio, USA.

11. HENRY J*3* KLASNER JR (Barbara O*2* Schellman, Johann "John"*1* Schellman) was born on 27 Apr 1905 in Michigan, USA. He died on 06 Mar 1985 in Hancock, Houghton Co., Michigan, USA (Age: 79). He married Ina B [Unknown] about 1930. She was born in 1898. She died in 1938.Ina B [Unknown] was buried in 1938 in Otisville, Genesee Co., Michigan, USA, at Smith Hill Cemetery

Henry J Klasner Jr. and Ina B [Unknown] had the following child:

    i.      JOHN*4* KLASNER was born about 1935 in Flint, Genesee Co., Michigan, USA. He married Gretchen [Unknown].

12. BARBARA L*3* KLASNER (Barbara O*2* Schellman, Johann "John"*1* Schellman) was born on 15 May 1908 in Michigan, USA. She died on 06 Sep 2001 in Flushing, Genesee Co., Michigan, USA (Kith Haven Nursing Home; Age: 93). She married Christian Brohn in 1934 in Flint, Genesee Co., Michigan, USA. He was born about 1906 in Michigan, USA. He died on 23 Oct 1971. Barbara L Klasner was buried 10 Sep 2001 in Flint, Genesee Co., Michigan, USA, at Sunset Hills Cemetery

---

BROHN, BARBARA L.

    Barbara L. Brohn, of Flint, age 93, Died Thursday, September 6, 2001 at Kith Haven Nursing Home. Funeral Service will be held at 11 AM Monday, September 10, 2001 at Emanuel Lutheran Church, G-6380 Beecher Road in Flint, Reverend Steven M. Lockman officiating. Burial in Sunset Hills Cemetery. Those desiring may make contributions to Emanuel Lutheran Church Building Fund. Visitation 6-9 PM Sunday at the Swartz Funeral Home, 125 West Hill Road. Mrs. Brohn will be at the church from 10:30 AM Monday until the time of the service.

    Mrs. Brohn was born in Hancock, Michigan on May 15, 1908. She married Christian R. Brohn in 1934 in Flint. She was a member of Emanuel Lutheran Church. Mrs. Brohn was employed by Sears, as an assistant cashier, for many years. Surviving are 2 sons, Gerald and wife Lois of Flushing, David and wife Celia of South Haven, MI; 8 grandchildren; 3 great - grandchildren; several nieces, nephews; many dear friends; special friends, Jean Otto and Dorothy McCanahan. She was preceded in death by her husband, Christian, on October 23, 1997; 2 sisters and 4 brothers. A heartfelt thanks to the staff and special niece Sue Parker, at Kith Haven for their wonderful care. ( pub. unk; abt 08 Sep 2001)

---

Christian Brohn and Barbara L Klasner had the following children:

22.    i.      GERALD LEE*4* BROHN was born on 03 Sep 1937 in Flint, Genesee Co., Michigan, USA. He died on 04 Nov 2011 in Flushing, Genesee Co., Michigan, USA. He married Lois Jean Glandorf on 23 Jun 1962 in Flint, Genesee Co., Michigan, USA.

    ii.     DAVID BROHN. He married Celia [Unknown].

13. CLARA J*3* VOLLMER (Paulina*2* Schellman, Johann "John"*1* Schellman) was born on 28 Jul 1904 in Michigan, USA. She died on 01 Oct 1994 in Akron, Summit Co., Ohio, USA (Age 90). She married (1) George H Repke about 1927. He was born about 1900. She married Alphonse Cyrille Cheney. He was born on 24 Dec 1901. He died on 07 Mar 1986.

Clara J Vollmer was buried in Hancock, Houghton Co., Michigan, USA, at Lakeside Cemetery. Alphonse Cyrille Cheney was buried in Houghton, Houghton Co., Michigan, USA, at Lakeside Cemetery.

George H Repke and Clara J Vollmer had the following children:

    i.    CLARICE PAULINE*4* REPKE was born about 1928 in Michigan, USA.

    ii.    RADERUK REPKE was born about 1937 in Michigan, USA.

14.  WALTER HERMAN*3* KETTENBEIL (Hannah*2* Schellman, Johann "John"*1* Schellman) was born on 03 Aug 1895 in Schoolcraft, Houghton Co., Michigan, USA. He died on 11 Jul 1977 in Laurium, Houghton Co., Michigan, USA (Age 81). He married Flossie Cantin about 1916. She was born about 1897 in Michigan, USA.

Walter Herman Kettenbeil WWI Draft Registration: Jun 1917 in Houghton Co., Michigan, USA

Walter Herman Kettenbeil and Flossie Cantin had the following children:

    i.    ZANE P*4* KETTENBEIL was born on 01 Jul 1926 in Michigan, USA.

    ii.    BRUCE KETTENBEIL was born about 1929 in Michigan, USA.

15.  EDNA*3* KETTENBIEL (Hannah*2* Schellman, Johann "John"*1* Schellman) was born in 1899 in Michigan, USA. She married Robert Porell. He was born about 1898 in Michigan, USA.

Robert Porell and Edna Kettenbiel had the following child:

    i.    ROBERT*4* PORELL JR was born about 1923 in Michigan, USA.

16.  HENRY*3* KETTENBEIL JR (Hannah*2* Schellman, Johann "John"*1* Schellman) was born on 21 Feb 1901 in Michigan, USA. He died in Apr 1970 in Lake Linden, Houghton Co., Michigan, USA (Age: 69). He married Margaret Birk. She was born on 08 Mar 1905 in Michigan, USA. She died in Jan 1992. Henry Kettenbeil Jr. was buried in Lake Linden, Houghton Co., Michigan, USA, at Maple Hill Cemetery. Margaret Birk was buried Jan 1992 in Lake Linden, Houghton Co., Michigan, USA, at Maple Hill Cemetery.

Henry Kettenbeil Jr. and Margaret Birk had the following child:

    i.    MARILYN*4* KETTENBEIL was born about 1932 in Michigan, USA.

17.  ELSA K.*3* KETTENBIEL (Hannah*2* Schellman, Johann "John"*1* Schellman) was born on 03 Mar 1903 in Michigan, USA. She died on 09 Dec 1993 in Portage, Kalamazoo Co., Michigan, USA (Age: 90). She married Garvin Peter Mitchell. He was born on 26 Aug 1897 in Hancock, Houghton Co., Michigan, USA. He died on 27 Dec 1985 in Oshtemo, Kalamazoo Co., Michigan, USA (Age: 88). Elsa K. Kettenbiel was buried in Houghton, Houghton Co., Michigan, USA, at Forest Hill Cemetery. Garvin Peter Mitchell was buried in Houghton, Houghton Co., Michigan, USA, at Forest Hill Cemetery

Garvin Peter Mitchell WWI Military Service: 14 Oct 1918 ; Age: 21

Garvin Peter Mitchell and Elsa K. Kettenbiel had the following children:

    i.    GARVIN CLYDE[4] MITCHELL was born on 18 Aug 1927 in Michigan, USA. He died on 09 Mar 2010 in St Cloud, Osceola Co., Florida, USA (Age: 82). Garvin Clyde Mitchell was buried in Anderson, Madison Co., Indiana, USA, at Maplewood Cemetery.

    ii.    JOANNE MITCHELL was born in 1932 in Michigan, USA.

---

GARVIN C. MITCHELL

ST. CLOUD, Fla. - Garvin C. Mitchell Aug. 18, 1927 - March 9, 2010ST. CLOUD, Fla. Garvin C. Mitchell, 82, St. Cloud, died March 9, 2010, at St. Cloud Regional Medical Center. He served with the U.S. Navy during World War II. Burial 2 p.m. Friday at Maplewood Cemetery in Anderson. Arrangements handled by Fisk Funeral Home & Crematory, St. Cloud, Fla.(Herald Bulletin, Anderson, IN, 05/26/2010).

---

18. HENRY GEORGE LINCOLN[3] TERP (Lydia[2] Schellman, Johann "John"[1] Schellman) was born on 12 Feb 1905 in St Paul, Ramsey Co., Minnesota, USA. He died in Apr 1980 in Green Bay, Brown Co., Wisconsin, USA (Age: 75). He married (1) Mary Eileen C [Unknown] about 1937. She was born on 11 Jun 1916 in Wisconsin, USA. She died on 01 Nov 1995 in Green Bay, Brown Co., Wisconsin, USA (Age: 79). He married (2) Mrs Henry G Terp [Unknown] between 1925-1930. She died before 1930.

Henry George Lincoln Terp and Mary Eileen C [Unknown] had the following child:

    i.    NANCY JO[4] TERP was born about 1938 in Wisconsin, USA.

19. LUCILLE S[3] TERP (Lydia[2] Schellman, Johann "John"[1] Schellman) was born on 07 Oct 1912 in Wisconsin, USA. She died on 18 May 2004 in Green Bay, Brown Co., Wisconsin, USA (Age: 91). She married Joseph P Baeb on 26 Dec 1933. He was born on 29 Jul 1908. He died on 27 May 1988 in Green Bay, Brown Co., Wisconsin, USA (Age: 80). Lucille S Terp was buried in Green Bay, Brown Co., Wisconsin, USA. Joseph P. Baeb was buried in Green Bay, Brown Co., Wisconsin, USA, at Ashwaubenon Moravian Cemetery.

---

LUCILLE BAEB

Mrs. Joseph (Lucille) Baeb, 91, Green Bay, died peacefully at home with her family at her side Tuesday, May 18, 2004. She was born Oct. 7, 1912, to the late Peter and Lydia (Shellman) Terp in Green Bay.

On Dec. 26, 1933, she married Joseph Baeb. He preceded her in death in 1988. Lucille had been a long-time standing member of West Side Moravian Church and its women's fellowship.

She enjoyed spending time with her children, grandchildren, relatives and friends.

Survivors include two daughters and one son-in-law, Judy (Allan) Schilling, Lakeville, Minn., and Barbara Johnson, Libertyville, Ill.; five grandchildren; nine great-grandchildren; one sister, Betty Berken, De Pere; three sisters-in-law; and many nieces and nephews.

In addition to her parents and husband, she was preceded in death by an infant son; seven brothers and one sister.

Friends may call from 4 to 8 p.m. Thursday, May 20, at Lyndahl Funeral Home, Lombardi Avenue at Ridge Road. visitation will continue after 10 a.m. Friday at West Side Moravian Church, 1707 S. Oneida St., where the funeral service will take place at 11 a.m. with the Rev. James Hicks officiating. Burial will be in Ashwaubenon Moravian Cemetery.

---

Joseph P Baeb and Lucille S Terp had the following children:

    i.      JUDY[4] BAEB. She married Allan Schilling.

    ii.     BARBARA BAEB. She married [Unknown] Johnson.

    iii.    EDWARD BAEB was born about 1932. He died on 28 Oct 1932 in Green Bay, Brown Co., Wisconsin, USA He was buried about 30 Oct 1932 in Green Bay, Brown Co., Wisconsin, USA, at Fort Howard Memorial Park.

20.  LESLIE IVEN JEPSON[3] TERP (Lydia[2] Schellman, Johann "John"[1] Schellman) was born on 21 Dec 1916 in Minnesota, USA. He died on 18 Dec 1977 in Los Angeles, Los Angeles Co., California, USA (Age: 60). He married Eunice [Unknown] about 1948. She was born about 1919 in Wisconsin, USA. Leslie Iven Jepson Terp was buried in Glendale, Los Angeles Co., California, USA, at Forest Lawn Memorial Park (Glendale).

Leslie Iven Jepson Terp and Eunice [Unknown] had the following child:

    i.      LESLIE P[4] TERP was born in 1956. He married Linda S Pace in 1976. She was born in 1952.

21.  HAROLD JAMES[3] TERP (Lydia[2] Schellman, Johann "John"[1] Schellman) was born on 05 Dec 1919 in Wisconsin, USA. He died on 28 Nov 2002 in Francis Creek, Manitowoc Co., Wisconsin, USA (Age: 80). He married Viola Ann Vincent on 14 Mar 1947 in Dubuque, Dubuque Co., Iowa, USA. She was born on 18 Apr 1928 in Wisconsin, USA. She died on 07 Mar 1992 (Age: 63). Harold James Terp was buried in Manitowoc, Manitowoc Co., Wisconsin, USA, at Evergreen Cemetery. Viola Ann Vincent was buried in Manitowoc, Manitowoc Co., Wisconsin, USA, at Evergreen Cemetery.

Harold James Terp WWII Military Service: Bet. 15 Oct 1940-24 Jun 1945 in Green Bay, Brown Co., Wisconsin, USA; National Guard, Field Artillery; Private; Age: 19; US Army; Sergeant.

Sandra Terp, a high school senior, was the driver of a vehicle that crashed into a flat car of a train preparing to pull out of the switching yard at the edge of town in Manitowoc, WI. The vehicle struck the right rear wheel of the flat car, preventing the vehicle from going under the train. The car left no skid marks on the road and it wasn't immediately known how fast the car had been going. The accident happened about 9 pm. Sandra died two hours later of severe head and chest injuries. Another girl in the car was killed on impact. Three other passengers sustained injuries that later caused the death of one of them as well.

93: Sandra Lynn Terp
Lincoln High School
1968 Yearbook
Manitowoc, Wisconsin

Harold James Terp and Viola Ann Vincent had the following child:

    i.      SANDRA LYNN[4] TERP was born about 1951. She died on 29 Apr 1968 in Manitowoc, Manitowoc Co., Wisconsin, USA (Car crashed into train).

    ii.

22.  GERALD LEE[4] BROHN (Barbara L[3] Klasner, Barbara O[2] Schellman, Johann "John"[1] Schellman) was born on 03 Sep 1937 in Flint, Genesse Co., Michigan, USA. He died on 04 Nov 2011 in Flushing, Genesee Co., Michigan, USA. He married Lois Jean Glandorf. They had three children.

Gerald Lee Brohn Military Service: Abt. 1955 ; US Army Reserves.

# DESCENDANTS OF AUGUST STEINER

### Generation 1

1. AUGUST[1] STEINER was born on 04 Jul 1836 in Germany. He died on 23 Jan 1902 in Chelsea, Taylor Co., Wisconsin, USA. He married Paulina Meisner in 1864. She was born on 23 Mar 1842 in Germany. She died on 29 Feb 1908 in Chelsea, Taylor Co., Wisconsin, USA (Probably). August Steiner was buried in Chelsea, Taylor Co., Wisconsin, USA, at Chelsea Cemetery. Paulina Meisner was buried in Chelsea, Taylor Co., Wisconsin, USA, at Chelsea Cemetery

94: Above: August
Steiner
Below: Pauline Steiner
Chelsea Cemetery
Chelsea, Taylor Co., WI

August Steiner and Paulina Meisner had the following children:

2.   i.   JOHN AUGUST[2] STEINER was born in 1852 in Tirol, Austria. He died in 1896 in Chelsea, Taylor Co., Wisconsin, USA (probably). He married Louise "Muna" Rouder. She was born in May 1852 in Tirol, Austria. She died in 1939 in Medford, Taylor Co., Wisconsin, USA.

    ii.   AUGUST STEINER was born 1868. He died in 1894. August Steiner was buried in Chelsea, Taylor Co., Wisconsin, USA; Chelsea Cemetery.

    iii.   ALBERT STEINER was born in Oct 1875 in Germany. He married Anna Erl on 02 Oct 1902 in Medford, Taylor Co., Wisconsin, USA. She was born in Germany.

    iv.   ANNA STEINER was born in Schoenwalde, Germany. She married Michael Gallagher on 23 Oct 1893 in Chelsea, Taylor Co., Wisconsin, USA. He was born in Donegal Co., Ireland. '

    v.   BERTHA STEINER was born in Germany. She married William Gebaueer on 11 Jan 1897 in Chelsea, Taylor Co., Wisconsin, USA. He was born in Germany.

### Generation 2

2. JOHN AUGUST[2] STEINER (August[1]) was born in 1852 in Tirol, Austria. He died in 1896 in Chelsea, Taylor Co. Wisconsin, USA. He married Louise "Muna" Rouder. She was born in May 1852 in Tirol, Austria. She died in 1939 in Medford, Taylor Co., Wisconsin. John August Steiner was buried in Chelsea, Taylor Co., Wisconsin, USA, at Chelsea Cemetery. Louise "Muna" Rouder was buried in Chelsea, Taylor Co., Wisconsin, USA, at Chelsea Cemetery.

John August Steiner and Louise "Muna" Rouder had the following children:

3.   i.   JOHN REINHARD[3] STEINER was born in May 1876 in Tirol, Austria. He died on 09 Oct 1944. He married Marie A Christman on 23 Jun 1901 in Medford, Taylor Co., Wisconsin, USA. She was born in Medford, Taylor Co., Wisconsin, USA.

    iii.   WILLIAM STEINER was born in Jun 1878 in Tirol, Austria.

4.    iii.    JOSEPH STEINER was born in Jan 1882 in Germany. He died on 09 Dec 1950 in Medford, Taylor Co., Wisconsin, USA (probably). He married Thekla Brandner. She died on 10 Apr 1964 in Medford, Taylor Co., Wisconsin, USA (probably).

5.    iv.    LOUIS STEINER was born on 13 May 1884 in Tirol, Austria (Germany). He died on 09 Mar 1962 in Taylor Co., Wisconsin, USA (Age: 77). He married Hattie Wapples. She was born about 1898 in Wisconsin, USA. She died before 1993.

6.    v.    MOLLIE STEINER was born in May 1887 in Wisconsin, USA. She died on 02 Mar 1981 in Medford, Taylor Co., Wisconsin, USA (Age 93). She married Otto Lange on 16 Sep 1909 in Medford, Taylor Co., Wisconsin, USA. He died on 09 Jan 1964.

7.    vi.    ANNA STEINER was born on 09 Aug 1890 in Marshfield, Fond du Lac Co., Wisconsin, USA. She died on 15 Mar 1946 in Marshfield, Fond du Lac Co., Wisconsin, USA (Age 56). She married Albert Philip Henry Grimm, son of Albert A Grimm and Mary S Schellman on 19 Aug 1908 in Medford, Taylor Co., Wisconsin, USA (Trinity Lutheran Church of Whittlesey). He was born on 24 Oct 1884 in Hancock, Houghton Co., Michigan, USA. He died on 14 Mar 1981 in Medford, Taylor Co., Wisconsin, USA Anna Steiner was buried in Chelsea, Taylor Co., Wisconsin, USA, at Chelsea Cemetery. Albert P. Grimm was buried in Chelsea, Taylor Co., Wisconsin, USA, at Chelsea Cemetery

    vii.    SOPHIE STEINER was born in Sep 1891 in Wisconsin, USA. She married Otto Lechner.

    viii.    REINHARD STEINER was born in May 1893 in Wisconsin, USA.

    ix.    FRANK STEINER was born in Aug 1895 in Wisconsin, USA.

95: John and Louise "Muna" Steiner
Chelsea Cemetery, Chelsea, Taylor Co., Wisconsin

## Generation 3

3.    JOHN REINHARD[3] STEINER (John August[2], August[1]) was born in May 1876 in Tirol, Austria. He died on 09 Oct 1944. He married Marie A Christman, daughter of Anton Christman and Minnie [Unknown], on 23 Jun 1901 in Medford, Taylor Co., Wisconsin, USA. She was born in Medford, Taylor Co., Wisconsin, USA.

John Reinhard Steiner and Marie A Christman had the following children:

    i.      DANIEL[4] STEINER was born about 1903.

    ii.     IRWIN STEINER was born about 1904.

    iii.   ALBERT STEINER was born about 1907.

4.    JOSEPH[3] STEINER (John August[2], August[1]) was born in Jan 1882 in Germany. He died on 09 Dec 1950 in Medford, Taylor Co., Wisconsin, USA (Probably). He married Thekla Brandner. She died on 10 Apr 1964 in Medford, Taylor Co., Wisconsin, USA (Probably).

96: Joseph and Thekla Steiner
Perkinstown, Taylor Co., WI

Joseph Steiner and Thekla Brandner had the following child:

8.    i.      HENRY J[4] STEINER was born on 29 Aug 1922 in Medford, Taylor Co., Wisconsin, USA. He died on 30 May 1995 in Marshfield, Fond du Lac Co., Wisconsin, USA. He married Darlene Anderson on 25 May 1957 in Golconda, Tasmania, Australia. She was born on 25 Jul 1932 in Medford, Taylor Co., Wisconsin, USA. She died on 11 Jul 1993 in Medford, Taylor Co., Wisconsin, USA.

5.    LOUIS[3] STEINER (John August[2], August[1]) was born on 13 May 1884 in Tirol, Austria (Germany). He died on 09 Mar 1962 in Taylor Co., Wisconsin, USA (Age: 77). He married Hattie Wapples. She was born about 1898 in Wisconsin, USA. She died before 1993.

97: Louis Steiner
Chelsea Cemetery
Chelsea, Taylor Co., WI

Louis Steiner and Hattie Wapples had the following children:

9.    i.      CHESTER LOUIS[4] STEINER was born on 24 Aug 1913 in Chelsea, Taylor Co., Wisconsin, USA. He died on 03 May 1993 in Shawano, Shawano Co., Wisconsin, USA (Shawano Community Hospital; Age 79). He married Helen Mae Donaldson on 15 Sep 1934 in Medford, Taylor Co., Wisconsin, USA (Whittlesey). She was born about 1915 in Wisconsin, USA. She died after May 1993.

10.   ii.    ALVERA STEINER was born about 1918 in Wisconsin, USA. She died before May 1993. She married Roland Strebig. He was born about 1911 in Wisconsin, USA.

    iii.   MARCELLA STEINER. She died after May 1993. She married Elmer Zuehlke.

    iv.    WALTER STEINER was born in 1912 and died an infant in 1912. He is buried in Chelsea, Taylor Co., Wisconsin, USA; Chelsea Cemetery.

6.    MOLLIE[3] STEINER (John August[2], August[1]) was born in May 1887 in Wisconsin, USA. She died on 02 Mar 1981 in Medford, Taylor Co., Wisconsin, USA (Age 93). She married Otto Lange on 16 Sep 1909 in Medford, Taylor Co., Wisconsin, USA. He died on 09 Jan 1964. Mollie Steiner was buried on 04 Mar 1981 in Medford, Taylor Co., Wisconsin.

MOLLIE LANGE

Funeral services were held Wednesday, March 4, at Trinity Lutheran Church, Whittlesey, , for Mollie Lange, 93, Town of Chelsea resident who died Monday morning at Memorial Hospital, Medford, where she had been a patient for five days. Rev. Jerome Newton officiated at the 2 p.m. services and burial took place in Medford Evergreen Cemetery. The body lay in state late Tuesday afternoon and evening at Hemer Funeral Home, Medford.

A native of Medford, the former Mollie Steiner was born May 18, 1887, and attended Medford area schools. She was married September 16, 1909, in Medford to Otto Lange who preceded her in death January 9 1964. She was a member of Trinity Lutheran congregation and it's Ladies Aid.

Surviving are three sons, Arthur of the Town of Chelsea, Louis of the Town of Molitor and Ervin of Clark County Health Care Center, Owen; two daughters, Lillian Streckert of Abbotsford and Latischa, Mrs. Maurice Egle, Town of Molitor; 10 grandchildren and 22 great grandchildren, and a sister, Sophie Lechner, Madras, Ore. In addition to her husband, Mrs. Lange was preceded in death by six brothers and three sisters. (Star News, Medford, WI; Mar1981)

Otto Lange and Mollie Steiner had the following children:

11.    i.    ERVIN O.[4] LANGE was born on 01 Apr 1912 in Chelsea, Taylor Co., Wisconsin, USA. He died on 11 Jul 1993 in Owen, Clark Co., Wisconsin, USA (Age 81). He married Evelyn Seibold in May 1936 in Tacoma, Pierce Co., Washington, USA.

       ii.    LOUIS G. LANGE was born on 01 Jan 1916. He died on 09 Aug 1984. He married Louise [Unknown] about Jul 1940. Louis G. Lange was buried 13 Aug 1984 in Medford, Taylor Co., Wisconsin, USA.

       iii.    ARTHUR LANGE.

       iv.    LILLIAN LANGE. She died after 1993. She married [Unknown] Strecker

12.    v.    LATISCHA LANGE. She married Maurice Egle on 30 Jun 1930 in Medford, Taylor Co., Wisconsin, USA. He was born on 18 Jan 1909 in Molitor, Taylor Co., Wisconsin, USA. He died on 13 Dec 1995 in Medford, Taylor Co., Wisconsin, USA (Age 86).

       vi.    ERNA LANGE. She died before 1984.

7.    ANNA[3] STEINER (John August[2], August[1]) was born on 09 Aug 1890 in Marshfield, Fond du Lac Co., Wisconsin, USA. She died on 15 Mar 1946 in Marshfield, Fond du Lac Co., Wisconsin, USA (Age 56). She married Albert Philip Henry Grimm, son of Albert A Grimm and Mary S Schellman on 19 Aug 1908 in Medford, Taylor Co., Wisconsin, USA (Trinity Lutheran Church of Whittlesey). He was born on 24 Oct 1884 in Hancock, Houghton Co., Michigan, USA. He died on 14 Mar 1981 in Medford, Taylor Co., Wisconsin, USA (Medford Hospital; Age 96). (See Descendants of Heinrich Ludwig Grimm)

Generation 4

8.    HENRY J[4] STEINER (Joseph[3], John August[2], August[1]) was born on 29 Aug 1922 in Medford, Taylor Co., Wisconsin, USA. He died on 30 May 1995 in Marshfield, Fond du Lac Co., Wisconsin, USA. He married Darlene Anderson on 25 May 1957 in Golconda, Tasmania, Australia. She was born on 25 Jul 1932 in Medford, Taylor Co., Wisconsin, USA. She died on 11 Jul 1993 in Medford, Taylor Co., Wisconsin, USA. Henry J Steiner was buried on 02 Jun 1995 in Medford, Taylor Co., WI, USA, at Evergreen Cemetery II. Darlene Anderson was buried on 04 Jul 1993 in Medford, Taylor Co., WI, USA, at Evergreen Cemetery II

Henry J Steiner and Darlene Anderson had the following child:

13.    i.    JOSEPH[5] STEINER was born about 1959. He married Janine [Unknown].

---

DARLENE A. STEINER (1932-1993)

Funeral services will be held at 11 a.m. on Wed, July 14, at Trinity Lutheran Church, Whittlesey, for Darlene Anita Steiner, 60, Town of Chelsea, who died Sunday evening, July 11, at memorial Nursing Home, Medford, where she had resided for the past 7-1/2 months.

Rev. Ronald Schultz will officiate and burial will be in Medford Evergreen Cemetery II. Pallbearers will be Roger Pinsch, Jerry Gardner, Tim and Dawn Ertl, and Kris and Tammy Salzwedel.

Hemer Funeral Home of Medford is in charge of the arrangements.

The former Darlene Anita Anderson was born July 25, 1932, at Medford to the late David and Alberta (Krickelberg) Anderson. She attended Medford area schools, graduating from Medford High School and Taylor county Normal School. She also received a Bachelor's degree from the University of Wisconsin, Eau Claire. She married Henry Steiner on May 25, 1957, at Golconia, Ill., and he survives.

She taught grade school in the Taylor and Clark county areas for eight years. In 1961, she and her husband moved to Harvard, Ill, where she taught grade school until retiring in in June of 1990. They then returned to the Medford area.

She was a member of Trinity Lutheran Church, Whittlesey and its Ladies Aid, St. Paul Lutheran Church of Harvard, Ill., Harvard Teachers Association, and Retired Teachers Association. Survivors also include a son, Joseph (Jan) Steiner of Crystal Lake, Ill., two brothers, Gerald (Sandy) of West Allis and Harlan of Medford; five sisters, Virginia (Ollie) Kitchen of Abbotsford, Jeanette (John) Reed of Medford, Sherrie (Mike) Ertl of Menominee Falls, Sandra (Richard) Salzwedel of Marshfield and Sheryl Anderson of Medford. (Star News, Medford, WI; n.d.g.)

---

9.    CHESTER LOUIS[4] STEINER (Louis[3], John August[2], August[1]) was born on 24 Aug 1913 in Chelsea, Taylor Co., Wisconsin, USA. He died on 03 May 1993 in Shawano, Shawano Co., Wisconsin, USA (Shawano Community Hospital; Age 79). He married Helen Mae Donaldson on 15 Sep 1934 in Medford, Taylor Co., Wisconsin, USA (Whittlesey). She was born about 1915 in Wisconsin, USA. She died after May 1993. Chester Louis Steiner was buried on 06 May 1993 in Kewaskum, Washington Co., Wisconsin, USA, at Lutheran Memorial Park Cemetery

---

CHESTER L. STEINER (1913-1993)

Town of Chelsea native, Chester L. Steiner, 79, Shawano, died Monday, May 3, at Shawano community Hospital. Funeral services were held Thursday afternoon, May 6, at the Miller funeral Home in Kewaskum. Rev. James Naumann of the Divine Savior Lutheran Church, Shawano, officiated and burial took place in Lutheran Memorial Park Cemetery.

He was born on August 24, 1913, in the town of Chelsea to the late Louis and Hatty (Wapples) Steiner. His marriage to Helen Mae Donaldson took place on September 15, 1934, in Whittlesey.

He was employed as a mechanic at Honeck Chevrolet in Kewaskum for 18 years, retiring in 1977. He was a member of the Divine Savior Lutheran Church in Shawano.

Survivors include his wife, Helen of Shawano; two sons, Kenneth (Marliss) of Germantown and Carl (Judy) of Kewaskum; two daughters, Irene (William) Seefeldt of Kewaskum and Eileen (Gerry) Grotzinger of Skokie, Ill.; a sister, Marcella (Elmer) Zuelke of Kewaskum; 16 grandchildren; and 14 great-grandchildren. He was also preceded in death by a brother, Walter; a sister, Alveria Strebig; a step-granddaughter; and a great-grandson. (Star News, Medford, WI; n.d.g.)

---

Chester Louis Steiner and Helen Mae Donaldson had the following children:

        i.    KENNETH[5] STEINER. He married Marliss [Unknown].

        ii.    CARL STEINER. He married Judy [Unknown].

        iii.    IRENE STEINER. She married William Seefeldt.

        iv.    EILEEN STEINER. She married Gerry Grotzinger.

10. ALVERA⁴ STEINER (Louis³, John August², August¹) was born about 1918 in Wisconsin, USA. She died before May 1993. She married Roland Strebig. He was born about 1911 in Wisconsin, USA.

Roland Strebig and Alvera Steiner had the following children:

    i.    EVELYNA⁵ STREBIG was born about 1935 in Wisconsin, USA.

    ii.    JACKIE STREBIG was born about 1938 in Wisconsin, USA.

11. ERVIN O.⁴ LANGE (Mollie³ Steiner, John August² Steiner, August¹ Steiner) was born on 01 Apr 1912 in Chelsea, Taylor Co., Wisconsin, USA. He died on 11 Jul 1993 in Owen, Clark Co., Wisconsin, USA (Age 81). He married Evelyn Seibold in May 1936 in Tacoma, Pierce Co., Washington, USA. Ervin O. Lange was buried on 13 Jul 1993 in Medford, Taylor Co., WI, USA, at Evergreen Cemetery

> **ERVIN O. LANGE**
>
> Ervin O. Lange, 81, Owen, died Sunday morning, July 11, at the Clark County Health Care Center, Owen, where he had been a resident since 1948. Funeral services were held Tuesday afternoon, July 13, at Hemer Funeral Home in Medford with Rev. Ronald Schultz officiating. Burial took place in Medford Evergreen Cemetery.
>
> He was born April 1, 1912, in the Town of Chelsea to Otto and Molly (Steiner) Lange. He attended Hillcrest School in the Town of Chelsea. He married Evelyn Seibold in May of 1936 in Tacoma, Wash., and they later divorced.
>
> He moved to Tacoma as a young man and was employed by Weyerhauser Company from 1936 to 1938. He then moved back to Taylor County where he farmed and was employed by the WPA, a federal government program during the 1930s and early 1940s.
>
> He was a former member of Trinity Lutheran Church in Whittlesey.
>
> Survivors include two daughters, Joyce Zentner, Tempe, Ariz., and June (Robert) Haynie, Dewey, Ariz., two sisters, Lillian Streckert, Abbottsford, and Latischa Egle, Medford; one brother, Arthur of Medford; ten grandchildren; and eight great-grandchildren. He was preceded in death by his parents, a sister, Erna Moore, and one brother, Louise Lange. (Star News, Medford, WI; July 1991

Ervin O. Lange and Evelyn Seibold had the following children:

    i.    JOYCE⁵ LANGE. She married [Unknown] Zentner.

    ii.    JUNE LANGE. She married Robert Haynie.

12. LATISCHA⁴ LANGE (Mollie³ Steiner, John August² Steiner, August¹ Steiner, Otto). She married Maurice Egle on 30 Jun 1930 in Medford, Taylor Co., Wisconsin, USA. He was born on 18 Jan 1909 in Molitor, Taylor Co., Wisconsin, USA. He died on 13 Dec 1995 in Medford, Taylor Co., Wisconsin, USA (Age 86). Maurice Egle was buried on 16 Dec 1995 in Medford, Taylor Co., Wisconsin, USA, at Evergreen Cemetery

Maurice Egle and Latischa Lange had the following children:

    i.    MARVIN⁵ EGLE. He married Barbara [Unknown].

    ii.    IRENE EGLE. She married Joe Sweda.

MAURICE EGLE (1909-1995)

Maurice Egle, 86, of the Town of Molitor, died Wednesday, December 13, at memorial Nursing Home in Medford where he had resided for three weeks. Funeral services were held Saturday, December 16, at Hemer Funeral Home in Medford with Rev. Warren Behling of St. Paul's Lutheran Church in Medford officiating.

Burial took place in Medford Evergreen Cemetery. Pallbearers were Mike and Marc Egle, Lynn and Jon Zevenbergen, and Lori and Rex Lloyd-Jones.

Mr. Egle was born January 18, 1909, in the Town of Molitor to Moritz and Emma Egle. He received his education in Town of Molitor elementary schools. His marriage to Latischa Lange took place on June 30, 1930, in Medford.

He worked in the logging camps, as a milk hauler, and then farmed for a period of time. He then worked at the Taylor County Highway Department until his retirement in 1974.

Survivors include his wife, Latischa of the Town of Molitor; a son, Marvin (Barbara) Egle of Ladysmith; a daughter, Irene (Joe) Sweda of Lublin; four grandchildren, and great-grandchild.. He was preceded in death by his parents, a sister, Monica Schreiner in 1991. (Star News, Medford, WI; 20 Dec 1995)

# DESCENDANTS OF ANDREW ANDERSON

## Generation 1

1. ANDREW[1] ANDERSON was born on 03 Apr 1847 in Norway. He died on 10 Feb 1928 in Medford, Taylor Co., Wisconsin, USA (Probably). He married Johanna Gunderson in 1872. She was born on 23 Apr 1841 in Norway. She died on 29 May 1903 in Medford, Taylor Co., Wisconsin, USA (Age 62). Andrew Anderson was buried in 10 Feb 1928 in Medford, Taylor Co., Wisconsin, USA; Medford Town Cemetery (Evergreen) Johanna Gunderson was buried in Medford, Taylor Co., Wisconsin, USA; Medford Town Cemetery (Evergreen).

Andrew Anderson immigrated to America in 1872 at the age of twenty-three. He was living on a farm in Little Black, Taylor Co., Wisconsin in 1880 with his wife Anna and his three oldest children.[67] In 1910, he was listed as a widower and living with his eldest son and his family in Little Black but no longer living with him in 1920.[68]

98: Andrew
Anderson
(circa unknown)

Receipt found among Clara Anderson Grimm's papers: *Received of Mrs. Frank Fray, $50.00 for perpetual care of Andrew Anderson's Lot No. 14 - Blk T in Evergreen Cemetery. Signed by Henry Geo. [Bachas] [Sec]. Dated 15 Aug 1955.*

Andrew Anderson and Johanna Gunderson had the following children (list may be incomplete):

2.  i. AUGUST NIKOLAUS[2] ANDERSON was born on 20 Mar 1875 in Green Bay, Brown Co., Wisconsin, USA. He died on 04 May 1945 in Medford, Taylor Co., Wisconsin, USA (Age 70). He married Mary Olson, daughter of Christopher Olson Sr. and Caroline Nelson on 22 Sep 1897 in Medford, Taylor Co., Wisconsin, USA. She was born on 15 Sep 1880 in Christiana, Norway. She died on 14 Jun 1955 in Deer Creek, Taylor Co., Wisconsin, USA (Medford Hospital; Age 74).

    ii. RACHE[L] ANDERSON was born in Mar 1877 in Wisconsin, USA.

    iii. ALBERT I ANDERSON was born on 29 Dec 1878 in Medford, Taylor Co., Wisconsin, USA. He died on 10 Jul 1954 in Everett, Snohomish Co., Washington, USA

99: Andrew and Johanna
Anderson
Evergreen Cemetery,
Medford, Taylor Co., WI

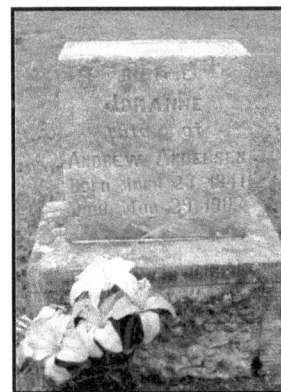

---

[67] Ancestry.com. *1880 United States Federal Census*. (Provo, UT, USA; Ancestry.com Operations Inc.) www.ancestry.com [Database Online]. Year: 1880. Little Black, Taylor Co., Wisconsin. ED: 189, p.9, Dwelling. 89, Family 89, L.36-40.
[68] Ancestry.com. *1910 United States Federal Census*. (Provo, UT, USA; Ancestry.com Operations Inc.) www.ancestry.com [Database Online]. Year: 1910. Little Black, Taylor Co., Wisconsin. ED: 171, p 7A, Dwelling 89, Family 92, L.19-24.

## Generation 2

2. AUGUST NIKOLAUS[2] ANDERSON (Andrew[1]) was born on 20 Mar 1875 in Green Bay, Brown Co., Wisconsin, USA. He died on 04 May 1945 in Medford, Taylor Co., Wisconsin, USA (Age 70). He married Mary Olson, daughter of Christopher Olson Sr. and Caroline Nelson on 22 Sep 1897 in Medford, Taylor Co., Wisconsin, USA. She was born on 15 Sep 1880 in Christiana, Norway. She died on 14 Jun 1955 in Deer Creek, Taylor Co., Wisconsin, USA (Medford Hospital; Age 74). August Nikolaus Anderson was buried on 07 May 1945 in Medford, Taylor Co., Wisconsin, USA; Evergreen Cemetery. Mary Olson was buried on 18 Jun 1955 in Medford, Taylor Co., Wisconsin, USA; Evergreen Cemetery.

100: August Anderson
(circa 1945)

101: August N. Anderson WWI draft registration, 1918; Taylor Co., Wisconsin.[69]

Mary Olson Anderson claimed her son, Robert, his wife, Eva, and their four children as dependents on her 1954 Income Tax Return. The children at the time were listed as Richard, Joyce, Diana, and Joan (possibly John). According to the *Schedule of Farm Income and Expenses (Form 1040F),* her gross profits for the year amounted to $2529.30 from the sale of livestock ($189.67) and produce raised ($2339.63). Her total deductions were $1248.22 for expenses ($1098.22) and depreciation of a barn acquired ten years earlier when she purchased the property ($150). Her total Adjusted Gross Income for 1954 was $1279.98. Seventy-three year old Mary checked "no" that she didn't pay someone else to prepare the forms for her. The forms were written and signed in pencil.[70]

1928 - 1978

In honor of the Fiftieth Wedding Anniversary of Art and Loretta Anderson

Their Children

Request the pleasure of your company at a Reception

On Sunday, the fourteenth of May Nineteen hundred and seventy eight From two until five o'clock in the afternoon

102: August and Mary Anderson family
(circa 1945)

103: Fiftieh wedding anniversary of Art & Loretta Anderson

[69] Ancestry.com. *United States, Selective Service System, World War I Selective Service System Draft Registration Cards, 1917-1918*, Washington, D.C.: National Archives and Records Administration; Database online. Registration Location: Taylor County, Wisconsin.
[70] Anderson, Mary nee Olson; *US Income Tax Forms 1040 and 1040F*; 19 Jan 1954; Prepared and signed by Mary Anderson.

August Nikolaus Anderson and Mary Olson had the following children:

i.     OLIVE[3] ANDERSON was born in 1900 in Wisconsin, USA.

3     ii.     ARTHUR CARL ANDERSON was born on 02 Jun 1903 in Wisconsin, USA. He died on 26 Nov 1998 in Okanogan, Okanogan Co., Washington, USA. He married Loretta Rachel Hoverson, daughter of Hulbert Hoverson and Helena Miller on 10 May 1928 in Newport, Pend Oreille Co., Washington, USA. She was born on 23 May 1912 in Tyler, Richland Co., North Dakota, USA. She died on 06 Jun 1991 in Okanogan, Okanogan Co., Washington, USA (Age 79).

iii.     EMMA ANDERSON was born about 1905 in Medford, Taylor Co., Wisconsin, USA. She died before Jul 1922 in Wisconsin, USA (probably); Tuberculosis; Age 12).

4     iv.     ELMER ANDERSON was born on 30 Mar 1907 in Medford, Taylor Co., Wisconsin, USA. He died on 24 Jan 1980 in Medford, Taylor Co., Wisconsin, USA (Age 72). He married Grace E. Clarkson, daughter of William Clarkson and Adeline Bollock on 10 Dec 1928 in Medford, Taylor Co., Wisconsin, USA. She was born on 20 May 1906 in Oaktown, Knox Co., Indiana, USA. She died on 18 Mar 1996 in Medford, Taylor Co., Wisconsin, USA (Age 89).

5     v.     MYRTLE ANDERSON was born in 1910 in Wisconsin, USA. She died before May 1997. She married John F Lorenz before 28 Dec 1930 in Wisconsin, USA (Courthouse (no town given). He was born on 11 Jan 1907 in Wisconsin, USA. He died in May 1972 in Medford, Taylor Co., Wisconsin, USA.

> **FUNERAL SET SATURDAY**
> At Holway Church For
> Mrs. Mary Anderson, 74
>
> Mrs. Mary Anderson, 74, Town of Deer Creek resident, died Tuesday at the Medford hospital. Funeral services will be at 2 o'clock Saturday afternoon at the Holway Lutheran church, with Rev. Max Wilhelm of Curtiss officiating.
>
> The body will lie in state at the Hartwig and Ruesch Funeral home in Medford from 10 a.m. Friday until an hour before services and at the church. Interment will be in Medford Evergreen cemetery. Pallbearers will be Paul Anderson Carl Anderson, Robert Sperl, Charles Peterson, Casper Olson Jr. and James Neuman Jr.
>
> The former Mary Olson was born in Christiana, Norway, September 15, 1880. She was four years old when she came to the United States with her parents, who after a few years settled in the town of Little Black. On September 22, 1897, she was married at Medford to August Anderson, who died May 4, 1945. For the past nine years she had been residing in the town of Deer Creek. She was a member of the Holway Lutheran Church.
>
> Children who survive her are Arthur and Florence, Mrs. Otto Anderson, Okanogan, Wash.; Elva, Mrs. George Drolshagen and Clara, Mrs. Alvin Grimm, Medford; Elmer and Robert, Stetsonville and Casper of Omak, Wash. Also surviving are three brothers, Casper Olson Withee; Christ Olson Jr., Creston, Can; and Anton Olson, Sask., Can; 31 grandchildren and 12 great-grandchildren.
>
> Three daughters preceded her in death and a sister and two brothers are also deceased. (Star News, Medford, WI; 16 Jun 1955)

6.     vi.     CLARA MATILDA ANDERSON was born on 09 Jan 1912 in Little Black, Taylor Co., Wisconsin, USA. She died on 05 May 1997 in Medford, Taylor Co., Wisconsin, USA (Age 85). She married Alvin Albert William Grimm, son of Albert Philip Henry Grimm and Anna Steiner on 09 Nov 1933 in Medford, Taylor Co., Wisconsin, USA (Whittlesey Lutheran Church Parsonage). He was born on 08 May 1909 in Chelsea, Taylor Co., Wisconsin, USA. He died on 24 Jun 2003 in Vancouver, Clark Co., Washington, USA (Age 94).

7.     vii.     ELVA MARIE ANDERSON was born on 21 May 1914 in Medford, Taylor Co., Wisconsin, USA. She died on 03 Oct 2001 in Medford, Taylor Co., Wisconsin, USA. She married George J Drolshagen on

01 May 1934 in Medford, Taylor Co., Wisconsin, USA. He was born on 28 Oct 1910 in Little Black, Taylor Co., Wisconsin, USA. He died on 03 Mar 1981 in Medford, Taylor Co., Wisconsin, USA.

8.  viii.  FLORENCE JOSEPHINE ANDERSON was born on 21 Jun 1918 in Medford, Taylor Co., Wisconsin, USA. She died on 12 Nov 1979 in Okanogan, Okanogan Co., Washington, USA (Age 61). She married Otto C Anderson, son of Oluf Anderson and Ingeborg Lovingen on 21 Oct 1939 in Medford, Taylor Co., Wisconsin, USA. He was born on 26 May 1915 in Medford, Taylor Co., Wisconsin, USA. He died on 01 Sep 1992 in Omak, Okanogan Co., Washington, USA (of pneumonia; Age 77).

9.  ix.  ROBERT MANUEL "BUD" ANDERSON was born on 01 Jun 1921 in Wisconsin, USA. He died on 15 Sep 2007 in Okanogan, Okanogan Co., Washington, USA. He married Florence Eva Clarkson before 1949 in Medford, Taylor Co., Wisconsin, USA (probably). She was born in 1923 in Wisconsin, USA. She died on 15 Jul 1974 in Okanogan, Okanogan Co., Washington, USA (probably).

10.  x.  CASPER DAVID ANDERSON was born on 03 Jan 1924 in Little Black, Taylor Co., Wisconsin, USA. He died on 05 May 1990 in Cambridge, Isanti Co., Minnesota, USA (Memorial Hospital; Age 66). He married Arlene Ruth Neumueller, daughter of Rudolph Neumueller and Helen Schwaubenhausen on 24 Aug 1946 in Medford, Taylor Co., Wisconsin, USA (Whittlesey). She was born on 04 Oct 1928 in Wisconsin, USA. She died on 11 Feb 2008 in Cambridge, Isanti Co., Minnesota, USA (Age 79).

104: August and Mary Anderson
Evergreen Cemetery
Medford, Taylor Co., WI

## Generation 3

3.  ARTHUR CARL[3] ANDERSON (August Nikolaus[2], Andrew[1]) was born on 02 Jun 1903 in Wisconsin, USA. He died on 26 Nov 1998 in Okanogan, Okanogan Co., Washington, USA. He married Loretta Rachel Hoverson, daughter of Hulbert Hoverson and Helena Miller on 10 May 1928 in Newport, Pend Oreille Co., Washington, USA. She was born on 23 May 1912 in Tyler, Richland Co., North Dakota, USA. She died on 06 Jun 1991 in Okanogan, Okanogan Co., Washington, USA (At home; Age 79). Arthur Carl Anderson was buried in Okanogan, Okanogan Co., Washington, USA, at Riverside Cemetery. Loretta Rachel Hoverson was buried on 10 Jun 1991 in Omak, Okanogan Co., Washington, USA, at Riverside Cemetery.

In 1940, Arthur Carl Anderson was renting a rural home with his wife and five children. He was employed as a rip sawyer at a box factor and had worked 44 weeks the previous year with an income of $557..[71]

---

[71] Ancestry.com. *1940 United States Federal Census*. (Provo, UT, USA; Ancestry.com Operations Inc.). www.ancestry.com [Database Online]. Year: 1940. Precinct 35, Okanogan Co, Washington, ED: 24, p 2A, Dwelling 34, L.32-38.

In Loving Memory of

LORETTA R. ANDERSON

May 23, 1912 - June 6, 1991

Services
June 10, 1991 - 2:00 P.M.

Barnes Elmway Chapel
Rev. John Ramsey, Officiate

Barbara Scarborough, Soloist
Ruth Rockey, Organist
"Amazing Grace"
"Sweet Bye & Bye"
"Whispering Hope"

Casket Bearers

Ocie Anderson    Danny Boiko
Mike Boiko    Gordon Boiko
Alex Boiko    Tommy Jones
Bob Jones    Ted Jones
Steve Jones    Kelly Lawson
Marty Lawson    Jamie Anderson
Scott Anderson

Concluding Services Riverside Cemetery

Barnes Elmway Chapel In Charge of
Arrangements

Arthur Carl Anderson and Loretta Rachel Hoverson had the following children:

11.  i. BERNHARD[4] ANDERSON was born in 1930 in Elk River,Clearwater Co., Idaho, USA. He married Bertha Lavonne Abel.

12.  ii. DONNA LEE ANDERSON was born on 02 Sep 1931 in Elk River, Clearwater Co.,Idaho, USA. She married Michael Boiko. He was born on 09 Nov 1923 in Washington, USA. He died on 18 May 1997 in Curlew, Ferry Co., Washington, USA.

13.  iii. DOLORES JEAN ANDERSON was born on 13 Sep 1933in Leavenworth, Chelan Co., Washington, USA. She married Thomas Griffth Jones on 23 May 1952 in Okanogan, Okanogan Co., Washington, USA. He was born on 18 May 1927 in Happy Hill (at home), Okanogan Co., Washington, USA.

14.  iv. DONALD MANUAL ANDERSON was born in 23 Mar 1936 in Leavenworth, Chelan Co., Washington, USA. He married Genon [Nmn] Jorgensen. She was born on 24 Dec 1937 in Malott, Okanogan Co., Washington, USA.

15.  v. NORMA GAYLE ANDERSON was born on 03 Nov 1929 in Leavenworth, Chalan Co., Washington, USA. She married Jimmy Carol Lawson on 17 Nov 1956 in Wenatchee, Chelan Co., Washington, USA. He was born on 06 Mar 1938 in Joy, White Co., Arkansas, USA.

16.  vi. GERALD "JERRY" EUGENE ANDERSON was born 12 Apr 1947 in Marshfield, Fond du Lac Co., Wisconsin, USA. He died in 19 Mar 2007 in Hoquiam, Grays Harbor Co., Washington, USA. He married Marilynn Kay Jaquish on 06 Dec 1965 in Omak, Okanogan Co., Washington, USA. She was born on 22 Jun 1948 in Omak, Okanogan Co. Washington, USA. Gerald Anderson is buried in Sunset Memorial Park, Hoquiam, Grays Harbor Co., Washington, USA.

LORETTA R. ANDERSON

OKANAGON - Loretta R. Anderson, 79, of Okanogan, died Thursday, June 6, 1991, in her home. She was born May 23, 1912, at Tyler, N.D., to Hulbert and Helena (Miller) Hoverson. She moved to Northport, Wash., with her family when she was young. She married Arthur C. Anderson May 10, 1928, at Ione, Wash. They lived at various locations in Idaho and Washington before moving to the Okanogan area in 1936. Mrs. Anderson worked in the local apple sheds and assisted her husband in orchard management. She was an active member and officer in the Okanogan Eagles Auxiliary for many years.

Survivors include her husband, at home; three sons, Bernard Anderson of Malott, Donald Anderson of Spokane and Gerald Anderson of Hoquaim; three daughters Donna Boiko of Curlew, Dolores Jones of Pine Creek, and Norma Lawson of Omak; 23 grandchildren; and 31 great-grandchildren. She was preceded in death by a brother and an infant grandson. Barnes Chapel is in charge of arrangements.

4. ELMER[3] ANDERSON (August Nikolaus[2], Andrew[1]) was born on 30 Mar 1907 in Medford, Taylor Co, Wisconsin, USA. He died on 24 Jan 1980 in Medford, Taylor Co., Wisconsin, USA (Memorial Nursing Home; Age 72). He married Grace E. Clarkson, daughter of William Clarkson and Adeline Bollock on 10 Dec 1928 in Medford, Taylor Co., Wisconsin, USA. She was born on 20 May 1906 in Oaktown, Knox Co., Indiana, USA. She died on 18 Mar 1996 in Medford, Taylor Co., Wisconsin, USA (Memorial Nursing Home; age 89). Elmer Anderson was buried on 26 Jan 1980 in Medford, Taylor Co., WI, USA; Evergreen Cemetery II. Grace E. Clarkson was buried on 20 Mar 1996 in Medford, Taylor Co., Wisconsin, USA; Evergreen Cemetery II.

Elmer Anderson was living in Medford, Taylor Co., Wisconsin, in a rural house he rented west of the railroad tracks. He lived there with his wife, Grace, and their six children. Elmer worked for the W.P.A. Sewer project as a sewer digger at the time. He had been employed for 36 weeks the previous year and had made $360. His son, Paul, had worked as a farm laborer for 8 weeks and had made $16. [72]

Elmer Anderson and Grace E. Clarkson had the following children:

17.     i.     PAUL BENTON[4] ANDERSON was born on 26 Apr 1925 in Hammel, Taylor Co., Wisconsin, USA. He died on 20 Feb 2006 in Medford, Taylor Co., Wisconsin, USA (Memorial Health Center; Age 80). He married Viola B. Neumueller on 11 Dec 1943 in Medford, Taylor Co., Wisconsin, USA. She was born on 19 Aug 1924 in Wisconsin, USA. She died on 03 Feb 2009 in Marshfield, Wood Co., WI, USA.

18.     ii.     CARL R ANDERSON was born on 05 Jun 1929 in Hammel, Taylor Co., Wisconsin, USA. He died on 30 Sep 2009 in Rib Lake, Taylor Co., Wisconsin, USA (Golden Living Center). He married Rose M. Neuman on 12 Feb 1955 in Stetsonville, Taylor Co., Wisconsin, USA. She died after 2009

19.     iii.     MARY ADELINE ANDERSON was born on 19 May 1931 in Medford, Taylor Co., Wisconsin, USA. She died on 23 Jan 2013 in Wausau, Marathon Co., Wisconsin, USA (Aspirus Wausau Hospital). She married Robert L. Sperl on 05 Jun 1948 in Stetsonville, Taylor Co., Wisconsin, USA (Sacred Heart Catholic Church). He was born on 06 Dec 1926 in Little Black, Taylor Co., Wisconsin, USA. He died on 28 Sep 2007 in Medford, Taylor Co., Wisconsin, USA (Memorial Nursing and Rehab Center).

20.     iv.     RUTH M ANDERSON was born on 26 May 1934 in Wisconsin, USA. She married Charles Peterson.

21.     v.     BETTY LOU ANDERSON was born on 21 Oct 1935 in Wisconsin, USA. She died on 26 Jan 1996 in Burbank, Cook Co., Illinois, USA. She married Robert G Bruton on 06 Jan 1956 in Cook Co., Illinois, USA.

22.     vi.     MARGARET ELLEN ANDERSON was born in 1938 in Wisconsin, USA. She married Frank Murphy about 1961.

        vii.     WALTER MILTON "WALLY" ANDERSON was born on 29 Dec 1940 in Wisconsin, USA. He died on 02 Feb 2012. He married Norma [Unknown].

        viii.     CHESTER ANDERSON was born on 19 May 1944. He died before 2006. He married Connie [Unknown].

        ix.     RUSSELL ANDERSON. He married Cheryl [Unknown].

---

[72] Ancestry.com. *1940 United States Federal Census*. (Provo, UT, USA; Ancestry.com Operations Inc.) www.ancestry.com [Database Online]. Year: 1940. Medford, Taylor Co., Wisconsin. ED: 60, p 3B, Dwelling 63, L. 76-83.

---

### RITES HELD JAN. 26 FOR E. ANDERSON

Patriarch of 77 descendants, Elmer Anderson, 72, Medford, died Thursday at Memorial Nursing Home in Medford where she had resided the past two weeks. The family consists of nine children, 48 grandchildren and 20 great-grandchildren.

Funeral services were conducted here Saturday morning at Hemer funeral home with Rev. Warren Behlin officiating. Interment took place in Evergreen cemetery II. Grandchildren served as pallbearers.

Hemer Funeral Home in Medford was in charge of arrangements.

Mr. Anderson was born March 30, 1907, at Medford and received his education in the Medford area schools. His marriage to Grace Clarkson, who survives, took place December 10, 1928, at Medford. He worked as a woodsman most of his early life. In 1957 he began employment with the Taylor county highway department and worked there until his retirement in 1971. Mr. Anderson was a member of Our Savior's Lutheran church, town of Holway.

In addition to his wife, grandchildren and great grandchildren, the surviving children are five sons, Paul, Carl, Walter, and Russell, all of Medford, and Chester, Chicago; four daughters, Mary, Mrs. Robert Sperl, Medford, Ruth, Mrs. Charles Peterson, Iron Ridge, Mrs. Betty Bruton, Chicago, and Margaret, Mrs. Frank Murphy, Horicon. Other survivors include three brothers, Arthur and Robert, both of Okanogan, Wash., and Casper, Cambridge, Minn., and two sisters, Alva, Mrs. George Drolshagen, and Clara, Mrs. Alvin Grimm, both of Medford.

Four sisters preceded him in death. (Star News, Medford, WI; abt 28 Jan 1980)

---

### GRACE E. ANDERSON (1906-1996)

Grace E. Anderson, 89, of Medford, died Monday, March 18, at Memorial Nursing Home in Medford where she had resided for eight years. Funeral services were held Wednesday, March 20, at St. Paul's Evangelical Lutheran Church in Medford with Rev. Lowell Bolstad officiating.

Burial was held in Medford Evergreen Cemetery II. Pallbearers were grandsons, David Peterson, Tim Sperl, Frank Murphy Jr., Terry Bruton, Brad Anderson, and Carl Anderson Jr.

Hemer Funeral Home in Medford was in charge of arrangements.

The former Grace E. Clarkson was born May 20, 1906, in Oaktown, Indiana, to William and Adeline (Bollock) Clarkson. She moved to Medford in her youth and attended Medford area schools.

Her marriage to Elmer Anderson took place on December 10, 1928, in Medford. She worked as a housewife and mother in her home for most of her life. She enjoyed crocheting, traveling, and her family. She was a member of St. Paul's Evangelican. Lutheran Church.

Survivors include three daughters, Mary (Robert) Sperl of Medford, Ruth (Charles) Peterson of Zimmerman, Minn., and Margaret (Frank) Murphy St. of Medford; five sons, Paul (Viola), Carl (Rosie), and Wally (Norma), all of Medford, Chester (Connie) of Chicago, and Russell (Cheryl) of Withee; 50 grandchildren; 92 great-grandchildren; and one great-great-grandchild.

She was preceded in death by her parents; her husband, Elmer on January 24, 1980; one daughter, Betty Bruton on January 26, 1996; six brother; three sisters; two grandchildren; and two great-grandchildren.

---

5. MYRTLE[3] ANDERSON (August Nikolaus[2], Andrew[1]) was born in 1910 in Wisconsin, USA. She died before May 1997. She married John F Lorenz before 28 Dec 1930 in Wisconsin, USA (Courthouse (no town given). He was born on 11 Jan 1907 in Wisconsin, USA. He died in May 1972 in Medford, Taylor Co., Wisconsin, USA. John F Lorenz military Service: 21 Feb 1941 in Milwaukee, Milwaukee Co., Wisconsin, USA

John F Lorenz and Myrtle Anderson had the following child:

i.    JOHN FRANK[4] LORENZ was born on 07 Nov 1930 in Wisconsin, USA.

105: Baptism Record for John Lorenz Jr.
Holway Lutheran Church,
Medford, Taylor Co., WI

6.    CLARA MATILDA ANDERSON Was Born On 09 Jan 1912 In Little Black, Taylor Co., Wisconsin, USA. She Died On 05 May 1997 In Medford, Taylor Co., Wisconsin, USA (Age 85). She Married Alvin Albert William Grimm, Son Of Albert Philip Henry Grimm And Anna Steiner On 09 Nov 1933 In Medford, Taylor Co., Wisconsin, USA (Whittlesey Lutheran Church Parsonage). He Was Born On 08 May 1909 In Chelsea, Taylor Co., Wisconsin, USA. He Died On 24 Jun 2003 In Vancouver, Clark Co., Washington, USA (Age 94). (See Descendants Of Heinrich Ludwig Grimm).

7.    ELVA MARIE[3] ANDERSON (August Nikolaus[2], Andrew[1]) Was Born On 21 May 1914 In Medford, Taylor Co., Wisconsin, USA. She Died On 03 Oct 2001 In Medford, Taylor Co., Wisconsin, USA. She Married George J Drolshagen On 01 May 1934 In Medford, Taylor Co., Wisconsin, USA. He Was Born On 28 Oct 1910 In Little Black, Taylor Co., Wisconsin, USA. He Died On 03 Mar 1981 In Medford, Taylor Co., Wisconsin, USA (Age 70). George J Drolshagen Was Buried On 05 Mar 1981 In Little Black, Taylor Co., Wisconsin, USA; St. Mary's Cemetery

GEORGE J. DROLSHAGEN

George J. Drolshagen, 70-year-old Town of Little Black resident, died Tuesday morning of an apparent heart attack at his home.

Funeral services will be conducted here at 10:30 a.m. Thursday, March 5, at Holy rosary Catholic Church with Rev. William Green officiating. Interment will take place in St. Mary's Cemetery, Town of Little Black. Nephews will serve as pallbearers.

The body lay in state at Hemer funeral Home Medford, where a prayer vigil was held Wednesday evening. Mr. Drolshagen was born October 28, 1910, in the Town of Little Black and attended the schools there. His marriage to Elva Anderson, who survives, took place May 1, 1934, at Medford.

He farmed in the Town of Little Black until the mid-1950s and then was employed by Miller Brothers Construction, doing road construction work. He had worked at the Dorchester Furniture Factory from 1960 until his retirement in 1973.

Mr. Drolshagen was a member of Holy Rosary Catholic Church.

In addition to his wife, he is survived by his mother, Mrs. Catherine Drolshagen, Medford; two sons, John, Medford, and Leighton, Dorchester; a daughter, Ruby, Mrs. James Neuman, Medford; a sister, Kunda, Mrs. Frank Brabeck, Owen; 13 grandchildren and three great-grandchildren. (Star News, Medford, WI; 5 March 1981)

George J Drolshagen And Elva Marie Anderson Had The Following Children:

23.    i.    RUBY KATHERINE[4] DROLSHAGEN Was Born On 28 Oct 1934 In Little Black, Taylor Co., Wisconsin, USA. She married James C Neuman On 21 Apr 1955 In Medford, Taylor Co., Wisconsin, USA. He was Born On 21 Apr 1924 In Greenwood, Clark Co., Wisconsin, USA. He Died On 06 Feb 1999 In Medford, Taylor Co., Wisconsin, USA.

24.    ii.    LEIGHTON E "LEE" DROLSHAGEN Was Born On 09 May 1939 In Wisconsin, USA. He Died On 01 Apr 2008 In Dorchester, Clark Co., Wisconsin, USA. He Married Beverly Kramer On 31 Mar 1973 In Taylor Co., Wisconsin, USA. She Was Born In 1942.

25.    iii.    JOHN A DROLSHAGEN was born on 28 Nov 1943. He married Charlotte A [Unknown]. She was born on 07 Mar 1944.

8.  FLORENCE JOSEPHINE[3] ANDERSON (August Nikolaus[2], Andrew[1]) was born on 21 Jun 1918 in Medford, Taylor Co., Wisconsin, USA. She died on 12 Nov 1979 in Okanogan, Okanogan Co., Washington, USA (Okanogan nursing home; Age 61). She married Otto C Anderson, son of Oluf Anderson and Ingeborg Lovingen on 21 Oct 1939 in Medford, Taylor Co., Wisconsin, USA. He was born on 26 May 1915 in Medford, Taylor Co., Wisconsin, USA. He died on 01 Sep 1992 in Omak, Okanogan Co., Washington, USA (Mid-Valley Hospital; of pneumonia; Age 77). Florence Josephine Anderson was buried on 15 Nov 1979 in Omak, Okanogan Co., Washington, USA; Riverside Cemetery. Otto C. Anderson was buried on 04 Sep 1992 in Omak, Okanogan Co., Washington, USA; Riverside Cemetery.

Military Service: for Otto C. Anderson: Abt. 1942 ; US Army, WWII; light machine gunner and rifleman.

---

FORMER RESIDENT MRS. ANDERSON DIES AT AGE 61

Funeral services were held Thursday, Nov. 15, at Precht-Harrison Chapel, Omak, Wash., for Mrs. Florence Anderson, 61, Okanogan, Wash., a former Medford resident who died November 12 in an Okanogan nursing home.

She was born here Jun 21, 1918 and received her education in the town of Little Black schools. Her marriage to Otto C. Anderson, who survives, took place October 21, 1939 at Medford. In 1949, they moved to Okanogan where she was a member of Our Savior's Lutheran Church.

In addition to her husband, she is survived by two sons, Wayne, Port Angeles, Wash., and Kenneth, Omak; a daughter, Mrs. Sharon Wells, Riverside, Wash.; four brothers, Art and Robert Anderson, both of Okanogan, Elmer Anderson, Medford, and Casper Anderson, Cambridge, Minn.; two sisters, Mrs. Alva Drolshagen and Mrs. Clara Grimm, both of Medford; nine grandchildren and a great grandchild. (Star News, Medford, WI; abt 16 Nov 1979)

---

Otto C Anderson and Florence Josephine Anderson had the following children:

26.     i.   WAYNE[4] ARTHUR ANDERSON was born 17 May 1938 in Medford, Taylor Co., Wisconsin, USA. He married (1) Nora Lee Bear in 1957 in Omak, Okanogan Co., Washington, USA. She was born on 04 Apr 1940 in Omak, Okanogan Co., Washington, USA. She died on 10 Oct 1989. He married (2) Carolyn Elizabeth Iverson in 1975 in Port Angeles, Clallam Co., Washington, USA. She was born on 10 Mar 1951 in Port Angeles, Clallam Co., Washington, USA. Nora Bear is buried in Mt. Angeles, Port Angeles, Clallam Co., Washington, USA (Age 49).

27.     ii.  KENNETH MELVIN ANDERSON was born 12 Nov 1941 in Medford, Taylor Co., Wisconsin, USA. He married (1) Janice Marie Rogers on 15 Mar 1961 in Okanogan Co., Washington, USA. She was born on 17 Aug 1944 in Omak, Okanogan Co., Washington, USA. He married (2) Jeanie Marie Hinderer about 1993. She was born on 27 May 1953 in Pullman, Whitman Co., Washigton, USA

28.     iii. SHARON LEE ANDERSON was born on May 10 1947 in Medford, Taylor Co., Wisconsin, USA. She married (1)[Unknown]. She married (2) Rodney Wells. Sharon had no children from either marriage.

9.  ROBERT MANUEL[3] "BUD" ANDERSON (August Nikolaus[2], Andrew[1]) was born on 01 Jun 1921 in Wisconsin, USA. He died on 15 Sep 2007 in Okanogan, Okanogan Co., Washington, USA (Valley Care Center). He married Florence Eva Clarkson before 1949 in Medford, Taylor Co., Wisconsin, USA (Probably). She was born in 1923 in Wisconsin, USA. She died on 15 Jul 1974 in Okanogan, Okanogan Co., Washington, USA (Probably). Florence Eva Clarkson was buried in Okanogan, Okanogan Co., Washington, USA; Riverside Cemetery.

---

*"Know All Men by These Presents, that the STATE BANK OF MEDFORD, Medford, Wisconsin...does hereby certify and acknowledge that a certain Chattel Mortgage bearing date on the 26th day of February, 1854, made and executed by Mrs. Mary Anderson, Robert Anderson, and Eva Anderson, his wife to State Bank of Medford and filed in the office of the Register of Deeds of the County of Taylor, in the State of Wisconsin on the 1st day of March, 1954...has been fully paid, satisfied and discharged. [Doc #79382].*

---

Robert Manuel "Bud" Anderson and Florence Eva Clarkson had the following children:

  i.  JOYCE[4] ANDERSON was born about 1950 in Deer Creek, Taylor Co., Wisconsin, USA (Possibly).

  ii.  RICHARD ANDERSON was born about 1952.

  iii.  DIANA ANDERSON was born about 1954.

  iv.  JOAN ANDERSON was born about 1955.

  v.  NANCY THERESA ANDERSON was born on 25 Sep 1956.

10. CASPER DAVID[3] ANDERSON (August Nikolaus[2], Andrew[1]) was born on 03 Jan 1924 in Little Black, Taylor Co., Wisconsin, USA. He died on 05 May 1990 in Cambridge, Isanti Co., Minnesota, USA (Memorial Hospital; Age 66). He married Arlene Ruth Neumueller, daughter of Rudolph Neumueller and Helen Schwaubenhausen on 24 Aug 1946 in Medford, Taylor Co., Wisconsin, USA (Whittlesey). She was born on 04 Oct 1928 in Wisconsin, USA. She died on 11 Feb 2008 in Cambridge, Isanti Co., Minnesota, USA (The Villages of North Branch; age 79). Casper David Anderson was buried 08 May 1990 in Cambridge, Isanti Co., Minnesota, USA; Cambridge Lutheran Cemetery. Arlene Ruth Neumueller was buried on 15 Feb 2008 in Cambridge, Isanti Co., Minnesota, USA; Cambridge Lutheran Cemetery.

Military Service of Casper David Anderson: Bet. Feb 1943-Feb 1946 ; US Army, 86th Infantry Division, WWII

---

CASPER D. ANDERSON

  Funeral services were conducted Tuesday afternoon, May 8, at the Cambridge Lutheran Church in Cambridge, Minn., for Casper D. Anderson, 66, Cambridge, a former Medford area resident who died Saturday, May 5, at Memorial Hospital in Cambridge.

  Interment took place in the Cambridge Lutheran Church where military rites were conducted by the Howard McCarty American Legion Post at Cambridge and the Isanti VFW Post at Isanti, Minn. Serving as pallbearers were Bob Patterson, Gene Bakke, Dave Clark, John Tumvall, Wendell Bjorklund and Tom Englund.

  Honorary pallbearers were grandsons, Troy, Jeff and Scott Travis, Kevin Anderson, Brian Peterson and John and Joseph Kirchberg.

  Mr. Anderson, son of the late August and Mary (Olson) Anderson, was born January 3, 1924, in the Town of Little Black and attended school in the Medford area.

  A World War II veteran, he entered the US Army in February of 1943 and served in Europe and the Philippines with the 86th Infantry Division. He received his discharge in February of 1946.

  His marriage to Arlene Neumueller, who survives, took place August 24, 1946, at Whittlesey.

  In 1958, the family moved to Cambridge where Mr. Anderson worked as a bricklayer in the Twin Cities and surrounding area.

  He was a member of the Cambridge American Legion Post and the Isanti VFW Post. His interests included hunting, fishing and woodworking.

  In addition to his wife, he is survived by a son, Allen, Cambridge; four daughters, Judy, Mrs. Mark Norman, also of Cambridge, Lois Kirchberg, Rush City, Minn., Lonna, Mrs. Glen Erickson, New London, Minn., and Sandy, Mrs. Keith Johnson, Isanti; 12 grandchildren and six step great-grandchildren. Other survivors include two sisters, Clara Grimm and Elva Drolshagen, both of Medford, two brothers, Arthur and Robert, both of Omak, Wash., and many nieces and nephews.

  He was also preceded in death by four sisters, a brother and a grandson. (Star News, Medford, WI; abt 9 May 1990).

---

Casper David Anderson and Arlene Ruth Neumueller had the following children:

28  i.  ALLEN LEE[4] ANDERSON was born on 18 Feb 1947 in Medford, Taylor Co., Wisconsin, USA. He died on 20 Apr 2002 in Princeton, Mille Lacs Co., Minnesota, USA. He married Diane Marie Brissette on 21 Mar 1970 in Isanti Co., Minnesota, USA. She was born on 13 Aug 1947 in Hennepin Co., Minnesota, USA.

29    ii.    LOIS ARLENE ANDERSON was born on 22 Aug 1948. She married (1) Kenneth John Kirchberg on 05 Jun 1971 in Isanti Co., Minnesota, USA. He was born on 09 Oct 1946 in Chisago Co., Minnesota, USA. She married (2) Lyle E Johnson on 12 Apr 1993 in Mille Lacs Co., Minnesota, USA. He was born in 1943.

    iii.    LONNA M ANDERSON was born on 28 May 1950. She married (1) Glen Dale Erickson on 26 Nov 1983 in Kandiyohi Co., Minnesota, USA. He was born on 07 Jun 1939 in Kandiyohi Co., Minnesota, USA. She married (2) Roger D Travis on 20 Jun 1970 in Isanti Co., Minnesota, USA. He was born on 13 Jan 1947. He died in Mar 1982.

    iv.    SANDRA RAE ANDERSON was born in 1954. She married Keith Howard Johnson on 22 Aug 1981 in Isanti, Isanti Co., Minnesota, USA (Route 2; "at their home"). He was born in 1945.

    v.    JUDY ANDERSON. She married Mark Norman.

---

ARLENE ANDERSON 1928-2008

Arlene Ruth Anderson, 79, Cambridge, Minn., died Monday, Feb. 11 at The Villages of North Branch. Funeral services will be held Friday, Feb. 15 at Cambridge Lutheran Church, with Pastor David Everett officiating. Mary Falk and Delores Oslund will serve as vocalists and Mary Kay O'Neill as organist.

Interment will be at Cambridge Lutheran Cemetery. Pallbearers will be Rick Hicks, Jon and Joseph Kirchberg and Jeff, Scott and Troy Travis

Visitation will be held Thursday, Feb 14 from 4 to 8 p.m. At Strike Funeral Homes, Cambridge Chapel and at the church on Friday from 1:00 p.m. until the time of the service..

---

## Generation 4

11.    BERNARD[4] ARTHUR ANDERSON was born 12 Jul 1929 in Elk River, Clearwater Co, Idaho, USA. He married Bertha Lavonne Abel, daughter of Bert Abel and Ethie [Unknown], after 1940. She was born on 09 Oct 1923 in Okanogan, Okanogan Co, Washington, USA. She died on 08 Mar 2005 in Okanogan, Okanogan Co, Washington, USA and is buried in Okanogan Valley Memorial Gardens in Omak, Okanogan Co., Washington. Bernard Arthur Anderson and Bertha Lavonne Abel had two children.

12.    DONNA LEE[4] ANDERSON (Arthur Carl[3], August Nikolaus[2], Andrew[1]) was born on 02 Sep 1931 in Elk River, Clearwater Co., Idaho, USA. She married Michael [Nmn] Boiko on 30 Oct 1952 in Okanogan, Okanogan Co., Washington, USA.. He was born on 09 Nov 1923 in Washington, USA. He died on 18 May 1997 in Curlew, Ferry Co., Washington, USA. They had four children.Military Service of Michael Boiko: Bet. 12 Feb 1943-26 Nov 1946; WWII Burial: Curlew, Ferry Co., Washington, USA.

13.    DOLORES JEAN[4] ANDERSON (Arthur Carl[3], August Nikolaus[2], Andrew[1]) was born in 13 Sep 1933 in Leavenworth, Chelan Co., Washington, USA. She married Thomas Griffth Jones ON 23 May 1952 in Okanogan, Okanogan Co., Washington, USA. They had seven children.

14.    DONALD MANUEL[4] ANDERSON (Arthur Carl[3], August Nikolaus[2], Andrew[1]) was born on 23 Mar 1936 in Leavenworth, Chelan Co., Washington, USA. He married Genon [Nmn] Jorgensen on 17 May 1958 in Okanogan, Okanogan Co., Washington, USA. She was born on 24 Dec 1937 in Malott, Okanogan Co., Washington, USA. They had two children.

15. NORMA GAYLE[4] ANDERSON (Arthur Carl[3], August Nikolaus[2], Andrew[1]) was born on 03 Nov 1938 in Leavenworth, Chelan Co, Washington, USA. She married Jimmy Carol Lawson on 17 Nov 1956 in Wenatchee, Chelan Co., Washington, USA. He was born on 06 Mar 1938 in Joy, White Co., Arkansas, USA. They had five children.

16. GERALD EUGENE "JERRY" ANDERSON was born 12 Apr 1947 in Marshfield, Fond du Lac Co., Wisconsin, USA. He died in 19 Mar 2007 in Hoquiam, Grays Harbor Co., Washington, USA. He married Marilynn Kay Jaquish on 06 Dec 1965 in Omak, Okanogan Co., Washington, USA. She was born on 22 Jun 1948 in Omak, Okanogan Co., Washington, USA.Gerald Anderson is buried in Sunset Memorial Park, Hoquiam, Grays Harbor Co., Washington, USA. They had three children.

---

GERALD E. ANDERSON

Hoquiam – Gerald E. Anderson, age 60, a resident of Hoquiam, died on Monday, March 19, 2007, at his home. Mr. Anderson was born on April 12, 1946, in Marshfield, Wisc. To Arthur Carl and Loretta Rachel (Hoverson) Anderson. At the age of 5, he moved with his family to Okanogan, Wash. In 1965 he graduated from Okanogan High School.

A memorial service was held at 1 p.m. on Saturday, March 24, 2007, at Saron Evangelical Lutheran Church in Hoquiam.

The family suggest that memorial donations be made to the Saron Lutheran Cancer Walk Tem, P.O. Box 517, Hoquiam, Wash. 98550.

Cremation arrangements are by the Coleman Mortuary in Hoquiam.

---

17. PAUL BENTON[4] ANDERSON (Elmer[3], August Nikolaus[2], Andrew[1]) was born on 26 Apr 1925 in Hammel, Taylor Co., Wisconsin, USA. He died on 20 Feb 2006 in Medford, Taylor Co., Wisconsin, USA (Memorial Health Center; Age 80). He married Viola B. Neumueller, daughter of Rudolph Neumueller and Helen [Unknown], on 11 Dec 1943 in Medford, Taylor Co., Wisconsin, USA. She was born on 19 Aug 1924 in Wisconsin, USA. She died on 03 Feb 2009 in Marshfield, Wood Co., Wisconsin, USA. Paul Benton Anderson was buried on 25 Feb 2006 in Medford, Taylor Co., Wisconsin, USA; Evergreen Cemetery II. They had two children.

---

PAUL ANDERSON (1925-2006)

Paul B. Anderson, 80, Medford, died Monday, Feb. 20 at Memorial Health Center Emergency Room. Funeral services will be held on Saturday, Feb 25 at 11 a.m. at Immanuel Evangelical Lutheran church in Medford, with Pastor John Melke officiating. Burial will be at Medford Evergreen Cemetery II. Pallbearers will be his grandsons, Brad and Travis Paulsrud, Brent and Troy Anderson, Mitchel Goerg and Great-grandson, Trevor Paulsrud.

Visitation will be on Friday, Feb. 24 from 4 to 8 p.m. at Hemer Funeral Home in Medford, and at the church on Saturday from 9 a.m. until the time of service.

Paul Anderson was born April 26, 1925 in the Town of Hammel to the late Elmer and Grace (Clarkson) Anderson. He attended Medford area schools and trade school in Merrill where he trained to be a welder. He married Viola B. Neumueller, who survives, on December 11, 1943, in Medford. He worked for William Buehler driving truck at the sawmill, and later began truck driving for Peterson and Sons and worked in the woods in the winter. In 1964 he and his son established Paul B. Anderson and Son Inc., which he co-owned and co-operated until semi-retirement in 1987. He then worked part time for Peterson and Sons until the fall of 2005.

He was a member of Immanuel Evangelical Lutheran Church and a former member of the We Whittlesey Whizzers Snowmobile Club. He enjoyed the outdoors and deer hunting.

In addition to his wife, survivors include a daughter, Carol Goerg of Medford; a son, Duane (Mary Lou) Anderson of Medford; three sisters, Mary (Bob) Sperl of Medford, Ruth (Charles) Peterson of Dorchester and Margaret (Frank) Murphy of Columbus.; three brothers, Carl (Rose) and Walter (Norma), both of Medford, and Russell (Cheryl) of Withee; six grandchildren; and five great-grandchildren.

In addition to his parents, he was preceded in death by a sister, Betty Bruton, and a brother, Chester. Memorials may be made to Immanuel Evangelical Lutheran Church. (Star News, Medford, WI; 23 Feb 1986)

---

18. CARL R[4] ANDERSON (Elmer[3], August Nikolaus[2], Andrew[1]) was born on 05 Jun 1929 in Hammel, Taylor Co., Wisconsin, USA. He died on 30 Sep 2009 in Rib Lake, Taylor Co., Wisconsin, USA (Golden Living Center). He married Rose M. Neuman on 12 Feb 1955 in Stetsonville, Taylor Co., Wisconsin, USA. She died after 2009. Carl R Anderson was buried on 02 Oct 2009. They had two children.

Military Service for Carl R. Sperl Breckinridge, Breckinridge Co., Kentucky, USA; U.S. Air Force, Camp Breckinridge. Carl's military address was given as: Clearing Company 501, Airborne Medical Bn, 101 Airborne Division. He served in the United States Air Force as a parachute jumper during the Korean War.

> CARL R ANDERSON:
>
> Carl Anderson (1929-2009)Carl R. Anderson, 80, Medford, died Wednesday, Sept. 30 at Golden Living Center in Rib Lake, where he had resided the past three months. Funeral services will be held Friday, Oct. 2 at 1:30 p.m. at Hemer Funeral Home in Medford, with Pastor Cathy Hinman officiating.
> Visitation will be held at the funeral home on Friday from 11:30 a.m. until the time of the service. Carl Anderson was born June 5, 1929 in the Town of Hammel to the late Elmer and Grace (Clarkson) Anderson. He attended Medford area schools.
> On February 12, 1955 in Stetsonville, he married Rose M. Neuman, who survives. He served in the United States Air Force as a parachute jumper during the Korean War. He then drove truck and hauled gravel for businesses in the Medford area for several years. He also did woodwork and logging for several years, then worked at Hurd as a muler until his retirement.
> He was a member of Klossner-Dietzler VFW Post No. 5729. He was an avid hunter and fisherman and enjoyed camping.
> In addition to his wife, survivors include two sons, Roger and Carl Jr., both of Medford; three sisters, Mary Sperl of Medford, Ruth (Charles) Peterson of Dorchester and Margaret (Frank) Murphy of Columbus; two brothers, Walter (Norma) of Medford and Russell (Cheryl) of Withee; two grandsons, Eric (Michelle) and Cory, both of Medford; and four great-grandsons, Bryce, Isaac, Dominic and Mason Anderson, all of Medford.
> In addition to his parents, he was preceded in death by a sister, Betty Bruton; and two brothers, Chester and Paul.
> In lieu of flowers, memorials can be made to his family to be designated at a later date.

19. MARY ADELINE[4] ANDERSON (Elmer[3], August Nikolaus[2], Andrew[1]) was born on 19 May 1931 in Medford, Taylor Co., Wisconsin, USA. She died on 23 Jan 2013 in Wausau, Marathon Co., Wisconsin, USA (Aspirus Wausau Hospital). She married Robert L. Sperl, son of Louis Sperl and Teresa Rothomer of Little Black, WI, on 05 Jun 1948 in Stetsonville, Taylor Co., Wisconsin, USA (Sacred Heart Catholic Church). He was born on 06 Dec 1926 in Little Black, Taylor Co., Wisconsin, USA. He died on 28 Sep 2007 in Medford, Taylor Co., Wisconsin, USA (Memorial Nursing and Rehab Center). Mary Adeline Anderson was buried on 28 Jan 2013 and her husband was buried on 02 Oct 2007. Both are buried in Medford, Taylor Co., Wisconsin, USA; Holy Rosary Catholic Church. They had twelve children. One died in infancy.

> SPERL-ANDERSON UNITED IN MARRIAGE SATURDAY
>
> Miss Mary Adeline Anderson, daughter of Mr. And Mrs. Elmer Anderson, town of Deer Creek, and Robert L. Sperl, son of Mr. and Mrs. Louis Sperl, town of Little Black, were united in marriage at 9 o'clock Saturday morning, June 5, by the Rev. Joseph A. Seeboth. The ceremony was performed in the Sacred heart Catholic Church in Stetsonville.
> Mrs. Henry Pernsteiner was matron of honor.... The bridesmaids were Marjorie Sperl and Ruth Anderson...and Carmella Baumer.
> Henry Pernsteiner, Gene Halopka, Don Johnson, and Carl Anderson attended the groom.
> Among those attending from away were Mr. and Mrs. Edgar Clarkson, Owen; Mr. and Mrs. Clarence Clarkson, Withee; Mr. and Mrs. Paul Anderson, Whittlesey; Mr. and Mrs. Charles Kramer and family, Kennan.
> The groom is a graduate of the Holy Rosary Catholic School and is presently employed by Peter Bootzin. Upon their return from a week's honeymoon in the West the bridal couple will make their home with the Louis Sperls. (Star News, Medford, WI; abt 6 Jun 1948)

MARY SPERL 1931-2013

Mary A. Sperl, 81, Medford, died on Wednesday, Jan. 23 at Aspirus Wausau Hospital while surrounded by her family, where she had been a patient the past six days. Funeral services were held on Monday, Jan. 28 at Holy Rosary Catholic Church in Medford, with Father Gerard Willger and Deacon Joseph Stefancin officiating. Interment of her cremated remains will take place at Holy Rosary Catholic Cemetery in Medford at a later date. Active pallbearers were Robby, Jeremy, Mike, Justin and Mathew Sperl, Joel Rausch, Brandon Riegert and Phil Curran. Honorary pallbearers were Bryce and Chase Sperl. Hemer Funeral Homes of Medford and Rib Lake assisted the family with arrangements.

The former Mary Anderson was born on May 19, 1931 in Medford to the late Elmer M. and Grace E. (Clarkson) Anderson. She attended Medford area schools.

On June 5, 1948 at Sacred Heart Catholic Church in Stetsonville, she married Robert L. Sperl, who preceded her in death on September 28, 2007. They farmed in Spencer from 1948 to 1955, then resided in the Town of Goodrich and later moved to the Town of Chelsea.

She was a member of Holy Rosary Catholic Church. She enjoyed canning, cooking, gardening, fishing, camping, crocheting, watching the Minnesota Vikings and the Big Joe Polka Show, reading medical articles and books, playing the dice game Chicken, and her cats.

Survivors include nine sons, Ron (Karleen) of Stetsonville, Danny (Sue), Bruce, Ricky (Nancy), Tim (Brenda), Jim (Cheryl) and Billy (Michelle), all of Medford, Jeff (Gail) of Manitowoc and Bobby (Gwen) of Abbotsford; two daughters, Nancy (Scott) Riegert of Dorchester and Sue (Tony) Rausch of Medford; two brothers, Wally (Norma) and Russell (Cheryl), both of Medford; two sisters, Ruth (Charles) Peterson of Dorchester and Margaret (Frank) Murphy of Medford; a sister-in-law, Rosie Anderson of Medford; 33 grandchildren and 36 great-grandchildren. In addition to her parents and husband, she was preceded in death by a grandson in infancy, Jaden Sperl in 2004; three brothers, Paul, Carl and Chester; a sister, Betty Bruton; and a daughter-in-law, Harriet Sperl in 1996.

ROBERT SPERL

Robert L. Sperl, 80, of the town of Chelsea died Sept. 28, 2007, at Memorial Nursing and Rehab Center in Medford where he had resided the last two days under the care of Hope Hospice.

Services will be held at 11 a.m. Tuesday at Holy Rosary Catholic Church in Medford. Interment will be in the Holy Rosary Catholic Cemetery. Visitation will be from 4 p.m. to 8 p.m. Monday at Hemer Funeral Home.

He was born Dec. 6, 1926, in Little Black, the son of Louis and Teresa (Rothomer) Sperl. On June 5, 1948, he married Mary Anderson at Sacred Heart Catholic Church in Stetsonville. He worked for the Taylor County Highway Department for many years until his retirement in 1972.

Survivors include his wife, Mary Sperl, of the town of Chelsea; nine sons, Ron (Karleen) Sperl of Stetsonville, Danny (Sue) Sperl of Medford, Bruce Sperl of Medford, Ricky (Nancy) Sperl of Medford, Jeff (Gail) Sperl of Manitowoc, Tim (Brenda) Sperl of Medford, Jim (Cheryl) Sperl of Medford, Billy (Michelle) Sperl of Medford and Bobby (Gwen) Sperl of Abbotsford; two daughters, Nancy (Scott) Riegert of Dorchester and Sue (Tony) Rausch of Medford; 33 grandchildren; 20 great-grandchildren; one brother, Ken Sperl of Medford; and three sisters, Eleanor Sherfield of Medford, Margie (Gene) Halopka of Abbotsford and Donna (Ben) Seidel of Medford. (Star News, Medford, Wisconsin)

20. RUTH M⁴ ANDERSON (Elmer³, August Nikolaus², Andrew¹) was born on 26 May 1934 in Wisconsin, USA. She married Charles Peterson. They had fifteen children.

21. BETTY LOU⁴ ANDERSON (Elmer³, August Nikolaus², Andrew¹) was born on 21 Oct 1935 in Wisconsin, USA. She died on 26 Jan 1996 in Burbank, Cook Co., Illinois, USA. She married Robert G Bruton on 06 Jan 1956 in Cook Co., Illinois, USA. They had one child.

22. MARGARET ELLEN⁴ ANDERSON (Elmer³, August Nikolaus², Andrew¹) was born in 1938 in Wisconsin, USA. She married Frank Murphy about 1961. They had two children.

23. RUBY KATHERINE[4] DROLSHAGEN (Elva Marie[3] Anderson, August Nikolaus[2] Anderson, Andrew[1] Anderson) was born on 28 Oct 1934 in Little Black, Taylor Co., Wisconsin, USA. She married James C Neuman on 21 Apr 1955 in Medford, Taylor Co., Wisconsin, USA. He was born on 21 Apr 1924 in Greenwood, Clark Co., Wisconsin, USA. He died on 06 Feb 1999 in Medford, Taylor Co., Wisconsin, USA. James C. Neuman was buried in Little Black, Taylor Co., Wisconsin, USA; St. Mary's Cemetery. They had six children. Military Service of James C. Neuman : 19 Jul 1945 ; US Navy (WWII)

24. LEIGHTON E[4] "LEE" DROLSHAGEN (Elva Marie[3] Anderson, August Nikolaus[2] Anderson, Andrew[1] Anderson) was born on 09 May 1939 in Wisconsin, USA. He died on 01 Apr 2008 in Dorchester, Clark Co., Wisconsin, USA. He married Beverly Kramer on 31 Mar 1973 in Taylor Co., Wisconsin, USA. She was born in 1942. Leighton E. Drolshagen was buried on 04 Apr 2008 in Lublin, Taylor Co., Wisconsin, USA; St Mary's Polish National Catholic. They had two children.

> LEIGHTON DROLSHAGEN 1939-2008
>
> Leighton "Lee" E. Drolshagen, 68, Dorchester, died Tuesday, April 1, 2008 at his home, surrounded by his loving family and Ministry Home Care Hospice of Marshfield. Funeral services will be held Friday, April 4 at 11 a.m. at Hemer Funeral Home in Medford, with Father Dennis Meulemans officiating. Interment will be at St. Mary's Catholic Cemetery in the Town of Little Black. Honorary pallbearers will be Melvin Mohan, Walter and Carl Anderson Sr., Dan Kagel, Louie Koffler, Donna Geiger and Brian Drolshagen. Active pallbearers will be Joe Drolshagen, Mike and Jeff Neuman, Rick Zoellick, Rick Crook and Al Prestebak. Visitation will be held at the funeral home on Thursday, April 3 from 4 to 7 p.m., with a 7 p.m. prayer service, and on Friday from 9 a.m. until the time of the service.

25. JOHN AUGUST[4] DROLSHAGEN (Elva Marie[3] Anderson, August Nikolaus[2] Anderson, Andrew[1] Anderson) was born on 28 Nov 1943 in Medford, Taylor Co., Wisconsin, USA. He married Charlotte Ann Tiller on 22 Jun 1963 in Medford, Taylor Co., Wisconsin, USA. She was born on 07 Mar 1944 in Racine, Racine Co., Wisconsin, USA. They had four children.

26. WAYNE ARTHUR[4] ANDERSON (Florence Josephine[3] Anderson, August Nikolaus[2] Anderson, Andrew[1] Anderson) was born on 17 may 1938 in Medford, Taylor Co., Wisconsin. He married (1) Nora Lee Bear in 1957 in Omak, Okanogan Co., Washington, USA. She was born on 04 Apr 1940 in Omak, Okanogan Co., Washington, USA. She died on 10 Oct 1989 in Vancouver, Clark Co., Washington, USA (Age 49). He married (2) Carolyn Elizabeth Iverson in 1975 in Port Angeles, Clallam Co., Washington, USA. She was born on 10 Mar 1951 in Port Angeles, Clallam Co., Washington, USA. Wayne Arthur Anderson and Nora Lee Bear had two children:

27. KENNETH MELVIN[4] ANDERSON (Florence Josephine[3] Anderson, August Nikolaus[2] Anderson, Andrew[1] Anderson) was born 12 Nov 1941 in Medford, Taylor Co., Wisconsin, USA. He married (1) Janice Marie Rogers on 15 Mar 1961 in Okanogan Co., Washington, USA. She was born on 17 Aug 1944 in Omak, Okanogan Co., Washington, USA. He married (2) Jeanie Marie Hinderer. She was born on 27 May 1953 in Pullman, Whitman Co., Washington, USA. Kenneth Melvin Anderson and Janice Marie Rogers had three children:

28. ALLEN LEE[4] ANDERSON (Casper David[3], August Nikolaus[2], Andrew[1]) was born on 18 Feb 1947 in Medford, Taylor Co., Wisconsin, USA. He died on 20 Apr 2002 in Princeton, Mille Lacs Co., Minnesota, USA. He married Diane Marie Brissette, daughter of John Donald Brissette and Corrine Marie Coburn, on 21 Mar 1970 in Isanti Co., Minnesota, USA. She was born on 13 Aug 1947 in Hennepin Co., Minnesota, USA. They had 1 child.

29. LOIS ARLENE⁴ ANDERSON (Casper David³, August Nikolaus², Andrew¹) was born on 22 Aug 1948. She married (1) Kenneth John Kirchberg on 05 Jun 1971 in Isanti Co., Minnesota, USA. He was born on 09 Oct 1946 in Chisago Co., Minnesota, USA. She married (2) Lyle E Johnson on 12 Apr 1993 in Mille Lacs Co., Minnesota, USA. He was born in 1943. They had two children.

## DESCENDANTS OF CHRISTOPHER OLSON SR.

### Generation 1

1. CHRISTOPHER[1] OLSON SR. was born in Mar 1844 in Norway. He married Caroline Nelson. She was born in Jul 1845 in Norway. She died in 1921. Caroline Nelson is buried in Perkinstown, Taylor Co., Wisconsin, USA.

Christopher Olson Sr. and Caroline Nelson had the following children:

106: Caroline Nelson Olson
Perkinstown, Taylor Co., WI
(ruler used for scale)

2.  i.  CHRISTOPHER[2] "CHRIST" OLSON JR was born on 18 Oct 1876 in Oslo, Norway. He died on Aug 1960 in Creston, British Columbia, Canada. He married Carrie Kiea Josephine Peterson, daughter of Christian Conrad Peterson and Maren Andrea Halvorsdatter on 04 Oct 1897 in Holway, Taylor Co., Wisconsin, USA. She was born on 21 May 1876 in Chicago, Cook Co., Illinois, USA. She died on 08 Jun 1964 in Creston, British Columbia, Canada.

3.  ii.  MARY OLSON was born on 15 Sep 1880 in Christiana, Norway. She died on 14 Jun 1955 in Deer Creek, Taylor Co., Wisconsin, USA (Medford Hospital; Age 74). She married August Nikolaus Anderson, son of Andrew Anderson and Johanna Gunderson on 22 Sep 1897 in Medford, Taylor Co., Wisconsin, USA. He was born on 20 Mar 1875 in Green Bay, Brown Co., Wisconsin, USA. He died on 04 May 1945 in Medford, Taylor Co., Wisconsin, USA (Age 70).

4.  iii.  ANTON OLSON was born in Dec 1884 in Kongsvinger, Norway. He died 25 Apr 1979 in Saskatoon, Saskatchewan, Canada. He married (1) Gena Olive Halvorson. She died in 1918. He married (2) Bessie [Unknown]. Anton Olson is buried in Preeceville Cemetery, Preeceville, Saskatchewan, Canada.

5.  iv.  CASPER OLSON SR was born on 12 Mar 1887 in Little Black, Taylor Co., Wisconsin, USA. He died on 17 Feb 1975 in Medford, Taylor Co., Wisconsin, USA. He married Alma C. Nelson. She was born in 1900 in Wisconsin, USA. She died in 1958 in Taylor Co., Wisconsin, USA.

   v.  NELS OLSON was born in Norway. He died before 1955. He married Engeborg Reighen on Apr 1899 in Medford, Taylor Co., Wisconsin, USA. She was born in Norway.

   vi.  BOY OLSON. He died before 1955.

   vii.  GIRL OLSON. She died before 1955.

### Generation 2

2 CHRISTOPHER[2] "CHRIST" OLSON JR (Christopher1 Sr.) was born on 18 Oct 1876 in Oslo, Norway. He died on 10 Aug 1960 in Creston, British Columbia, Canada. He married Carrie Kiea Josephine Peterson, daughter of Christian Conrad Peterson and Maren Andrea Halvorsdatter, on 04 Oct 1897 in Holway, Taylor Co., Wisconsin, USA. She was born on 21 May 1876 in Chicago, Cook Co., Illinois, USA. She died on 08 Jun 1964 in Creston, British Columbia, Canada.

Christopher "Christ" Olson Jr. and Carrie Kiea Josephine Peterson had the following children:

i.    CHARLES MELVIN[3] OLSON was born on 27 Jan 1901 in Greenbush, Mille Lacs Co., Minnesota, USA. He died on 08 Aug 1989 in Vancouver, British Columbia, Canada. He married Agnes Elise Alvis on 20 Oct 1922 in Saskatchewan, Canada (Rama?).

ii.   ANNA CHRISTINE OLSON was born on 27 Apr 1902 in Medford, Taylor Co., Wisconsin, USA. She died on 01 Jan 1998 in Saskatchewan, Canada (Nipiwin?).

107: Chris and Carrie Olson (circa 1947)

iii.  EDWARD OLIVER OLSON was born on 29 Nov 1903 in Little Black, Taylor Co., Wisconsin, USA. He died on 10 Jun 1973 in Bremerton, Kitsap Co., Washington, USA (Age: 69). He married Vivian Pearl Mcavany on 20 Jun 1933 in Unity, Saskatchewan, Canada. She was born on 09 Feb 1914 in Clark Mills, Oneida Co., New York, USA. She died in Feb 1994.

iv.   ELSIE MARIE OLSON was born on 24 Jan 1906 in Medford, Taylor Co., Wisconsin, USA. She died on 21 Mar 1984 in Tacoma, Pierce Co., Washington, USA.

5.   v.    GILBERT THEODORE OLSON was born on 03 Sep 1908 in Medford, Taylor Co., Wisconsin, USA. He died on 26 Aug 1944 in Steilacoom, Pierce Co., Washington, USA (Fort Steilacoom); Age: 36). He married Leona A Miller on 24 Feb 1936 in Stevens Co., Washington, USA. She was born about 1919 in Washington, USA.

vi.   CARRIE MATHILDA OLSON was born on 04 Oct 1909 in Medford, Taylor Co., Wisconsin, USA. She died in Aug 1971 in Nanaimo, British Columbia, Canada.

vii.  NELS DANIEL OLSON was born on 07 Nov 1911 in Medford, Taylor Co., Wisconsin, USA. He died on 13 Jun 1955 in Cusick, Pend Oreille Co., Washington, USA. Nels Daniel Olson was buried in Ione, Pend Oreille Co., Washington, USA

viii. HELEN ELEANOR OLSON was born on 21 Aug 1913 in Buchanan, Saskatchewan, Canada. She died on 29 Aug 1995 in Tacoma, Pierce Co., Washington, USA.

ix.   EMMA A OLSON was born on 12 Nov 1914 in Saskatchewan, Canada. She died in 2007 in Alberta, Canada.

x.    ARTHUR DAVID OLSON was born on 28 Apr 1918 in Buchanan, Saskatchewan, Canada. He died on 21 Jul 1921 in Buchanan, Saskatchewan, Canada.

xi.   CLARENCE D. OLSON was born on 18 Jan 1922 in Newport, King Co., Washington, USA. He died on 17 Sep 2007 in Nanaimo, British Columbia, Canada.

3. MARY OLSON was born on 15 Sep 1880 in Christiana, Norway. She died on 14 Jun 1955 in Deer Creek, Taylor Co., Wisconsin, USA (Medford Hospital; Age 74). She married August Nikolaus Anderson, son of Andrew Anderson and Johanna Gunderson on 22 Sep 1897 in Medford, Taylor Co., Wisconsin, USA. He was born on 20 Mar 1875 in Green Bay, Brown Co., Wisconsin, USA. He died on 04 May 1945 in Medford, Taylor Co., Wisconsin, USA (Age 70). (See Descendants of Andrew Anderson)

4. ANTON[2] OLSON was born in Dec 1884 in Kongsvinger, Norway. He died 25 Apr 1979 in Saskatoon, Saskatchewan, Canada. He married (1) Gena Olive Halvorson. She died in 1918. He married (2) Bessie [Unknown]. Anton Olson is buried in Preeceville Cemetery, Preeceville, Saskatchewan, Canada.

108: Mary Olson (circa 1945)

Anton Olson had the following children (by which spouse unknown):

    i.    ARTHUR 3 OLSON.

    ii.    GILBERT OLSON

    iii.    BRUCE OLSON

5. CASPER[2] OLSON SR (Christopher1 Sr.) was born on 12 Mar 1887 in Little Black, Taylor Co., Wisconsin, USA. He died on 17 Feb 1975 in Medford, Taylor Co., Wisconsin, USA. He married Alma C. Nelson, daughter of Thomas Nelson and Catherine [Unknown]. She was born in 1900 in Wisconsin, USA. She died in 1958 in Taylor Co., Wisconsin, USA. Casper Olson Sr. was buried in Perkinstown, Taylor Co., Wisconsin, USA; Perkinstown Cemetery. Alma C. Nelson was buried in Perkinstown, Taylor Co., Wisconsin, USA; Perkinstown Cemetery.

109: Casper Olson Sr.
(circa unknown)

Casper Olson Sir and Alma C. Nelson had the following children:

    i.    ALVIN LESTER[3] OLSON was born on 05 Mar 1927 in Wisconsin, USA. He died on 08 Mar 2011 in Arlington, Tarrant Co., Texas, USA (Age 84). He married (1) Delois C. [Unknown] about 1951 (Married 44 yrs.). She was born on 04 Jan 1928 in Texas, USA (Probably). She died on 08 Jun 1995 in Arlington, Tarrant Co., Texas, USA. He married (2) Vivian P Nichols on 30 Aug 1997 in Tarrant Co, Texas, USA. She was born on 23 May 1939. Alvin Lester Olson was buried 10 Mar 2011 in Arlington, Tarrant Co., Texas, USA; Moore Memorial Gardens Cemetery

ALVIN LESTER OLSON (1927 - 2011)

    Alvin L. Olson, 84, passed away Tuesday, March 8, 2011. Funeral: 3:30 p.m. Thursday in Moore Funeral Home Chapel. Interment will follow in Moore Memorial Gardens. Visitation: 6 to 8 p.m. Wednesday at Moore Funeral Home.
    Alvin was preceded in death by previous spouse of 44 years, Delois Olson of Arlington; his parents, Casper Olson and Alma Nelson; brother, Casper Olson Jr.; sisters, Katherine Singleton and Doris Faude, all of Medford, Wis.; sons, Lawrence Brown and J. Anthony Brown; and daughter, Kathy Fogle, all of Arlington.
    Survivors: His wife, Vivian Ann Olson; daughter, Vivian D. Klemstein; stepchildren, John Parker and Terry Dyer; brothers, Gene Olson and his wife, Judy, and Edwin Olson of Medford, Wis.; six grandchildren; 16 great-grandchildren; and one great-great-grandchild. (Star-Telegram on March 9, 2011)

    ii.    KATHERINE CAROLINE OLSON was born on 15 Oct 1928 in Wisconsin, USA. She died on 16 Mar 1975 in Medford, Taylor Co., Wisconsin, USA. She married Basil Orlando Singleton on 01 May 1948 in Medford, Taylor Co., Wisconsin, USA. He was born on 01 Jan 1907 in Hanover, Jackson Co., Michigan, USA. He died on 01 Jan 1975 in Maplehurst, Taylor Co., Wisconsin, USA.

iii.   DORIS OLSON was born in 1931 in Wisconsin, USA. She died before Mar 2011. She married [Unknown] Faude.

iv.   EDWIN OLSON was born in 1934 in Wisconsin, USA. He died after 2011.

v.   CASPER OLSON JR. was born on 08 Jan 1936 in Wisconsin, USA. He died on 09 Jan 2004 in Withee, Clark Co., Wisconsin, USA. He married Shirley [Unknown].She was born in 1942. Casper Olson Jr. was buried in  Perkinstown, Taylor Co., Wisconsin, USA; Perkinstown Cemetery.

vi.   EUGENE D OLSON was born on 09 Aug 1938, Wisconsin, USA. He died after 2011. He married Judy [Unknown] about 1960.

110: Casper and Alma Grimm Perkinstown, Taylor Co., WI

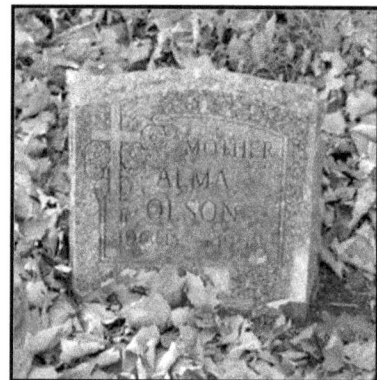

**6.**   GILBERT THEODORE[3]  OLSON (Christoper2 "Christ" Jr., Christopher1 Sr.) was born on 03 Sep 1908 in Medford, Taylor Co., Wisconsin, USA. He died on 26 Aug 1944 in Steilacoom, Pierce Co., Washington, USA (Fort Steilacoom); Age 36. He married Leona A. Miller on 24 Feb 1936 in Stevens Co., Washington, USA. She was born about 1919 in Washington, USA.

**7.**   KATHERINE CAROLINE[3] OLSON (Casper[2] Sr., Christopher[1] Sr.) was born on 15 Oct 1928 in Wisconsin, USA. She died on 16 Mar 1975 in Medford, Taylor Co., Wisconsin, USA. She married Basil Orlando Singleton on 01 May 1948 in Medford, Taylor Co., Wisconsin, USA. He was born on 01 Jan 1907 in Hanover, Jackson Co., Michigan, USA. He died on 01 Jan 1975 in Maplehurst, Taylor Co., Wisconsin, USA. Katherine Caroline Olson was buried in Perkinstown, Taylor Co., Wisconsin, USA; Perkinstown Cemetery. Basil Orlando Singleton was buried in Perkinstown, Taylor Co., Wisconsin, USA; Perkinstown Cemetery.

Basil Orlando Singleton WWII Military Service: 13 Oct 1942 in Milwaukee, Milwaukee Co., Wisconsin, USA; US Army; Served in Pacific SW

Basil Orlando Singleton and Katherine Caroline Olson had the following children:

i.   SHARON[4] SINGLETON.

ii.   CHILD SINGLETON. Died before 1975.

iii.   CHILD SINGLETON. Died before 1975.

B. SINGLETON DIES; RITES HELD SATURDAY

Funeral services were held Saturday afternoon at Hemer Funeral Home, Medford, for Basil O. Singleton, 67, who died New Year's Day after suffering an apparent heart attack at his home in the town of Maplehurst. Mr. Singleton, who was declared dead on arrival at Memorial hospital shortly after noon, had been in ill health for some time.

Rev. Warren Behling, St. Paul's Lutheran Church, Medford, officiated at services and burial with full military rites took place in Perkinstown community Cemetery. The body lay in state at the funeral home Friday afternoon and evening.

Serving as pallbearers were Ernest Westrich, Edwin Petz, Lowell Clarke, Henry Mayer, Kenneth Emmerich and Ed Smith.

Basil Orland Singleton was born January 3, 1907 in Hanover County, Michigan. His marriage to the former Katherine Olson who survives took place at Medford May 1, 1948. The couple lived at Eli, Minn., for 16 years and moved to Taylor County in 1968. He served in the army during World War II, spending several years in the southwest Pacific theater of operations. He was a woodsman and farmer and also was engaged in the blacksmith trade. Ill health forced his retirement six years ago. He was a member of Klossner-Dietzler Veterans of Foreign Wars post, Medford.

In addition to his wife, Mr. Singleton is survived by a daughter, Sharon Singleton, Owen; one grandchild; three sisters, Mrs. Bessie Westrich and Mrs. Daisy Moyer of Medford and Ruth, Mrs. Clarence Thompson, Stetsonville, and a brother, Richard, Isabelle, Minn. He was preceded in death by two children, a sister and six brothers. (The Star News, Medford, WI; Jan 1975)

8. GILBERT THEODORE[3] OLSON (Christoper[2] "Christ" Jr., Christopher[1] Sr.) was born on 03 Sep 1908 in Medford, Taylor Co., Wisconsin, USA. He died on 26 Aug 1944 in Steilacoom, Pierce Co., Washington, USA (Fort Steilacoom); Age 36. He married Leona A. Miller on 24 Feb 1936 in Stevens Co., Washington, USA. She was born about 1919 in Washington, USA.

Gilbert Theodore Olson and Leona A Miller had the following children:

i. JACKIE B[4] OLSON was born about 1937 in Washington, USA.

ii. DELORIS RUTH OLSON was born about 1939 in Washington, USA.

# BIBLIOGRAPHY

**Title:** **Census Records (State)**

Citation: 1855 Wisconsin State Census Record for Heinrich Ludwig Grimm (Provo, UT, USA, Ancestry.com Operations Inc), www.ancestry.com, 1855 State Census Record; Wisconsin, Compiled Census and Census Substitutes Index, 1820-1890; Jackson, Ron V., Accelerated Indexing Systems, comp., Wisconsin Census, 1820-1890. [Database online].

Citation: 1857-1892 WA State Census for L Penrose (Provo, UT, USA, Ancestry.com Operations Inc, 2012), www.ancestry.com, Washington State and Territorial Censuses, 1857-1892; [Database online]. Washington, Washington Territorial Census Rolls, 1857-1892, Olympia, Washington: Washington State Archives.

Citation: 1905 WI State Census Albert Grimm Sr. (Provo, UT, USA, Ancestry.com Operations Inc), 2007. www.ancestry.com, Wisconsin, State Censuses, 1895 and 1905 [Database online].

Citation: 1905 WI State Census for Alma Nelson (Provo, UT, USA, Ancestry.com Operations Inc), 2007. www.ancestry.com, Wisconsin, State Censuses, 1895 and 1905 [Database online].

Citation: 1905 WI State Census for August N Anderson (Provo, UT, USA, Ancestry.com Operations Inc, 2007). www.ancestry.com, Wisconsin, State Censuses, 1895 and 1905 [Database online].

Citation: 1905 WI State Census for August N Anderson (Provo, UT, USA, Ancestry.com Operations Inc, 2007), www.ancestry.com, Wisconsin, State Censuses, 1895 and 1905 [Database online[,

Citation: 1905 WI State Census for Lydia (Grimm) Schubert (Provo, UT, USA, Ancestry.com Operations Inc, 2007), www.ancestry.com, Wisconsin, State Censuses, 1895 and 1905 [Database online]. 1st Ward (Hammel); Pg. 4, line 34-36, Family 65

Citation: Washington State Census for Caroline T (Grimm) Pederson (Provo, UT, USA, Ancestry.com Operations Inc, 2006), www.ancestry.com, Washington State and Territorial Censuses, 1857-1892.

**Title:** **Census Records (United States Federal Census) 1870**

Citation: 1870 United States Federal Census Record for John and Barbara Schellman. (Provo, UT, USA, Ancestry.com Operations Inc, 2009), www.ancestry.com, [Database online].Year: 1870; Hancock, Houghton Co, Michigan; Roll: M593_674; Pg: 672; Image 185; FHL: 552173; 1870 U.S. census, population schedules. NARA #M593; Washington, D.C.; National Archives and Records Administration.

Citation: 1870 United States Federal Census Record for Augusta Emma Fischer (Provo, UT, USA, Ancestry.com Operations Inc, 2009), www.ancestry.com, [Database online].Year: 1870; Mosel, Sheboygan Co, Wisconsin; M593; Page: 158A; Image 319; FHL #553239.

Citation: 1870 United States Federal Census Record for Wilhelmina Schalk. (Provo, UT, USA, Ancestry.com Operations Inc, 2009), www.ancestry.com [Database online].Year: 1870; Mosel, Sheboygan Co, Wisconsin; Page: 169A; Image 341; FHL 5532239. Pg 24; Line 19-22

Citation: 1880 US Federal Census for Andrew Anderson (Provo, UT, USA, Ancestry.com Operations Inc, 2010), www.ancestry.com, [Database online]. Year: 1880. Little Black, Taylor Co, Wisconsin; Roll 1448; FHL #1255448; Pg 381A, ED 189.

Citation: 1880 US Federal Census for Franziscus "Frank" G Grimm (Provo, UT, USA, Ancestry.com Operations Inc), www.ancestry.com, [Database online].Westbury, Buchanan Co, Iowa; Roll 329; FHF #1254329; Image 606A; ED 97; Pg. 9A; Line 13-19; Dwelling 82; Family 82.

Citation: 1880 US Federal Census for Henry Ludwig Grimm (Provo, UT, USA, Ancestry.com Operations Inc), www.ancestry.com, [Database online].Year: 1880; Westbury, Buchanan Co, Iowa; Roll: 329; FHL #1254329; Image 513; Pg 606A; ED 097; Line 6-12; Dwelling #81; Family #81;

Citation: 1880 US Federal Census for John Schellman (Provo, UT, USA, Ancestry.com Operations Inc, 2010), www.ancestry.com, Year: 1880; Hancock, Houghton Co, Michigan; T623 FHL #124581; Image 0475; ED 14; Pg. 399B

Citation: 1900 US Federal Census for Albert Grimm (Provo, UT, USA, Ancestry.com Operations Inc), www.ancestry.com, [Database online].Year: 1900; Medford, Taylor Co.,Wisconsin; T623; Page: 6B; ED: 0181; FHL #: 1241819.

Citation: 1900 US Federal Census for Albert Grimm (Provo, UT, USA, Ancestry.com Operations, Inc.), www.ancestry.com. [Database online].Year: 1900; Medford, Taylor Co, Wisconsin; T623; Page: 6B; ED: 0181; FHL #: 1241819.

Citation: 1900 US Federal Census for Albert I Anderson (Provo, UT, USA, Ancestry.com Operations Inc, 2012), www.ancestry.com, [Database online].Year: 1900; Grover, Taylor Co, Wisconsin; T623, Page: 1B; ED: 0178; FHL #1241819.

Citation: 1900 US Federal Census for Andrew Anderson (Provo, UT, USA, Ancestry.com Operations Inc), www.ancestry.com, [Database online].Year: 1900; Medford, Taylor Co, Wisconsin; T623. FHL# 1241819; ED: 181; Page: 9A.

Citation: 1900 US Federal Census for Anna (Grimm) Bacon (Provo, UT, USA, Ancestry.com Operations Inc), www.ancestry.com, [Database online].Year: 1900; Portland Ward 10, Multnomah Co, Oregon. T623, Pg: 8B; ED: 0081; FHL #:1241351.

Citation: 1900 US Federal Census for Anna (Grimm) Schmelzer (Provo, UT, USA, Ancestry.com Operations Inc), www.ancestry.com, [Database online].1900; Mount Angel, Marion Co, Oregon; . FHL #1241349; ED: 0137; Pg: 13B.

Citation: 1900 US Federal Census for Anna Steiner (Provo, UT, USA, Ancestry.com Operations Inc), www.ancestry.com, [Database online].Year: 1900; Chelsea, Taylor Co, Wisconsin; T623; Page: 6B; ED: 0177; FHL #1241819.

Citation: 1900 US Federal Census for August N Anderson (Provo, UT, USA, Ancestry.com Operations Inc, 2000), www.ancestry.com, [Database online].Year: 1900; Little Black, Taylor Co, Wisconsin. T623; Page: 10B; ED: 0179; FHL #1241819:

Citation: 1900 US Federal Census for August Steiner (Provo, UT, Ancestry.com, 2012), www.ancestry.com, [Database online].Year: 1900; Chelsea, Taylor Co, Wisconsin; Roll: T623; FHL #1241819; ED: 0177; Pg. 7A

Citation: 1900 US Federal Census for Barbara O Klasner (Provo, UT, USA, Ancestry.com Operations Inc, 2004), www.ancestry.com, [Database online]. Year: 1900; Hancock, Houghton Co, MI; FHL #: 1240714; ED: 0183; Page: 9A.

Citation: 1900 US Federal Census for Bernhart Grimm (Provo, UT, USA, Ancestry.com Operations Inc), www.ancestry.com, [Database online].Year: 1900; Mount Angel, Marion Co, Oregon; Roll: T623; Page: 16A; ED: 0137; FHL #: 1241349.

Citation: 1900 US Federal Census for Caroline (Grimm) Penrose (Provo, UT, USA, Ancestry.com Operations Inc), www.ancestry.com, [Database online].Year: 1900; Spring Valley, Polk Co, O; T623; FHL #1241351; ED: 0172; Pg: 4A.

Citation: 1900 US Federal Census for Caroline (Schellman) Wambsganss (Provo, UT, USA, Ancestry.com Operations Inc, 2004), www.ancestry.com, 1900 US Federal Census; [Database online].Year: 1900; Wayne, Allen Co, Indiana; Roll: 359; FHL #1240359; ED: 37; Page: 16A;

Citation: 1900 US Federal Census for Christopher Olson (Provo, UT, USA, Ancestry.com Operations Inc, 2004), www.ancestry.com, [Database online].Year: 1900; Little Black, Taylor Co, Wisconsin; Roll: T623; FHL #1241819. ED: 179; Page: 11A.

Citation: 1900 US Federal Census for Frank A Grimm (Provo, UT, USA, Ancestry.com Operations Inc), www.ancestry.com, [Database online].Year: 1900 Mount Angel, Marion Co, Oregon; Roll: T623. FHL #: 1241349; ED 137; Page: 20A.

Citation: 1900 US Federal Census for Frank Grimm (Provo, UT, USA, Ancestry.com Operations Inc), www.ancestry.com, [Database online].Year: 1900 Monitor, Marion Co, Oregon; Roll: T623. FHL #: 1241349; ED: 137; Pg: 7A.

Citation: 1900 US Federal Census for Frederick T Grimm (Provo, UT, USA, Ancestry.com Operations Inc), www.ancestry.com, [Database online].Year: 1900 Maple Grove, Manitowoc Co, Wisconsin; T623. FHL #1241797; ED 80; Pg. 5A

Citation: 1900 US Federal Census for Hannah Schellman (Provo, UT, USA, Ancestry.com Operations Inc, 2004), www.ancestry.com, US Federal Census; [Database online]. Year: 1900; Schoolcraft, Houghton Co, Michigan; Roll: 715; FHL #1240715; ED: 0196; Pg 17B.

Citation: 1900 US Federal Census for Louis Grimm (Provo, UT, USA, Ancestry.com Operations Inc), www.ancestry.com, [Database online].Year: 1900 Portland Ward 10, Multnomah Co, Oregon. T623. FHL #1241351; ED: 81; Pg: 8B.

Citation: 1900 US Federal Census for Louisa (Rouder) Steiner (Provo, UT, USA, Ancestry.com Operations Inc), www.ancestry.com, Year: 1900 Chelsea, Taylor Co, Wisconsin; Roll: 1819; FHL #1241819; ED: 177; Page: 6B.

**Title:** **Census Records (United States Federal Census) 1910**

Citation: 1910 US Federal Census for Albert Grimm (Provo, UT, USA, Ancestry.com Operations Inc, 2006), www.ancestry.com, [Database online].Year: 1910 Chelsea, Taylor Co, Wisconsin; T624. FHL #1375750; ED: 167; Pg: 3B.

Citation: 1910 US Federal Census for Albert Grimm Sr. (Provo, UT, USA, Ancestry.com Operations Inc 2006), www.ancestry.com, [Database online].Year: 1910 Medford, Taylor Co, WI; T624. FHL: #1375750. ED: 174; Pg. 1A.

Citation: 1910 US Federal Census for Andrew Anderson (Provo, UT, USA, Ancestry.com Operations Inc 2006), www.ancestry.com, Year: 1910 Little Black, Taylor Co, Wisconsin; T624; FHL #: 1375750; ED: 171; Page 7A

Citation: 1910 US Federal Census for Anna (Grimm) Bacon (Provo, UT, USA, Ancestry.com Operations Inc, 2006), www.ancestry.com, [Database online].Year: 1910 Acequia, Lincoln Co, ID; T624; FHL #1374239; ED: 0298; Pg:12A

Citation: 1910 US Federal Census for Anna (Grimm) Schmelzer (Provo, UT, USA, Ancestry.com Operations Inc 2006), www.ancestry.com, [Database online].Year: 1910 Anaheim, Orange Co, CA; T624; FHL #1374103; ED: 0043; Pg: 12B

Citation: 1910 US Federal Census for August N Anderson (Provo, UT, USA, Ancestry.com Operations Inc, 2006), www.ancestry.com, [Database online].Year: 1910 Little Black, Taylor Co, WI. T624. FHL #1375750; ED: 0171; Pg: 7A

Citation: 1910 US Federal Census for Barbara Schellman (Provo, UT, USA, Ancestry.com Operations Inc), www.ancestry.com, Year: 1910 Hancock Ward 3, Houghton Co, Michigan; T624. FHL #1375295. Page: 10A; ED: 0119.

Citation: 1910 US Federal Census for Caroline (Grimm) Penrose (Provo, UT, USA, Ancestry.com Operations Inc), www.ancestry.com, [Database online].Year: 1910 Silver, Lake Co, Oregon; T624. FHL #1375295; ED: 138; Pg. 6B.

Citation: 1910 US Federal Census for Caroline (Schellman) Wambsganss (Provo, UT, USA, Ancestry.com Operations Inc, 2006), www.ancestry.com, Year: 1910 Fort Wayne Ward 6, Allen Co, Indiana; T624. Page: 5A; ED: 0048; FHL #: 1374352.

Citation: 1910 US Federal Census for Christopher Olson (Provo, UT, USA, Ancestry.com Operations Inc ), www.ancestry.com, [Database online].Year: 1910 Little Black, Taylor Co, Wisconsin; T624; FHL #1375750; ED: 171; Pg. 7A.

Citation: 1910 US Federal Census for Elizabeth (Wambsganss) Weber (Provo, UT, USA, Ancestry.com Operations Inc, 2006), www.ancestry.com, [database on-line].2006. Year: 1910 New Orleans, Orleans Co, Louisiana; ED: 236; Pg 3A.

Citation: 1910 US Federal Census for Frederick P.E. Wambsganss (Provo, UT, USA, Ancestry.com Operations Inc, 2006), www.ancestry.com, [Database online]. Year 1910 New Orleans Ward 15, Orleans Co, Louisiana; T624. ED: 234; Precinct 5; House: #438, Dwelling: 344; Family 347; Lines 37-39.

Citation: 1910 US Federal Census for Frederick T Grimm (Provo, UT, USA, Ancestry.com Operations Inc), www.ancestry.com, [Database online].Year: 1910 Maple Grove, Manitowoc Co, Wisconsin. T624. FHL #1375731; ED: 32; Pg: 5B.

Citation: 1910 US Federal Census for Hannah (Schellman) Kettenbeil (Provo, UT, USA, Ancestry.com Operations Inc, 2006), www.ancestry.com, Year: 1910; Schoolcraft, Houghton Co, Michigan; T624. FHL #1374660; ED: 128: Pg:13A

Citation: 1910 US Federal Census for Henry Klasner (Provo, UT, USA, Ancestry.com Operations Inc, 2006), www.ancestry.com, Year: 1910 Hampton, Keweenaw Co, Michigan; Roll: T624. FHL #1374239; ED: 152; Pg.3B.

Citation: 1910 US Federal Census for Henry W Grimm (Provo, UT, USA, Ancestry.com Operations Inc), www.ancestry.com, [Database online].Year: 1910 Heyburn, Lincoln Co, Idaho; T624. FHL #1374239; ED: 208; Pg: 18A.

Citation: 1910 US Federal Census for Hueston Rosebrook (Provo, UT, USA, Ancestry.com Operations Inc), www.ancestry.com, [Database online].Year: 1910 Portland Ward 9, Multnomah Co, Oregon. T624. FHL #1375302. ED: 218: Page: 9A.

Citation: 1910 US Federal Census for John S Schellman (Provo, UT, USA, Ancestry.com Operations Inc, 2006), www.ancestry.com, Year: 1910 Hancock Ward 3, Houghton Co, Michigan. T624. FHL #1374659; ED: 119; Pg. 10A.

Citation: 1910 US Federal Census for John Steiner (Provo, UT, USA, Ancestry.com Operations Inc), www.ancestry.com, ED: 174; p.15B, Dwelling 293, Family 297

Citation: 1910 US Federal for Lillian Ann (Penrose) Nelson. (Provo, UT, USA, Ancestry.com Operations Inc), www.ancestry.com, Year: 1910; Census Place: Willamette, Yamhill, Oregon; Roll: T624_1291; Page: 4B; ED: 0300; FHL microfilm: 1375304.

Citation: 1910 US Federal Census for Louisa (Rouder) Blankenburg (Provo, UT, USA, Ancestry.com Operations Inc), www.ancestry.com, [Database online].Year: 1910 Little Black, Taylor Co, Wisconsin. FHL #1375750; ED: 171; Pg 7A.

Citation: 1910 US Federal Census for Lydia (Grimm) Schubert (Provo, UT, Ancestry.com Operations Inc), www.ancestry.com, [Database online].Year: 1910 Lambert, Red Lake Co, Minnesota; T624. FHL #1374703; ED: 235; Pg. 3B.

Citation: 1910 US Federal Census for Lydia (Schellman) Terp (Provo, UT, USA, Ancestry.com Operations Inc, 2006), www.ancestry.com, Year: 1910 Green Bay Ward 7, Brown Co, Wisconsin; T624. FHL #1375750; ED: 20; Page: 6B.

Citation: 1910 US Federal Census for Pauline (Schellman) Vollmer (Provo, UT, USA, Ancestry.com Operations Inc, 2006), www.ancestry.com, [database on-line]. 2006. Year: 1910. Hancock Ward 3, Houghton Co, Michigan; T624. FHL #: 1374659. ED: 119; .Pg: 8A.

Citation: 1910 US Federal Census for Rose (Grimm) Schubert (Provo, UT, USA, Ancestry.com Operations Inc), www.ancestry.com, [Database online]. 2006. Year: 1910 Browning, Taylor Co, Wisconsin; T624. FHL #1375750; ED: 166; Page: 5A.

Citation: 1910 US Federal Census for Theodore Olson (Provo, UT, USA, Ancestry.com Operations Inc), www.ancestry.com, [Database online]. 2006. Year: 1910 Little Black, Taylor Co, Wisconsin; T624. FHL #: 1375750; ED: 171; Page: 7A.

**Title:** **Census Records (United States Federal Census) 1920**

Citation: 1920 Federal Census for John Schellman (Provo, UT, USA, Ancestry.com Operations Inc), www.ancestry.com, [Database online]. Year: 1920 Hancock Ward 3, Houghton Co, Michigan

Citation: 1920 US Federal Census for Adolph H Grimm (Provo, UT, USA, Ancestry.com Operations Inc, 2010), www.ancestry.com, Year: 1920 Maple Grove, Manitowoc Co, Wisconsin; T625. Image 750; ED: 113; Pg. 7B.

Citation: 1920 US Federal Census for Albert Grimm (Provo, UT, USA, Ancestry.com Operations Inc), www.ancestry.com, [Database online].Year: 1920 Chelsea, Taylor Co, Wisconsin; T625. Image: 69. ED: 203; Pg. 6B.

Citation: 1920 US Federal Census for Albert Grimm Sr. (Provo, UT, Ancestry.com Operations Inc, 2012), www.ancestry.com, [Database online].Year: 1920 Lambert, Red Lake Co, Minnesota; T625. Image: 1106; ED 230; Pg. 8A.

Citation: 1920 US Federal Census for Anna (Grimm) Bacon (Provo, UT, USA, Ancestry.com Operations Inc), www.ancestry.com, [Database online].Year: 1920 Paul, Minidoka Co, Idaho; T625. Image: 754; ED: 204; Pg. 7A

Citation: 1920 US Federal Census for Anna M (Grimm) Schmeltzer (Provo, UT, USA, Ancestry.com Operations Inc 2010) www.ancestry.com, [Database online].Year: 1920 Oakdale, Stanislaus Co, Calif; T625. Image 1166; ED: 179; Pg: 8B.

Citation: 1920 US Federal Census for August N Anderson (Provo, UT, USA, Ancestry.com Operations Inc, 2010), www.ancestry.com, [Database online].Year: 1920 Little Black, Taylor Co, Wisconsin. T625 Img: 187; ED: 209; Pg.1A

Citation: 1920 US Federal Census for Barbara (Schellman) Klasner (Provo, UT, USA, Ancestry.com Operations Inc, 2010), www.ancestry.com, [database on-line]. Year: 1920 Hancock Ward 3, Houghton Co, Michigan; T625. "Klossner". Page 68; House: 811; Dwelling: 88: Family: 120.

Citation: 1920 US Federal Census for Caroline (Grimm) Penrose (Provo, UT, USA, Ancestry.com Operations Inc 2010), www.ancestry.com, [Database online].Year: 1920 Bend, Deschutes Co, Oregon; T625. Image: 424; ED: 35; Pg. 4B

Citation: 1920 US Federal Census for Caroline (Schellman) Wambsganss (Provo, UT, USA, Ancestry.com Operations Inc, 2010), www.ancestry.com, [Database online].Year: 1920; Fort Wayne Ward 6; Allen Co, Indiana. T625. ED: 58; Page: 16B; Dwelling: 382; Family: 394; Lines: 62-64.

Citation: 1920 US Federal Census for Carrie M Olson (Provo, UT, USA, Ancestry.com Operations Inc 2010), www.ancestry.com, [Database online].Year: 1920 West Ione, Pend Oreille Co, Washington. T625. Image: 632; ED: 109; Pg: 5B.

Citation: 1920 US Federal Census for Charles H L Strebig (Provo, UT, Ancestry.com Operations Inc, 2012), www.ancestry.com, Year: 1920 Hammel, Taylor Co, Wisconsin; T625. Image 147; ED: 207; Pg. 1A.

Citation: 1920 US Federal Census for Charles Henry Doriot (Provo, UT, USA, Ancestry.com Operations Inc), www.ancestry.com, Year: 1920 Flambeau, Vilas Co, Wisconsin. T625.

Citation: 1920 US Federal Census for Christopher Olson Jr. (Provo, UT, USA, Ancestry.com Operations Inc), www.ancestry.com, [Database online]. 1920 West Ione, Pend Oreille Co, WA. T625. Img: 632. ED: 109; Pg: 5B.

Citation: 1920 US Federal Census for Edward Grimm (Provo, UT, USA, Ancestry.com Operations Inc), www.ancestry.com, [Database online].Year: 1920 Heyburn, Minidoka Co, Idaho; T625. Image: 738; ED: 203; Pg. 17A.

Citation: 1920 US Federal Census for Elizabeth (Wambsganss) Weber (Provo, UT, USA, Ancestry.com Operations Inc, 2010), www.ancestry.com, [database on-line]. Year: 1920 Marshall, Harrison Co, Texas; ED: 57; Pg: 19B.

Citation: 1920 US Federal Census for Frank A Grimm (Provo, UT, USA, Ancestry.com Operations Inc), www.ancestry.com, Year: 1920 Paul, Minidoka Co, Idaho; Roll: T625. Image: 762; ED: 204; Pg: 11A.

Citation: 1920 US Federal Census for Frederick P.E, Wambsganss (Provo, UT, USA, Ancestry.com Operations Inc, 2010), www.ancestry.com, [Database online].Year: 1920 Fort Wayne Ward 6, Allen Co., Indiana. T625. ED: 58; Page: 16B; Dwelling: 382: Family: 394; Lines: 62-64.

Citation: 1920 US Federal Census for Frederick T Grimm (Provo, UT, USA, Ancestry.com Operations Inc), www.ancestry.com, [Database online].Year: 1920 Maple Grove, Manitowoc Co, Wisconsin. T625. Image: 746; ED: 113; Pg. 5B.

Citation: 1920 US Federal Census for Gustav Grimm (Provo, UT, USA, Ancestry.com Operations Inc), www.ancestry.com, [Database online].Year: 1920 Lessor, Polk Co, Minnesota; T625. Image: 614; ED: 182; Pg. 1A.

Citation: 1920 US Federal Census for Henry Grimm (Provo, UT, USA, Ancestry.com Operations Inc), www.ancestry.com, [Database online].Year: 1920 Paul, Minidoka Co, Idaho; T625. Image: 774; ED: 204: Pg: 17A.

Citation: 1920 US Federal Census for Ida (Bruns) Grimm (Provo, UT, USA, Ancestry.com Operations Inc), www.ancestry.com, [Database online].Year: 1920 Paul, Minidoka Co, Idaho; T625. ED: 204; Pg. 5B.

Citation: 1920 US Federal Census for J Maynard Doriot (Provo, UT, USA, Ancestry.com Operations Inc), www.ancestry.com, [Database online].Year: 1920 Flambeau, Vilas Co, Wisconsin; T625. Image: 488; ED: 224; Pg.13A.

Citation: 1920 US Federal Census for John Lorenz (Provo, UT, USA, Ancestry.com Operations Inc, 2006), www.ancestry.com, [Database online].Year: 1920 Medford, Taylor Co, Wisconsin; T625. Image: 327; ED: 215; Pg. 4A.

Citation: 1920 US Federal Census for Lydia (Schellman) Terp (Provo, UT, USA, Ancestry.com Operations Inc 2010), www.ancestry.com, Year: 1920. Green Bay Ward 7, Precinct 1, Brown Co, Wisconsin. "Terf". T625. Image: 958; ED: 32; Page 5A; House: #2322 Broadway; Dwelling: 12; Family: 12; Lines 47-53.

Citation: 1920 US Federal Census for Monroe Grimm (Provo, UT, USA, Ancestry.com Operations Inc 2010), www.ancestry.com, [Database online].Year: 1920 Paul, Minidoka Co, Idaho; T625. Image: 774; ED: 204; Pg: 17A.

Citation: 1920 US Federal Census for Orville Grimm (Provo, UT, USA, Ancestry.com Operations Inc), www.ancestry.com, [Database online].Year: 1920 Lambert, Red Lake Co, Minnesota; T625. Image: 1106; ED: 230; Pg. 8A.

Citation: 1920 US Federal Census for Pauline (Schellman) Vollmer (Provo, UT, USA, Ancestry.com Operations Inc, 2010), www.ancestry.com, [Database on-line]. Year: 1920 Hancock Ward 3, Houghton Co, Michigan; T625. ED: 149; Pg 5A

Citation: 1920 US Federal Census for Walter Herman Kettenbeil (Provo, UT, USA, Ancestry.com Operations Inc, 2010), www.ancestry.com, [database on-line]. Year: 1920; Schoolcraft, Houghton Co, Michigan. T625; Image: 911; ED: 169; Pg. 10B.

**Title:** **Census Records (United States Federal Census) 1930**

Citation: 1930 US Federal Census for Adolph Grimm (Provo, UT, USA, Ancestry.com Operations Inc 2002), www.ancestry.com, [Database online].Year: 1930 Maple Grove, Manitowoc Co, Wisconsin. Roll: 2581; FHL #: 2342315; Image: 134; ED: 28; Pg. 6A.

Citation: 1930 US Federal Census for Albert Grimm (Provo, UT, USA, Ancestry.com Operations Inc 2002), www.ancestry.com, [Database online].Year: 1930 Chelsea, Taylor Co, Wisconsin; Roll: 2614. FHL #: 2342348; Image: 33; ED: 3; Pg: 3B.

Citation: 1930 US Federal Census for Albert Grimm Sr. (Provo, UT, Ancestry.com Operations Inc., 2002), www.ancestry.com, [Database online].Year: 1930 Lambert, Red Lake Co, Minn; Roll: 1113. FHL #: 2340848; Image: 934: ED: 7; Pg. 4B.

Citation: 1930 US Federal Census for Alvin E Grimm (Provo, UT, USA, Ancestry.com Operations Inc, 2002), www.ancestry.com, Year: 1930 Los Angeles, Los Angeles, Calif; Roll: 165; FHL #: 2339900; Img: 73; ED: 761; Pg 1A

Citation: 1930 US Federal Census for Anna (Grimm) Bacon McKee (Provo, UT, USA, Ancestry.com Operations Inc 2002), www.ancestry.com,[Database online]. Portland, Multnomah Co, Oregon. ED: 547; Pg. 2A; Line 87-91; Dwelling 101; Family 102.

Citation: 1930 US Federal Census for Anna (Grimm) Schmelzer (Provo, UT, USA, Ancestry.com Operations Inc 2002), www.ancestry.com, [Database online].Year: 1930 Santa Rosa, Sonoma Co, California; FHL #: 2339957; Image: 873; ED: 56; Pg. 2B.

Citation: 1930 US Federal Census for Arlene R Nuemueller (Provo, UT, USA, Ancestry.com Operations Inc, 2002), www.ancestry.com, [Database online].Year: 1930 Chelsea, Taylor Co, Wisconsin; Roll: 2614; FHL #: 2342348: Image: 38; ED: 3; Pg. 6A.

Citation: 1930 US Federal Census for August N Anderson (Provo, UT, USA, Ancestry.com Operations Inc, 2002), www.ancestry.com, [Database online].Year: 1930 Little Black, Taylor Co, Wisconsin; Roll: 2614; FHL #2342348; Image: 165: ED: 14; Pg. 3A.

Citation: 1930 US Federal Census for Barbara Klasner (Provo, UT, USA, Ancestry.com Operations Inc, 2002), www.ancestry.com, [Database online].Year: 1930 Flint, Genesee Co, Michigan; Roll: 987; FHL #2340722; Image: 70; ED: 52; Pg: 14B.

Citation: 1930 US Federal Census for Beatrice F Menkenmaier (Provo, UT, USA, Ancestry.com Operations Inc 2002), www.ancestry.com, [Database online].Year: 1930 Fort Rock, Lake Co, Oregon; Roll: 1943. FHL #: 2341677; Image: 1063; ED: 17; Pg. 1A.

Citation: 1930 US Federal Census for Caroline (Schellman) Wambsganss (Provo, UT, USA, Ancestry.com Operations Inc, 2002), www.ancestry.com, [Database online] Year: 1930. Fort Wayne, Allen Co, Indiana; Roll: 575; FHL #: 2340310; Image: 402; ED: 25; Pg. 17B.

Citation: 1930 US Federal Census for Carrie (Grimm) Penrose (Provo, UT, USA, Ancestry.com Operations Inc, 2002), [Database online].Year: 1930 Precinct 11, Yamhill, Oregon; Roll: 1958; FHL #: 2341692; Image: 152; ED: 15; Pg. 5A.

Citation: 1930 US Federal Census for Casper Olson (Provo, UT, USA, Ancestry.com Operations Inc), www.ancestry.com, [Database online].Year: 1930 Holway, Taylor Co, Wisconsin; Roll: 2614; FHL# 2342348; Image: 147; ED: 12; Pg. 7A.

Citation: 1930 US Federal Census for Clara (Vollmer) Repke (Provo, UT, USA, Ancestry.com Operations Inc, Houghton Co, Michigan; Roll 994. Image: 58; ED: 25; Pg. 4A.

Citation: 1930 US Federal Census for Edward C Grimm (Provo, UT, USA, Ancestry.com Operations Inc), www.ancestry.com, [Database online].Year: 1930 Anaheim, Orange, California; Roll: 180; FHL #: 2339915; Image: 752: ED: 2; Pg. 1A.

Citation: 1930 US Federal Census for Elaine A Pleith (Provo, UT, USA, Ancestry.com Operations Inc 2002), www.ancestry.com, [Database online].Year: 1930 Tigard, Washington Co, Oregon; FHL #: 2341691; Image: 985; ED: 56: Pg. 4A.

Citation: 1930 US Federal Census for Elizabeth (Wambsganss) Weber (Provo, UT, USA, Ancestry.com Operations Inc, 2002), www.ancestry.com, [Database on-line]. Year: 1930. Precinct 3, Harrison Co, Texas; ED: 17; Pg. 12B.

Citation: 1930 US Federal Census for Elmer H Grimm (Provo, UT, USA, Ancestry.com Operations Inc 2002). Year: 1930 Phoenix Precinct 8, Maricopa Co., Arizona; FHL #: 2339792; Image: 966; ED: 71-11; Pg. 2B; House: #1301 West Monroe; Dwelling: 29; Family: 45; Lines: 60-61.

Citation: 1930 US Federal Census for Erma (Grimm) Krausse (Provo, UT, USA, Ancestry.com Operations Inc, 2002), www.ancestry.com, [database on-line]. Year: 1930; Molitor, Taylor Co, Wisconsin. T626 Roll: 2614; FHL #: 2342348; Image: 290: ED: 21; Pg. 2B.

Citation: 1930 US Federal Census for Evadna (Bacon) Rosebrook (Provo, UT, USA, Ancestry.com Operations Inc), www.ancestry.com, [Database online].Year: 1930 Anaheim, Orange Co, California; T626, Roll: 180; FHL #: 2339915; Image: 752; ED: 2; Pg. 1A.

Citation: 1930 US Federal Census for Florence Eva Clarkson (Provo, UT, USA, Ancestry.com Operations Inc, 2002), www.ancestry.com, [Database online].Year: 1930 Hammel, Taylor Co, Wisconsin; T626. Roll: 2614; FHL #: 2342348; Image: 129; ED: 11; Pg. 4A.

Citation: 1930 US Federal Census for Frederick P.E. Wambsganss (Provo, UT, USA, Ancestry.com Operations Inc, 2002), www.ancestry.com, [Database online]. Year: 1930 Fort Wayne Ward 6, Block 267, Allen Co, Indiana. T626. ED: 25; Page: 1A; House: #2322 Broadway; Dwelling: 12; Family: 12; Lines: 42-53.

Citation: 1930 US Federal Census for Frederick T Grimm (Provo, UT, USA, Ancestry.com Operations Inc 2002), www.ancestry.com, [Database online].Year: 1930 Reedsville, Manitowoc Co, Wisconsin; T626. Roll: 2581; FHL #: 2342315; Image: 243; ED: 32: Pg. 6B.

Citation: 1930 US Federal Census for George Drohlshagen (Provo, UT, USA, Ancestry.com Operations Inc, 2002), www.ancestry.com, [Database online]. Year: 1930. Little Black, Taylor Co, Wisconsin. T626. FHL #: 2342348; Image 183; ED: 14: Pg. 12A.

Citation: 1930 US Federal Census for Glen Marion Co. Propst (Provo, UT, USA, Ancestry.com Operations Inc 2002) www.ancestry.com, [Database online].Year: 1930 Portland, Multnomah Co, Oregon; T626. Roll: 1952; FHL #:2341686; Image: 652; ED: 354; Pg. 1A.

Citation: 1930 US Federal Census for Gustav Grimm (Provo, UT, USA, Ancestry.com Operations Inc 2002), www.ancestry.com, [Database online].Year: 1930 Lessor, Polk Co, Minn; T626. Roll: 1113; FHL #: 2340848; Img: 354; ED: 53; Pg.1B.

Citation: 1930 US Federal Census for Helen Donaldson (Provo, UT, USA, Ancestry.com Operations Inc, 2002), www.ancestry.com, Year: 1930 Molitor, Taylor Co, Wisconsin; T626. FHL# 2342348; Image: 289; ED: 21; Pg. 2A.

Citation: 1930 US Federal Census for Henry Grimm (Provo, UT, USA, Ancestry.com Operations Inc), www.ancestry.com, [Database online].Year: 1930 Paul, Minidoka Co, Idaho; T626. Roll: 402; FHL #: 2340137; Image: 137; ED: 7; Pg: 2B.

Citation: 1930 US Federal Census for Henry J Klasner Jr. (Provo, UT, USA, Ancestry.com Operations Inc, 2002), www.ancestry.com, [Database online].Year: 1930; Hancock, Houghton Co, Michigan. T626. Roll 994; Image: 58; ED: 25; Pg 4A ED 25

Citation: 1930 US Federal Census for Henry Kettenbeil (Provo, UT, USA, Ancestry.com Operations Inc, 2002), www.ancestry.com, Year: 1930 Schoolcraft, Houghton Co, MI; T626. FHL #2340729; Image: 446; ED: 37; Pg. 5A

Citation: 1930 US Federal Census for Hilda C Schmelzer (Provo, UT, USA, Ancestry.com Operations Inc 2002), www.ancestry.com, [Database online].Year: 1930 Santa Rosa, Sonoma Co, California; T626. Roll: 222; FHL # 2339957; Image: 752; ED: 50; Pg. 3B.

Citation: 1930 US Federal Census for Howard H Vollmer (Provo, UT, USA, Ancestry.com Operations Inc, 2002), www.ancestry.com, [Database online].Year: 1930; Hancock, Houghton Co, Michigan. T626. Image: 58: ED: 25: Pg 4A.

Citation: 1930 US Federal Census for John S Schellman (Provo, UT, USA, Ancestry.com Operations Inc, 2002), www.ancestry.com, [Database online]. Year: 1930 Hancock, Houghton Co, Michigan. T626. Roll: 994; FHL #: 2340729; Image: 58; ED: 25; Pg. 4A.

Citation: 1930 US Federal Census for Lydia (Grimm) Strebig (Provo, UT, Ancestry.com Operations Inc 2002), www.ancestry.com, [Database online].Year: 1930 Hammel, Taylor Co, Wisconsin; T626. Roll: 2614; FHL # 2342348; Image: 127; ED: 11; Pg. 3A.

Citation: 1930 US Federal Census for Lydia (Schellman) Terp (Provo, UT, USA, Ancestry.com Operations, Inc, 2006), www.ancestry.com, [Database online]. Year: 1930. Green Bay, Brown Co, Wisconsin; T626. Roll: 2562; FHL #: 2342296; Image: 74; ED: 15; Pg. 18B.

Citation: 1930 US Federal Census for Lydia (Schellman) Terp (Provo, UT, USA, Ancestry.com Operations, Inc, 2006), www.ancestry.com, [Database online]. Year: 1930 Green Bay, Brown Co, Wisconsin. T626. Roll: 2562; FHL # 2342296; Image: 74; ED: 15; Pg. 18B

Citation: 1930 US Federal Census for Marion Co. V Dyce (Provo, UT, USA, Ancestry.com Operations Inc, T626. Roll: 2562; FHL #: 2342296; Image: 803; ED: 36; Pg. 17A.

Citation: 1930 US Federal Census for Mathilda (Grimm) Koch (Provo, UT, USA, Ancestry.com Operations Inc 2002), www.ancestry.com, [Database online].Year: 1930 Paul, Minidoka Co, Idaho; T626. Roll: 402; FHL #: 2340137; Image 148; ED: 8: Pg. 4A.

Citation: 1930 US Federal Census for Maynard Doriot (Provo, UT, USA, Ancestry.com Operations Inc 2002), www.ancestry.com, [Database online].Year: 1930 Merrill, Lincoln Co, Wisconsin; T626. Roll: 2580; FHL #: 2342314; Image: 592; ED: 8; Pg: 7A.

Citation: 1930 US Federal Census for Mildred (Grimm) Johns (Provo, UT, USA, Ancestry.com Operations Inc 2002) Roll: 1954; FHL #: 2341688; Image 1031; ED: 547; Pg. 2B.

Citation: 1930 US Federal Census for Myrtle (Anderson) Lorenz (Provo, UT, USA, Ancestry.com Operations Inc, 2002), www.ancestry.com, [Database online].Year: 1930 Little Black, Taylor Co, Wisconsin. T626. Roll: 2614; FHL #: 2342348; Image: 165: ED: 14; Pg: 3A.

Citation: 1930 US Federal Census for Myrtle (Klasner) Joos (Provo, UT, USA, Ancestry.com Operations Inc, 2002) T626. Roll: 1020; FHL #: 2340755; Image: 480; ED: 10; Pg. 16B.

Citation: 1930 US Federal Census for Otto William Grimm (Provo, UT, USA, Ancestry.com Operations Inc), www.ancestry.com, [Database online].Year: 1930 Manitowoc Co, Manitowoc Co, Wisconsin; T626. Roll: 2581; FHL #: 2342315; Image: 1019; ED: 22; Pg: 1A

Citation: 1930 US Federal Census for Reinhard Grimm (Provo, UT, USA, Ancestry.com Operations Inc.2002), www.ancestry.com, [Database online].Year: 1930 Maple Grove, Manitowoc Co, Wisconsin. T626. Roll: 2581; FHL #: 2342315; Image: 133; ED: 28; Page: 5B.

Citation: 1930 US Federal Census for Robert Porell (Provo, UT, USA, Ancestry.com Operations Inc, 2002), [Database online]. T626. Roll: 994; FHL #: 2340729; Image: 410; ED: 36; Pg: 5A

Citation: 1930 US Federal Census for Viola (Grimm) Bill (Provo, UT, USA, Ancestry.com Operations Inc, 2002), www.ancestry.com, [Database online].Year: 1930 Paul, Minidoka Co, Idaho; T626. Roll: 402; FHL #: 2340137; Image: 137; ED: 7; Page: 2B.

Citation: 1930 US Federal Census for Walter Herman Kettenbeil (Provo, UT, USA, Ancestry.com Operations Inc, 2002), www.ancestry.com, 1930 US Federal Census [Database online].Michigan, Houghton Co, Schoolcraft Twp., Lake Lindon Village; T626. ED 36, p. 8B; Line 77; Dwelling: 180; Fam: 202.

Citation: 1930 US Federal Census for Wilbert Grimm (Provo, UT, USA, Ancestry.com Operations Inc 2002), www.ancestry.com, [Database online].Year: 1930 Portland, Multnomah Co, Oregon; T626. FHL #: 2341688; Image: 1050; ED: 548; Pg: 3A.

Citation: 1930 US Federal Census for Will M Grimm (Provo, UT, USA, Ancesrty.com Operations Inc 2002), www.ancestry.com, [Database online].Year: 1930 Lambert, Red Lake Co, Minn.; T626. FHL #: 2340848; Image: 934; ED: 7; Pg: 4B.

Citation: 1930 US Federal Census for William A Wambsganss (Provo, UT, USA, Ancestry.com Operations Inc, 2002), www.ancestry.com, [Database online].Year: 1930 Lakewood, Cuyahoga, Ohio; T626. Roll: 1787; FHL #: 2341521; Image: 66; ED: 647; Page: 16B.

Citation: 1930 US Federal Census for William A Wambsganss (Provo, UT, USA, Ancestry.com Operations Inc, 2002), www.ancestry.com, [Database online].Year: 1930 Lakewood, Cuyahoga, Ohio; T626; Roll: 1787; FHL #: 2341521; Image: 66; ED: 647; Page: 16B.

Citation: 1930 US Federal Census for William Grimm (Provo, UT, USA, Ancestry.com Operations Inc), www.ancestry.com, [Database online].Year: 1930 Monitor, Marion Co, Oregon; T626. FHL #: 2341681; Image: 1068; ED: 42: Pg: 5B.

Citation: 1930 US Federal Census for William John Vollmer (Provo, UT, USA, Ancestry.com Operations Inc, 2002), www.ancestry.com, [Database online].Year: 1930 Superior, Douglas, Wisconsin; T626. Roll: 2570; FHL # 2342304; Image: 488; ED: 33; Pg.17B.

Citation: 1930 US Federal Census for Wilma (Grimm) Huffman (Provo, UT, USA, Ancestry.com Operations Inc), www.ancestry.com, [Database online].Year: 1930 Portland, Multnomah Co, Oregon; T626. Roll: 1953; FHL #: 2341687; Image: 567; ED: 434; Page: 5B.

**Title:**    **Census Records (United States Federal Census) 1940**

Citation: 1940 US Federal Census for Adolph H Grimm (Provo, UT, USA, Ancestry.com Operations Inc, 2012), www.ancestry.com, [Database online].Year: 1940 Maple Grove, Manitowoc Co, Wisconsin; T627; ED: 34; Pg: 3B

Citation: 1940 US Federal Census for Alvera (Steiner) Strebig (Provo, UT, USA, Ancestry.com Operations Inc 2012), www.ancestry.com, [Database online].Year: 1940 Chelsea, Taylor Co, Wisconsin; T627. #4528; ED: 60-3; Page: 6A.

Citation: 1940 US Federal Census for Alvera (Steiner) Strebig (Provo, UT, USA, Ancestry.com Operations Inc 2012), www.ancestry.com, [Database online].Year: 1940 Chelsea, Taylor Co, Wisconsin; T627_4528; ED: 60-3; Page: 6A.

Citation: 1940 US Federal Census for Alvin E Grimm (Provo, UT, USA, Ancestry.com Operations Inc, 2012), www.ancestry.com, [Database online].Year: 1940 Los Angeles, Los Angeles Co, California; T627; ED: 60-1123 Pg: 5A.

Citation: 1940 US Federal Census for Alvin Grimm (Provo, UT, USA, Ancestry.com Operations Inc, 2006), www.ancestry.com, [Database online].Year: 1940 Chelsea, Taylor Co, Wisconsin; T627_4528; ED: 60-3; Page: 5B.

Citation: 1940 US Federal Census for Anna (Grimm) Schmelzer (Provo, UT, USA, Ancestry.com Operations Inc 2012), www.ancestry.com, [Database online].Year: 1940 Santa Rosa, Sonoma Co, California; T627; ED: 49-52; Page: 11B.

Citation: 1940 US Federal Census for Anna (Grimm) Stansbery (Provo, UT, USA, Ancestry.com Operations Inc, 2012), www.ancestry.com, [Database online].Year: 1940 Portland, Multnomah Co, Oregon; T627; ED: 37-443; Page: 8A.

Citation: 1940 US Federal Census for Anton Grimm (Provo, UT, USA, Ancestry.com Operations Inc 2012), www.ancestry.com, [Database online].Year: 1940 Maple Grove, Manitowoc Co, Wisconsin. T627_4495; ED: 36-34; Page: 3B.

Citation: 1940 US Federal Census for Arthur Carl Anderson (Provo, UT, USA, Ancestry.com Operations Inc, 2012), www.ancestry.com, [Database online].Year: 1940 Riverside, Okanogan Co, Wash,; T627_ 4353; ED: 24-56; Pg: 2A.

Citation: 1940 US Federal Census for August N Anderson (Provo, UT, USA, Ancestry.com Operations Inc, 2012), www.ancestry.com, [Database online].Year: 1940 Chelsea, Taylor Co, Wisconsin; T627. Roll: 4528; ED: 60-3; Pg: 5A.

Citation: 1940 US Federal Census for Barbara (Schellman) Klasner (Provo, UT, USA, Ancestry.com Operations Inc, 2012), www.ancestry.com, [database on-line]. 2012. Year: 1940 Hancock, Houghton Co, Michigan; ED: 31-25; Page: 6A.

Citation: 1940 US Federal Census for Barbra L (Klasner) Brohn (Provo, UT, USA, Ancestry.com Operations Inc, 2012), www.ancestry.com, [Database online].Year: 1940 Flint, Genesee Co, Michigan; T627 Roll: 1892; ED: 85-12Page: 3A.

Citation: 1940 US Federal Census for Bertha (Grimm) Buxton (Provo, UT, USA, Ancestry.com Operations Inc, 2012), www.ancestry.com, [Database online].Year: 1940 Portland, Multnomah Co, Oregon; T627; ED: 37-379; Page: 9A.

Citation: 1940 US Federal Census for Carrie (Grimm) Penrose (Provo, UT, USA, Ancestry.com Operations Inc), www.ancestry.com, [Database online].Year: 1940 Hopewell, Yamhill Co, Oregon; T627; ED: 36-16; Page: 5B.

Citation: 1940 US Federal Census for Carrie (Grimm) Penrose (Provo, UT, USA, Ancestry.com Operations Inc 2012), www.ancestry.com, [Database online].Year: 1940 Hopewell, Yamhill Co, Oregon; T626. ED: 36-16; Page: 5B.

Citation: 1940 US Federal Census for Casper Olson (Provo, UT, USA, Ancestry.com Operations Inc 2012), www.ancestry.com, [Database online].Year: 1940 Hammel, Taylor Co, Wisconsin; T627_4528 ED: 60-12; Page: 2B.

Citation: 1940 US Federal Census for Clara (Vollmer) Repke (Provo, UT, USA, Ancestry.com Operations Inc, 2012), www.ancestry.com, [Database online].Year: 1940 Hancock, Houghton Co, Michigan; T627. ED: 31-25; Page: 5B.

Citation: 1940 US Federal Census for Clara Grimm (Provo, UT, USA, Ancestry.com Operations Inc, 2012), www.ancestry.com, [Database online].Year: 1940 Stettin, Marathon Co, Wisconsin; T627_4497; ED: 37-52; Page: 11B.

Citation: 1940 US Federal Census for Clara Repke (Provo, UT, USA, Ancestry.com Operations Inc 2012), www.ancestry.com, [Database online].Year: 1940 Hancock, Houghton Co, Michigan; T627. ED: 31-25; Page: 5B.

Citation: 1940 US Federal Census for Douglas Grimm (Provo, UT, USA, Ancestry.com Operations Inc 2012), www.ancestry.com, [Database online].Year: 1940 Lambert, Red Lake Co, Minnesota; T627_1951; ED: 63-7; Page: 4B.

Citation: 1940 US Federal Census for Douglas Grimm (Provo, UT, USA, Ancestry.com Operations Inc 2012), www.ancestry.com, [Database online].Year: 1940 Lambert, Red Lake Co, Minnesota; T627_1951; ED: 63-7; Page: 4B.

Citation: 1940 US Federal Census for Edward C Grimm (Provo, UT, USA, Ancestry.com Operations Inc, 2012), www.ancestry.com, [Database online].Year: 1940 Fullerton, Orange Co, California; T627_272 ED: 30-33; Page: 16B; Line 59-61; Dwelling: 144; Family: 507

Citation: 1940 US Federal Census for Elmer Anderson (Provo, UT, USA, Ancestry.com Operations Inc, 2012), www.ancestry.com, [Database online]. Year: 1940 Medford, Taylor Co, Wisconsin. T627. ED: 60-20; Page: 3B.

Citation: 1940 US Federal Census for Esther (Penrose) Propst (Provo, UT, USA, Ancestry.com Operations Inc 2012), www.ancestry.com, [Database online].Year: 1940 Portland, Multnomah Co, Oregon; T627. ED: 37-300; Pg: 61B.

Citation: 1940 US Federal Census for Ethel (Klasner) Funkey (Provo, UT, USA, Ancestry.com Operations Inc, 2012), www.ancestry.com, [database on-line]. 2012. Year: 1940 Ontonagon, Ontonagon Co, Michigan; T627_1806; ED: 66-12B; Page: 3A; D: 66-12B.

Citation: 1940 US Federal Census for Evadna (Bacon) Rosebrook Spencer (Provo, UT, USA, Ancestry.com Operations Inc 2012), www.ancestry.com, [Database online].Year: 1940 Holbrook, Multnomah Co, Oregon; T627_3377; ED: 26-42; Page: 4A.

Citation: 1940 US Federal Census for Florence Eva Clarkson (Provo, UT, USA, Ancestry.com Operations Inc, 2012), www.ancestry.com, [Database online].Year: 1940 Little Black, Taylor Co, Wisconsin. T627. ED: 60-15; Page: 18B.

Citation: 1940 US Federal Census for Frederick P.E. Wambsganss (Provo, UT, USA, Ancestry.com Operations Inc, 2012), www.ancestry.com, [Database online]. Year: 1940 Fort Wayne Ward 6, Block 267; Allen Co., Indiana. T627. ED: 40; Page: 14 A; House: #2322 Broadway; Dwelling: 300; Lines: 15-20.

Citation: 1940 US Federal Census for George Drohlshagen (Provo, UT, USA, Ancestry.com Operations Inc, 2012), www.ancestry.com, [Database online]. Year: 1940 Little Black, Taylor Co, Wisconsin. T627. ED: 60-15; Page: 11B.

Citation: 1940 US Federal Census for Gust Grimm (Provo, UT, USA, Ancestry.com Operations Inc 2012), www.ancestry.com, [Database online].Year: 1940 Macleay, Marion Co, Oregon; T627_3373; ED: 24-37; Pg: 4A

Citation: 1940 US Federal Census for Hannah (Schellman) Kettenbeil (Provo, UT, USA, Ancestry.com Operations Inc 2012) Year: 1940 Hancock Ward 1, Houghton Co, Michigan. T627_1757; ED: 31-23; Pg; 4B; Lines: 70-75. Living with sister and brother-in-law, Garvin Mitchell.

Citation: 1940 US Federal Census for Henry G L Terp (Provo, UT, USA, Ancestry.com Operations Inc, 2012), www.ancestry.com, [Database online].Year: 1940 Green Bay, Brown, Wisconsin; T627_4459; ED: 5-24; Pg. 14A.

Citation: 1940 US Federal Census for Henry Kettenbeil (Provo, UT, USA, Ancestry.com Operations Inc, 2012), www.ancestry.com, [Database online].Year: 1940 Schoolcraft, Houghton Co, Michigan; Roll: 1757; ED: 31-40; Pg 6B.

Citation: 1940 US Federal Census for Hilda (Schmelzer) Cook (Provo, UT, USA, Ancestry.com Operations Inc 2012), www.ancestry.com, [Database online].Year: 1940 Santa Rosa, Sonoma Co, California; T627; ED: 49-52; Pg. 11B.

Citation: 1940 US Federal Census for Hildegarde Wambsganss (Provo, UT, USA, Ancestry.com Operations Inc, 2012), www.ancestry.com, [Database online]. 2012. Year: 1940 Perry, Allen, Indiana; T626 Roll: 1025; ED: 2-20; Pg 17B.

Citation: 1940 US Federal Census for Howard H Vollmer (Provo, UT, USA, Ancestry.com Operations Inc, 2012), www.ancestry.com, [database on-line]. 2012. Year: 1940 Hancock, Houghton Co, Michigan. T627. ED: 25; Pg. 63A

Citation: 1940 US Federal Census for Ida C Grimm (Provo, UT, USA, Ancestry.com Operations Inc), www.ancestry.com, [Database online].Year: 1940 Portland, Multnomah Co, Oregon; T627 Roll: 3394; ED: 37-493B; Pg. 61A.

Citation: 1940 US Federal Census for J Maynard Doriot (Provo, UT, USA, Ancestry.com Operations Inc 2012), www.ancestry.com, [Database online].Year: 1940 Mercer, Iron Co, Wisconsin; T627_4484 ED: 26-12; Page 1B.

Citation: 1940 US Federal Census for John S Schellman (Provo, UT, USA, Ancestry.com Operations Inc, 2012), www.ancestry.com, [Database online].Year: 1940 Hancock, Houghton Co, Michigan T627_1757; ED: 31-25; Pg. 5B.

Citation: 1940 US Federal Census for Lawrence A Grimm (Provo, UT, USA, Ancestry.com Operations Inc, 2012), www.ancestry.com, [Database online].Year: 1940 Portland, Multnomah Co, Oregon; T627_3393; ED: 37-457; Pg. 1A.

Citation: 1940 US Federal Census for Leona (Grimm) Arronson (Provo, UT, USA, Ancestry.com Operations Inc 2012), www.ancestry.com, [Database online].Year: 1940 Portland, Multnomah Co, Oregon; T627 ED: 37-493B; Pg. 3B.

Citation: 1940 US Federal Census for Leona (Grimm) Arronson (Provo, UT, USA, Ancestry.com Operations Inc), www.ancestry.com, [Database online].Year: 1940 Portland, Multnomah Co, Oregon; T627 ED: 37-493B; Pg. 3B.

Citation: 1940 US Federal Census for Leonard Grimm (Provo, UT, USA, Ancestry.com Operations Inc 2012), www.ancestry.com, [Database online].Year: 1940 Los Angeles, Los Angeles Co, California; T627. ED: 768; Pg. 15B.

Citation: 1940 US Federal Census for Louis Steiner (Provo, UT, USA, Ancestry.com Operations, Inc., 2012), www.ancestry.com, [Database online].Year: 1940 Chelsea, Taylor Co, Wisconsin; T627_4528 ED: 60-3; Pg. 6A.

Citation: 1940 US Federal Census for Lova Jean Grimm (Provo, UT, USA, Ancestry.com Operations Inc, 2012), www.ancestry.com, [Database online].Year: 1940 Butteville, Marion Co, Oregon; Roll: T627_3373; ED: 24-7: Pg. 1B.

Citation: 1940 US Federal Census for Lydia (Grimm) Strebig (Provo, UT, USA, Ancestry.com Operations Inc, 2012), www.ancestry.com, [Database online].Year: 1940 Hammel, Taylor Co, Wisconsin; T627_4528 ED: 60-12; Pg. 7B.

Citation: 1940 US Federal Census for Lydia (Schellman) Terp (Provo, UT, USA, Ancestry.com Operations Inc, 2012), www.ancestry.com, [Database online].Year: 1940 Allouez, Brown Co, Wisconsin; T627 Roll: 4459; ED: 5-1A; Pg 10B

Citation: 1940 US Federal Census for Mathilda (Grimm) Koch (Provo, UT, USA, Ancestry.com Operations Inc 2012), www.ancestry.com, [Database online].Year: 1940 Paul, Minidoka Co, Idaho; T627_751. ED: 34-8; Pg. 6B

Citation: 1940 US Federal Census for Michael Boiko (Provo, UT, USA, Ancestry.com Operations Inc, 2012).www.ancestry.com, [Database online].Year: 1940 East Republic, Ferry Co, Washington; T627_4338. ED: 10-6; Pg. 2A.

Citation: 1940 US Federal Census for Mildred (Grimm) Johns (Provo, UT, USA, Ancestry.com Operations Inc, 2012), www.ancestry.com, [Database online].Year: 1940 Portland, Multnomah Co, Oregon; T627. ED: 37-110; Pg. 4A.

Citation: 1940 US Federal Census for Monroe Grimm (Provo, UT, USA, Ancestry.com Operations Inc 2012), [Database online].Year: 1940 Paul, Minidoka Co, Idaho; T627_751; ED: 34-9; Page 1B.

Citation: 1940 US Federal Census for Myrtle (Klasner) Joos (Provo, UT, USA, Ancestry.com Operations Inc, 2012), www.ancestry.com, [Database online].Year: 1940 Ontonagon, Ontonagon Co, Michigan. T627. ED: 66-11; Pg. 25A.

Citation: 1940 US Federal Census for Otto C Anderson (Provo, UT, USA, Ancestry.com Operations Inc, 2012), www.ancestry.com, [Database online].Year: 1940 Grover, Taylor Co, Wisconsin; T627_4528. ED: 60-10; Page: 2A

Citation: 1940 US Federal Census for Verna (Bacon) Teuber (Provo, UT, USA, Ancestry.com Operations Inc 2012), www.ancestry.com, [Database online]. Year: 1940 San Francisco, San Francisco Co, CA; T627. ED: 38-472; Pg. 66B.

Citation: 1940 US Federal Census for Viola (Grimm) Bill (Provo, UT, USA, Ancestry.com Operations Inc 2012), www.ancestry.com, [Database online].Year: 1940 Paul, Minidoka Co, Idaho; T627_751; ED: 34-8. Page: 5A

Citation: 1940 US Federal Census for Viola B. Neumueller (Provo, UT, USA, Ancestry.com Operations Inc., 2012), www.ancestry.com, [Database online]. Year: 1940 Chelsea, Taylor Co, Wisconsin. T627 Roll: 4528; ED: 60-3; Pg: 1A.

Citation: 1940 US Federal Census for Violet Vincent (Provo, UT, USA, Ancestry.com Operations Inc, 2012), www.ancestry.com, [Database online]. Year: 1940 Duck Creek, Brown Co, Wisconsin; T627_4461; ED: 5-50; Page: 21A.

Citation: 1940 US Federal Census for Violette (Grimm) Ferden (Provo, UT, USA, Ancestry.com Operations Inc), www.ancestry.com, [Database online]. Year: 1940 Reddick, Kankakee Co, Illinois; T627_824; ED: 46-48; Pg. 2A.

Citation: 1940 US Federal Census for Wilbert Grimm (Provo, UT, USA, Ancestry.com Operations Inc 2012), www.ancestry.com, [Database online].. 1940 Portland, Multnomah Co, Oregon; T627 Roll: 3389; ED: 37-246; Pg. 8B.

Citation: 1940 US Federal Census for William Adolph Wambsganss (Provo, UT, USA, Ancestry.com, 2012), www.ancestry.com, [database on-line]. Year: 1940 Lakewood, Cuyahoga Co, Ohio. T627_3055; ED: 18-195; Pg. 9B.

Citation: 1940 US Federal Census for William Grimm (Provo, UT, Ancestry.com Operations Inc., 2012), www.ancestry.com, [Database online]. Year: 1940 Lambert, Red Lake Co, Minnesota; T627_1951; ED: 63-7; Pg. 4A.

Citation: 1940 US Federal Census for William Klasner (Provo, UT, USA, Ancestry.com Operations Inc, 2012), www.ancestry.com, [database on-line]. Year: 1940; Saginaw, Saginaw Co, Michigan; T627_1814; ED: 73-65; Pg. 21A.

Citation: 1940 US Federal Census for Wilma (Grimm) Huffman (Provo, UT, USA, Ancestry.com Operations Inc), www.ancestry.com, [Database online].Year: 1940 Portland, Multnomah Co, Oregon; T627_3394; ED: 37-486; Pg. 6B.

Citation: 1940 US Federal Census for Woodrow J Terp (Provo, UT, USA, Ancestry.com Operations Inc 2012), www.ancestry.com, Year: 1940 Green Bay, Brown Co, Wisconsin; T627_4460; ED: 5-43; Pg. 13A

**Title:** **Address Book of Clara Anderson Grimm**

Citation: Address Book of Clara Anderson Grimm (Chelsea, WI, Clara Grimm, n.d.g.), In possession of Tracy Doriot, Washougal, WA. Entries in small green address book once belonging to Clara Anderson Grimm; n.d.g.

**Title:** **Anniversary Announcements**

Citation: Anniversary Announcement for Alvin & Clara Grimm (Medford, Taylor Co, Wisconsin, USA, The Star News, abt Aug 1983); Golden Wedding Anniversary: "...married 50 years next November..."

Citation: Anniversary Announcement for Art & Loretta Anderson (Okanogan, Okanogan Co, WA, Art and Loretta Anderson, abt 14 May 1978); In possession of Tracy Doriot, Washougal, WA 14 May 1978. "In honour of [their] fiftieth wedding anniversary..."

Citation: Anniversary Announcement for LaVern & Nora Grimm (McIntosh, Polk Co, MN, LaVern & Nora Grimm, Oct 1986), Copy in possession of Tracy Doriot, Washougal, WA.11 Oct 1986; Invitation to50th wedding anniversary reception, at Immanuel Lutheran Church, McIntosh, MN.

Citation: Anniversary Announcement for Louis & Louise Lange, Abt May 1982; (Stetsonville, WI). In copy in Possession of Tracy Doriot, Washougal, WA. 40th wedding anniversary.

Citation: Anniversary Announcement for Lucille Grimm and Vernon Frey (Stetsonville, WI, Children of Mr. and Mrs. Vernon Frey, abt Jul 1982), Abt May 1982; Copy in possession of Tracy Doriot, Washougal, WA. "...in celebration of their 40th wedding anniversary."

**Title:** **Autobiographies, Biographies, Histories**

Citation: Everett Grimm, Autobiography of Everett Grimm's Military Service (Middlebury, IN, 03 Mar2005), (Copy in possession of Tracy Doriot, Washougal, WA) Five typed pages.

Citation: Biographical Note about Annie Steiner Grimm, n.d.g.; Typewritten paragraph found among Clara Grimm's papers

**Title:** **Baptism Records**

Citation: Baptism Record for Alvin Albert William Grimm (Trinity Lutheran Church at Whittlesey Parish, Rev. Richard E. Heschkle, 02 July 1909), (Copy in possession of Tracy Doriot, Washougal, WA) Barbara Schellman and Wilhelm Grimm, godparents. Document written in Germany.

Citation: Baptism Record for Clara M. Anderson (Holway, Taylor Co, WI, Our Saviour Lutheran Church, 05 May 1912), (In possession of Tracy Doriot, Washougal, WA) Seal-Certified; Copied from official church records by Pastor, Rev. R.L. Tellock; Sponsors were Tina Halverson, Casper Olson and Oscar Nelson. ...was baptized at church now known as "Our Saviour Lutheran Church, Holway, Taylor Co, WI "

Citation: Baptismal Certificate of John F. Lorenz (Medford, Taylor Co, WI, Holway Lutheran Church, W.L. Anderson (Pastor), 1931), (In possession of Tracy Doriot, Washougal, WA.) 15 Apr 1931. Holway Lutheran Congregation, Medford, WI.

**Title:** **Birth Records**

Citation: Birth Record for August Nikolaus Anderson (Provo, UT, USA, Ancestry.com Operations Inc, 2011), www.ancestry.com, "Wisconsin Births and Christenings, 1826–1926." Index. [Database online]FamilySearch, Salt Lake City, Utah, 2009, 2010. Index entries derived from digital copies of original and compiled records.

Citation: Birth Record for Augusta Emma Fischer (Provo, UT, USA, Ancestry.com Operations, Inc., 2011), www.ancestry.com, Wisconsin, Births and Christenings Index, 1826-1908 [database on-line]. Original data: "Wisconsin Births and Christenings, 1826–1926." Index. FamilySearch, Salt Lake City, Utah, 2009, 2010. Index entries derived from digital copies of original and compiled records.

Citation: Birth Record for Caroline Grimm (Provo, UT, Ancestry.com Operations Inc, 2012), www.ancestry.com, Wisconsin, Births and Christenings Index, 1826-1908 [database on-line]. Original data: "Wisconsin Births and Christenings, 1826–1926." Index. FamilySearch, Salt Lake City, Utah, 2009, 2010. Index entries derived from digital copies of original and compiled records.

Citation: Birth Record for Diane Marie Brissette (Provo, UT, USA, Ancestry.com Operations Inc, 2004), www.ancestry.com, Minnesota Births and Christenings, 1840–1980 [Database online]. Original data: "Minnesota Births and Christenings, 1840–1980." Index. FHL #1008260. FamilySearch, Salt Lake City, Utah, 2009, 2010. Index entries derived from digital copies of original and compiled records.

Citation: Birth Record for Donald L. Grimm (Provo, UT, USA, Ancestry.com Operations Inc, 2004), www.ancestry.com, Minnesota Birth Index, 1935-2002; [Database online].

Citation: Birth Record for Elsie Olson (Provo, UT, USA, Ancestry.com Operations, Inc., 2011), www.ancestry.com, Wisconsin, Births and Christenings Index, 1826-1908 [database on-line]. Original data: "Wisconsin Births and Christenings, 1826–1926." Index. FamilySearch, Salt Lake City, Utah, 2009, 2010. Index entries derived from digital copies of original and compiled records.

Citation: Birth Record for Ethel Klasner (Provo, UT, USA, Ancestry.com Operations Inc, 2011), www.ancestry.com, Minnesota Births and Christenings, 1840–1980 [Database online]. Original data: "Minnesota Births and Christenings, 1840–1980." Index. FHL #1008260. FamilySearch, Salt Lake City, Utah, 2009, 2010. Index entries derived from digital copies of original and compiled records.

Citation: Birth Record for Glen Dale Erickson (Provo, UT, USA, Ancestry.com Operations Inc, 2004), www.ancestry.com, Minnesota Births and Christenings, 1840–1980 [Database online] Original data: "Minnesota Births and Christenings, 1840–1980." Index. FHL #1008260. FamilySearch, Salt Lake City, Utah, 2009, 2010. Index entries derived from digital copies of original and compiled records.

Citation: Birth Record for Gustave Alphonse Weber (Provo, UT, USA, Ancestry.com Operations Inc, 2005), www.ancestry.com, New Orleans, Louisiana Birth Records Index, 1790-1899 [database on-line]. New Orleans, Louisiana Birth Records Index, 1790-1899; Volume: 82; Page #: 554. 2002. Original data: State of Louisiana, Secretary of State, Division of Archives, Records Management, and History. Vital Records Indices. Baton Rouge, LA.

Citation: Birth Record for Henry G L Terp (Provo, UT, USA, Ancestry.com Operations Inc, 2011), www.ancestry.com, Minnesota, Births and Christenings Index, 1840-1980; [Database online].FHL1309045/1309134. Original source: "Minnesota Births and Christenings, 1840–1980." Index. FamilySearch, Salt Lake City, Utah, 2009, 2010.

Citation: Birth Record for Jon M Kirchberg (Provo, UT, USA, Ancestry.com Operations Inc, 2004), www.ancestry.com, Minnesota Department of Health; Minnesota Birth Index, 1935-2002 [Database online].

Citation: Birth Record for Joseph P Kirchberg (Provo, UT, USA, Ancestry.com Operations Inc, 2007), www.ancestry.com, Minnesota Births and Christenings, 1840–1980 [Database online]. Original data: "Minnesota Births and Christenings, 1840–1980." Index. FHL #1008260. FamilySearch, Salt Lake City, Utah, 2009, 2010.

Citation: Birth Record for Kenneth John Kirchberg (Provo, UT, USA, Ancestry.com Operations Inc, 2004), www.ancestry.com, Minnesota Birth Index, 1935-2002; [Database online].

Citation: Birth Record for Myrtle Klasner (Provo, UT, USA, Ancestry.com Operations Inc, 2011), www.ancestry.com, Minnesota Births and Christenings, 1840–1980 [Database online]. Original data: "Minnesota Births and Christenings, 1840–1980." Index. FHL # 1008260. FamilySearch, Salt Lake City, Utah, 2009, 2010. Index entries derived from digital copies of original and compiled records.

Citation: Birth Record for Philip Wambsganss (Provo, UT, USA, Ancestry.com Operations Inc), www.ancestry.com, Michigan Births and Christenings Index, 1867-1911.

Citation: Birth Record for Siegfried Krausse (Provo, UT, USA, Ancestry.com Operations Inc, 2011), www.ancestry.com, Wisconsin, Births and Christenings Index, 1826-1908 [database on-line]. Original data: "Wisconsin Births and Christenings, 1826–1926." Index. FamilySearch, Salt Lake City, Utah, 2009, 2010. Index entries derived from digital copies of original and compiled records. FHL: 1305594

Citation: Birth Record for Walter Herman Kettenbeil (Provo, UT, USA, Ancestry.com Operations Inc), www.ancestry.com, Michigan, Births and Christenings Index, 1867-1911 [database on-line]. FHL: 1009346. Original data: "Michigan Births and Christenings, 1775-1995." Index. FamilySearch, Salt Lake City, Utah, 2009, 2010. Index entries derived from digital copies of original and compiled records.

Citation: Birth Record for Wilbert Terp (Provo, UT, USA, Ancestry.com Operations Inc, 2000), www.ancestry.com, Wisconsin Births, 1820-1907 [Database online].County: Brown; Reel #0021; Record: 001857; Wisconsin Department of Health and Family Services. Wisconsin Vital Record Index, pre-1907. Madison, WI, USA: Wisconsin Department of Health and Family Services Vital Records Division.

**Title:** **Birth/Christening Records**

Citation: Birth/Christening Record for Henry George Lincoln Terp (Provo, UT, USA, Ancestry.com Operations Inc, 2011), www.ancestry.com, Minnesota, Births and Christenings Index, 1840-1980[Database online]. Minnesota Births and Christenings, 1840–1980." Index. FamilySearch, Salt Lake City, Utah, 2009, 2010. Index entries derived from digital copies of original and compiled records.

Citation:   Birth/Christening Record for Wilbert Terp (Provo, UT, USA, Ancestry.com Operations Inc, 2011), www.ancestry.com, Wisconsin, Birth and Christenings, 1826-1908. [Database online]. #1299480; Wisconsin, Birth and Christenings, 1826-1908. Index. FamilySearch, Salt Lake City, UT, 2009, 2010.

Citation:   Birth/Christening Record for William Adolph Wambsganss (Index) (Provo, UT, USA, Ancestry.com Operations Inc, 2011), www.ancestry.com, Ohio, Births and Christenings Index, 1800-1962 [database online] 2011. "Ohio Births and Christenings, 1821-1962." Index. FamilySearch, Salt Lake City, Utah, 2009, 2011. Index entries derived from digital copies of original and compiled records.

Citation:   Birth/Christenings for Garvin Peter Mitchell (Provo, UT, USA, Ancestry.com Operations Inc, 2011), www.ancestry.com, Michigan, Births and Christenings Index, 1867-1911; Original data: "Michigan Births and Christenings, 1775–1995." Index. FamilySearch, Salt Lake City, Utah, 2009, 2010. Index entries derived from digital copies of original and compiled records.

Citation:   Births/Christening for Rubin Kettenbeil (Provo, UT, USA, Ancestry.com Operations Inc, 2011), www.ancestry.com, Michigan, Births and Christenings Index, 1867-1911 [Database online]. Original source: "Michigan Births and Christenings, 1775–1995." Index. FamilySearch, Salt Lake City, Utah, 2009, 2010. Index entries derived from digital copies of original and compiled records.

**Title:**   **Border Crossing Records**

Citation:   Border Crossing Record for Carrie Peterson 1932 (Provo, UT, USA, Ancestry.com Operations Inc, 2010), www.ancestry.com, Border Crossings From Canada to U.S., 1895-1954; National Archives and Records Administration; Washington, D.C.; Manifests of Alien Arrivals at Porthill, Idaho, 1923-1952; National Archives # Publication: A3462; Record Group Title: Records of the Immigration and Naturalization Service.

Citation:   Border Crossing Record for Carrie Peterson 1946 (Provo, UT, USA, Ancestry.com Operations Inc), www.ancestry.com, Border Crossings From Canada to U.S., 1895-1954; National Archives and Records Administration; Washington, D.C.; Manifests of Alien Arrivals at Porthill, Idaho, 1923-1952; National Archives # Publication: A3462; Record Group Title: Records of the Immigration and Naturalization Service.

Citation:   Border Crossing Record for Clarence Olson 1938 (Provo, UT, USA, Ancestry.com Operations Inc), www.ancestry.com, Border Crossings From Canada to U.S., 1895-1954; National Archives and Records Administration; Washington, D.C.; Manifests of Alien Arrivals at Porthill, Idaho, 1923-1952; National Archives # Publication: A3462; Record Group Title: Records of the Immigration and Naturalization Service.

Citation:   Border Crossing Record for Nels Olson 1929 (Provo, UT, USA, Ancestry.com Operations Inc), www.ancestry.com, Border Crossings From Canada to U.S., 1895-1954; National Archives and Records Administration; Washington, D.C.; Manifests of Alien Arrivals at Porthill, Idaho, 1923-1952; National Archives # Publication: A3462; Record Group Title: Records of the Immigration and Naturalization Service.

Citation:   Border Crossing Record for Nels Pederson (Provo, UT, USA, Ancestry.com Operations Inc, 2012), www.ancestry.com, Border Crossings From Canada to U.S., 1895-1954; [Database online].Records of the Immigration and Naturalization Service, RG 85, Washington, D.C.: National Archives and Records Administration; National Archives and Records Administration; Washington, D.C.; Manifests of Alien Arrivals at Havre, Loring, Opheim, Raymond, Turner, Westby, and White Tail, Montana, 1924-1956; National Archives # Publication: A3448; Record Group Title: Records of the Immigration and Naturalization Service.

**Title:**   **Business Records**

Citation:   Business Registration and License for Doriot Construction (State of Washington, Unknown), (In possession of Tracy Doriot, Washougal, WA), Sole Proprietorship;

Citation:   K.W.R.L. Maintenance Facility Dedication (Woodland, WA, K.W.R.L. Pupil Transportation Co-op), (Copy in possession of Tracy Doriot, Washougal, WA). K.W.R.L Maintenance Facility Dedication; La Center, Clark Co, Washington; 1999.

**Title:**   **Cemetery Land Deeds**

Citation:   Cemetery Land Deed for Andrew Anderson (Medford, Taylor Co, WI, State of Wisconsin, County of Taylor Co,Town of Medford, 21 May 1906), In possession of Tracy Doriot, Washougal, WA. 21 May 1906; Purchased Lot 14, Blk T in Medford Town Cemetery (now Evergreen) for $5.00"...Andrew Anderson and his heirs forever,...expressly for burial purposes and no other."

Citation:   Cemetery Land Deed for Johanna (?) Anderson (Medford, Taylor Co, WI, State of Wisconsin, County of Taylor Co, Town of Medford, 19 Jun 1903), (In possession of Tracy Doriot, Washougal, WA). 19 Jun 1903, Purchased Lot 14, Block T for $5.00 in the Town Cemetery (Evergreen), Medford, Taylor Co, Wisconsin.

**Title:**   **Confirmation Records**

Citation:   Confirmation Record for Clara M. Anderson (Holway, Taylor Co, WI, Holway Lutheran Congregation, 31 Oct 1926), (In possession of Tracy Doriot, Washougal WA). Confirmation Record; Holway Lutheran Congregation; Holway, Taylor Co, Wisconsin; 31 Oct 1926. Record for Clara M Anderson.

Citation:   Confirmation Card For Leroy Krausse (Medford, Taylor Co, WI, St. Paul Lutheran Church, 16 May1943), (Copy in possession of Tracy Doriot, Washougal, WA).Confirmation Card; St. Paul Lutheran Church, Medford, Taylor Co, Wisconsin; 16 May 1943.

**Title:** **Death Certificates**

Citation: Death Certificate for Clara Matilda Grimm (Unknown, State of Wisconsin, Dept. of Health and Social Services, Register of Deeds, 8 May 1997), (In possession of Tracy Doriot, Washougal, WA) 8 May 1997; Vol 32, p. 35

Citation: Death Certificate for Horace C Teuber (Seattle, WA, Washington State Department of Health, Division of Vital Statistics, Dec 1948), Washington State Dept. of Health, Division of Vital Statistics Seattle, WA, Death Certificate; State of Washington, Department of Health, Division of Vital Statistics, Seattle, Washington; Rec #20802; Seattle, King Co, Washington.

**Title:** **Death of Otto Anderson (letter)**

Citation: Death of Otto Anderson (letter) (Okanogan, WA, Ruth Anderson (spouse), 10 Sep 1992), (In possession of Tracy Doriot, Washougal, WA). Letter regarding death of Otto Anderson; Okanogan, Okanogan Co, Washington; 10 Sep 1992; Author: Ruth Anderson (written to Clara and Alvin Grimm).

**Title:** **Death Records**

Citation: Death Record for Albert A Grimm (Index) (Provo, UT, USA, Ancestry.com Operations Inc, 2001), www.ancestry.com, Minnesota, Death Index, 1908-2002.

Citation: Death Record for Albert I. Anderson (Index) (Provo, UT, USA, Ancestry.com Operations Inc, 2008), www.ancestry.com, Washington Death Index, 1940-1996 [Database online].2002.Original data: Washington State Department of Health. State Death Records Index, 1940-1996. Washington State Archives, Olympia, Washington.

Citation: Death Record for Albert P Grimm (Index) (Provo, UT, USA, Ancestry.com Operations Inc, 2007), www.ancestry.com, Wisconsin Death Index, 1959-1997 [database on-line]. Original data: Wisconsin Vital Records Office. Wisconsin Death Index, 1959-67, 1969-97. Madison, Wisconsin, USA: Wisconsin Department of Health.

Citation: Death Record for Allen Lee Anderson (Index) (Provo, UT, USA, Ancestry.com Operations Inc, 2004), www.ancestry.com, Minnesota, Death Index, 1908-2002 [database on-line]. 2001.Original data: State of Minnesota. Minnesota Death Index, 1908-2002. Minneapolis, MN, USA: Minnesota Department of Health.

Citation: Death Record for Alvin E Grimm (Index) (Provo, UT, USA, Ancestry.com Operations Inc, 2011), www.ancestry.com, California, Death Index, 1940-1997 [Database online].2000. Original data: State of California. California Death Index, 1940-1997. Sacramento, CA, USA: State of California Department of Health Services, Center for Health Statistics.

Citation: Death Record for Anna Margaret Schmelzer (Index) (Provo, UT, USA, Ancestry.com Operations Inc, 2000), www.ancestry.com, California, Death Index, 1940-1997 [Database online].2000. Original data: State of California. California Death Index, 1940-1997. Sacramento, CA, USA: State of California Department of Health Services, Center for Health Statistics. 2010.

Citation: Death Record for Anton H Grimm (Index) (Provo, UT, USA, Ancestry.com Operations Inc, 2007), www.ancestry.com, Wisconsin Death Index, 1959-1997 [database on-line]. Original data: Wisconsin Vital Records Office. Wisconsin Death Index, 1959-67, 1969-97. Madison, Wisconsin, USA: Wisconsin Department of Health.

Citation: Death Record for Basil Orlando Singleton (Index) (Provo, UT, USA, Ancestry.com Operations Inc, 2000), www.ancestry.com, Wisconsin Vital Records Office, Wisconsin Death Index, 1959-67, 1969-97, Madison, Wisconsin, USA: , Wisconsin Department of Health; [Database online].

Citation: Death Record for Beatrice Francis Schroder (Index) (Provo, UT, USA, Ancestry.com Operations Inc, 2000), www.ancestry.com, Oregon, Death Index, 1898-2008 [database on-line]. 2000. Oregon State Library; 1966-1970 Death Index; Reel Title: Oregon Death Index A-L; Year Range: 1931-1941. Original data: State of Oregon. Oregon Death Index, 1903-1998. Salem, OR, USA: Oregon State Archives and Records Center. Oregon Death Indexes, 1903-1970. Salem, OR, USA: Oregon State Library. Oregon Death Indexes, 1971-2008. Salem, OR, USA: Oregon State Library.

Citation: Death Record for Bernhart Grimm (Index) (Provo, UT, USA, Ancestry.com Operations Inc), www.ancestry.com, Oregon, Death Index, 1898-2008; State of Oregon, Oregon Death Index,1903-1998, Salem, OR, USA: Oregon State Archives and Records Center; [Database online].

Citation: Death Record for Bernice A Terp (Index) (Provo, UT, USA, Ancestry.com Operations Inc, 2007), www.ancestry.com, Wisconsin Death Index, 1959-1997 [database on-line]. Original data: Wisconsin Vital Records Office. Wisconsin Death Index, 1959-67, 1969-97. Madison, Wisconsin, USA: Wisconsin Department of Health.

Citation: Death Record for Caroline (Schellman) Wambsganss (Index) (Provo, UT, USA, Ancestry.com Operations Inc, 2010), www.ancestry.com, Ohio Obituary Index, 1830s-2011, 2010. Original data: Hayes Presidential Center Obituary Indexers and Volunteers. "Ohio Obituary Index." Database. Rutherford B. Hayes Presidential Center. http://index.rbhayes.org/hayes/index/; 2009.

Citation: Death Record for Carrie T (Grimm) Penrose (Index) (Provo, UT, USA, Ancestry.com Operations Inc, 2000), www.ancestry.com, Oregon, Death Index, 1898-2008 [database on-line]. 2000. Oregon State Library; 1966-1970 Death Index; Reel Title: Oregon Death Index A-L; Year Range: 1931-1941. Original data: State of Oregon. Oregon Death Index, 1903-1998. Salem, OR, USA: Oregon State Archives and Records Center. Oregon Death Indexes, 1903-1970. Salem, OR, USA: Oregon State Library. Oregon Death Indexes, 1971-2008. Salem, OR, USA: Oregon State Library.

Citation: Death Record for Casper D Anderson (Index) (Provo, UT, USA, Ancestry.com Operations Inc, 2007), www.ancestry.com, Minnesota, Death Index, 1908-2002; [Database online].State of Minnesota, Minnesota Death Index, 1908-2002, Minneapolis, MN, USA: Minnesota Department of Health.

Citation: Death Record for Casper Olson (Index) (Provo, UT, USA, Ancestry.com Operations Inc, 2007), www.ancestry.com, Wisconsin Death Index, 1959-1997 [database on-line]. Original data: Wisconsin Vital Records Office. Wisconsin Death Index, 1959-67, 1969-97. Madison, Wisconsin, USA: Wisconsin Department of Health.

Citation: Death Record (Index) for Louis Steiner (Provo, UT, USA, Ancestry.com Operations Inc, 2007), www.ancestry.com, [Database online].

Citation: Death Record for Christopher Olson (Index) (Provo, UT, USA, Ancestry.com Operations Inc, 2012), www.ancestry.com, British Columbia, Canada, Death Index 1872-1990.

Citation: Death Record for Clara (Vollmer) Cheney (Index) (Provo, UT, USA, Ancestry.com Operations Inc), www.ancestry.com, Ohio Deaths, 1908-1932, 1938-1944, and 1958-2002; [Database online]; Cert#081929.

Citation: Death Record for Clara J Cheney (Index) (Provo, UT, USA, Ancestry.com Operations Inc, 2010), www.ancestry.com, Ohio, Deaths, 1908-1932, 1938-2007 [Database online].Certificate: 081929; Volume: 30000; Original data: Ohio. Division of Vital Statistics. Death Certificates and Index, December 20, 1908-December 31, 1953. State Archives Series 3094. Ohio Historical Society, Ohio; Ohio Department of Health. Index to Annual Deaths, 1958-2002. Ohio Department of Health, State Vital Statistics Unit, Columbus, OH, USA.

Citation: Death Record for Cletus Berken (Index) (Provo, UT, USA, Ancestry.com Operations Inc, 2007), www.ancestry.com, Wisconsin Vital Records Office, Wisconsin Death Index, 1959-67, 1969-97, Madison, Wisconsin, USA: , Wisconsin Department of Health; [Database online].

Citation: Death Record for Delois Olson (Index) (Provo, UT, USA, Ancestry.com Operations Inc), www.ancestry.com, Texas Death Index, 1903-2000; [Database online].Texas Department of Health, Texas Death Indexes, 1903-2000, Austin, TX, USA: Texas Department of Health, State Vital Statistics Unit.

Citation: Death Record for Douglas Lavern Grimm (Index) (Provo, UT, USA, Ancestry.com Operations Inc, 2005), www.ancestry.com, Minnesota, Death Index, 1908-2002 [database on-line]. 2001.Original data: State of Minnesota. Minnesota Death Index, 1908-2002. Minneapolis, MN, USA: Minnesota Department of Health.

Citation: Death Record for Duane Ervin Grimm (Index) (Provo, UT, USA, Ancesty.com Operations Inc, 2001), www.ancestry.com, Montana, Death Index, 1868-2011; [Database online].State of Montana, Montana Death Index, 1868-2011, Helena, Montana: State of Montana Department of Public Health and Human Services, Office of Vital Statistics.

Citation: Death Record for Edward C Grimm (Index) (Provo, UT, USA, Ancestry.com Operations Inc, 2000), www.ancestry.com, California, Death Index, 1940-1997 [Database online].2000. Original data: State of California. California Death Index, 1940-1997. Sacramento, CA, USA: State of California Department of Health Services, Center for Health Statistics.

Citation: Death Record for Elmer Anderson (Index) (Provo, UT, USA, Ancestry.com Operations Inc., 2011), www.ancestry.com, Wisconsin Vital Records Office, Wisconsin Death Index, 1959-67, 1969-97, Madison, Wisconsin, USA, Wisconsin Department of Health; [Database online]..

Citation: Death Record for Elmer H Grimm (Index) (Provo, UT, USA, Ancestry.com Operations Inc, 2000), www.ancestry.com, Oregon, Death Index, 1898-2008; [Database online]. Oregon State Library; Oregon Death Indexes, 1971-2008; Reel Title: State of Oregon Death Index; Year Range: 1991-2000.

Citation: Death Record for Elmore A Johns (Index) (Provo, UT, USA, Ancestry.com Operations Inc), www.ancestry.com, Oregon State Library; Oregon Death Index 1931-1941; Reel Title: Oregon Death Index A-Kl; Year Range: 1951-1960.

Citation: Death Record for Elsa K Mitchell (Index) (Provo, UT, USA, Ancestry.com Operations, Inc., 2011), www.ancestry.com, Michigan, Deaths and Burials Index, 1867-1995 [database on-line]. 2011. Original data: "Michigan Deaths and Burials, 1800–1995." Index. FamilySearch, Salt Lake City, Utah, 2009, 2010. Index entries derived from digital copies of original and compiled records.

Citation: Death Record for Elsie (Grimm) Pederson (Index) (Provo, UT, USA, Ancestry.com Operations Inc, 2012), www.ancestry.com, Oregon, Death Index, 1898-2008 [database on-line]. 2000. Oregon State Library; 1966-1970 Death Index; Reel Title: Oregon Death Index A-L; Year Range: 1931-1941. Original data: State of Oregon. Oregon Death Index, 1903-1998. Salem, OR, USA: Oregon State Archives and Records Center. Oregon Death Indexes, 1903-1970. Salem, OR, USA: Oregon State Library. Oregon Death Indexes, 1971-2008. Salem, OR, USA: Oregon State Library.

Citation: Death Record for Emily (Kreidt) Grimm (Index) (Provo, UT, USA, Ancestry.com Operations Inc, 2000), www.ancestry.com, Oregon State Library; Oregon Death Index 1903-1920; Reel Title: Oregon Death Index A-L; Year Range: 1903-1920.

Citation: Death Record for Ethel (Klasner) Funkey (Index) (Provo, UT, USA, Ancestry.com Operations Inc, 1998), www.ancestry.com, Michigan Department of Vital and Health Records. Michigan, Deaths, 1971-1996 [database on-line]. 1998. Original data: Michigan Department of Vital and Health Records. Michigan Death Index. Lansing, MI, USA.

Citation: Death Record for Evadna I (Bacon) Spencer (Index) (Provo, UT, USA, Ancestry.com Operations Inc, 2000), www.ancestry.com, Oregon, Death Index, 1898-2008; State of Oregon, Oregon Death Index, 1903-1998, Salem, OR, USA: Oregon State Archives and Records Center; [Database online].

Citation: Death Record for Evert Nels Pederson (Index) (Provo, UT, USA, Ancestry.com Operations Inc, 2007), www.ancestry.com, Oregon, Death Index, 1898-2008 [database on-line]. 2000. Oregon State Library; 1966-1970 Death Index; Reel Title: Oregon Death Index.

Citation: Death Record for Frank A. Grimm (Index) (Provo, UT, USA, Ancestry.com Operations Inc, 2003), www.ancestry.com, Idaho, Death Index, 1890-1962 [database on-line]. 2003. Original data: Bureau of Health Policy and Vital Statistics. Idaho Death Index, 1911-51. Boise, ID, USA: Idaho

Citation: Death Record for Fredricka Schellman (Index) (Provo, UT, USA, Ancestry.com Operations Inc, 2011), www.ancestry.com, Michigan, Deaths and Burials Index, 1867-1995 [database on-line]. Index entries derived from digital copies of original and compiled records.

Citation: Death Record for Gavin P Mitchell (Provo, UT, USA, Ancestry.com Operations Inc, 1998), www.ancestry.com, Michigan, Deaths, 1971-1996 [Database online].Michigan Department of Vital and Health Records. Michigan Death Index. Lansing, MI, USA.

Citation: Death Record for George J Drohlshagen (Index) (Provo, UT, USA, Ancestry.com Operations Inc, 2007), www.ancestry.com, Wisconsin Death Index, 1959-1997 [database on-line]. Original data: Wisconsin Vital Records Office. Wisconsin Death Index, 1959-67, 1969-97. Madison, Wisconsin, USA: Wisconsin Department of Health.

Citation: Death Record for George Menkenmaier (Index) (Provo, UT, USA, Ancestry.com Operations Inc, 2000), www.ancestry.com, Oregon, Death Index, 1898-2008 [database on-line]. 2000. Oregon State Library; 1966-1970 Death Index; Reel Title: Oregon Death Index.

Citation: Death Record for Gilbert T Olson (Index) (Provo, UT, USA, Ancestry.com Operations Inc), www.ancestry.com, Wisconsin Death Index, 1959-1997 [database on-line].

Citation: Death Record for Gustav A Grimm (Index) (Provo, UT, USA, Ancestry.com Operations Inc, 2000), www.ancestry.com, Oregon, Death Index, 1898-2008 [database on-line]. 2000. Oregon State Library; 1966-1970 Death Index; Reel Title: Oregon Death Index.

Citation: Death Record for Harriet L Klasner (Index) (Provo, UT, USA, Ancestry.com Operations Inc, 1998), www.ancestry.com, Minnesota, Death Index, 1908-2002; [Database online].State of Minnesota, Minnesota Death Index, 1908-2002, Minneapolis, MN, USA: Minnesota Department of Health.

Citation: Death Record for Hazel Menkenmaier (Index) (Provo, UT, USA, Ancestry.com Operations Inc, 2000), www.ancestry.com, Oregon, Death Index, 1898-2008 [database on-line]. 2000. Oregon State Library; 1966-1970 Death Index; Reel Title: Oregon Death Index A-L; Year Range: 1931-1941.

Citation: Death Record for Henry George Terp (Index) (Provo, UT, USA, Ancestry.com Operations Inc, 2007), www.ancestry.com, Wisconsin Death Index, 1959-1967, 1969-1997; [Database online].Cert#008884;

Citation: Death Record for Henry J Klasner (Index) (Provo, UT, USA, Ancestry.com Operations Inc, 1998), www.ancestry.com, Michigan Department of Vital and Health Records. Michigan, Deaths, 1971-1996[database on-line].

Citation: Death Record for Herman F Grimm (Index) (Provo, UT, USA, Ancestry.com Operations Inc, 2000), www.ancestry.com, Oregon, Death Index, 1898-2008; [Database online] .Original Source: Oregon State Library; Death Index Portland 1915-1924; Reel Title: Oregon Death Index Portland A-Z; Year Range: 1915-1924.

Citation: Death Record for Hollie F Schroder (Index) (Provo, UT, USA, Ancestry.com Operations Inc, 2000), www.ancestry.com, Oregon, Death Index, 1898-2008 [database on-line]. 2000. Oregon State Library; 1966-1970 Death Index; Reel Title: Oregon Death Index.

Citation: Death Record for Howard H Vollmer (Index) (Provo, UT, USA, Ancestry.com Operations Inc, 1998), www.ancestry.com, [database on-line].Michigan Department of Vital and Health Records. Michigan, Deaths, 1971-1996

Citation: Death Record for Ida (Bruns) Grimm (Index) (Provo, UT, USA, Ancestry.com Operations Inc, 2007), www.ancestry.com, Oregon, Death Index, 1898-2008; [Database online].State of Oregon; Oregon Death Index, 1903-1998, Salem, OR, USA: Oregon State Archives and Records Center.

Citation: Death Record for James E Huffman (Index) (Provo, UT, USA, Ancestry.com Operations Inc, 2000), www.ancestry.com, Oregon, Death Index, 1898-2008 [database on-line]. Oregon State Library; 1966-1970 Death Index; Reel Title: Oregon Death Index.

Citation: Death Record for James Maynard Doriot (Index) (Provo, UT, USA, Ancestry.com Operations Inc, 2000), www.ancestry.com, Oregon, Death Index, 1898-2008 [database on-line]. Oregon State Library; 1966-1970 Death Index; Reel Title: Oregon Death Index A-L; Year Range: 1931-1941.

Citation: Death Record for Johanna Anderson (Provo, UT, USA, Ancestry.com Operations Inc, 2000), www.ancestry.com, Wisconsin Death Index, 1959-1997 [Database online].Cert #017122;

Citation: Death Record for John Lincoln Klasner (Index) (Provo, UT, USA, Ancestry.com Operations, Inc., 2012), www.ancestry.com, Genesee County, Michigan, Death Index, 1867-1930 [Database online]. Vol 9; p. 312; record #655; Flint Genealogy Society, Flint, Michigan. Accessed 1 Sep 2013.

Citation: Death Record for John Lorenz (Index) (Provo, UT, USA, Ancestry.com Operations Inc, 2007), www.ancestry.com, Wisconsin Vital Records Office, Wisconsin Death Index, 1959-67, 1969-97, Madison, Wisconsin, USA. Wisconsin Department of Health; [Database online].

Citation: Death Record for John N Domnisse (Index) (Provo, UT, USA, Ancestry.com Operations Inc, 2010), www.ancestry.com, Oregon, Death Index, 1898-2008; Oregon State Library; 1966-1970 Death Index; Reel Title: State of Oregon Death Index; Year Range: 1971-1980

Citation: Death Record for Joseph P Baeb (Index) (Provo, UT, USA, Ancestry.com Operations Inc, 2007), www.ancestry.com, Wisconsin Vital Records Office, Wisconsin Death Index, 1959-67, 1969-97, Madison, Wisconsin, USA, Wisconsin Department of Health; [Database online].

Citation: Death Record for Katherine Singleton (Index) (Provo, UT, USA, Ancestry.com Operations Inc, 2007), www.ancestry.com, Wisconsin Vital Records Office, Wisconsin Death Index, 1959-67, 1969-97, Madison, Wisconsin, USA. Wisconsin Department of Health; [Database online].

Citation: Death Record for Kenneth Morris Pederson (Index) (Provo, UT, USA, Ancestry.com Operations Inc, 2005), www.ancestry.com, Oregon, Death Index, 1898-2008; Oregon State Library; Oregon Death Indexes, 1971-2008; Reel Title: State of Oregon Death Index; Year Range: 2001-2005.

Citation: Death Record for Lawrence A Grimm (Index) (Provo, UT, USA, Ancestry.com Operations Inc, 2012), www.ancestry.com, Oregon State Library; Oregon Death Indexes, 1971-2008; Reel Title: State of Oregon Death Index; Year Range: 1981-1990.

Citation: Death Record for Leona (Grimm) Arronson (Index) (Provo, UT, USA, Ancestry.com Operations Inc, 2000), www.ancestry.com, Oregon, Death Index, 1898-2008 [database on-line]. Oregon State Library; 1966-1970 Death Index; Reel Title: Oregon Death Index.

Citation: Death Record for Leslie I Terp (Index) (Provo, UT, USA, Ancestry.com Operations Inc, 2000), www.ancestry.com, California, Death Index, 1940-1997; [Database online]. State of California. California Death Index, 1940-1997. Sacramento, CA, USA: State of Calif. Department of Health Services, Center for Health Statistics. Date: 1977-12-18.

Citation: Death Record for Lewis E Penrose (Index) (Provo, UT, USA, Ancestry.com Operations Inc, 2000), www.ancestry.com, Oregon, Death Index, 1898-2008 [database on-line]. Oregon State Library; 1966-1970 Death Index; Reel Title: Oregon Death Index.

Citation: Death Record for Logan J Bacon (Index) (Provo, UT, USA, Ancestry.com Operations Inc), www.ancestry.com, Idaho Death Index, 1911-51; Bureau of Health Policy and Vital Statistics, Idaho Death Index, 1911-51, Boise, ID, USA: Idaho Department of Health and Welfare; [Database online].

Citation: Death Record for Louis Steiner (Index) (Provo, UT, USA, Ancestry.com Operations Inc, 2007), www.ancestry.com, Wisconsin Vital Records Office, Wisconsin Death Index, 1959-67, 1969-97, Madison, Wisconsin, USA: , Wisconsin Department of Health; [Database online].

Citation: Death Record for Margaret (Birk) Kettenbeil (Index) (Provo, UT, USA, Ancestry.com Operations Inc, 1998), www.ancestry.com, Michigan Department of Vital and Health Records. Michigan, Deaths, 1971-1996 .

Citation: Death Record for Marian Virginia (Terp) Dyce (Index) (Provo, UT, USA, Ancestry.com Operations Inc, 2000), www.ancestry.com, California, Death Index, 1940-1997 [Database online].Los Angeles; Date: 28 Jun 1993; Social Security: 396034208.

Citation: Death Record for Mary C. Brandes (Provo, UT, USA, Ancestry.com Operations Inc, 2010), www.ancestry.com, Ohio, Deaths, 1908-1932, 1938-2007; Certificate: 080841; Volume: 27896; Ohio. Division of Vital Statistics. Death Certificates and Index, December 20, 1908-December 31, 1953.

Citation: Death Record for Mary Eileen Terp (Index) (Provo, UT, USA, Ancestry.com Operations Inc, 2007), www.ancestry.com, Wisconsin Death Index, 1959-1997 [Database online].No. 013455;

Citation: Death Record for Mathilda (Grimm) Koch (Index) (Provo, UT, USA, Ancestry.com Operations Inc), www.ancestry.com, Idaho, Death Index, 1890-1962 [Database online].

Citation: Death Record for Merle Elton Crabb (Index) (Provo, UT, USA, Ancestry.com Operations Inc, 2007), www.ancestry.com, Wisconsin Vital Records Office, Wisconsin Death Index, 1959-67, 1969-97, Madison, Wisconsin, USA. Wisconsin Department of Health; [Database online].

Citation: Death Record for Mildred I Grimm (Index) (Provo, UT, USA, Ancestry.com Operations Inc, 2000), www.ancestry.com, Oregon, Death Index, 1898-2008; Oregon State Library; Oregon Death Index1931-1941; Reel Title: Oregon Death Index A-Kl; Year Range: 1951-1960. includes

Citation: Death Record for Nels Olson (Index) (Provo, UT, USA, Ancestry.com Operations Inc, 2007), www.ancestry.com, Washington Death Index, 1940-1996 [Database online].

Citation: Death Record for Nels Pederson (Index) (Provo, UT, USA, Ancestry.com Operations Inc, 2010), www.ancestry.com, Oregon, Death Index, 1898-2008 [database on-line].

Citation: Death Record for Nora (Bear) Anderson. (Provo, UT, USA, Ancestry.com Operations Inc. 2010) www.ancestry.com.. Washington Death Index, 1940-1996 [database on-line]. 2002. Vancouver, Clark Co., Washington; Cert #025994. Original data: Washington State Department of Health. State Death Records Index, 1940-1996. Microfilm. Washington State Archives, Olympia, Washington.

Citation: Death Record for Otto C Anderson (Index) (Provo, UT, USA, Ancestry.com Operations Inc, 2002), www.ancestry.com, Wisconsin Vital Records Office, Wisconsin Death Index, 1959-67, 1969-97, Madison, Wisconsin, USA. Wisconsin Department of Health; [Database online].

Citation: Death Record for Otto Grimm (Index) (Provo, UT, USA, Ancestry.com Operations Inc, 2007), www.ancestry.com, Wisconsin Death Index, 1959-1997 [database on-line].

Citation: Death Record for Ralph F Spencer (Index) (Provo, UT, USA, Ancestry.com Operations Inc, 2011), www.ancestry.com, Oregon, Death Index, 1898-2008 [database on-line]. 2000. Oregon State Library; 1966-1970 Death Index; Reel Title: Oregon Death Index.

Citation: Death Record for Raymond Paul Schubert (Provo, UT, USA, Ancestry.com Operations Inc, 2001), www.ancestry.com, Minnesota, Death Index, 1908-2002 [database on-line]. Cert #021392; Rec#2472773.

Citation: Death Record for Reinhard Grimm (Index) (Provo, UT, USA, Ancestry.com Operations Inc, 2007), www.ancestry.com, Wisconsin Death Index, 1959-1997 [database on-line].

Citation: Death Record for Reuben Kettenbeil (Index) (Provo, UT, USA, Ancestry.com Operations Inc, 2010), www.ancestry.com, The Library of Michigan; Michigan Death Records, 1897-1920; Rolls: 1-302; Archive Barcode/Item Number: 30000008530952; Roll: 57; Cert #28.

Citation: Death Record for Reuben Kettenbeil (Index) (Provo, UT, USA, Ancestry.com Operations Inc, 2011), www.ancestry.com, Michigan, Deaths and Burials Index, 1867-1995 [database on-line]. Index entries derived from digital copies of original and compiled records.

Citation: Death Record for Robert J Terp (Index) (Provo, UT, USA, Ancestry.com Operations Inc, 2007), www.ancestry.com, Wisconsin Death Index, 1959-1997 [Database online].Cert #017122;

Citation: Death Record for Robert L Grimm (Index) (Provo, UT, USA, Ancestry.com Operations Inc), www.ancestry.com, California, Death Index, 1940-1997 [Database online].

Citation: Death Record for Rosa (Otjen) Grimm (Index) (Provo, UT, USA, Ancestry.com Operations Inc, 2003), www.ancestry.com, Idaho Death Index, 1911-51; [Database online].

Citation: Death Record for Shirley B Evanoff (Index) (Provo, UT, USA, Ancestry.com Operations Inc, 2006), www.ancestry.com, California, Death Index, 1940-1997 [Database online].

Citation: Death Record for Susan (Schneider) Schellman (Index) (Provo, UT, USA, Ancestry.com Operations Inc, 2010), www.ancestry.com, Michigan, Death Records, 1897-1920; The Library of Michigan; Michigan Death Records, 1897-1920; Rolls: 1-302; Archive Barcode/Item Number: 30000008533261; Roll #: 224; Cert# 122.

Citation: Death Record for Verna (Bacon) Field (Index) (Provo, UT, USA, Ancestry.com Operations Inc, 2000), www.ancestry.com, California, Death Index, 1940-1997; State of California. California Death Index, 1940-1997. Sacramento, CA, USA: State of California Dept. of Health Services, Center for Health Statistics. Date: 1967-09-19.

Citation: Death Record for Viola (Grimm) Bill (Index) (Provo, UT, USA, Ancestry.com Operations Inc, 2003), www.ancestry.com, Idaho, Death Index, 1890-1962 [Database online].

Citation: Death Record for Walter H Kettenbeil (Index) (Provo, UT, USA, Ancestry.com Operations Inc, 1998), www.ancestry.com, [database on-line].Michigan Department of Vital and Health Records. Michigan, Deaths, 1971-1996

Citation: Death Record for Wilbert Louis Grimm (Index) (Provo, UT, USA, Ancestry.com Operations State of California. California Death Index, 1940-1997. Sacramento, CA, USA: State of California Inc, 2000), www.ancestry.com, California, Death Index, 1940-1997 [Database online].

Citation: Death Record for Wilhelm A Grimm (Index) (Provo, UT, USA, Ancestry.com Operations Inc, 2000), www.ancestry.com, Oregon, Death Index, 1898-2008 [database on-line]. Oregon State Library; 1966-1970 Death Index; Reel Title: Oregon Death Index. Original data: State of Oregon. Oregon Death Index, 1903-1998. Salem, OR, USA: Oregon Death Indexes, 1903-1970. Salem, Oregon, USA Oregon State Library. Oregon Death Indexes1971-2008. Salem, OR, USA

Citation: Death Record for William Max Grimm (Index) (Provo, UT, USA, Ancestry.com Operations Inc, 2001), www.ancestry.com, Minnesota, Death Index, 1908-2002; [Database online].State of Minnesota, Minnesota Death Index, 1908-2002, Minneapolis, MN, USA: Minnesota Department of Health.

Citation: Death Record for William Schellman (Index) (Provo, UT, USA, Ancestry.com Operations Inc, 1998), www.ancestry.com, Michigan Department of Vital and Health Records. Michigan, Deaths, 1971-1996[database on-line]. 1998. Original data: Michigan Department of Vital and Health Records. Michigan Death Index. Lansing, MI, USA.

Citation: Death Record for Wilma (Grimm) Huffman (Index) (Provo, UT, USA, Ancestry.com Operations Inc, 2000), www.ancestry.com, Oregon, Death Index, 1898-2008 [database on-line]. Oregon State Library; 1966-1970 Death Index; Reel Title: Oregon Death Index. Original data: State of Oregon. Oregon Death Index, 1903-1998. Salem, OR,

Citation: Death Record for Woodrow J Terp (Index) (Provo, UT, USA, Ancestry.com Operations Inc, 2000), www.ancestry.com, California, Death Index, 1940-1997 [Database online].Los Angeles; 1983-06-22. Source Information: State of California. California Death Index, 1940-1997. Sacramento, CA, USA: State of California Department of Health Services, Center for Health Statistics.

Citation:    Death Report of Clara Anderson Grimm, n.d., Hemer Funeral Service, Inc., Medford, WI. (Copy in possession of Tracy Doriot, Washougal, WA).

Citation:    Funeral Arrangements for Mary Olson Anderson (Medford, Taylor Co, WI, Hartwig and Ruesch Funeral Home, abt Jun 16 1955), (Copy in possession of Tracy Doriot, Washougal, WA).Funeral Arrangement Order; Hartwig and Ruesch Funeral Home; purchase by Mrs. Alvin Grimm; Medford, Taylor Co, Wisconsin.

Citation:    Funeral Car List Booklet for August Anderson (Marshfield, Taylor Co, WI, Felker Bros., Mfg. Co, 7 May 1945), In possession of Tracy Doriot, Washougal, WA. Funeral Car Passenger Booklet; Marshfield, Marshfield, Taylor Co, Wisconsin; notation of spouse's date of birth and death.

Citation:    Military Burial Register for Alfred Schubert (Provo, UT, USA, Ancestry.com Operations, Inc., 2012), www.ancestry.com, [Database online]. p. 350, entry #3.; "...shipped to Medford, Wis." www.ancestry.com, U.S., Burial Registers, Military Posts and National Cemeteries, 1862-1960; [Database online].

**Title:    Death Records (Veterans Administration)**

Source information for all following VA Death Record citations: (Provo, UT, USA, Ancestry.com Operations Inc, 2010), www.ancestry.com, U.S., Department of Veterans Affairs BIRLS Death File, 1850-2010; database online; Beneficiary Identification Records Locator Subsystem (BIRLS) Death File

Citation:    VA Death Record for Garvin Mitchell

Citation:    VA Death Record for Harold J Terp

Citation:    VA Death Record for James Neuman

Citation:    VA Death Record for Leroy Krausse

Citation:    VA Death Record for Lloyd G. Schubert

Citation:    VA Death Record for Melvin Pederson

Citation:    VA Death Record for Michael Boiko

**Title:    Divorce Records**

Citation:    Divorce Record (Index) for Danny Robert Sperl (Provo, UT, USA, Ancestry.com Operations Inc, 2006), www. Ancestry.com. Wisconsin Divorce Index, 1965-1984 [database on-line]. 2008. Cert #003524.Original data: Wisconsin Department of Health and Family Services. Wisconsin Divorce Index, 1965-1984. Madison, WI, USA: Wisconsin Department of Health and Family Services.

Citation:    Divorce Record (Index) for Leslie P Terp (Provo, UT, USA, Ancestry.com Operations Inc), www.ancestry.com, California Divorce Index, 1966-1984 [Database online]. State file #159618; Dissolution File #014125; Original source: State of California. California Divorce Index, 1966-1984. Microfiche. Center for Health Statistics, California department of Health Services, Sacramento, CA.

Citation:    Divorce Record (Index) for Lois A Kirchberg (Provo, UT, USA, Ancestry.com Operations Inc, 2006), www.ancestry.com, Minnesota, Divorce Index, 1970-1995; [Database online].Minnesota Statewide Divorce Index, 1970-1995, St Paul, MN, USA: Minnesota Department of Health.

**Title:    Education Records**

Citation:    Commencement Program for Gladys Ann Grimm (Medford, WI, Medford High School, 20 May1952), (Copy in possession of Tracy Doriot, Washougal, WA.) Commencement Program; Medford High School,1952 Class Roll; "In the order of receiving diplomas....Gladys Grimm"; Medford, Taylor Co, WI

Citation:    Education Record of Clara Anderson (Medford, Taylor Co, WI, Department of Education, 1927), (In possession of Tracy Doriot, Washougal, WA). High School Diploma; Medford High School, Medford, Taylor Co, WI; 10 Jun 1927.

Citation:    Graduation Certificate Gardiner Flying Services (Madison, WI, State of Wisconsin State Aeronautics Commission, 04 Jun 1948), Copy in possession of Tracy Doriot, Washougal, WA. Private Pilot License; Gardinier Flying Services; State of Wisconsin State Aeronautics Commission; Madison, Dane Co, Wisconsin..

Citation:    Pecos Army Flying School Yearbook (Seattle, WA, Army and Navy Publishing Co, Inc., 1942). (Copy in possession of Tracy Owen Doriot, Washougal, WA). 1942; Army Air Forces West Coast Training Center.

Citation:    US School Yearbook for Sandra Terp (Provo, UT, USA, Ancestry.com Operations Inc, 2010), www.ancestry.com, U.S. School Yearbooks [database on-line]. Original data: Yearbook: Flambeau 1968, Lincoln High School. Manitowoc Co, Manitowoc Co, Wisconsin

**Title:    Family Genealogies**

Kratz Family Genealogy for Adolph Grimm Line (dkratz0849@sheglobalnet.com, Donald Kratz, 23 Dec 2010), WorldConnect.com, Kratz Family Genealogy; WorldConnect.rootsweb.ancestry.com; [Database online]. http://worldconnect.rootsweb.ancestry.com/cgi-bin/igm.cgi?op=GET&db=k632&id=I09027.

**Title:    Family Group Sheets**

Citation:    Family Group Sheet from Bernice Krausse Kuklinsky (Marshall, WI, Bernice Krausse, 15 Feb 2000), (In possession of Tracy Doriot, Washougal, WA). Family Group Sheet (handwritten) Marshall, Taylor Co, Wisconsin; submitted by Bernice Krausse Kuklinsky.

Citation:    Family Group Sheet from Elaine Krausse McNeil (Marshall, Dane Co, WI, Elaine Krausse McNeil, 05 Feb 2000), (In possession of Tracy Doriot, Washougal, WA). Family Group Sheet (handwritten), Marshall, Taylor Co, Wisconsin; submitted by Elaine Krausse McNeil.

**Title:** **Family Portrait Christmas Card of LaVern Grimm Family**

Citation: Family Portrait Christmas Card of LaVern Grimm Family, 1986; (In possession of Tracy Doriot, Washougal, WA).Members identified on back of photo; Grimm, Johnson, Mandt.

**Title:** **Funeral Records**

Citation: Funeral Arrangements for Mary Olson Anderson (Medford, Taylor Co, WI, Hartwig and Ruesch Funeral Home, abt 16 Jun 1955), (Copy in possession of Tracy Doriot, Washougal, WA).Funeral Arrangement Order; Hartwig and Ruesch Funeral Home; purchase by Mrs. Alvin Grimm; Medford, Taylor Co, Wisconsin.

**Title:** **Gravesites**

Citation: Gravesite for Adolph Koch (Provo, UT, USA, Ancestry.com Operations, Inc., 2011), www.ancestry.com, Idaho, Find A Grave Index, 1850-2012; [Database online]. Record added: Aug 02, 2005. Find A Grave Memorial# 11466812. Paul, Minidoka Co., Idaho; Paul Cemetery; Accessed 02 Dec 2013.

Citation: Gravesite for Adolph Koch Jr. (Provo, UT, USA, Ancestry.com Operations Inc, 2011), www.ancestry.com, Paul Cemetery, Paul, Minidoka Co, Idaho, Find A Grave Index, 1850-2012; Record added: Aug 02, 2005; Find A Grave Memorial# 11466812 [Database online]. Accessed 02 Dec 2013.

Citation: Gravesite for Albert A Grimm (Provo, UT, USA, Ancestry.com Operations Inc, 2012), www.ancestry.com, Immanuel Lutheran Cemetery, McIntosh, Polk Co, Minnesota, Find A Grave Index, 1800-2012 [website]. Record added: Jul 07, 2012 Find A Grave Memorial# 93233668; Accessed 18 January 2013.

Citation: Gravesite for Alfred E Arronson (Provo, UT, USA, Ancestry.com Operations Inc, 2012), www.ancestry.com, Skyline Memorial Gardens, Portland, Multnomah Co, Oregon, Find A Grave Index, 1819-2012; [Database online]. Plot: Old Rugged Cross 260 B 1; Record added: Feb 06, 2013; Find A Grave Memorial# 104729173

Citation: Gravesite for Alma (Nelson) Olson (Provo, UT, USA, Ancestry.com Operations Inc, 2010), www.ancestry.com, Perkinstown Cemetery, Perkinstown, Taylor Co, Wisconsin, Find A Grave [website]. 2010. Record added: Oct 27, 2011; Find A Grave Memorial# 79401813.

Citation: Gravesite for Alphonse Cyrille Cheney (Provo, UT, USA, Ancestry.com Operations Inc, 2012), www.ancestry.com, Michigan, Find A Grave [website]. Plot: Sec 11, Lot 131; Record added: Nov 02, 2011; Find A Grave Memorial# 79779037; Lakeside Cemetery, Hancock, Houghton Co, Michigan; Plot: Section 11 Lot 131; Accessed 29 Aug 2013.

Citation: Gravesite for Alvin L Olson (Provo, UT, USA, Ancestry.com Operations Inc), www.ancestry.com, Selected U.S. Headstone Photos [Database online].

Citation: Gravesite for Alvin Lester Olson (Provo, UT, USA, Ancestry.com Operations IN, 2012), www.ancestry.com, Texas, Find A Grave Index, 1761-2012 [Database online].Record added: Mar 09, 2011; Find A Grave Memorial# 66666895; Moore Memorial Gardens; Arlington, Tarrant Co, Texas; Accessed 02 Dec 2013.

Citation: Gravesite for Amos Bill (Provo, UT, USA, Web: Idaho, Find A Grave Index, 1850-2012, 2011), www.ancestry.com, Idaho, Find A Grave Index, 1850-2012; [Database online]. Record added: Aug 02, 2005; Find A Grave Memorial# 11466821; Paul Cemetery; Paul, Minidoka Co, Idaho. Accessed 02 Dec 2013.

Citation: Gravesite for Andrew Anderson (Provo, UT, USA, Ancestry.com Operations Inc, 2010), www.ancestry.com, Evergreen Cemetery, Medford, Taylor Co, Wisconsin; Lot 14, Block T. (Photo: Maryellen Anderson, Vancouver, WA; Oct 2003).

Citation: Gravesite for Anna (Duesing) Grimm (Provo, UT, USA, Ancestry.com Operations Inc), www.ancestry.com, Minnesota, Find a Grave Index: 1800-2012; [Database online]. Record added: Aug 30, 2010 Find A Grave Memorial# 57935891; Immanuel Lutheran Cemetery, Paul, Minidoka Co., Minnesota. Accessed 02 Dec 2013.

Citation: Gravesite for Anna (Grimm) Bacon (Provo, UT, USA, Ancestry.com Operations, Inc.), www.ancestry.com, Oregon, Find A Grave Index, 1819-2012; [Database online].Record added: Oct 20, 2010; Find A Grave Memorial# 60385958. Rose City Cemetery; Portland, Multnomah Co, Oregon. Accessed 02 Dec 2013.

Citation: Gravesite for Anton H Grimm (Provo, UT, USA, Ancestry.com Operations Inc, 2010), www.ancestry.com, Wisconsin, Find A Grave Index, 1836-2012; [website]. 2010. Record added: Jun18, 2012; Find A Grave Memorial# 92163893. St. John-St. James Lutheran Cemetery, Reedsville, Manitowoc Co., Wisconsin. Accessed 02 Dec 2013.

Citation: Gravesite for Arka (Antrim) Penrose Lawrence. (Provo, UT, USA, Ancestry.com Operations Inc, 2012), www.ancestry.com, Oregon, Find A Grave Index, 1819-2012; [website] 2010. Record added: Jan 13, 2005. Find A Grave Memorial# 10318852. Hopewell Cemetery, Dayton, Yamhill Co., Oregon. Accessed 02 Dec 2013.

Citation: Gravesite for August N and Mary (Olson) Anderson (Photo: Maryellen Anderson, 2003), Evergreen Cemetery; Medford, Taylor Co, Wisconsin. (Photo by Maryellen Anderson, Vancouver, WA, Oct 2003).

Citation: Gravesite for August Steiner (Medford, Taylor Co, WI, 2003), Chelsea Cemetery, Medford, Taylor Co, Wisconsin. (Photo by Maryellen Anderson, Vancouver, WA, Oct 2003).

Citation: Gravesite for Barbara (Klasner) Brohn (Provo, UT, USA, Ancestry.com Operations Inc, 2012), www.ancestry.com, Michigan, Find A Grave Index, 1805-2012 [website]. Record added: Feb 10, 2010. Find A Grave Memorial# 47956274. Sunset Hills Cemetery; Flint, Genesee Co., Michigan. Accessed 1 Sep 2013.

Citation: Gravesite for Basil Orlando Singleton (Provo, UT, USA, Ancestry.com Operations Inc., 2000), www.ancestry.com, Wisconsin, Find A Grave [website]. 2010. Record added: May 16, 2007 Find A Grave Memorial# 19396160. Perkinstown Cemetery, Perkinstown, Taylor Co, Wisconsin. Accessed 02 Dec 2013.

Citation: Gravesite for Bernice A Terp (Provo, UT, USA, Ancestry.com Operations Inc, 2011), www.ancestry.com, Wisconsin: Find A Grave [Database online]. Record added: Feb 18, 2009 Find A Grave Memorial# 33978896. Woodlawn Cemetery; Allouez, Brown Co., Michigan. Accessed 02 Dec 2013.

Citation: Gravesite for Bertha Lavonne Abel (Provo, UT, USA, Ancestry.com Operations Inc, 2011), www.ancestry.com, Washington: Find A Grave [Database online]. Okanogan Valley Memorial Gardens, Omak, Okanogan Co., Washington; Recorded: 29 Sep 2009. Find A Grave Memorial #42505788. Accessed 10 Dec 2013.

Citation: Gravesite for Carl F Schmelzer (Provo, UT, USA, Ancestry.com Operations Inc, 2012), www.ancestry.com, California, Find A Grave Index, 1775-2012; [Database online]. Odd fellows Lawn Cemetery (Sec: C); Santa Rosa, Sonoma Co, CA. Accessed 02 Dec 2013.

Citation: Gravesite for Caroline (Schellman) Wambsganss (Provo, UT, USA, Ancestry.com Operations Inc), www.ancestry.com, Indiana, Find A Grave [website]. Recorded: May 17, 2010; Find A Grave Memorial# 52500201; Concordia Lutheran Cemetery; Fort Wayne, Allen Co., Indian. Accessed 29 Aug 2013.

Citation: Gravesite for Carrie T (Grimm) Penrose (Provo, UT, USA, Ancestry.com Operations Inc, 2012), www.ancestry.com, Oregon, Find A Grave Index, 1819-2012; [Database online]. Record added: Jan 17, 2005. Find A Grave Memorial# 10338169. "Teresa Carrie Grimm Penrose". Hopewell Cemetery, Dayton, Yamhill Co, Oregon. Accessed 02 De 2013.

Citation: Gravesite for Casper Olson Jr. (Provo, UT, USA, Ancestry.com Operations Inc, 2010), www.ancestry.com, Wisconsin, Find A Grave Index, 1836-2012; [website]. 2010. Record added: Oct27, 2011; Find A Grave Memorial# 79401840. Perkinstown Cemetery, Perkinstown, Taylor Co, Wisconsin. Accessed 02 Dec 2013.

Citation: Gravesite for Casper Olson Sr. (Provo, UT, USA, Ancestry.com Operations Inc, 2010), www.ancestry.com, Wisconsin, Find A Grave Index, 1836-2012; [website]. 2010. Record added: Oct27, 2011; Find A Grave Memorial# 79401794; Perkinstown Cemetery, Perkinstown, Taylor Co, Wisconsin. Accessed 02 Dec 2013.

Citation: Gravesite for Charles Henry Louis Strebig (Provo, UT, USA, Ancestry.com Operations Inc, 2010), www.ancestry.com, Wisconsin, Find A Grave [website]. 2010. Record added: Apr 11, 2008 Find A Grave Memorial# 25936559.

Citation: Gravesite for Chester Louis Steiner (Provo, UT, USA, Ancestry.com Operations Inc, 2010), www.ancestry.com, Wisconsin, Find A Grave [website]. 2010. Recorded: Sep 25, 2012 Find A Grave Memorial# 97774868; Lutheran Memorial Park (Sect: B Lot 14), Kewaskum, Washington Co, Wisconsin. Accessed 02 Dec 2013.

Citation: Gravesite for Clara (Vollmer) Cheney (Provo, UT, USA, Ancestry.com Operations Inc, 2012), www.ancestry.com, Michigan, Find A Grave Index, 1805-2012 [website]. Record added: Jun 01, 2011 Find A Grave Memorial# 70710347; Lakeside Cemetery (Plot: Sec 11, Lot 131), Hancock, Houghton Co, Michigan. Accessed 29 Aug 2013.

Citation: Gravesite for Claude H. Klasner (Provo, UT, USA, Ancestry.com Operations, Inc., 2012), www.ancestry.com, Michigan, Find A Grave Index, 1805-2012 [database on-line]. Record added: Sep 15, 2012; Find A Grave Memorial # 97127320.Woodland Cemetery, Jackson, Jackson Co, Michigan. Accessed: 1 Sep 2013.

Citation: Gravesite for Cleo (Grimm) Zemke (Provo, UT, USA, Ancestry.com Operations Inc, 2012), www.ancestry.com, Web: Idaho, Find A Grave Index, 1850-2012; [Database online]. Record added: Jul 06, 2012 Find A Grave Memorial# 93199837. Paul Cemetery, Paul, Minidoka Co, Minnesota. Accessed 02 Dec 2013.

Citation: Gravesite for Donna (Anderson) Boiko (Provo, UT, USA, Ancestry.com Operations Inc, 2012), www.ancestry.com, Washington, Find A Grave Index, 1821-2012; Record added: Jul 06, 2012 Find A Grave Memorial# Record added: May 09, 2010. Find A Grave Memorial# 52187583 [Database online]. Curlew Cemetery, Curlew, Ferry Co, Washington. Accessed 02 Dec 2013.

Citation: Gravesite for Douglas L Fritz (Provo, UT, USA, Ancestry.com Operations Inc, 2011), www.ancestry.com, Indiana, Find A Grave Index, 1800-2012 [website]. Recorded: 16 May 2010; Find A Grave Memorial# 52451831. Concordia Cemetery Gardens, Fort Wayne, Allen Co, Indiana. Retrieved 30 August 2013.

Citation: Gravesite for Douglas L Grimm (Provo, UT, USA, Ancestry.com Operations Inc, 2012), www.ancestry.com, Minnesota, Find A Grave Index, 1800-2012; [Database online]. Record added: Aug 30, 2010. Find A Grave Memorial# 57935985; Immanuel Lutheran Church, McIntosh, Polk Co, Minnesota. Accessed 02 Dec 2013.

Citation: Gravesite for Edward Baeb (Infant) (Provo, UT, USA, Ancestry.com Operations Inc, 2011), www.ancestry.com, Wisconsin: Find A Grave [website]. Record added: Jan 30, 2012 Find A Grave Memorial# 84200086. Fort Howard Memorial Park, Green Bay, Brown Co, Wisconsin. Accessed 02 Dec 2013.

Citation: Gravesite for Elfrieda (Wambsganss) Baals (Provo, UT, USA, Ancestry.com Operations Inc, 2012), www.ancestry.com, Indiana, Find A Grave, 1800-2012 [website]. Record added: Aug 12, 2010 Find A Grave Memorial# 56978071; Concordia Cemetery Gardens, Fort Wayne, Allen Co, Indiana. Obituary printed in the News-Sentinel, Fort Wayne, Indiana, on 28 Feb 1992, included. Retrieved 30 August 2013.

Citation: Gravesite for Elizabeth (Schneider) Grimm (Provo, UT, USA, Ancestry.com Operations Inc, 20112), www.ancestry.com, Web: Oregon, Find A Grave Index, 1819-2012; [Database online].Record added: May 08, 2012; Memorial# 89817881. Trinity Lutheran Church, Mount Angel, Marion Co, Oregon. Accessed 02 Dec 2013.

Citation: Gravesite for Elizabeth (Wambsganss) Weber (Provo, UT, USA, Ancestry.com Operations Inc, 2010), www.ancestry.com, Texas, Find A Grave, [website]. 2010. 1968 Record added: May 06, 2007; Find A Grave Memorial# 19266373. Algoma Cemetery South (Plot: Sec: South Side), Marshall, Harrison Co., Texas. Retrieved 30 August 2013.

Citation: Gravesite for Ella K. [Unknown] Grimm. (Provo, UT, USA, Ancestry.com Operations Inc, 2012), www.ancestry.com, Oregon, Find A Grave Index, 1819-2012; [Database online]. Record added: Mar 24, 2010. Find A Grave Memorial# 50161674. City View Cemetery (Sec: R), Salem, Marion Co, Oregon. Accessed 02 Dec 2013.

Citation: Gravesite for Elmore A Johns (Provo, UT, USA, Ancestry.com Operations Inc), www.ancestry.com, National Cemetery Administration. U.S. Veterans Gravesites, ca.1775-2006 [database on-line]. Provo, UT, USA: Ancestry.com Operations Inc, 2006; Original data: National Cemetery Administration Nationwide Gravesite Locator. Willamette National Cemetery, Portland, Multnomah Co, Oregon. Accessed 02 Dec 2013.

Citation: Gravesite for Ethel (Klasner) Funkey (Provo, UT, USA, Ancestry.com Operations Inc, 2012), www.ancestry.com, Michigan, Find A Grave Index, 1805-2012 [database on-line].Record added: Feb 11, 2010; Find A Grave Memorial# 48002882. Birch Run Cemetery, Birch Run, Saginaw Co, Michigan. Accessed 1 Sep 2013.

Citation: Gravesite for Florence (Clarkson) Anderson (Provo, UT, USA, Ancestry.com Operations, Inc., 2007), www.ancestry.com, Washington, Find A Grave Index, 1821-2012 [Database online]. Record added: Oct 06, 2009. Find A Grave Memorial# 42758459. Riverside Cemetery, Okanogan, Okanogan Co, Washington. Accessed 02 Dec 2013.

Citation: Gravesite for Florence (Laurin) Vollmer Ronseth (Provo, UT, USA, Ancestry.com Operations Inc), www.ancestry.com, Wisconsin, Find A Grave [website]. Recorded: Sep 7, 2011; Find A Grave Memorial# 76149590; Calvary Cemetery, Superior, Douglas Co, Wisconsin. Accessed 29 Aug 2013.

Citation: Gravesite for Florence Anderson (Provo, UT, USA, Ancestry.com Operations Inc, 2010), www.ancestry.com, Washington, Find A Grave [website] 2010. Record added: Oct 06, 2009; Find A Grave Memorial# 42758459. "Anderson - Otto C. 1915; Florence J. 1918-1979 - Together Forever". Riverside Cemetery, Okanogan, Okanogan Co., Washington. Accessed 02 Dec 2013.

Citation: Gravesite for Franziscus "Frank" Grimm Sr. (Provo, UT, USA, Ancestry.com Operations Inc, 2010), www.ancestry.com, Web: Oregon, Find A Grave Index, 1819-2012 [database on-line]. Provo, UT, USA: Ancestry.com Operations, Inc., 2012. Record added: Nov 06, 2010; Memorial #61747693; Rose City Cemetery, Portland, Multnomah Co., Oregon. Accessed 02 Dec 2013.

Citation: Gravesite for Frederick P W Wambsganss (Provo, UT, USA, Ancestry.com Operations Inc, 2012), www.ancestry.com, Indiana, Find A Grave, 1800-2012 [website]. Record added: Dec 29, 2012; Find A Grave Memorial# 102800522. Original source: Wellman Funeral Home. Greenlawn Memorial Park, Fort Wayne, Allen Co, Indiana. Records Retrieved 30 August 2013

Citation: Gravesite for Frederick P.E. Wambsganss. (Provo, UT, USA, Ancestry.com Operations Inc, 2012), www.ancestry.com, Indiana, Find A Grave Index, 1800-2012; [website]. Record added: May 17, 2010; Find A Grave Memorial# 52500212; Concordia Cemetery Gardens, Fort Wayne, Allen Co, Indiana. Accessed 29 Aug 2013.

Citation: Gravesite for Garvin C Mitchell (Provo, UT, USA, Ancestry.com Operations Inc, 2012), www.ancestry.com, Indiana, Find A Grave Index, 1800-2012 [Database online].Record added: May 26, 2010; Find A Grave Memorial# 52863785; Maplewood Cemetery, Anderson, Madison Co., Indiana. Accessed 29 August 2013.

Citation: Gravesite for George E Menkenmaier (Provo, UT, USA, Ancestry.com Operations Inc, 2012), www.ancestry.com, Oregon, Find A Grave Index, 1819-2012; [website]. Record added: Jun 24, 2007; Find A Grave Memorial #20058467. Burns Cemetery, Burns, Harney Co., Oregon. Accessed 02 Dec 2013.

Citation: Gravesite for Gerald Eugene Anderson (Provo, UT, USA, Ancestry.com Operations Inc, 2012), www.ancestry.com, Washington, Find A Grave Index, 1819-2012; [website]. Record added 06 Apr 2010; Find A Grave Memorial #50708276. Sunset Memorial Park, Hoquiam, Grays Harbor Co., Washington. Accessed 11 Dec 2013.

Citation: Gravesite for Gust A Grimm (Provo, UT, USA, Ancestry.com Operations Inc, 2012), www.ancestry.com, Oregon, Find A Grave Index, 1819-2012; [Database online]. Record added: Mar 24, 2010. Find A Grave Memorial# 50161672. City View Cemetery (Sec: R), Salem, Marion Co, Oregon. Accessed 02 Dec 2013.

Citation: Gravesite for Gustave Alphonse Weber (Provo, UT, USA, Ancestry.com Operations Inc, 2010), www.ancestry.com, Texas, Find A Grave, [website]. 2010. 1968 Record added: May 06, 2007; Find A Grave Memorial# 19266374. Algoma Cemetery South (Sec: South Side) Marshall, Harrison Co., Texas. Retrieved 30 August 2013.

Citation: Gravesite for Harold J Terp (Provo, UT, USA, Ancestry.com Operations Inc, 2006), www.ancestry.com, US Veterans Gravesites, circa 1775-2006 [Database online].National Archives and Records Administration. U.S. World War II Army Enlistment Records, 1938-1946 [database on-line]. Original data: Electronic Army Serial Number Merged File, 1938-1946 [Archival Database]; ARC: 1263923. World War II Army Enlistment Records; Records of the National Archives and Records Administration, Record Group 64; National Archives at College Park. College Park, Maryland, U.S.A.

Citation: Gravesite for Harold James Terp (Provo, UT, USA, Ancestry.com Operations Inc, 2012), www.ancestry.com, Wisconsin, Find A Grave [Database online].Recorded: 11 Aug 2012 Find A Grave Memorial# 95221828; Evergreen Cemetery (Plot: V-18-7-4), Manitowoc, Manitowoc Co., Wisconsin. Accessed 02 Dec 2013.

Citation: Gravesite for Harriet [Unknown] Klasner (Provo, UT, USA, Ancestry.com Operations Inc, 2011), www.ancestry.com, Michigan, Find A Grave Index, 1805-2012 [database on-line]. 2012 Record added: Sep 15, 2012. Find A Grave Memorial #97127399. Woodland Cemetery, Jackson, Jackson Co., Michigan. Accessed 1 Sep 2013

Citation: Gravesite for Hazel (Grimm) Menkenmaier (Provo, UT, USA, Ancestry.com Operations Inc, 2012), www.ancestry.com, Oregon, Find A Grave Index, 1819-2012; [Database online]. Record added: Oct 25, 2008. Find A Grave Memorial# 30869504. Greenwood Cemetery, Bend, Deschutes Co., Oregon. Accessed 02 Dec 2013.

Citation: Gravesite for Henry Kettenbeil Jr. (Provo, UT, USA, Ancestry.com Operations Inc, 2012), www.ancestry.com, Michigan, Find A Grave Index, 1805-2012 [Database online]. Record added: Feb 11, 2010. Find A Grave Memorial# 48003102. Maple Hill Cemetery (Schoolcraft Twp.), Lake Linden, Houghton Co., Michigan. Accessed 02 Dec 2013.

Citation: Gravesite for Henry W Grimm (Provo, UT, USA, Ancestry.com Operations Inc), www.ancestry.com, Web: Idaho, Find A Grave Index, 1850-2012; [Database online]. Record added: Aug 13, 2005. Find A Grave Memorial# 11529013. Paul Cemetery, Paul, Minidoka Co., Idaho. Accessed 02 Dec 2013.

Citation: Gravesite for Herman F Grimm (Provo, UT, USA, Ancestry.com Operations Inc, Provo, UT, USA), www.ancestry.com, Web: Oregon, Find A Grave Index, 1819-2012. Record added: May 08, 2012, Find A Grave Memorial# 89817886. Trinity Lutheran Cemetery, Mount Angel, Marion Co., Oregon. Accessed 02 Dec 2013.

Citation: Gravesite for Hildegarde (Wambsganss) Nelson (Provo, UT, USA, Ancestry.com Operations Inc, 2012), www.ancestry.com, Colorado, Find A Grave, [website] Record added: Nov 01, 2010; Find A Grave Memorial# 60961210. Steamboat Springs Memorial Cemetery (Historical Site #5RT791), Steamboat Springs, Routt Co., Colorado. Retrieved 30 August 2013.

Citation: Gravesite for Hueston "Hugh" Rosebrook (Provo, UT, USA, Ancestry.com Operations Inc, 2011), www.ancestry.com, Washington, Find A Grave Index, 1821-2012; [Database online]. Record added: Jun 29, 2012. Find A Grave Memorial# 92773759. Holy Cross Cemetery, Spokane, Spokane Co., Washington. Accessed 02 Dec 2013.

Citation: Gravesite for Ida (Bruns) Grimm (Provo, UT, USA, Ancestry.com Operations Inc, 2012), www.ancestry.com, Oregon, Find A Grave Index, 1819-2012; [Database online]. Record added: Nov 16, 2010. Find A Grave Memorial# 61747629. Rose City Cemetery, Portland, Multnomah Co., Oregon. Accessed 02 Dec 2013.

Citation: Gravesite for Ina B [___] Klasner (Provo, UT, USA, Ancestry.com Operations Inc, 2012), www.ancestry.com, Michigan, Find A Grave Index, 1805-2012 [database on-line]. Record added: Oct 02, 2007; Find A Grave Memorial# 21895912. Accessed 1 Sep 2013.

Citation: Gravesite for Jack D Baals (Provo, UT, USA, Ancestry.com Operations Inc, 2012), www.ancestry.com, Indiana, Find A Grave [website]. Record added: Aug 12, 2010; Find A Grave Memorial# 56972458; Concordia Cemetery Gardens, Fort Wayne, Allen Co., Indiana. Retrieved 30 August 2013.

Citation: Gravesite for Jack Vernon Smith (Provo, UT, USA, Ancestry.com Operations Inc, 2011), www.ancestry.com, Indiana, Find A Grave Index, 1800-2012 [website] Record added: Sep 01, 2011; Find A Grave Memorial# 75796789. Greenlawn Memorial Park, Fort Wayne, Allen Co., Indiana. Accessed 30 Aug 2013.

Citation: Gravesite for James C Neuman (Provo, UT, USA, Ancestry.com Operations Inc, 2006), www.ancestry.com, National Cemetery Administration. U.S. Veterans Gravesites, ca.1775-2006[database on-line]. Provo, UT, USA: Ancestry.com Operations Inc, 2006. National Cemetery Administration, Nationwide Gravesite Locator; Medford, Taylor Co., Wisconsin. Accessed 02 Dec 2013.

Citation: Gravesite for James E Huffman (Provo, UT, USA, Ancestry.com Operations Inc, 2012), www.ancestry.com, Oregon, Find A Grave Index, 1819-2012; [Database online]. Record added: Jun 22, 2008. Find A Grave Memorial# 27740991. Willamette National Cemetery, Portland, Multnomah Co., Oregon. Accessed 02 Dec 2013.

Citation: Gravesite for James M Doriot (Provo, UT, USA, Ancestry.com Operations Inc, 2012), www.ancestry.com, Washington, Find A Grave Index, 1821-2012; [Database online]. Record added: Feb 16, 2010. Find A Grave Memorial# 48223906. Ridgefield Cemetery, Ridgefield, Clark Co., Washington. Accessed 02 Dec 2013.

Citation: Gravesite for James Terry Neuman (Provo, UT, USA, Ancestry.com Operations, Inc., 2005), www.ancestry.com, Wisconsin, Find A Grave Index, 1836-2012 [database on-line]. Provo, UT, USA: Ancestry.com Operations, Inc., 2012. Record added: Nov 02, 2012. Find A Grave Memorial# 100066785. St. Mary's Cemetery, Stetsonville, Taylor Co., Wisconsin. Accessed 1 Sep 2013.

Citation: Gravesite for Johanna Anderson (Medford, Taylor Co, WI, Evergreen Cemetery Medford, Taylor Co, WI; 2003), (Photo: Maryellen Anderson, Vancouver, WA, Oct 2003),.Evergreen Cemetery, Medford, Taylor Co, WI; .Lot 14, Block T. Johanna "mother" ; "wife of Andrew Anderson".

Citation: Gravesite for John and Louisa (Rouder) Steiner (Photo: Maryellen Anderson, Vancouver, WA, Oct 2003), Chelsea Cemetery, Medford, Taylor Co, WI.

Citation: Gravesite for John S Schellman (Provo, UT, USA, Ancestry.com, 2012), www.ancestry.com, Michigan, Find A Grave Index, 1805-2012 [website]; Record added: Feb 11, 2010; Find A Grave Memorial# 47985650. Lakeside Cemetery, Hancock, Houghton Co., Michigan. Accessed 02 Dec 2013.

Citation: Gravesite for John Schellman (Provo, UT, USA, Ancestry.com Operations Inc, 2012), www.ancestry.com, Michigan, Find A Grave Index, 1805-2012 [Database online]. Record added: Feb 23, 2010. Find A Grave Memorial# 48665124. Hancock, Houghton Co, Michigan; St Joseph Cemetery (defunct). Accessed 02 Dec 2013.

Citation: Gravesite for Joseph P Baeb (Provo, UT, USA, Ancestry.com Operations Inc, 2012), www.ancestry.com, Wisconsin: Find A Grave, 1836-2012; [website]; Record added: Apr 04, 2012 Find A Grave Memorial# 88057415. Ashwaubenon Moravian Cemetery, Green Bay, Brown Co., Wisconsin. Accessed 02 Dec 2013.

Citation: Gravesite for Katherine Caroline (Olson) Singleton (Provo, UT, USA, Ancestry.com Operations Inc, 2010), www.ancestry.com, Wisconsin, Find A Grave [website]. 2010. Record added: May 16, 2007; Find A Grave Memorial# 19396168. Perkinstown Cemetery, Perkinstown, Taylor Co., Wisconsin. Accessed 02 Dec 2013.

Citation: Gravesite for Kenneth M Pederson (Provo, UT, USA, Ancestry.com Operations Inc, 2012), www.ancestry.com, Oregon, Find A Grave Index, 1819-2012; [website]. 2010. Record added: Jun 13, 2010. Find A Grave Memorial# 53621140. City View Cemetery, Salem, Marion Co., Oregon. Accessed 02 Dec 2013.

Citation: Gravesite for Laverne Grimm (Provo, UT, USA, Ancestry.com Operations Inc, 2012), www.ancestry.com, Minnesota, Find A Grave Index, 1800-2012; [Database online]. Record added: Jul 07, 2012; Find A Grave Memorial# 93225784. Immanuel Lutheran Cemetery, McIntosh, Polk Co., Minnesota. Accessed 02 Dec 2013.

Citation: Gravesite for Lawrence A Grimm (Provo, UT, USA, Ancestry.com Operations Inc, 2012), www.ancestry.com, Oregon, Find A Grave Index, 1819-2012; [website]. 2010. Record added: Sep 24, 2012; Find A Grave Memorial# 97698483. River View Cemetery (Sec 132, Lot 150, Grave 3), Portland, Multnomah Co., Oregon. Accessed 4 February 2013.

Citation: Gravesite for Leighton E Drolshagen (Provo, UT, USA, Ancestry.com Operations Inc, 2011), www.ancestry.com, Wisconsin, Find A Grave [website]. 2010. Record added: Nov 02, 2012 Find A Grave Memorial# 100066856. St. Mary's Cemetery, Stetsonville, Taylor Co., Wisconsin. Accessed 02 Dec 2013.

Citation: Gravesite for LeRoy E Funkey (Provo, UT, USA, Ancestry.com Operations Inc, 2012), www.ancestry.com, Michigan, Find A Grave Index, 1805-2012 [website]. 2012. Record added: Feb 11, 2010; Find A Grave Memorial# 48002766. Birch Run Cemetery, Birch Run, Saginaw Co., Michigan. Accessed 1 Sep 2013.

Citation: Gravesite for Leroy S Krausse (Provo, UT, USA, Ancestry.com Operations Inc, 2012), www.ancestry.com, Wisconsin, Find A Grave. [Website]. Record added: Jan 05, 2013; Find A Grave Memorial# 103112229. St. Joseph's Cemetery, Edgerton, Taylor Co., Wisconsin. Accessed 02 Dec 2013.

Citation: Gravesite for Leslie Ivan Jepson Terp (Provo, UT, USA, Ancestry.com Operations, Inc., 2012), www.ancestry.com, California, Find A Grave Index, 1775-2012 [website]; Record Added: 22 Feb 2012; Find A Grave Memorial #8553174. Forest Lawn Memorial Park (Plot: Meditation, Lot 1489, Space 1), Glendale, Los Angeles Co., California. Accessed 02 Dec 2013.

Citation: Gravesite for Lewis Penrose (Provo, UT, USA, Ancestry.com Operations Inc, 2012), www.ancestry.com, Oregon, Find A Grave Index, 1819-2012; [website] 2010. Record added: Jan 17, 2005. Find A Grave Memorial# 10338175. Hopewell Cemetery, Dayton, Yamhill Co., Oregon. Accessed 02 Dec 2013.

Citation: Gravesite for Lloyd G. Schubert (Provo, UT, USA, Ancestry.com Operations Inc, 2006), www.ancestry.com, National Cemetery Administration; U.S. Veterans Gravesites, ca.1775-2006; [Database online]. Medford, Taylor Co., Wisconsin. Accessed 02 Dec 2013.

Citation: Gravesite for Logan J Bacon (Provo, UT, USA, Ancestry.com Operations Inc, 2010), www.ancestry.com, Oregon, Find A Grave Index, 1819-2012; [Database online]. Record added: Oct20, 2010; Find A Grave Memorial# 60385483.

Citation: Gravesite for Louis Steiner (Photo: Maryellen Anderson, Vancouver, WA, Oct 2003), Chelsea Cemetery, Medford, Taylor Co, Wisconsin

Citation: Gravesite for Lucille (Terp) Baeb (Provo, UT, USA, Ancestry.com Operations, Inc., 2011), www.ancestry.com, Wisconsin: Find A Grave: 1836-2012; [website]; Record added: Dec 13, 2010; Find A Grave Memorial# 62896918. Ashwaubenon Moravian Cemetery, Green Bay, Brown Co., Wisconsin. Accessed 02 Dec 2013.

Citation: Gravesite for Lydia (Schellman) Terp (Provo, UT, USA, Ancestry.com Operations Inc), www.ancestry.com, Wisconsin: Find A Grave [Database online]. Record added: Feb 23, 2010; Find A Grave Memorial# 48664620; Woodlawn Cemetery, Brown Co, Wisconsin; Obituary included. Accessed 02 Dec 2013.

Citation: Gravesite for Lydia Grimm Strebig (Provo, UT, USA, Ancestry.com Operations, Inc., 2012), www.ancestry.com, Wisconsin, Find A Grave Index, 1836-2012; [website]. Record added: Apr11, 2008; Find A Grave Memorial# 25936422. Evergreen Cemetery, Medford, Taylor Co., Wisconsin. Accessed 02 Dec 2013.

Citation: Gravesite for Maren (Terp) Crabb (Provo, UT, USA, Ancestry.com Operations, Inc., 2012), www.ancestry.com, Wisconsin: Find A Grave, 1836-21012. [Database online]. Record added: Apr 09, 2012; Find A Grave Memorial# 88263924. Ashwaubenon Moravian Cemetery, Green Bay, Brown Co., Wisconsin. Accessed 02 Dec 2013.

Citation: Gravesite for Maren (Terp) Crabb (Provo, UT, USA, Ancestry.com Operations, Inc., 2013), www.ancestry.com, BillionGraves.com Burial Index (website); [Database online]. Green Bay, Brown Co., WI. Accessed 02 Dec 2013.

Citation: Gravesite for Margaret (Birk) Kettenbeil (Provo, UT, USA, Ancestry.com Operations Inc), www.ancestry.com, Michigan, Find A Grave Index, 1805-2012 [database on-line]. Record added: Feb 11, 2010 Find A Grave Memorial# 48003276; Maple Hill Cemetery, Lake Linden, Houghton Co., Wisconsin. Accessed 29 August 2013.

Citation: Gravesite for Mary (Rodenbeck) Wambsganss (Provo, UT, USA, Ancestry.com Operations Inc, 2010), www.ancestry.com, Indiana, Find A Grave Index, 1800-2012; [website]. Record added: May17, 2010; Find A Grave Memorial# 52500221; Concordia Lutheran Cemetery, Fort Wayne, Allen Co., Indiana. Accessed 29 Aug 2013.

Citation: Gravesite for Mary (Schellman) Grimm (Provo, UT, USA, Ancestry.com Operations Inc, 2010), Minnesota Find A Grave [Website]; Record added: Aug 30, 2010; Find A Grave Memorial#57935974; Immanuel Lutheran Cemetery, McIntosh, Polk Co., Minnesota. Mary "Marie" (Schellman) Grimm. Accessed 02 Dec 2013.

Citation: Gravesite for Mathilda Koch (Provo, UT, USA, Ancestry.com Operations Inc, 2011). [Database online]. www.ancestry.com, Web: Idaho, Find A Grave Index, 1850-2012; Record added: Aug 02, 2005; Find A Grave Memorial # 11466809. Paul Cemetery, Paul, Minidoka Co., Idaho. Accessed 02 Dec 2013.

Citation: Gravesite for Merle E Crabb (Provo, UT, USA, Ancestry.com Operations Inc, 2011), www.ancestry.com, Wisconsin: Find A Grave. [Database online]. Record added: Apr 09, 2012; Find A Grave Memorial # 88263890. Ashwaubenon Moravian Cemetery, Green Bay, Brown Co., Wisconsin. Accessed 02 Dec 2013.

Citation: Gravesite for Merle E. Crabb (Provo, UT, USA, Ancestry.com Operations Inc, 2013), www.ancestry.com, BillionGraves.com Burial Index [website]. Green Bay, Brown Co., Wisconsin. Accessed 02 Dec 2013.

Citation: Gravesite for Michael Boiko (Provo, UT, USA, Ancestry.com Operations Inc, 2012), www.ancestry.com, Washington, Find A Grave Index, 1821-2012; [Database online].Record added: Oct 04, 2004; Find A Grave Memorial # 9553065. Curlew City Cemetery, Curlew, Ferry Co., Washington. Accessed 02 Dec 2013..

Citation: Gravesite for Mildred I Grimm (Provo, UT, USA, Ancestry.com Operations Inc, 2005), www.ancestry.com, Oregon, Find A Grave Index, 1819-2012; [Database online]. Record added: Jul 08, 2012. Find A Grave Memorial # 93263993. Mountain View Cemetery (Sec.K, Blk 8, Lot 11, Grave C), Oregon City, Clackamas Co, Oregon. Accessed 02 Dec 2013.

Citation: Gravesite for Monroe Henry Grimm (Provo, UT, USA, Ancestry.com Operations Inc, 2011), www.ancestry.com, Web: Idaho, Find A Grave Index, 1850-2012; [Database online]. Record added: Jun 25, 2012. Find A Grave Memorial# 92533511. Paul Cemetery, Paul, Minidoka Co., Idaho. Accessed 02 Dec 2013.

Citation: Gravesite for Myrtle "Mert" (Klasner) Joos (Provo, UT, USA, Ancestry.com Operations Inc, 2012), www.ancestry.com, Michigan, Find A Grave Index, 1805-2012 [database on-line]. 2012. Record added: Feb 24, 2010; Find A Grave Memorial# 48699184; River View Cemetery, Okanogan, Okanogan Co., Washington. Accessed 1 Sep 2013.

Citation: Gravesite for Nels D Olson (Provo, UT, USA, Ancestry.com Operations Inc, 2012), www.ancestry.com, Washington, Find A Grave Index, 1821-2012; [Database online].Record added: May 20, 2009; Find A Grave Memorial# 37298429. Riverside Cemetery, Ione, Pend Oreille, Washington. Accessed 02 Dec 2013.

Citation: Gravesite for Nora (Bear) Anderson (Provo, UT, USA, Ancestry.com Operations Inc, 2012) www.ancestry.com. Washington, Find A Grave Index, 1821-2012 [database on-line]. 2012. Mt. Angeles Memorial Park (Plot: Garden of Matthew), Port Angeles, Clallam Co., Washington. Find A Grave. Find A Grave. Recorded: 03 Jun 2007; Find A Grave Memorial #19698914. Accessed 14 Dec 2013.

Citation: Gravesite for Nora (Nelson) Grimm (Provo, UT, USA, Ancestry.com Operations Inc, 2010), www.ancestry.com, Minnesota, Find A Grave [website]. 2010. Record added: Jul 07, 2012 Find A Grave Memorial# 93225784. Immanuel Lutheran Church, McIntosh, Polk Co., Minnesota. Accessed 02 Dec 2013.

Citation: Gravesite for Otto C Anderson (Provo, UT, USA, Ancestry.com Operations, Inc., 2002), www.ancestry.com, Washington, Find A Grave Index, 1821-2012 [Database online]. Record added: Oct 06, 2009; Find A Grave Memorial# 42758412. River View Cemetery, Okanogan, Okanogan Co, Washington. Accessed 02 Dec 2013.

Citation: Gravesite for Otto Grim (Provo, UT, USA, Ancestry.com Operations Inc), www.ancestry.com, [Database online]. Manitowoc County Cemetery (Hospital Section), Manitowoc, Manitowoc Co., Wisconsin. Data retrieved 13 Aug 2013.

Citation: Gravesite for Paul Benton Anderson (Provo, UT, USA, Ancestry.com Operations Inc, 2010), www.ancestry.com, Wisconsin, Find A Grave Index, 1836-2012 [website].Record added: Feb 07, 2011; Find A Grave Memorial# 65319095.

Citation: Gravesite for Paul W Nelson (Provo, UT, USA, Ancestry.com Operations Inc, 2012), www.ancestry.com, Colorado, Find A Grave, 1855-2012 [website] Record added: Nov 01, 2010; Find A Grave Memorial# 60961234. Steamboat Springs Cemetery, Steamboat Springs, Routt Co., Colorado. Retrieved 30 August 2013.

Citation: Gravesite for Paulina Steiner (Photo: Maryellen Anderson, Vancouver, WA; Oct 2003). Chelsea Cemetery, Medford, Taylor Co, Wisconsin

Citation: Gravesite for Peter Hansen Terp (Provo, UT, USA, Ancestry.com Operations Inc, 2012), www.ancestry.com, Wisconsin, Find A Grave [website]. Record added: Feb 23, 2010; Find A Grave Memorial# 48664875. Woodlawn Cemetery, Allouez, Brown Co., Wisconsin. Accessed 02 Dec 2013.

Citation: Gravesite for Philipp Wambsganss Jr. (Provo, UT, USA, Ancestry.com Operations Inc, 2010), www.ancestry.com, Indiana, Find A Grave Index, 1800-2012; [website]. Record added: Apr 23, 2010; Find A Grave Memorial# 51506966 Concordia Lutheran Cemetery, Fort Wayne, Allen Co, Indiana; Accessed 29 Aug 2013.

Citation: Gravesite for Raymond Paul Schubert (Provo, UT, USA, Ancestry.com Operations Inc, 2013), www.ancestry.com, Wisconsin, Find A Grave Index, 1836-2012 [database on-line]. Provo, UT, USA: Ancestry.com Operations, Inc., 2012. Rec# 19651725; Nola Cemetery, Park Falls (Block O, Lot 54), Price, Wisconsin. Added 31 May 2007.

Citation: Gravesite for Rev. Phillip Wambsganss (Provo, UT, USA, Ancestry.com Operations Inc, 2012), www.ancestry.com, Web: Indiana, Find A Grave Index, 1800-2012; [website]. Record added: May 17, 2010; Find A Grave Memorial# 52500282; Concordia Lutheran Cemetery, Fort Wayne, Allen Co, Indiana. Accessed 29 Aug 2013.

Citation: Gravesite for Robert J Terp (Provo, UT, USA, Ancestry.com Operations Inc, 2006), www.ancestry.com, Wisconsin: Find A Grave [Database online]. Woodlawn Cemetery, Brown Co, Wisconsin; Record added: Jan 12, 2012 Find A Grave Memorial# 83354359. Woodlawn Cemetery, Allouez, Brown Co., Wisconsin. Accessed 02 Dec 2013.

147

Citation:   Gravesite for Robert L Grimm (Provo, UT, USA, Ancestry.com Operations Inc, 2012), www.ancestry.com, California, Find A Grave Index, 1775-2012; [Database online]. Record added: Oct 06, 2008; Find A Grave Memorial# 30374813. Lawncrest, Redding Shasta Co, California. Accessed 02 Dec 2013.

Citation:   Gravesite for Roger D Travis (Provo, UT, USA, Ancestry.com Operations Inc, 2012), www.ancestry.com, Minnesota, Find A Grave Index, 1800-2012;[Database online].Record added: Apr 26, 2008; Find A Grave Memorial# 26406680. Lebanon Cemetery, New London, Kandiyohi Co., Minnesota. Accessed 02 Dec 2013.

Citation:   Gravesite for Ronald Lester Zemke (Provo, UT, USA, Ancestry.com Operations Inc, 2012), www.ancestry.com, Idaho, Find A Grave Index, 1850-2012; [website] Record added: Jul 06, 2012; Find A Grave Memorial # 93199908. Paul Cemetery, Paul, Minidoka Co., Idaho. Accessed 02 Dec 2013.

Citation:   Gravesite for Rosa Wambsganss (Provo, UT, USA, Ancestry.com Operations Inc, 2010), www.ancestry.com, Indiana, Find A Grave Index, 1800-2012; [website]. Record added: May 17, 2010; Find A Grave Memorial# 52500252; Concordia Lutheran Cemetery, Fort Wayne, Allen Co., Indiana, Accessed 29 Aug 2013.

Citation:   Gravesite for Rosette (Grimm) Evans (Provo, UT, USA, Ancestry.com Operations Inc, 2013), www.ancestry.com

            Gravesite for  Leo Leon Bill (Provo, UT, USA, Ancestry.com Operations Inc, 2011), www.ancestry.com, Idaho, Find A Grave Index, 1850-2012; [website].Record added: Jun 01, 2008. Find A Grave Memorial# 27247040; Paul Cemetery (Plot J-8), Paul, Minidoka Co., Idaho. Accessed 02 Dec 2013.

Citation:   Gravesite for Ruth V. (Hofhine) Grimm. (Provo, UT, USA, Ancestry.com Operations Inc, 2011), www.ancestry.com, Web: Idaho, Find A Grave Index, 1850-2012; [Database online]. Record added: Jun 25, 2012. Find A Grave Memorial# 92533677. Record added: Jun 25, 2012Find A Grave Memorial# 92533677; Paul Cemetery, Paul, Minidoka Co., Idaho. Accessed 02 Dec 2013.

Citation:   Gravesite for Sandra Lynn Terp (Provo, UT, USA, Ancestry.com Operations Inc, 2012), www.ancestry.com, Wisconsin, Find A Grave [Database online]. Record added: Aug 11, 2012 Find A Grave Memorial# 95221829; Evergreen Cemetery (Plot: V-18-7-6), Manitowoc, Manitowoc Co., Wisconsin. Accessed 02 Dec 2013.

Citation:   Gravesite for Susan (Schneider) Schellman (Provo, UT, USA, Ancestry.com Operations Inc, 2012), www.ancestry.com, Web: Michigan, Find A Grave Index, 1805-2012. Record added: Feb 09, 2010; Find A Grave Memorial# 47924435. Lakeside Cemetery, Hancock, Houghton Co., Michigan. Accessed 24 August 2013.

Citation:   Gravesite for Venita Terp (Provo, UT, USA, Ancestry.com Operations Inc, 2012), www.ancestry.com, Wisconsin, Find A Grave, 1936-2012 [website]. Record added: Jan 30, 2012; Find A Grave Memorial# 84213332 Fort Howard Memorial Cemetery, Green Bay, Brown Co., Wisconsin. Accessed 02 Dec 2013.

Citation:   Gravesite for Viola (Grimm) Bill (Provo, UT, USA, Ancestry.com Operations, Inc., 2005), www.ancestry.com, Idaho, Find A Grave Index, 1850-2012; [website]. 2010. Record added: Aug 02, 2005; Find A Grave Memorial# 11466817. Paul Cemetery, Paul, Minidoka Co., Idaho. Accessed 02 Dec 2013.

Citation:   Gravesite for Viola A Terp (Provo, UT, USA, Ancestry.com Operations Inc, 2012), www.ancestry.com, Wisconsin, Find A Grave [Database online].Record added: Aug 11, 2012 Find A Grave Memorial# 95221830; Evergreen Cemetery (Plot: V-18-7-5), Manitowoc, Manitowoc Co., Wisconsin. Accessed 02 Dec 2013.

Citation:   Gravesite for Violet (Grimm) Ferden (Provo, UT, USA, Ancestry.com Operations Inc, 2012), www.ancestry.com, Minnesota, Find A Grave Index, 1800-2012; [website]; Record added: Jul 07, 2012. Find A Grave Memorial# 93236305. Immanuel Lutheran Cemetery, McIntosh, Polk Co., Minnesota. Accessed 02 Dec 2013.

Citation:   Gravesite for Wilhelmina (Schalk) Grimm (Provo, UT, USA, Ancestry.com Operations Inc, 2012), www.ancestry.com, Oregon, Find A Grave Index, 1819-2012; [website] 2010. Record added: Oct 20, 2010. Find A Grave Memorial# 60386372. Rose City Cemetery, Portland, Multnomah Co., Oregon. Accessed 02 Dec 2013.

Citation:   Gravesite for William "Bill" Terp (Provo, UT, USA, Ancestry.com Operations Inc, 2012), www.ancestry.com, Wisconsin, Find A Grave [Database online]. Record added: Jan 30, 2012; Find A Grave Memorial# 84213333. Rose City Cemetery, Portland, Multnomah Co., Oregon. Accessed 02 Dec 2013.

Citation:   Gravesite for William Adolph "Bill" Wambsganss (Provo, UT, USA, Ancestry.com Operations, Inc., 2012), www.ancestry.com, Ohio, Find A Grave Index, 1787-2012 [website]. Fort Howard Memorial Cemetery (Plot: Section 30, Lot 218, Grave 2), Green Bay, Brown Co., Wisconsin. Accessed 02 Dec 2013.

Citation:   Gravesite for William John Vollmer (Provo, UT, USA, Ancestry.com Operations Inc, 2012), www.ancestry.com, Wisconsin, Find A Grave [website]. Record: Nov 20, 2009; Find A Grave Memorial# 44600014; Calvary Cemetery, Superior, Douglas Co., Wisconsin. Accessed 29 Aug 2013.

Citation:   Gravesite for William Joos (Provo, UT, USA, Ancestry.com Operations Inc, 2012), www.ancestry.com, Michigan, Find A Grave Index, 1805-2012 [website]. Record added: 24 Feb 2010. Find A Grave Memorial# 48698857; Riverside Cemetery, Ontonagon, Ontonagon Co., Michigan. Obituary included. Accessed 1 Sep 2013.

Citation:   Gravesite for Wilma (Grimm) Huffman (Provo, UT, USA, Ancestry.com Operations Inc, 2000), www.ancestry.com, Oregon, Find A Grave [website] 2010. Record added: Jun 22, 2008; Find A Grave Memorial# 27741037. Willamette National Cemetery, Portland, Multnomah Co., Oregon. Accessed 02 Dec 2013.

Citation:   Headstone Application for LeRoy E Funkey (Provo, UT, USA, Ancestry.com Operations Inc, 2012),www.ancestry.com, U.S., Headstone Applications for Military Veterans, 1925-1963 [database on-line].National Archives and Records

Administration; Washington, D.C.; Applications for Headstones for U.S. military veterans, 1925-1941; National Archives # Publ. A1, 2110-C; Record Group Title: Records of the Office of the Quartermaster General; RG #92. 2012.

Citation: Headstone Application of Adolph Koch Jr. (Provo, UT, USA, Ancestry.com Operations Inc, 2012), www.ancestry.com, U.S., Headstone Applications for Military Veterans, 1925-1963 [Database online]. National Archives and Records Administration; Washington, D.C.; Applications for Headstones for U.S. military veterans, 1925-1941; National Archives # Publ: A1, 2110-C; Record Group Title: Records of the Office of the Quartermaster General; RG# 92. 2012.

Citation: Headstone Application of Alfred Schubert (Provo, UT, USA, Ancestry.com Operations Inc, 2012), www.ancestry.com, U.S., Headstone Applications for Military Veterans, 1925-1963 [Database online]. National Archives and Records Administration; Washington, D.C.; Applications for Headstones for U.S. military veterans, 1925-1941; National Archives # Publ: A1, 2110-C; Record Group Title: Records of the Office of the Quartermaster General; RG#: 92. 2012.

**Title:** **History of Manitowoc County Wisconsin, 1911-1912**

Citation: Falge, Dr. L, History of Manitowoc County Wisconsin, 1911-1912 (Manitowoc County Wisconsin Genealogy, unknown), Manitowoc County Wisconsin Genealogy, People who Lived in Manitowoc County, Wisconsin Primarily before [1901]; Manitowoc Frederich "Fred" T Grimm. http://www.2manitowoc.com/.County Personal Sketches; Fred T. Grimm; v.2, p.321-322; Retrieved 19 August 2013.

**Title:** **Income Tax Returns**

Citation: Income Tax Return for Mary Anderson (Rt. 1, Stetsonville, Taylor Co, WI, Mary Anderson, 19 Jan1954). (In possession of Tracy Doriot, Washougal, WA). US Income Tax Forms 1040 and 1040F; 19 Jan 1954; Prepared and signed by Mary Anderson.

**Title:** **Land and Residency Records**

Citation: Chattel Mortgage for Mary Anderson and Robert Anderson (son) (Medford, Taylor Co, WI, Register of Deeds of the County of Taylor Co.26 Feb 1954), (In possession of Tracy Doriot, Washougal, WA). Dates created and satisfied; executioners; Doc #79382. "...by Mrs. Mary Anderson, Robert Anderson, and Eva Anderson, his wife." Certified and acknowledged by State Bank of Medford, Medford, WI.

Citation: Land Record for Frederich T Grimm (Provo, UT, USA, Ancestry.com Operations Inc, 2010), www.ancestry.com, U.S., Indexed County Land Ownership Maps 1860-1918; [database on-line]. 2010. Collection #G&M_79; Roll # 79. Westburg, Buchanan Co., IA, 1886.Original data: Various publishers of County Land Ownership Atlases.

Citation: Real Property Description for Gladys A. Doriot (Vancouver, Clark Co, WA, Clark County Property Information, Unknown), Clark County Records Office, Vancouver, WA, Regular  parcel, #101 of Frederick Shobert DLC; Legal Description: SW 1/4, S19, T4N, R1E, Ridgefield, Clark Co, WA http://gis.clark.wa.gov/applications/gishome/property.

Citation: Residence Record of Adolph Grimm (Chicago, IL, Geo. A. Ogle & Co. Publishers and Engravers, unknown), Manitowoc County Wisconsin Genealogy, Manitowoc County Marriages [website]; Original Source: 1921 Manitowoc County Patron Directory from Stanedar Atlas of Manitowoc County Wisconsin; Farmer, Sect. 27, Maple Grove, PO Reedsville. Farmer, Sect. 27, Maple Grove, PO Reedsville; "came to County 1892".

**Title:** **Licenses**

Citation: Driver's License for James Maynard Doriot (State of Washington). (In possession of Tracy Doriot, Washougal, WA), Driver's License issued by State of Washington.

Citation: Drivers Licenses for Clara (Anderson) Grimm (Madison, WI, State of Wisconsin).(In possession of Tracy Doriot, Washougal, WA), 1983-1995 Wisconsin Driver's Licenses (3)..

Citation: Special Resident Fishing License for Clara Grimm (Madison, WI, State of Wisconsin, Dept. of Natural Resources, 04 Jan 1977), (In possession of Tracy Doriot, Washougal, WA).

Citation: Taylor County Older Adult ID Card for Clara Grimm (Taylor County, Wisconsin, n.d.g.), (In possession of Tracy Doriot, Washougal, WA)

**Title:** **Marriage Records**

Citation: Marriage Certificate of Myrtle Anderson & John Lorenz (In possession of Tracy Doriot, Washougal, WA). 28 Dec n.y.g.

Citation: Marriage Record for Albert Steiner (Madison, WI, Vezzetti, Judy, 2001), State Historical Society of Wisconsin, Madison, Wisconsin, Compiled by Judy Vezzetti; Appendix by Barry C. Noonan; Proofread by members of the Taylor County Genealogical Society, Medford, Wisconsin; Vol. 1, p. 7175; 11 Jan 1897.

Citation: Marriage Record for Alvin Grimm and Clara Anderson (Chelsea, Taylor Co, WI, State of Wisconsin, Dept. of Health, Bureau of Vital Statistics, 09 Nov 1933), (In possession of Tracy Doriot, Washougal, WA).6 Nov 1933; License #1601, County of Taylor Co, Township of Chelsea, WI; witnesses: Arthur Lange and Elva Anderson.

Citation: Marriage Record for Alvin L Olson (Provo, UT, USA, Ancestry.com Operations Inc, 2006), www.ancestry.com, Texas Marriage Collection, 1814-1909 and 1966-2002; [Database online].

Citation: Marriage Record for Anna Steiner (Madison, WI, Vezzetti, Judy, 2001), State Historical Society of Wisconsin, Madison, Wisconsin, Compiled by Judy Vezzetti; Appendix by Barry C. Noonan; Proofread by members of the Taylor County Genealogical Society, Medford, Wisconsin; Vol. 1, p. 138; 23 Oct 1893.

Citation: Marriage Record for Arthur C. Anderson & Loretta Hoverson (Provo, UT, USA, Ancestry.com Operations, Inc., 2012), www.ancestry.com, Washington, Marriage Records, 1865-2004; [Database Online].

Citation: Marriage Record For August Anderson & Mary Olson (Madison, WI, Vezzetti, Judy, 2001), State Historical Society of Wisconsin, Madison, Wisconsin, Compiled by Judy Vezzetti; Appendix by Barry C. Noonan; Proofread by members of the Taylor County Genealogical Society, Medford, Wisconsin; Vol. 1, p. 187, 22 Sep 1897.

Citation: Marriage Record for Bernice F Krausse (Provo, UT, USA, Ancestry.com Operations Inc, 2005), www.ancestry.com, Wisconsin Marriages, 1973-1997; [Database online].Wisconsin Department of Health and Family Services. Wisconsin Marriages, 1973-1978; Wisconsin Marriages, 1979-1997. Wisconsin, USA: Wisconsin Department of Health and Family Services.

Citation: Marriage Record for Caroline Schellman, Marriage Records 1878 – 1915, St. John's Lutheran Church, Sherman Twp., Sheboygan Co, WI; http://www.vorpahlfamily.com/genealogy//docs/StJohnSC/StJohnSCMarriages1878.htm.

Citation: Marriage Record for Christopher Olson (Oleson) Jr. (Madison, WI, Vezzetti, Judy; 2001) State Historical Society of Wisconsin, Madison, Wisconsin; Compiled by Judy Vezzetti; Appendix by Barry C. Noonan; Proofread by members of Taylor County Genealogical Society, Medford, Wisconsin; Vol. 1, p. 183; 04 Oct 1897.

Citation: Marriage Record for Danny R Sperl (Provo, UT, USA, Ancestry.com Operations Inc, 2011), www.ancestry.com, Wisconsin Department of Health and Family Services, Wisconsin Marriages, 1973-1978; Wisconsin Marriages, 1979-1997, Wisconsin, USA: Wisconsin Department of Health and Family Services; [Database online].

Citation: Marriage Record for Elaine (Krausse) Mason (Provo, UT, USA, Ancestry.com Operations Inc, 2005), www.ancestry.com, Wisconsin Marriages, 1973-1997 [database on-line]. Original data: Wisconsin Department of Health and Family Services. Wisconsin Marriages, 1973-1978; Wisconsin Marriages, 1979-1997. Wisconsin, USA: Wisconsin Department of Health and Family Services.

Citation: Marriage Record for Elizabeth (Wambsganss) Weber (Provo, UT, USA, Ancestry.com Operations Inc, 2005), www.ancestry.com, Indiana, Marriage Collection, 1800-1941 [database on-line]. 2005 Allen County, Indiana; Index to Marriage Record, Indiana 1824 - 1920, Incl, W.P.A.; County Clerk's"; Book: 33; Page: 197.

Citation: Marriage Record for Elmer H Grimm (Provo, UT, USA, Ancestry.com Operations Inc, 2007), www.ancestry.com, California, Marriage Index, 1960-1985 [Database online].2007.

Citation: Marriage Record for Eunice Evelyn Wambsganss (FamilySearch.com, unknown), FamilySearch.com, Indiana, Marriages, 1811-1959. 1950. Film # 002130536; DFN 004205257; # 00630; Batch#M02145-7; p. 468. Officiated by Fred Wambsganss. Retrieved 30 Aug 2013 from https://familysearch.org/pal:/MM9.1.1/XX22-YSG.

Citation: Marriage Record for Evadna Bacon & Hugh Rosebrook (Provo, UT, USA, Ancestry.com Operations Inc), www.ancestry.com, Washington, Marriage Records, 1865-2004 [database on-line]. 2012.

Citation: Marriage Record for Fred T Grimm (Manitowoc Co, WI, Manitowoc County Wisconsin Genealogy, Manitowoc County Wisconsin Genealogy, Manitowoc County Marriages Pre-1907; Manitowoc County Wisconsin Genealogy; [Website].

Citation: Marriage Record for Frederick P.E. Wambsganss (Provo, UT, USA, Ancestry.com Operations Inc, 2005), www.ancestry.com, Indiana, Marriage Collection, 1800-1941 [database on-line]. 2005. Allen County, Indiana; Index to Marriage Record, Indiana 1824 - 1920 Incl, W.P.A.; County Clerk's "O" Book: 28; Page: 339.

Citation: Marriage Record for Hannah (Wambsganss) Hitzeman (Provo, UT, USA, Ancestry.com Operations Inc, 2005), www.ancestry.com, Indiana, Marriage Collection, 1800-1941 [database on-line]. 2005. Allen County, Indiana; Index to Marriage Record, Indiana 1824 - 1920 Incl, W.P.A.; County Clerk's O; Book: 43; Page: 422.

Citation: Marriage Record for Hazel G Penrose (Provo, UT, USA, Ancestry.com Operations Inc, 2000), www.ancestry.com, Oregon, Marriage Indexes, 1906-1924, 1946-2008; [Database online].State of Oregon, Oregon, Marriage Indexes, 1906-1924, 1946-2008, Portland, OR, USA: Oregon Health Division, Center for Health Statistics.

Citation: Marriage Record for James Doriot and Gladys Grimm (Provo, UT, USA, Ancestry.com Operations Inc, 2006), www.ancestry.com, Nevada, Marriage Index, 1956-2005.

Citation: Marriage Record for John Reinhard Steiner (Madison, WI, Vezzetti, Judy, 2001), State Historical Society of Wisconsin, Madison, Wisconsin, Compiled by Judy Vezzetti; Appendix by Barry C. Noonan; Proofread by members of the Taylor County Genealogical Society, Medford, Wisconsin; Vol. 1, p. 239; 23 Jun 1901.

Citation: Marriage Record for Leighton Drohlshagen & Beverly Kramer (Provo, UT, USA, Ancestry.com Operations Inc, 2005), www.ancestry.com, Wisconsin Marriages, 1973-1997 [database on-line]. Original data: Wisconsin Department of Health and Family Services. Wisconsin Marriages, 1973-1978; Wisconsin Marriages, 1979-1997. Wisconsin, USA: Wisconsin Department of Health and Family Services.

Citation: Marriage Record for Lois A Anderson (Provo, UT, USA, Ancestry.com Operations Inc, 2007), www.ancestry.com, Minnesota, Marriage Collection, 1958-2001; [Database online].

Citation: Marriage Record for Lois A Anderson (Provo, UT, USA, Ancestry.com Operations Inc, 2007), www.ancestry.com, Minnesota, Marriage Collection, 1958-2001; [Database online].

Citation: Marriage Record for Lois A Kirchberg and Lyle Johnson (Provo, UT, USA, Ancestry.com Operations Inc, 2007), www.ancestry.com, Minnesota, Marriage Collection, 1958-2001; [Database online].

Citation: Marriage Record for Lonna M Anderson & Glen Erickson (Provo, UT, USA, Ancestry.com Operations Inc, 2007), www.ancestry.com, Minnesota, Marriage Collection, 1958-2001 [database on-line]. 2007.

Citation: Marriage Record for Louise (Rouder) (Madison, WI, Vezzetti, Judy, 2001), State Historical Society of Wisconsin, Madison, WI, Compiled by Judy Vezzetti; Appendix by Barry C. Noonan; Proofread by members of the Taylor County Genealogical Society. Vol. 1, p243; 26 Sep 1901.

Citation: Marriage Record for Mathilda A Grimm & Adolph Koch (Provo, UT, USA, Ancestry.com Operations Inc, 2011), www.ancestry.com, Western States Marriage Index, 1809-2011; Database online. Western States Marriage Index, Brigham Young University–Idaho.

Citation: Marriage Record for Matilda Grimm & Adolph Koch (Provo, UT, USA, Ancestry.com Operations Inc, 2005), www.ancestry.com, Idaho, Marriage Index, 1842-1996; [Database online].Upper Snake.

Citation: Marriage Record for Melvin Propst (Provo, UT, USA, Ancestry.com Operations, Inc, 2000), www.ancestry.com, Oregon, Marriage Indexes, 1906-1924, 1946-2008; [Database online].

Citation: Marriage Record for Mildred (Grimm) Johns (Provo, UT, USA, Ancestry.com Operations Inc), www.ancestry.com, Oregon State Library; Oregon Marriage Indexes, 1906-2006; Reel: 5; Years: 1946-1955.

Citation: Marriage Record for Mildred A Grimm (Provo, UT, USA, Ancestry.com Operations Inc, 2000), www.ancestry.com, Oregon, Marriage Indexes, 1906-1924, 1946-2008; [Database online].Oregon State Library; Oregon Marriage Indexes, 1906-2006; Reel: 4; Years: 1921-1924.

Citation: Marriage Record for Monroe Grimm (Provo, UT, USA, Ancestry.com Operations Inc, 2011), www.ancestry.com, Idaho, Marriage Index, 1842-1996; [Database online].

Citation: Marriage Record for Nancy Sperl & Kenneth Reigert (Provo, UT, USA, Ancestry.com Operations Inc, 2005), www.ancestry.com, Wisconsin Marriages, 1973-1997 [database on-line].

Citation: Marriage Record for Phillip Wambsganss Jr. (Provo, UT, USA, Ancestry.com Operations Inc, 2005), www.ancestry.com, Indiana, Marriage Collection, 1800-1941 [database on-line]. 2005. Allen County, Indiana; Index to Marriage Record, Indiana 1824 - 1920 Incl, W. P. A. Original Record Located County Clerk's O; Book: 36; Page: 27.

Citation: Marriage Record for Reinhard Grimm (Chicago, IL, George A. Ogle & Co. Publishers and Engravers, Publ. Date unknown), Manitowoc County Wisconsin Genealogy, Manitowoc, Manitowoc Co, Wisconsin; 06 July 1918.

Citation: Marriage Record for Ricky A Sperl (Provo, UT, USA, Ancestry.com Operations Inc., 2005), www.ancestry.com, Wisconsin Marriages, 1973-1997 [database on-line].

Citation: Marriage Record for Robert Lee Sperl (Provo, UT, USA, Ancestry.com Operations Inc, 2005), www.ancestry.com, Wisconsin Marriages, 1973-1997 [database on-line]. Department of Health and Family Services. Wisconsin Marriages, 1973-1978; Wisconsin Marriages, 1979-1997. Wisconsin, USA: Wisconsin Department of Health and Family Services.

Citation: Marriage Record for Roger D Travis (Provo, UT, USA, Ancestry.com Operations Inc, 2007), www.ancestry.com, Minnesota, Marriage Collection, 1958-2001; [Database online].

Citation: Marriage Record for Shirley Pederson (Provo, UT, USA, Ancestry.com Operations, Inc, 2000), www.ancestry.com, Oregon, Marriage Indexes, 1906-1924, 1946-2008; [Database online].

Citation: Marriage Record for Verna Bacon & Horace Teuber (Provo, UT, USA, Ancestry.com Operations, Inc.), www.ancestry.com, Washington, Marriage Records, 1865-2004 [database on-line].

Citation: Marriage Record for Viola Grimm & Amos Bill (Provo, UT, USA, Ancestry.com Operations Inc, 2005), www.ancestry.com, Idaho, Marriage Index, 1842-1996; [Database online].

Citation: Marriage Record for Vivian P Nichols (Provo, UT, USA, Ancestry.com Operations Inc, 2006), www.ancestry.com, Texas Marriage Collection, 1814-1909 and 1966-2002; [Database online].

Citation: Marriage Record for William A Wambsganss & Effie Mulholland (Index) (Provo, UT, USA, Ancestry.com Operations, Inc., 2010), www.ancestry.com, Cuyahoga County Archive; Cleveland, Ohio; Cuyahoga County, Ohio, Marriage Records, 1810-1973; Volume: Vol 104-105; Page: 200; Year Range: 1917 Apr - 1917 Aug.

Citation: Marriage Record for William J. Sperl (Provo, UT, USA, Ancestry.com Operations Inc, 2005), www.ancestry.com, Wisconsin Marriages, 1973-1997 [database on-line].

**Title:** **Mayoral Record for Gladys (Grimm) Doriot**

Citation: Mayoral Record for Gladys (Grimm) Doriot (Ridgefield, WA, City of Ridgefield, Retrieved from internet 03 Apr 2004), Ridgefieldwash.com, City of Ridgefield [website] 2004. City of Ridgefield Council Members; Mayoral position. Ridgefield, Clark Co, Washington. Accessed Aug 2013. http://www.ridgefieldwash.com/government.htm.

**Title:** **Medical Records**

Citation: Medicare Health Insurance Card for Clara Grimm (Medicare Health Administration, 01 Jan 1977), (In possession of Tracy Doriot, Washougal, WA). Medicare Health Insurance Card; State of Wisconsin

**Title:** **Membership & Affiliation Records**

Citation: Bricklayers & Allied Craftsman Membership Card for Alvin Grimm (Washington, D.C., International Union of Bricklayers & Allied Craftsman, Jun 1959),( In possession of Tracy Doriot, Washougal, WA.); I.U. #011805, Local 6, BAC Local #18; Wisconsin.

Citation: Business Card for Gladys Doriot (Ridgefield, WA, Gladys A. Doriot, Unknown), (In possession of Tracy Doriot, Washougal, WA.).; City of Ridgefield; Mayor.

Citation: Membership Dues Book (UBCJA) for Alvin Grimm (Medford, WI, United Brotherhood of Carpenters and Joiners of America, 14 Sep 1948), (In possession of Tracy Doriot, Washougal, WA). Local Union #1025; 30 Dec 1952.

Citation: Professional Baseball Players, 1876-2004; (Provo, UT, USA, Ancestry.com Operations Inc, 2004), www.ancestry.com, Baseball Almanac, comp, Professional Baseball Players, 1876-2004; 2004. Original data: Biographical baseball data provided by Baseball Almanac reproduced courtesy of the Library of Congress, Washington, D.C.

Citation: Union Withdrawal Card for Alvin Grimm (Medford, WI, United Brotherhood of Carpenters and Joiners of America, 30 Dec 1952), (In possession of Tracy Doriot, Washougal, WA).

**Title:** **Memorial Cards**

Citation: Memorial Card for Albert Philip Grimm (Medford, Taylor Co, WI, Hemer Funeral Service, Inc., Mar1981), (In possession of Tracy Doriot, Washougal, WA) Evergreen Cemetery, Medford, Taylor Co, Wisconsin; 14 Mar 1981.

Citation: Memorial Card for Alvin W. Grimm (Medford, WI, Trinity Lutheran Church, Oct 2003), (In possession of Tracy Doriot, Washougal, WA) Hemer Funeral Home Service; Medford, Taylor Co, Wisconsin; 03 Oct 2003.

Citation: Memorial Card for Annie Duesing Grimm (McIntosh, MN, Reese-Hoialmen Funeral Home, Feb1979), (In possession of Tracy Doriot, Washougal, WA) Internment at Immanuel Cemetery, McIntosh, MN

Citation: Memorial Card for Casper David Anderson (Cambridge, Isanti Co, MN, Carlson Funeral Home, 5 May 1990), (In possession of Tracy Doriot, Washougal, WA) Carlson Funeral Home; Cambridge, Isanti Co, Minn

Citation: Memorial Card for Clara M. Grimm, Memorial Card; Hemer Funeral Home; Medford, Taylor Co, Wisconsin; (In possession of Tracy Doriot, Washougal, WA) Interment at Trinity Lutheran Church Cemetery.

Citation: Memorial Card for Darlene A Steiner (Medford, Wisconsin, 14 Jul 1993), (In possession of Tracy Doriot, Washougal, WA), Medford, Taylor Co, Wisconsin.

Citation: Memorial Card for David J. Neuman (Medford, Taylor Co, WI, Hemer Funeral Services, Inc; Abt 23 Mar 1990), (In possession of Tracy Doriot, Washougal, WA). Hemer Funeral Services; Medford, Taylor Co, Wisconsin; Interment at St. Mary's Cemetery.

Citation: Memorial Card for Elmer Anderson (Medford, Taylor Co, WI, Hemer Funeral Service, Inc, 26 Jan, 1980), (In possession of Tracy Doriot, Washougal, WA) Hemer Funeral Home; Medford, Taylor Co, Wisconsin; Interment at Evergreen Cemetery II

Citation: Memorial Card for Erma Grimm Krausse (Edgerton, WI, Bruni-Nygaard-Ward, 02 Jun 1991), (In possession of Tracy Doriot, Washougal, WA) Bruni-Nygaard-Ward; Edgerton, Wisconsin

Citation: Memorial Card for Ervin Lange (Medford, WI, Hemer Funeral Service, Inc, 13 Jul 1993), (In possession of Tracy Doriot, Washougal, WA), Hemer Funeral Home; Medford, Taylor Co, Wisconsin

Citation: Memorial Card for George Drolshagen (Medford, Taylor Co, WI, Hemer Funeral Home, abt 04 Mar 1981), (In possession of Tracy Doriot, Washougal, WA) Hemer Funeral Home; Medford, Taylor Co, Wisconsin

Citation: Memorial Card for Gertrud Grimm (Middlebury, Indiana, Miller Funeral Home, Mar 1996), (In possession of Tracy Doriot, Washougal, WA), Miller Funeral Home; Middlebury, Indiana; "In Memory of Mrs. Gertrud "Trudl" E. Grimm".

Citation: Memorial Card for Grace Clarkson Anderson (Medford, Taylor Co, WI, Hemer Funeral Service, Inc., 20 18 Mar 1996), (In possession of Tracy Doriot, Washougal, WA) Hemer Funeral Home; Medford, Taylor Co, WI

Citation: Memorial Card for Johanna Anderson (n. a. given, n. pub. given, Abt 27 May 1903), (In possession of Tracy Doriot, Washougal, WA)

Citation: Memorial Card for Loretta (Hoverson) Anderson (Okanogan, Okanogan Co, WA, Barnes Elmway Chapel 10 Jun 1991), (In possession of Tracy Doriot, Washougal, WA). Barnes Elmway Chapel; Okanogan, Okanogan, Washington.

Citation: Memorial Card for Louis G. Lange, Memorial Card; Medford, Taylor Co, Wisconsin; (In possession of Tracy Doriot, Washougal, WA). Interment at Evergreen Cemetery II; 13 Aug 1984.

Citation: Memorial Card for Maurice Egle, Memorial Card; Medford, Taylor Co, Wisconsin; (In possession of Tracy Doriot, Washougal, WA) Interment at Evergreen Cemetery; 16 Dec 1995.

Citation: Memorial Card for Mollie Steiner Lange (Medford, WI, Hemer Funeral Service, Inc, 4 Mar1981), (In possession of Tracy Doriot, Washougal, WA) Hemer Funeral Home; Medford, Taylor Co, Wisconsin; Evergreen Cemetery.

Citation: Memorial Card for Nora Irene Nelson Grimm (McIntosh, Polk Co, Minnesota, Carlin-Hoialmen Funeral Home, 13 April 1995), (In possession of Tracy Doriot, Washougal, WA).

Citation: Memorial Card for Otto Anderson (Okanogan, Okanogan Co, WI, Barnes Elmway Chapel, 04 Sep 1992), (In possession of Tracy Doriot, Washougal, WA). Barnes Elmway Chapel; Okanogan, Okanogan Co, Washington; Interment at Riverside Cemetery.

Citation: Memorial Card for William Max Grimm (McIntosh, WI, Carlin-Hoialmen Funeral Home, 24 Feb 1990), (In possession of Tracy Doriot, Washougal, WA). Carlin-Hoialmen Funeral Home; McIntosh, Polk Co, Minnesota

**Title:** **Memorial Sermons**

Citation: Memorial Sermon for Alvin Grimm (Medford. WI, Rev. Randal Jeppesen, Oct 2003), Copy in possession of Tracy Doriot, Washougal, WA). Memorial Service; Rev. Randal Jeppesen, Trinity Lutheran Church; Medford, Taylor Co, Wisconsin; Oct 2003.

Citation: Memorial Service of Albert P. Grimm, (Whittlesey, Taylor Co, WI, Rev. Jerome Newton (Possibly), abt 14 Mar 1981), (In possession of Tracy Doriot, Washougal, WA) Memorial Service (probably); .

Citation:   Memorial Service Program for Alvin Grimm (Medford, Taylor Co, Wisconsin, USA, Trinity Lutheran Church (Whittlesey), 03 Oct 2003), (In possession of Tracy Doriot, Washougal, WA) Memorial Service; "Order of Worship"; Trinity Lutheran Church (Whittlesey); Medford, Taylor Co, Wisconsin

Citation:   Memorial Service Program for Casper David Anderson (Cambridge, MN, Cambridge Lutheran Church, 08 May 1990), (In possession of Tracy Doriot, Washougal, WA).Memorial Service; Cambridge Lutheran Church; Cambridge, Minnesota; Arrangements by Carlson Funeral Home.

Citation:   Presidential Memorial Certificate for James Maynard Doriot, "...honors the memory of James Maynard Doriot.". Signed: William J. Clinton.

**Title:**   **Naturalization Records**

Citation:   Naturalization Record (Index) for Henry Ludwig Grimm (Provo, UT, USA, Ancestry.com Operations, Inc., 2010), www.ancestry.com, U.S. Naturalization Record Indexes, 1791-1992 (Indexed in World Archives Project) [Database online]. Selected U.S. Naturalization Records, Washington D.C.: National Archives and Records Administration.

**Title:**   **News Articles**

Citation:   News Article #1 for Gladys Doriot (La Center, WA, Lewis River News, 20 Jan 1993), (Copy in possession of Tracy Doriot, Washougal, WA) Jan 1993; "Warriors of the Road"; Robert Yelas, Reporter

Citation:   News Article about Sandra Lynn Terp (Provo, UT, USA, Ancestry.com Operations Inc),www.ancestry.com, Manitowoc Herald Times, Manitowoc Co, Wisconsin; 30 April 1968; Front page

Citation:   News Article for Auction Sale of Robert Anderson Farm (Medford, Taylor Co, WI, The Star News, 18 Jun (1960), Copy in possession of Tracy Doriot, Washougal, WA. "Robert Anderson, Former Owner...Auction Finance Dept., State Bank of Medford, WI".

Citation:   News Article for Carl Anderson (Recruit) (Medford, Taylor Co, WI, The Star News, date unknown) (Copy in possession of Tracy Doriot, Washougal, WA). "Recruit Carl Anderson".

Citation:   News Article for William Grimm 100th Birthday (unknown, n. p. given, 1986), Copy in possession of Tracy Doriot, Washougal, WA) 12 Mar 1986; n.pub.

Citation:   News Article for William Grimm 98th Birthday (Publ. Unknown, Date Unknown, 1986), (Copy in possession of Tracy Doriot, Washougal, WA).

**Title:**   **Obituaries**

Citation:   Obituary for Adolph H Grimm (Manitowoc Co, WI, Manitowoc Times, 10 Jun 1970), Two Rivers Reporter T-13.

Citation:   Obituary for Adolph Koch (Twin Falls, ID, Times News, Jan 1985), "Adolph Koch ... married Mathilda Grimm"

Citation:   Obituary for Alma (Bauman) Grimm (Portland, OR, The Oregonian, 30 April 1961).

Citation:   Obituary for Alvin Lester Olson (Arlington, TX, Star-Telegram, 09 Mar 2011),

Citation:   Obituary for Alvin W. Grimm (Medford, WI, Star News, 2003), Obituary for Alvin W. Grimm.

Citation:   Obituary for Alvin W. Grimm (Vancouver, Clark Co, Washington, USA, The Columbian Newspaper, abt 26 Jun 2003), (Copy in possession of Tracy Doriot, Washougal, WA).

Citation:   Obituary for Anna (Grimm) Stansbery (Portland, OR, The Oregonian, Aug 1952),

Citation:   Obituary for Annie Steiner Grimm (Medford, Taylor Co, WI, The Star News, abt 15 Mar 1946), (Copy in possession of Tracy Doriot, Washougal, WA). "Mrs. Albert Grimm, 56 Buried Here Yesterday".

Citation:   Obituary for Anton H. Grimm (Sheboygan Co. Press, 26 Jun 1977)

Citation:   Obituary for Anton Olson (Sturgis, Saskatchewan, Canada, n.publ. g., n.d.g.); suesaunders55, Randall/Furden/Halverson/Potter Family Tree Site, Public Family Tree, Ancestry.com. Accessed 15 Dec 2013; http://trees.ancestry.com/tree/1546213

Citation:   Obituary for Arlene (Neumueller) Anderson (Medford, WI, The Star News, 14 Feb 2008)

Citation:   Obituary for Barbara L (Klasner) Brohn (Provo, UT, USA, Ancestry.com Operations Inc, 2012), www.ancestry.com, Michigan, Find A Grave Index, 1805-2012 [database on-line]. Record added: Feb 10, 2010. Find A Grave Memorial# 47956274. Obituary included.

Citation:   Obituary for Basil Orlando Singleton (Medford, WI, Star News, Jan 1975)

Citation:   Obituary for Bertha (Grimm) Doblie (Portland, OR, The Oregonian, 25 Dec 2011), www.ancestry.com

Citation:   Obituary for Betty L. (Anderson) Bruton (Provo, UT, USA, Ancestry.com Operations Inc, 2001), www.ancestry.com, John Stoddard, comp.; Chicago Tribune, Chicago, IL, USA: Chicago Tribune Obituary Index, 1988-1997; [Database online].

Citation:   Obituary for Carl R Anderson (Medford, WI, Star News, 01 Oct 2009), United States Obituary Collection; [Database online].

Citation:   Obituary for Casper David Anderson (Medford, Taylor Co, WI, The Star News, abt 05 May 1990), (Copy in possession of Tracy Doriot, Washougal, WA)

Citation:   Obituary for Chester L. Steiner (Medford, WI, Star News, abt May 7 1993), (Copy in possession of Tracy Doriot, Washougal, WA).

Citation:   Obituary for Clara M. Grimm, 2 news articles, Bet. May 6 -11, 1997; Star News, Medford, WI. (Copy in possession of Tracy Doriot, Washougal, WA)

Citation:  Obituary for Darlene (Anderson) Steiner (Medford, WI, Star News, abt July 12 1993). (Copy in possession of Tracy Doriot, Washougal, WA)

Citation:  Obituary for Elfrieda (Wambsganss) Baals (Provo, UT, USA, Ancestry.com Operations Inc, 2012). www.ancestry.com, News-Sentinel (Fort Wayne, Indiana) 28 Feb 1992; Included on Indiana, Find A Grave, 1800-2012; Record added: Aug 12, 2010; Find A Grave Memorial# 56978071; Retrieved 30 August 2013.

Citation:  Obituary for Elizabeth (Terp) Berken (Provo, UT, USA, Ancestry.com Operations Inc, 2011), www.ancestry.com, Green Bay Press-Gazette; Green Bay, WI; 28 Feb 2008.

Citation:  Obituary for Elmer Anderson (Medford, Taylor Co., WI, The Star News, aft 26 Jan 1980). ( Copy in possession of Tracy Doriot, Washougal, WA).Abt. 27 Jan 1980. Rites Held Jan. 26 for E. Anderson".

Citation:  Obituary for Emma (Fischer) Grimm (Sheboygan Co. Press, 09 Mar 1939).

Citation:  Obituary for Erma Grimm Krausse (Medford, Taylor Co, WI, Star News, 06 Jun 1991). (Copy in possession of Tracy Doriot; Washougal, WA). "Erma H. Krausse (1911-1991)".

Citation:  Obituary for Ervin O. Lange (Medford, WI, Star News, abt 14 Jul 1993). (Copy in possession of Tracy Doriot, Washougal, WA)

Citation:  Obituary for Evadna Bacon Spencer (Portland, OR, The Oregonian, 17 Jan 1968).

Citation:  Obituary for Florence Anderson (Medford, Taylor Co, WI, The Star News, 15 Nov 1979), (Copy in possession of Tracy Doriot; Washougal, WA).

Citation:  Obituary for Frederick P.E. Wambsganss (Provo, UT, USA, Ancestry.com Operations Inc, 25 Nov 1957), www.ancestry.com, Allen County, Indiana, Obituary Index, 1841-2010 [database on-line]. 2010. Original data: Fort Wayne and Allen County, Indiana Area Obituary Index, 1841 August 2011; Allen County Public Library. Printed in Fort Wayne Journal Gazette. Retrieved 30 August 2013 from http://friendsofallencounty.org/search_obits1900.php

Citation:  Obituary for George Drolshagen (Medford, Taylor Co., WI, The Star News, 06 Mar 1981). (Copy in possession of Tracy Doriot, Washougal, WA)

Citation:  Obituary for Gerald Lee Brohn (Provo, UT, USA, Ancestry.com Operations Inc, 2011), www.ancestry.com, Obituary; Flint Journal (Flint, Michigan) 05 Nov 2011 http://www.milive.com/.

Citation:  Obituary for Gertrud Grimm (Publ. Unk, 09 Mar 1996). (Copy in possession of Tracy Doriot, Washougal, WA)

Citation:  Obituary for Gladys (Grimm) Doriot (Vancouver, Clark Co, WA, The Columbian, 9 Mar 2011). (Copy in possession of Tracy Doriot, Washougal, WA).

Citation:  Obituary for Grace Clarkson Anderson (Medford, Taylor Co, WI, The Star News, abt 18 Mar 1996), (Copy in possession of Tracy Doriot, Washougal, WA).

Citation:  Obituary for Henry J. Steiner (Medford, WI, Star News).

Citation:  Obituary for Henry William Grimm (Rupert, Idaho, Rupert News, 20 Dec 1945).

Citation:  Obituary for Ida C. (Bruns) Grimm (Portland, OR, The Oregonian, 4 Nov 1961).

Citation:  Obituary for Jack D Baals (Provo, UT, USA, Ancestry.com Operations Inc, 2012), www.ancestry.com, Journal Gazette (Fort Wayne, Indiana) 21 Jun 2003; Obituary printed at Indiana, Find A Grave, 1800-2012; Record added: Aug 12, 2010; Find A Grave Memorial# 56972458; Retrieved 30 August 2013.

Citation:  Obituary for Jack Vernon Smith (Provo, UT, USA, Ancestry.com Operations Inc, 2011), www.ancestry.com, News-Sentinel, The (Fort Wayne, Indiana) 13 November 1990; Attached to Indiana, Find A Grave, 1800-2012; Record added: Sep 01, 2011; Find A Grave Memorial# 75796789. Accessed 30 Aug 2013

Citation:  Obituary for James Maynard Doriot (Vancouver, WA, The Columbian Newspaper (probably). (Copy in possession of Tracy Doriot, Washougal, WA). Publ. unknown, n.d.

Citation:  Obituary for Leighton Lee Drolshagen (Medford, WI, The Star News, 03 Apr 2008) (Copy in possession of Tracy Doriot, Washougal, WA).

Citation:  Obituary for Leo L. Bill (Twin Falls, ID, Times News, Jun 1997).

Citation:  Obituary for Loretta (Hoverson) Anderson (Okanogan, WA (Probably), n. pub. given, abt 06 Jun1991). (Copy in possession of Tracy Doriot, Washougal, WA).

Citation:  Obituary for Lucille (Terp) Baeb (Provo, UT, USA, Ancestry.com Operations Inc, 2011). www.ancestry.com, Wisconsin: Find A Grave: 1836-2012; [website]; Record added: Dec 13, 2010 Find A Grave Memorial# 62896918; Obituary included.

Citation:  Obituary for Lydia (Schellman) Terp (Provo, UT, USA, Ancestry.com Operations Inc), www.ancestry.com, Wisconsin: Find A Grave [Database online]. Woodlawn Cemetery, Brown Co, Wisconsin; Record added: Feb 23, 2010; Find A Grave Memorial# 48664620; Obituary included.

Citation:  Obituary for Margaret B Wambsganss (Provo, UT, USA, Ancestry.com Operations Inc, 2005), www.ancestry.com, Allen County, Indiana, Obituary Index, 1841-2010 [database on-line]. 2010. Printed 04 Mar 1972. Original data: Fort Wayne and Allen County, Indiana Area Obituary Index, 1841 - August 2011; Allen County Public Library. Retrieved 30 August 2013 from http://friendsofallencounty.org/search_obits1900.php.

Citation:  Obituary for Mary (Anderson) Sperl (Medford, WI, Star News, abt 24 Jan 2013) "Funeral Set Saturday at Holway Church for Mrs. Mary Anderson, 74".

154

Citation: Obituary for Maurice Egle, 20 Dec 1995; The Star News, Medford, WI). (Copy in possession of Tracy Doriot, Washougal, WA).

Citation: Obituary for Mollie Steiner Lange (Medford, WI, Star News, May 1981). (Copy in possession of Tracy Doriot, Washougal, WA).

Citation: Obituary for Orville Gust Grimm (McIntosh, MN, Tri-Times, 15 Feb 2005)

Citation: Obituary for Otto C. Anderson (N. pub., n.d.g.), (Copy in possession of Tracy Doriot, Washougal, WA).

Citation: Obituary for Paul B. Anderson (Medford, Taylor Co, WI, The Star News, 26 Feb 2006), (Copy in possession of Tracy Doriot, Washougal, WA).

Citation: Obituary for Reinhard Franz Grimm (Manitowoc Co, WI, Herald-Times, 01 Jun 1966)

Citation: Obituary for Robert L. Sperl (Wisconsin Rapids, WI, Daily Tribune, 01 Oct 2007).

Citation: Obituary for Robert Manuel Anderson (Omak, WA, Omak-Okanogan County Chronicle, 26 Sep2007)

Citation: Obituary for Rose Penrose Stoutenburg (Dayton, OR, Dayton Tribune, 25 Jun 1975).

Citation: Obituary for Tammy Thompson Anderson (Hoquiam, WA (http://www.meaningfulfunerals.net/fh/obituaries; Jan 2011) Accessed 13 Dec 2013.

Citation: Obituary for Vernon J. Frey (Sheboygan Co, WI, Sheboygan Co. Press, 23 Nov 2004), [Database online]. Newspaper: Daily Tribune; Publication Date: 1 10 2007; Publication Place: Wisconsin Rapids , WI

Citation: Obituary for William A Grimm (Portland, OR, The Oregonian, 24 Sep 1952). "GRIMM ---William A"Obituary for William Adolph Wambsganss Jr. (AP, 11 Dec 1985). "Bill Wambsganss Dies at 91; Made a Triple Play in Series."

**Title:** **Passenger & Immigration Records**

Citation: Passenger & Immigration Record for Henry Ludwig Grimm (Provo, UT, USA, Ancestry.com Operations Inc, 2010), www.ancestry.com, Passenger and Immigration Lists Index, 1500s-1900s[Database online].Place: Port uncertain; Year: 1848; Page Number: .Filby, P. William, ed., Passenger and Immigration Lists Index, 1500s-1900s, Farmington Hills, MI, USA: Gale Research.

Citation: Passenger Record for Henry Ludwig Grimm (Provo, UT, USA, Ancestry.com Operations Inc, 2003), www.ancestry.com, New York, Passenger and Immigration Lists, 1820-1850 [Database online].New York, Registers of Vessels Arriving at the Port of New York from Foreign Ports, 1789-1919, Washington, D.C.: National Archives and Records Administration.

**Title:** **Personal Knowledge (Interviews)**

Citation: Personal Knowledge of Bernard Arthur Anderson (Moses Lake, WA, 12 Dec 2013) Personal interview with Maryellen Anderson (author).

Citation: Personal Knowledge of Danny Robert Sperl (Medford, WI, 15 Dec 2013) Personal interview with Maryellen Anderson (author).

Citation: Personal Knowledge of Dolores Anderson Jones (Omak, WA, 12 Dec 2013) Personal interview with Maryellen Anderson (author).

Citation: Personal Knowledge of Donald Manual Anderson (Okanogan, WA, 12 Dec 2013) Personal interview with Maryellen Anderson (author).

Citation: Personal Knowledge of Donna Anderson Boiko (Curlew, WA, 12 Dec 2013) Personal interview with Maryellen Anderson (author).

Citation: Personal Knowledge of Everett Grimm (Middlebury, IN Jan 2000). Personal interview with Maryellen Anderson (author).

Citation: Personal Knowledge of Gladys Grimm Doriot (Ridgefield, WA, Jan 2000), Personal Interview with Maryellen Anderson ( author).

Citation: Personal Knowledge of Kenneth Melvin Anderson (Omak, WA, 15 Dec 2013) Personal Interview with Maryellen Anderson ( author).

Citation: Personal Knowledge of Marilynn Jaquish Anderson (Hoquiam, WA, 12 Dec 2013) Personal interview with Maryellen Anderson (author).

Citation: Personal Knowledge of Norma Anderson Lawson (Brewster, WA, 12 Dec 2013) Personal interview with Maryellen Anderson (author).

Citation: Personal Knowledge of Ruby Drohlshagen Neuman (Medford, WI, 02 Jul 2005). Personal interview with Maryellen Anderson (author).

Citation: Personal Knowledge of Ruth Anderson Perterson (Medford, WI, 12 Dec 2013) Personal interview with Maryellen Anderson (author).

Citation: Personal Knowledge of Tracy Owen Doriot (Washougal, WA, Tracy Doriot), Personal interview with Maryellen Anderson (author).

Citation: Personal Knowledge of Wayne Arthur Anderson (Port Angeles, WA) Personal Interview with Maryellen Anderson ( author).

**Title:** **Probate Records**

Citation: Application for Informal Administration for James R. Doriot (Madison, WI, Thomas Lindow, 02 Nov 2002), State of Wisconsin, Dane County Circuit Court Madison, WI, (Copy in possession of Tracy Doriot, Washougal, WA) Atty: Croak, Gonzalez & Eckerle, 4703 Monona Dr., Madison, WI 53716.

**Title:** **Public Member Trees (Ancestry.com)**

Citation: Public Member Tree for Carrie Kiea Josephine Peterson (Provo, UT, USA, Ancestry.com Operations Inc, 2006), www.ancestry.com, Public Member Tree. [Database online].

Citation: Public Member Tree for Ed Olivus Olson (Provo, UT, USA, Ancestry.com Operations Inc, 2006), www.ancestry.com, Public Member Tree. [Database online]. Alternate name.

Citation: Public Member Tree for Elsie Maria Grimm (Provo, UT, USA, Ancestry.com Operations Inc, 2006), www.ancestry.com, Public Member Tree. [Database online]. Furlong Family Tree; http://trees.ancestry.com/tree/40071523

Citation: Public Member Tree for Emma A. Olson (Provo, UT, USA, Ancestry.com Operations Inc, 2006), www.ancestry.com, Public Member Tree. [Database online]. Pederson-Petterson-Christiansen-Wold-Olsen-Jensdatter-Nord Family Tree; http://trees.ancestry.com/tree/1747318/person/-971449703; marriage date and place.

Citation: Public Member Tree for Herman Grimm (Provo, UT, USA, Ancestry.com Operations Inc, 2006), www.ancestry.com, Public Member Tree. [Database online]. White/Poggeman Family Tree; http://trees.ancestry.com/tree/4524382/person/326041559.

Citation: Public Member Tree for Lillian A. Penrose (Provo, UT, USA, Ancestry.com Operations Inc, 2006), www.ancestry.com, Public Member Tree. [Database online].

Citation: Public Member Tree for Wilma (Grimm) Huffman (Scappoose, OR, huffmanmj, 2011), www.ancestry.com, Palmer/Huffman Family Tree; [Database online].Ancestry.com/tree/1982011/.

**Title:** **Social Security Records**

Citation: Social Security Benefit Statement for Alvin Grimm (Dept. of the Treasury, Internal Revenue Service, 1995). (Copy in possession of Tracy Doriot, Washougal, WA).

Citation: Social Security Card of Clara (Anderson) Grimm (Social Security Administration, n.d.g.). (In possession of Tracy Doriot, Washougal, WA).

**Title:** **Social Security Records (Social Security Death Index**

Source information for all following SSDI records: (Provo, UT, USA, Ancestry.com Operations Inc, 2006). [Database online]. U.S. Social Security Death Index 1935-Current; Social Security Administration. Social Security Death Index, Master File. Social Security Administration.

Citation: SSDI for Adolph Koch; Issue State: Idaho; Issue Date: Before 1951.

Citation: SSDI for Albert P Grimm. Issue State: Wisconsin; Issue Date: 1955-1956

Citation: SSDI for Alfred E. Arronson .Issue State: Oregon; Issue Date: Before 1951.

Citation: SSDI for Allen L. Anderson .Issue State: Minnesota; Issue Date: 1965.

Citation: SSDI for Alvin E Grimm. Issue State: California; Issue Date: Before 1951.

Citation: SSDI for Alvin Lester Olson. Issue State: Wisconsin; Issue Date: Before 1951.

Citation: SSDI for Alvin Schubert. Issue State: Montana; Issue Date: Before 1951.

Citation: SSDI for Alvin W. Grimm. Issue State: Wisconsin; Issue Date: Before 1951

Citation: SSDI for Amos Bill. Issue State: Idaho; Issue Date: Before 1951.

Citation: SSDI for Anton Grimm Issue State: Wisconsin; Issue Date: 1956-1957.

Citation: SSDI for Arlene (Nuemueller) Anderson. Issue State: Minnesota; Issue Date: 1960.

Citation: SSDI for Arthur Carl Anderson. Issue State: Washington; Issue Date: Before 1951.

Citation: SSDI for Barbara L. Klasner. Issue State: Michigan; Issue Date: Before 1951.

Citation: SSDI for Basil O. Singleton. Issue State: Wisconsin; Issue Date: Before 1951.

Citation: SSDI for Bernice A Terp. Issue State: Wisconsin; Issue Date: 1964.

Citation: SSDI for Bertha (Abel) Anderson. Issue State: Washington; Issue Date: Bef. 1951.

Citation: SSDI for Bertha (Grimm) Doblie. Issue State: Oregon; Issue Date: Before 1951.

Citation: SSDI for Betty (Anderson) Bruton. Issue State: Wisconsin; Issue Date: 1953-1954.

Citation: SSDI for Betty (Sapp) Grimm. Issue State: Oregon; Issue Date: Before1951.

Citation: SSDI for Caroline W Grimm. Issue State: Pennsylvania; Issue Date: Before 1951.

Citation: SSDI for Casper D Anderson. Issue State: Wisconsin; Issue Date: Before 1951.

Citation: SSDI for Casper Olson. Issue State: Wisconsin; Issue Date: Before 1951.

Citation: SSDI for Casper Olson Jr. Issue State: Wisconsin; Issue Date: 1952-1953.

Citation: SSDI for Chester L Steiner. Issue State: Wisconsin; Issue Date: Before 1951.

Citation: SSDI for Clara (Anderson) Grimm. .Issue State: Wisconsin; Issue Date: 1969.

Citation: SSDI for Clara J. Cheney. Issue State: Michigan; Issue Date: Before 1951.

Citation: SSDI for Claude Klasner. Issue State: Pennsylvania. Issue Date: Before 1951.

Citation: SSDI for Cleo (Grimm) Zemke. Issue State: Idaho; Issue Date: Before 1951.

Citation: SSDI for Cletus J Berken. Issue State: Wisconsin; Issue Date: Before 1951.
Citation: SSDI for Delois C. Olson. Issue State: Texas; Issue Date: Before 1951
Citation: SSDI for Douglas Grimm. Issue State: Minnesota; Issue Date: 1959.
Citation: SSDI for Douglas L. Fritz. Issue State: Indiana; Issue Date: Before 1951.
Citation: SSDI for Duane Ervin Grimm. Issue State: Minnesota; Issue Date: 1951.
Citation: SSDI for Edward Oliver Olson. Issue State: Washington; Issue Date: Before 1951.
Citation: SSDI for Effie (Mulholland) Wambsganss. Issue State: Ohio; Issue Date: 1964.
Citation: SSDI for Eileen C. Terp. Issue State: Wisconsin; Before 1951
Citation: SSDI for Elmer Anderson. Issue State: Wisconsin; Issue Date: Before 1951.
Citation: SSDI for Elmer H Grimm. Issue State: Arizona; Issue Date: Before 1951.
Citation: SSDI for Elsa K. Kettenbiel. Issue State: Michigan; Issue Date: 1964.
Citation: SSDI for Elsie M. Pederson. Issue State: Oregon; Issue Date: Before 1951.
Citation: SSDI for Elva (Anderson) Drohlshagen. Issue State: Wisconsin; Issue Date: Before 1951.
Citation: SSDI for Erma (Grimm) Krausse. Issue State: Wisconsin; Issue Date: 1956-1957.
Citation: SSDI for Ethel (Klasner) Funkey. Issue State: Michigan; Issue Date: 1951.
Citation: SSDI for Eunice E. (Wambsganss) Smith. Issue State: Indiana; Issue Date: Before 1951.
Citation: SSDI for Evert N. Pederson. Issue State: Washington; Issue Date: Before 1951.
Citation: SSDI for Garvin C. Mitchell Issue State: Michigan; Issue Date: Before 1951.
Citation: SSDI for Garvin Peter Mitchell Issue State: Michigan; Issue Date: Before 1951.
Citation: SSDI for George Drohlshagen. Issue State: Wisconsin; Issue Date: Before 1951.
Citation: SSDI for Gerald Eugene Anderson. Issue State: Washington; Issue Date: 1961.
Citation: SSDI for Gladys Ann Grimm. Issue State: Wisconsin; Issue Date: 1951-1952.
Citation: SSDI for Gustav A. Grimm. Issue State: Oregon; Issue Date: Before 1951.
Citation: SSDI for Hannah (Wambsganss) Hitzman. Issued: Indiana; Bef 1951.
Citation: SSDI for Harold J. Terp Issue State: Wisconsin; Issue Date: Before 1951.
Citation: SSDI for Henry A Bill. Issue State: Idaho; Issue Date: Before 1951.
Citation: SSDI for Henry J Klasner Jr. Issue State: Michigan; Issue Date: Before 1951.
Citation: SSDI for Henry Kettenbeil Jr. Issue State: Michigan; Issue Date: Before 1951.
Citation: SSDI for Henry Terp. Issue State: Wisconsin; Before 1951.
Citation: SSDI for Hilda Cook. Issue State: California; Issue Date: Before 1951.
Citation: SSDI for Hollie F. Schroder. Issue State: Washington; Issue Date: Before1951.
Citation: SSDI for Howard Vollmer. Issue State: Michigan; Issue Date: Before 1951.
Citation: SSDI for Hueston "Hugh" Rosebrook. Issue State: Oregon; Issue Date: Before1951.
Citation: SSDI for Jack Vernon Smith. Issue State: Indiana; Issue Date: Before 1951.
Citation: SSDI for James C Neuman. Issue State: Wisconsin; Issue Date: Before 1951.
Citation: SSDI for James E Huffman. Issue State: Oregon; Issue Date: Before1951.
Citation: SSDI for James M. Doriot. Issue State: Wisconsin; Issue Date: Before 1951.
Citation: SSDI for James T Neuman. Issue State: Wisconsin; Issue Date: 1971.
Citation: SSDI for John Lorenz. Issue State: Michigan; Issue Date: Before 1951.
Citation: SSDI for John N Domnisse. Issue State: Oregon; Issue Date: Before 1951.
Citation: SSDI for John W Terp. Issue State: Wisconsin; Before 1951.
Citation: SSDI for Joseph P Baeb. Issue State: Wisconsin; Issue Date: Before 1951.
Citation: SSDI for Kathleen C. Terp. Issue State: Minnesota; Issue Date: Before 1951.
Citation: SSDI for Kenneth M. Pederson. Issue State: Washington; Issue Date: Before 1951.
Citation: SSDI for Kenneth R. Hunt. Issue State: Oregon; Issue Date: Before 1951.
Citation: SSDI for Laurin Cook. Issue State: California; Issue Date: 1955.
Citation: SSDI for Lavern Albert Grimm. Issue State: Minnesota; Issue Date: Before 1951.
Citation: SSDI for Lawrence A Grimm. Issue State: Oregon; Issue Date: Before 1951.
Citation: SSDI for Leighton E. Drolshagen. Issue State: Wisconsin; Issue Date: 1956.
Citation: SSDI for Leo L. Bill. Issue State: Idaho; Issue Date: 1951-1952.
Citation: SSDI for Leona (Grimm) Arronson. Issue State: Oregon; Issue Date: Before 1951.
Citation: SSDI for Leonard Grimm. Issue State: California; Issue Date: Before 1951.
Citation: SSDI for Leonard R Grimm (Provo, UT, USA, Ancestry.com Operations Inc, 2000), www.ancestry.com, California, Death Index, 1940-1997, [Database online]. State of California, California Death Index, 1940-1997, Sacramento, CA, USA: State of California Department of Health. Services, Center for Health Statistics
Citation: SSDI for Leroy Siegfried Krausse. Issue State: Wisconsin; Issue Date: Before 1951
Citation: SSDI for Leslie Terp. Issue State: Wisconsin; Issue Date: Before 1951.
Citation: SSDI for Lloyd G Schubert. Issue State: Wisconsin; Issue Date: Before 1951.
Citation: SSDI for Lucille S Terp. Issue State: Wisconsin; Issue Date: Before 1951.

Citation: SSDI for Lydia Strebig. Issue State: Wisconsin; Issue Date: 1963.
Citation: SSDI for Maren R. Crabb. Issue State: Wisconsin; Issue Date: Before 1951.
Citation: SSDI for Max I. Doblie Issue State: Oregon; Issue Date: Before 1951.
Citation: SSDI for Melvin Pederson. Issue State: Washington; Issue Date: Before 1951.
Citation: SSDI for Merle E Crabb. Issue State: Wisconsin; Issue Date: Before 1951.
Citation: SSDI for Michael Boiko. Issue State: Washington; Issue Date: Before 1951.
Citation: SSDI for Mollie (Steiner) Lange. Issue State: Wisconsin; Issue Date: before 1951.
Citation: SSDI for Monroe Grimm. Issue State: Idaho; Issue Date: Before 1951.
Citation: SSDI for Nels Olson. Issue State: Washington; Issue Date: Before 1951.
Citation: SSDI for Otto C Anderson. Issue State: Wisconsin; Issue Date: Before 1951.
Citation: SSDI for Paul Benton Anderson. Issue State: Washington; Issue Date: Before 1951.
Citation: SSDI for Paul Hitzeman. Issue State: Indiana; Issue Date: Before 1951. .
Citation: SSDI for Paul W Nelson. Issue State: Colorado; Issue Date: Before 1951.
Citation: SSDI for Ralph Spencer. Issue State: Railroad Board (Issued Through); Issue Date: Before 1951.
Citation: SSDI for Raymond Paul Schubert. Issue State: Wisconsin; Issue Date: bef 1951. .
Citation: SSDI for Reinhard Grimm. Issue State: Wisconsin; Issue Date: 1956.
Citation: SSDI for Robert L Sperl Issue State: Wisconsin; Issue Date: 1951.
Citation: SSDI for Robert L. Grimm. Issue State: Oregon; Issue Date: Before 1951.
Citation: SSDI for Robert Manuel Anderson Issue State: Wisconsin; Issue Date: Before 1951.
Citation: SSDI for Robert Terp Issue State: Wisconsin; Issue Date: Before 1951.
Citation: SSDI for Roger Travis Issue State: Minnesota; Issue Date: 1964.
Citation: SSDI for Ronald Lester Zemke. Issue State: Idaho; Issue Date: Before 1951.
Citation: SSDI for Roy Stoutenburg. Issue State: Oregon; Issue Date: Before 1951.
Citation: SSDI for Siegfried Krausse. Issue State: Wisconsin; Issue Date: Before 1951.
Citation: SSDI for Venita Terp. Issue State: Wisconsin; Issue Date: Before 1951.
Citation: SSDI for Vernon J Frey. Issue State: Wisconsin; Issue Date: Before 1951.
Citation: SSDI for Viola (Vincent) Terp. Issue State: Wisconsin; Issue Date: Before 1951.
Citation: SSDI for Viola R. Anderson. Issue State: Wisconsin; Issue Date: 1974.
Citation: SSDI for Violette M. Ferden. Issue State: Illinois; Issue Date: 1963-1964.
Citation: SSDI for Walter Kettenbeil. Issue State: Michigan; Issue Date: Before 1951.
Citation: SSDI for Walter Milton Anderson Issue State: Wisconsin; Issue Date: 1957.
Citation: SSDI for Wilbert Louis Grimm. Issue State: Oregon; Issue Date: Before 1951.
Citation: SSDI for William Max Grimm. Issue State: Minnesota; Issue Date: Before 1951.
Citation: SSDI for William Terp. Issue State: Wisconsin; Before 1951.
Citation: SSDI for William A. Wambsganss Issue State: Ohio; Issue Date: Before 1951.
Citation: SSDI for Wilma (Grimm) Huffman. Issue State: Oregon; Issue Date: Before 1951.
Citation: SSDI for Woodrow Terp. Issue State: Wisconsin; Issue Date: Before 1951.
**Title:** **Sworn Affidavit by Anna (Grimm) McKee**
Citation: Sworn Affidavit by Anna (Grimm) McKee (Portland, OR, State of Oregon, County of Multnomah Co,07 Jan 1943), date and place of her birth and sibling's birth; names of parents. "...our father's name was Frank Grimm and mother's maiden name was Minnie Shelk."
**Title:** **Unemployment Records**
Citation: Unemployment Record for Robert Anderson (Medford, Taylor Co, WI, Wisconsin State Employment Service, Unemployment Compensation Dept., Jan 1961),(In possession of Tracy Doriot, Washougal, WA). Wisconsin State Employment Service; Unemployment Compensation Dept.; (Jan 1961).
**Title:** **U.S. City Directory Records**
Source information for all following U.S. City Directory Records: (Provo, UT, USA, Ancestry.com Operations Inc, 1950), www.ancestry.com, U.S. City Directories, 1821-1989 [database on-line]. 2011
Citation: US City Directory for Alma (Bauman) Grimm. Portland, OR, 1931 p. 537.
Citation: US City Directory for Barbara L Klasner. Flint, Michigan, City Directory, 1934; p. 399.
Citation: US City Directory for Bernard Grimm. R.L. Polk & Co's Directory of Clatsop County 1904 Alphabetical List of Tax Payers; p. 293
Citation: US City Directory for Claude H Klasner. Pottsville, Pennsylvania, City Directory, 1941 p. 206; 1950. p. 162.
Citation: US City Directory for Cletus J Berken. Green Bay, Wisconsin, City Directory, 1946; p. 82.
Citation: US City Directory for Elmer H Grimm San Diego, California, City Directory 1933, p. 268.
Citation: US City Directory for Evadna (Bacon) Rosebrook Residence (1929, 1934) Portland, Oregon, City Directory; p. 1464.
Citation: US City Directory for Gladys (Grimm) Doriot. Bend, Oregon, City Directory, 1955, p. 86. Pilot Butte Inn, waitress.
Citation: US City Directory for Glen M Propst, San Jose, California, City Directory, 1955, p. 127.
Citation: US City Directory for Henry Kettenbeil Jr. Calumet, Michigan, City Directory, 1930; p. 237.

Citation: US City Directory for Jack V Smith; Fort Wayne, Indiana, City Directory, 1960, p. 934.
Citation: US City Directory for James M. Doriot. Seattle, Washington, City Directory, 1942, (Carpenter, TSDD) p. 295 ; Bend, Oregon, City Directory, 1959, p. 152 (laborer, Oregon Woodwork)
Citation: US City Directory for John Domnisse. Portland, Oregon, City Directory, 1953, p. 289.
Citation: US City Directory for Joseph Baeb Green Bay, Wisconsin, City Directory, 1937; p. 46.
Citation: US City Directory for Lawrence A Grimm Portland, Oregon, City Directory; 1929. 1933. 1955.
Citation: US City Directory for Leona (Grimm) Arronson. Portland, Oregon, City Directory, 1955, p. 55.
Citation: US City Directory for Leroy S Krausse. Janesville, Wisconsin, City Directory, 1959, p. 224.
Citation: US City Directory for Louis A Grimm. Portland, Oregon, City Directory; 1899, p. 329; 1916, p. 537; 1918, p. 523.
Citation: US City Directory for Lydia (Schellman) Terp. Green Bay, Wisconsin, City Directory, 1935, p. 551; 1941, p. 619; 1949, p. 502.
Citation: US City Directory for Melvin Pederson. Salem, Oregon, City Directory, 1977, p. 339.
Citation: US City Directory for Minnie Grimm. Portland, Oregon, City Directory; 1918, p. 523.
Citation: US City Directory for Mildred (Grimm) Domnisse. Portland, Oregon, City Directory, 1953, p. 289; Astoria City Directory, 1959, p. 131.
Citation: US City Directory for Monroe Grimm. Eureka, California, City Directory, 1958, p. 203.
Citation: US City Directory for Nels Pederson. Spokane, Washington, City Directory, 1940, p. 592.
Citation: US City Directory for Rev Philip Wambsganss Fort Wayne, Indiana, City Directory; 1918; p. 1222.
Citation: US City Directory for Robert J Terp. Fond Du Lac, Wisconsin, City Directory, 1942; p. 338.
Citation: US City Directory for Verna (Bacon) Teuber Seattle, Washington, City Directory, 1932, p. 1419; 1934, p. 1411.
Citation: US City Directory for Violette Ferden. Bloomington, Illinois, City Directory, 1946, p. 123.
Citation: US City Directory for Walter Kettenbeil. Calumet, Michigan, City Directory, 1930; p. 237.
Citation: US City Directory for Wilbert W Terp Green Bay, Wisconsin, City Directory, 1925; p. 374.
Citation: US City Directory for William Klasner. Flint, Michigan, City Directory, 1934; p. 399.
Citation: US City Directory for Winifred (Wambsganss) Fritz Fort Wayne, Indiana, City Directory, 1946; p. 199. 1960; p. 335.
**Title:** **U.S. Public Records**
Source information for all following citations for U.S. Public Records: (Provo, UT, USA, Ancestry.com Operations Inc, 2010), www.ancestry.com, U.S. Public Records Index, Volume 1 & 2; [Database online]. Voter Registration Lists, Public Record Filings, Historical Residential Records, and Other Household Database Listings
Citation: US Public Record for Alvin L Olson. Residence (1993) Arlington, Tarrant Co., Texas.
Citation: US Public Record for Casper Olson. Residence (2004) Withee, Clark Co., Wisconsin.
Citation: US Public Record for Chester Anderson. Birthdate; Residence (1980) Chicago, Cook Co., Illinois.
Citation: US Public Record for Donna L Boiko. Residence (1991) Curlew, Ferry Co., Washington.
Citation: US Public Record for Elaine L Krausse. Residence (1988) Stoughton, Dane Co., Wisconsin.
Citation: US Public Record for Duane Grimm. Residence (n.d.g.) Great Falls, Cascade Co., Montana.
Citation: US Public Record for Eugene D Olson. Residence (n.d.g.) Medford, Taylor Co., Wisconsin.
Citation: US Public Record for Everett R Grimm. Residence (1981) Middlebury, Elkhart Co., Indiana.
Citation: US Public Record for Evert N Pederson. Name; Birthdate; Residence (1993) Salem, Marion Co., Oregon.
Citation: US Public Record for Gladys A Doriot. Residence (1955) Bend, Deschutes Co., Oregon.
Citation: US Public Record for Glen M Propst. Residence (1930) Portland, Multnomah Co., Oregon; (1955) San Jose, Los Angeles Co., California; (1993) Paradise, Butte Co., California (n.d.g.) Yountville, Napa Co., California.
Citation: US Public Record for Hueston "Hugh" L Rosebrook. Residence (1929) Portland, Multnomah Co., Oregon.
Citation: US Public Record for John Drolshagen. Residence (1981) Medford, Taylor Co., Wisconsin.
Citation: US Public Record for John W Terp. Residence (1935, 1993) Lake Forest, California.
Citation: US Public Record for Joseph Alex Boiko. Birthdate. Residence (n.d.g.) Curlew, Ferry Co., Washington.
Citation: US Public Record for Julie (Purdem) Doriot. Birthdate. Residence (1985) Ridgefield, Clark Co., Washington.
Citation: US Public Record for Kenneth J Kirchberg. Residence (1987) Rush City, Chisago Co., Minnesota.
Citation: US Public Record for Lauretta J (Hodge) Bill. Birthdate.
Citation: US Public Record for Leo L Bill. Residence (1940) Rupert, Minidoka Co., Idaho.
Citation: US Public Record for Lois (Anderson) Kirchberg. Residence (1986) Isle, Mille Lacs, Minnesota; (1990) Rush City, Chisago Co., Minnesota.
Citation: US Public Record for Maren R (Crabb) Terp. Residence (1920, 1958) Green Bay, Brown Co, Wisconsin; (1940) Allouez, Brown Co., Wisconsin
Citation: US Public Record for Melvin Pederson. Residence (1977) Salem, Marion Co., Oregon.
Citation: US Public Record for Melvin R Propst. Residence (1940) Portland, Multnomah Co., Oregon.
Citation: US Public Record for Merle E Crabb: Residence (1978) Green Bay, Brown Co., Wisconsin.
Citation: US Public Record for Nancy T Anderson. Residence (n.d.g.) Omak, Okanogan Co., Washington.
Citation: US Public Record for Orrin L Doriot. Residence (1990) Ridgefield, Clark Co., Washington.
Citation: US Public Record for Susan A Boiko. Residence (1995) Curlew, Ferry Co., Washington.

Citation: US Public Record for Timothy J Krausse. Residence (1987, 1993) Edgerton, Taylor Co., Wisconsin.
Citation: US Public Record for Tracy Doriot. Residence (1988) Vancouver, Clark Co., Washington.
Citation: US Public Record for Vivian P Nichols. Residence (1992); Keslo, Clatsop Co., Washington.
Citation: US Public Record for Zane P Kettenbeil. Residence (1952); Lake Linden, Michigan.

**Title:** **Voter Registration Records**
Citation: Voter Registration Record for Hilda Schmelzer (Provo, UT, USA, Ancestry.com Operations Inc, 2008), www.ancestry.com, California, Voter Registrations, 1900-1968; [Database online].
Citation: Voter Registration Record for Leonard R Grimm (Provo, UT, USA, Ancestry.com Operations Inc). www.ancestry.com, California, Voter Registrations, 1900-1968; [Database online]. State of California, United States, Great Register of Voters, Sacramento, California: California State Library.

**Title:** **Warranty Deed Records**
Citation: Warranty Deed for Mary and Robert Anderson (son) (Medford, Taylor Co, WI, Register of Deeds, State of Wisconsin, Taylor County, 10 Mar 1945), (In possession of Tracy Doriot, Washougal, WA), Doc #120791; Vol. 111 of Deeds on p. 179; Bruno and Elizabeth Pechstein, grantors, to Mary Anderson and Robert Anderson, grantees.
Citation: Warranty Deed for Robert Anderson (Medford, Taylor Co, WI, Register of Deeds Office, State of Wisconsin, Taylor County, 04 Aug 1955),(In possession of Tracy Doriot, Washougal, WA). Vol 124 of deeds, p. 403; Doc #146832. "This indenture made by Robert Anderson, grantor of Town of Deer Creek, Taylor County, Wisconsin, hereby convey(s) and warrant(s) to Eva Anderson...."

**Title:** **Wedding Anniversaries and Announcements**
Citation: Wedding Anniversary for Casper & Arlene Anderson (Cambridge, MN, Casper and Arlene Anderson, Aug 1981). (Copy in possession of Tracy Doriot, Washougal, WA).22 Aug 1981. 35th anniversary.
Citation: Wedding Anniversary for Paul and Viola Anderson (Medford, Taylor Co, WI, Paul and Viola Anderson, Dec 1993), (Copy in possession of Tracy Doriot, Washougal, WA)
Citation: Wedding Announcement for Mary Anderson and Robert Sperl (Medford, Taylor Co, WI, The Star News, 17 Jun 1948), (Copy in possession of Tracy Doriot, Washougal, WA).
Citation: Wedding Invitation for Albert Grimm and Annie Steiner, "Mrs. John Steiner...marriage of her daughter...."

**Title:** **WWI Civilian Draft Registration**
Source information for all following citations for WWI Civilian Draft Registration Records: (Provo, UT. USA, Ancestry.com Operations Inc, 2000), www.ancestry.com, Banks, Ray, comp., World War I Civilian Draft Registrations; [Database online].
Citation: WWI Civilian Draft Registration for Ludwig "Louis" Alexander Grimm; Sep 1918; Rupert, Minidoka Co., Idaho.
Citation: WWI Civilian Draft Registrations for Albert I. Anderson; 1918; Snohomish Co, Washington.
Citation: WWI Civilian Draft Registrations for James E Huffman. Registration: Columbia County, Oregon.

**Title:** **WWI Draft Registration Cards**
Source information for all following citations for WWI Draft Registration Cards: (Provo, UT, USA, Ancestry.com Operations Inc, 2005), www.ancestry.com, United States, Selective Service System, World War I Selective Service System Draft Registration Cards, 1917-1918, Washington, D.C.: National Archives and Records Administration [Database online]. M1509
Citation: WWI Draft Registration for Adolph Grimm Registration: Taylor 172County, Wisconsin.
Citation: WWI Draft Registration for Albert Grimm. Registration: Taylor County, Wisconsin.
Citation: WWI Draft Registration for Albert I. Anderson. Registration: Snohomish County, Washington.
Citation: WWI Draft Registration for Alfred Schubert. Registration: Red Lake County, Minnesota.
Citation: WWI Draft Registration for Anton Grimm. Registration: Manitowoc County, Wisconsin.
Citation: WWI Draft Registration for August Nikolaus Anderson. Registration: Taylor County, Wisconsin.
Citation: WWI Draft Registration for Charles H Strebig. Registration: Wisconsin, Taylor County. Roll: 1674995.
Citation: WWI Draft Registration for Edward C Grimm. Registration Location: Minidoka County, Idaho
Citation: WWI Draft Registration for Elmore A Johns. Registration: Oregon; Multnomah County., Roll:1852145
Citation: WWI Draft Registration for George E Menkenmaier. Registration: Lake County, Oregon.
Citation: WWI Draft Registration for Gustav Grimm. Registration: Polk County, Minnesota.
Citation: WWI Draft Registration for Gustave Alphonse Weber. Registration; Harrison County, Texas; Roll: 1953527.
Citation: WWI Draft Registration for Henry William Grimm Registration: Minidoka County, Idaho.
Citation: WWI Draft Registration for Hugh L Rosebrook. Registration: Multnomah County, Oregon.
Citation: WWI Draft Registration for John N Domnisse. Registration: Multnomah County, Oregon.
Citation: WWI Draft Registration for LeRoy E Funkey: Registration Houghton County, Michigan.
Citation: WWI Draft Registration for Louis Alexander Grimm. Registration: Minidoka County, Idaho.
Citation: WWI Draft Registration for Nils Pederson. Registration: Polk County, Minnesota.
Citation: WWI Draft Registration for Otto William Grimm. Registration Location: Manitowoc County, Wisconsin.
Citation: WWI Draft Registration for Paul F Schubert. Registration: Taylor County, Wisconsin.
Citation: WWI Draft Registration for Paul W Hitzeman. Registration: Allen County, Indiana. .

Citation: WWI Draft Registration for Reinhard F Grimm. Registration: Manitowoc County, Wisconsin.

Citation: WWI Draft Registration for Walter Herman Kettenbeil. Registration: Houghton County, Michigan.

Citation: WWI Draft Registration for William John Vollmer. Registration: Houghton County, Michigan.

Citation: WWI Draft Registration for Willie Grimm. Registration: Polk Co., Minnesota.

Citation: WWI Enlistment Record for William A Wambsganss (Ohio Soldiers in WWI, 1917-1918); Fort Wayne, Allen Co., Indiana.

**Title:** **WWII Enlistment Records**

Source information for all following citations for WWII Enlistment Records except where noted: (Provo, UT, USA, Ancestry.com Operations Inc, 2012), www.ancestry.com, U.S. World War II Army Enlistment Records, 1938-1946; [Database Online]. National Archives and Records Administration. Electronic Army Serial # Merged File, 1938-1946 [Archival Database]; ARC: 1263923World War II Army Enlistment Records; Records of the National Archives and Records Administration, Record Group 64; National Archives at College Park, College Park, MD.

Citation: WWII Army Enlistment Record for Adolph Koch Jr., Enlistment date: 21 Mar 1944; Enlistment place: Fort Douglas.

Citation: WWII Army Enlistment Record for Basil O. Singleton; Enlistment date: 13 Oct 1942; Enlistment place: Milwaukee, Milwaukee Co, Wisconsin.

Citation: WWII Army Enlistment Record for Elmer H Grimm. Enlistment date: 17 Mar 1941; Enlistment place: Oregon.

Citation: WWII Army Enlistment Record for Henry A Bill; Enlistment date: 20 May 1943; Enlistment place: Pocatello, Bannock Co., Idaho.

Citation: WWII Army Enlistment Record for James M Doriot; Enlistment date: 15 Oct 1942; Enlistment place: Tacoma, Pierce Co., Washington.

Citation: WWII Army Enlistment Record for John F Lorenz; Enlistment date: 21 Feb 1941; Enlistment place: Milwaukee, Milwaukee Co., Wisconsin.

**Title:** **WWII Draft Registration Records**

Source information for all following citations for WWII Registration Records: (Provo, UT, USA, Ancestry.com Operations Inc, 2010), www.ancestry.com, U.S. World War II Army Enlistment Records, 1938-1946; [Database Online]. National Archives and Records Administration. Original data: Electronic Army Serial Number Merged File, 1938-1946 [Archival Database]; ARC: 1263923. World War II Army Enlistment Records; Records of the National Archives and Records Administration, Record Group 64; National Archives at College Park. College Park, Maryland, U.S.A.

Citation: WWII Draft Registration for Adolph H Grimm. Local board: Reedville, Wisconsin.

Citation: WWII Draft Registration for Albert I. Anderson. Local board: Snohomish, Washington.

Citation: WWII Draft Registration for Albert Philipp Grimm Local board: Chelsea, Wisconsin.

Citation: WWII Draft Registration for Anton H Grimm Local board: Maple Grove, Wisconsin.

Citation: WWII Draft Registration for Casper Olson Local board: Molitor, Wisconsin.

Citation: WWII Draft Registration for Elmore A Johns. (The National Archives Pacific Alaska Region (Seattle); Seattle, Archive #563991;Box # 62)

Citation: WWII Draft Registration for Frederick Phillip Ernst Wambsganss (Fourth Registration Draft Cards; (WWII); State Headquarters: Oregon; Records of the Selective Service System; RGN: #147)

Citation: WWII Draft Registration for Gustav A Grimm Local board: Salem, Oregon.

Citation: WWII Draft Registration for Henry William Grimm Local board: Paul, Idaho

Citation: WWII Draft Registration for James Maynard Doriot E Local board: Portland, Oregon.

Citation: WWII Draft Registration for John N Domnisse (NARA Pacific Alaska Region (Seattle); Seattle, Washington; Fourth Registration Draft Cards (WWII); State Headquarters: Oregon; Records of the Selective Service System; RGN #: 147; Archive #563991; Box #: 32).

Citation: WWII Draft Registration for Laurin F Cook Local board: Sonoma, California.

Citation: WWII Draft Registration for Nels (NARA Pacific Alaska Region (Seattle); Seattle, Washington; Fourth Registration Draft Cards (WWII); State Headquarters: Washington; Records of the Selective Service System; RGN #147; Archive # 563992; Box # 158).

Citation: WWII Draft Registration for Reinhard F Grimm Local board: Maple Grove, Wisconsin.

Citation: WWII Draft Registration for William John Vollmer (NARA Washington, D.C.; World War II Draft Cards (Fourth Registration) State Headquarters: Wisconsin; Records of the Selective Service System, 1940-; RGN #: 147; Box #: 325; # Series: M2126; # Roll: 109).

Citation: WWII Enlistment Record for Harold J Terp; National Archives and Records Administration. U.S. World War II Army Enlistment Records, 1938-1946 [database on-line]. Provo, UT, USA: Ancestry.com Operations Inc, 2005.Green Bay, Brown Co., Wisconsin.

# ABOUT THE AUTHOR

I was first bitten by the genealogy bug in the mid-1970's after watching the hit mini-series <u>Roots</u> by Alex Haley on television. The acute phase of my addiction occurred during the pre-computer age when there was no internet or social network available. Forms and charts were handwritten or typed on a typewriter. Research and trying to obtain a single piece of information was a long, drawn out process and extremely time consuming by today's standards. It was conducted mostly through visiting repositories and libraries, making telephone calls and letter writing. Correspondence could take months to get a response back and the results were often negative.

One never really recovers from genealogy once infected. It develops into a chronic obsession. It's like a case of malaria but with recurring bouts of enthusiastic research. An early symptom of neophyte genealogists is the tendency to focus on filling out forms and charts rather than on the family history behind the data. I missed many opportunities to ask questions that are so obvious to me in retrospect today due to my own exuberance and eagerness in those early days. I survived that phase and, fortunately, had the foresight to save every letter and document I ever received or collected. I learned that genealogy is not just about collecting names and dates. I learned to ask the right questions and ferret out the answers I was looking for. Moreover, I progressed from being the one asking the questions to being the one others ask the questions from.

My passion has led others to request my help in locating long lost relatives who don't realize that they are missing and resolving various family history questions. I was able to unite two sisters who didn't know that each other existed. I found another's brother who hadn't been heard from in thirty years. He was dying when I found him but he was able to reconnect with his siblings for the last few months of his life. I also resolved and brought closure to a family regarding a ten-year wrongful death mystery. The most satisfying moment, however, was when I finally located a person who I had been searching over twenty years at the request of a distant relative. It's moments like these – when I am able to share in the joy and happy tears of those I have been able to help – that I understand why I enjoy this avocation so much.

Genealogy and family history continues to be a life-long passion for me. I am always happy to share my research with others interested in the common pursuit of discovering our ancestry.

Maryellen Anderson
manderson620@gmail.com